THE MAN
IN THE ARENA

THE MAN IN THE ARENA

VANGUARD FOUNDER JOHN C. BOGLE AND HIS LIFELONG BATTLE TO SERVE INVESTORS FIRST

Edited by

KNUT A. ROSTAD

WILEY

For general information on our other products and services or for technical support, please contact our Customer Care Department within the United States at (800) 762-2974, outside the United States at (317) 572-3993 or fax (317) 572-4002.

Wiley publishes in a variety of print and electronic formats and by print-on-demand. Some material included with standard print versions of this book may not be included in e-books or in print-on-demand. If this book refers to media such as a CD or DVD that is not included in the version you purchased, you may download this material at http://booksupport.wiley.com. For more information about Wiley products, visit www.wiley.com.

ISBN 978-1-118-65076-9 (Hardcover)
ISBN 978-1-118-65080-6 (ePDF)
ISBN 978-1-118-65073-8 (ePub)

Printed in the United States of America
10 9 8 7 6 5 4 3 2 1

I rank this Bogle invention—the index fund—along with the invention of the wheel, the alphabet, Gutenberg printing, and wine and cheese: a mutual fund that never made Bogle rich but elevated the long-term returns of the mutual-fund owners. Something new under the sun.

PAUL A. SAMUELSON, NOBEL LAUREATE,
ON THE SIGNIFICANCE OF THE INDEX FUND

CONTENTS

FOREWORD

WHERE HAVE THE heroes gone?

In years past, sports legends, crusaders, war veterans, and business leaders who were successful and gifted became larger than life. They inspired us. They were heroes. Heroes used to live right, (mostly) follow the rules, be humble and still do amazing things. Heroes illuminated our paths. Heroes provided, by example, guidance that could bring order to the chaos of our own decision making.

That breed appears to be gone. Instead, today many accomplished and successful people often appear to flout the rules and live in an exclusive world where showing their wealth is more important than doing good.

This book is about one of the very few individuals, I believe, who deserves hero status today. Jack Bogle is a hero for all seasons—to millions of ordinary investors, as well as to extraordinarily accomplished and famous people (as you will see in this book).

What it means that Jack Bogle is my hero may be best seen reiterated in Jack's own hero.

Jack Bogle has written about his heroes and identifies quite a few over his lifetime, but one stands out: Walter Morgan, whom Jack calls "my greatest mentor." Morgan hired Jack in 1951 and entrusted him with the leadership of the company in 1965. Of Morgan, Jack wrote, "I could not begin to do justice to all of Walter Morgan's fine qualities—intelligence, grace, ambition, generosity. . . . He inspired me and challenged me to do my best. His high values—especially his unyielding integrity and uncompromising honesty—reinforced my own values and made me a better person."

In Jack's tribute to Morgan, I see my tribute to Jack. Jack founded a company based on the premise that the interests of the shareholders come first, and that all people should be given a break, encouraged, and respected. He has tirelessly worked for and championed the little guy. He has taken on powerful interests without regard for his own career risk. He continues fighting, while most of his peers have long since fled to more leisurely pursuits.

His success is best measured by two metrics: first, the success of others, and second, the diffusion of his ideas. The first might be said to be measured in the collective market share of index mutual funds, the second by the nation's movement toward what he terms a "fiduciary society." It is this challenge that, I think, keeps Jack going to the office. The significant personal wealth he might have accumulated if he had chosen a more common path does not concern him. He exudes the sense that he has more than "Enough."

His humility, as much as his efforts *and* success, is inspirational.

Most readers of this book probably have not met Jack. While the book portrays the mettle of the man, and the clarity, quality, and impact of his ideas, it may not fully convey his presence. It is a book, after all, not a flesh-and-blood human being.

Jack's presence is summarized easily: The perfect actor to portray Jack would have been Jimmy Stewart (although perhaps Walter Brennan would have been needed for some voice-over work in order to capture how the pitch of his voice rises when he is emphasizing a point).

Jack's style matches and reflects his substance; they dance in a virtuous circle with each other. This interplay is easily seen in his writing. Jack has written much, all of it clear, simple, and eloquent. His analysis is always straightforward. His ideas have such power that ornamentation would get in the way. It would be a shame to camouflage their steel.

When you know a hero personally, when the hero is not just a name, all the better. You are inspired to be your best; you would never want to let him down.

I feel blessed to know Jack Bogle. I admit it: Jack is my hero, my Walter Morgan. On behalf of the millions who share this sentiment, I say thank you, Jack Bogle. And thank you, Walter Morgan.

Andrew Golden
President, Princeton University Investment Company

INTRODUCTION

THIS BOOK DESCRIBES John C. (Jack) Bogle's lifework and what it means—his legacy, if you will. It does so in two ways: first, through Bogle's own words on topics that matter most to him—Vanguard, indexing, the mutual fund industry, corporate governance, and a fiduciary society; second, through the voices of many others whose lives he has touched with his words and deeds. The result is a snapshot of Bogle's lifelong quest to build a better world for investors, and a compendium of commentary from investors, colleagues, and admirers alike.

Bogle began his mission in 1951 with his senior thesis at Princeton University on the mutual fund industry. Right away, Bogle observed that "the principal role of the mutual fund should be to serve its shareholders." The embodiment of this conviction only began to take its full form 23 years later with the founding of Vanguard. As Bogle explained in a 1999 speech, Vanguard is about *stewardship*: "The one great idea that explains what Vanguard is, who we are, and what we do. Serving the shareholder first; acting as trustee, in a fiduciary capacity. Mutual funds of the investor, by the investor, for the investor. This is a company that stands for something. Something bigger than mere commercial success. Something called character."

Bogle launched the world's first index mutual fund in 1975. Its simple concept was that passively investing in the entire market over the long term at lower costs will provide superior returns than more expensive active management. The index fund was largely ridiculed by the industry—"Bogle's folly" and "un-American."

Not the Most Popular Guy on Wall Street

Former Federal Reserve Chairman Paul Volcker underscored Bogle's "un-American" philosophy when he wrote, years later, that Vanguard's first index fund was "supported by plain evidence: that most active money managers most of the time will not be able to beat the market. Very few funds can consistently outperform the averages. "That's not an easy conclusion for money managers to accept," noted Volcker dryly. "Bogle has not won many popularity contests among his professional colleagues."

Un-American or not, investors *like* indexing. At of the end of 2012, the share of equity fund assets that were invested in all index funds (traditional index funds and exchange-traded funds [ETFs]) was 27 percent. The average expense ratio for Vanguard's index funds, for example, in 2012 was 0.10 percent. If Vanguard had charged the industry average expense ratio of 1.15 percent in 2012 on shareholders' average assets of $1.64 trillion, their net returns would have been $19 billion less.

These savings have endured over time. Kenneth French, professor of finance at the Tuck School of Business at Darmouth University, released a study in 2008 that compared the "fees, expenses, and trading costs society pays to invest in the U.S. stock market with an estimate of what would be paid if everyone invested passively." Averaging 1980 to 2006, French found that investors paid 0.67 percent by not investing actively. In 2006 alone, the total cost of active management was $101.6 billion. French explains that the more than $100 billion estimate of the cost of active management is "probably low, but I am trying to be conservative." And, apparently, he was conservative. French received four e-mails challenging his results—all from industry professionals who complained that his estimates were too low. "I am happy with that outcome," he says.

INNOVATIONS THAT TRANSFORM, WORDS FOR REFORM

Vanguard and indexing are, no doubt, *business* successes. But they are much more. They are *innovation*s that transformed individual investing to benefit millions of investors. How transformative? Nobel laureate Paul Samuelson put it simply when he compared the index fund to the invention of the wheel and the Gutenberg printing press. Add to Bogle's innovations his words on *reform* of the mutual fund industry, in corporate governance and a fiduciary society, and Bogle becomes, in the eyes of most mutual fund executives, more a Ralph Nader than an industry colleague.

That Bogle is viewed more as a crusader than a business leader may be obvious, as Chairman Volcker suggested when he noted that Bogle would not win a popularity contest among his peers. Yet, an acclaimed book by Harvard Business School (HBS) professors Anthony J. Mayo and Nitin Nohria, *In Their Time: The Greatest Business Leaders of the Twentieth Century* (2005), may provide the academic evidence. It identifies the factors associated with great business leaders. Seven thousand business executives, HBS alumni, were surveyed to evaluate and rank a list of 1,000 CEOs and founders (including Bogle) to develop a list of a top 100 ranking of great American executives. Although Bogle did not make the "top 100" in this survey, in 1999 *Fortune* magazine named him one of the investment industry's four "giants of the 20th century."

Others have noted *Fortune*'s "giant." Much commentary on Jack Bogle is noteworthy for its sheer intensity. From Vanguard shareholders and crew members to colleagues and to leaders in academia and financial regulation, the messengers are ardent, their messages clear: Jack Bogle—entrepreneur, visionary, fighter, industry reformer—evokes intense passion. Praise from individuals across diverse walks of life underscores Bogle's vision, clarity, integrity, persistence, honesty, and humility. His zeal to put investors first and to restore a sensibility that certain shared values matter greatly to the nation moves his admirers and inspires Bogle to continue. Forever the optimist, Bogle has no doubt those shared values can be restored.

The virtual parade of admirers that has formed around Bogle's lifework is led by, some would argue, the two most acclaimed leaders of our day in the world of investing and in the public life of the world—Warren Buffett and President Bill Clinton. This speaks much of the man who is Jack Bogle.

THE BOGLE LEGACY

In the most recent of his 10 books, *The Clash of the Cultures: Investment vs. Speculation*, Bogle reflects on his experiences over his career, the opportunities and challenges he has faced, and the mistakes he made during his quest to build a better world for investors. In so doing, he cites President Theodore Roosevelt's inspiring words about "The Man in the Arena":

> It is not the critic who counts; not the man who points out how the strong man stumbles, or where the doer of deeds could have done them better. The credit belongs to the man who is actually in the arena, whose face is marred by dust and sweat and blood; who strives valiantly; who errs, who comes short again and again, because there is no effort without error and shortcoming; but who does actually strive to do the deeds; who knows great enthusiasms, the great devotions; who spends himself in a worthy cause; who at the best knows in the end the triumph of high achievement, and who at the worst, if he fails, at least fails while daring greatly, so that his place shall never be with those cold and timid souls who neither know victory nor defeat.

These words resonate with Bogle as one who freely admits that, as a pursuer of "a worthy cause," he "comes short again and again." Be it the Republican New York state assemblyman who tried to clean up state politics or the president who called on Congress to break up the trusts, Theodore Roosevelt, the innovator and reformer, did not hesitate to challenge major interest groups. Roosevelt sought a "square deal" for the American people. Similarly, Bogle seeks a "fair shake" for the American investor. Bogle, "The Man in the Arena," has been judged favorably in his time. And history, finally, will judge the legacy Jack Bogle will leave behind.

Knut A. Rostad*, Editor

---

* Knut A. Rostad is president of the Institute for the Fiduciary Standard.

PART I

THE JOHN C. BOGLE LEGACY FORUM—A VISION FOR RESTORING TRUST

O N A COLD Tuesday in January 2012, some of the most highly respected legal and financial minds in the country gathered in the heart of Wall Street at the Museum of American Finance to wrestle with a fundamental question: "Restoring Investor Trust in Financial Markets: Does Jack Bogle Offer a Prescription?"

The John C. Bogle Legacy Forum was cochaired by former chairman of the Federal Reserve Board Paul A. Volcker and former Securities and Exchange Commission (SEC) chairman Arthur Levitt Jr. Chairman Volcker set the tone for the forum with panel topics that are "relevant, provocative, unsettled." Chairman Levitt noted of the program speakers, "This event brings together the best-known financial figures to honor a visionary in global finance. Jack Bogle has given investors throughout the world more wisdom and good financial judgment than any person in the history of markets."

Volcker and Levitt led a host committee that included Sheila C. Bair, John Biggs, Alan Blinder, William Donaldson, Peter Fitzgerald, Andrew Golden, Roger G. Ibbotson, Burton G. Malkiel, and David F. Swensen.

The Forum was spearheaded by the Institute for the Fiduciary Standard, co-organized by the CFA Institute and the Museum of American Finance, and sponsored by Bloomberg Link. The Tuesday session began with the reading of a welcome letter from William Jefferson Clinton, 42nd president of the United States, who succeeded Bogle as chairman of the board of the National Constitution Center and wrote the foreword to Bogle's 2008 book *Enough. True Measures of Money, Business, and Life.*

On the evening before the Forum, a small dinner was held for the speakers. Dinner hostess Maria Eleanor Lagomasino welcomed and thanked the speakers. Tamar Frankel raised her glass to salute the honoree for his "down-to-earth wisdom." William Isaac spoke of the eternal values that Bogle articulated and lived by. The evening ended with remarks by Jack Bogle's son, John, which began with this greeting: "Good evening. My name is John C. Bogle Jr., and I run a hedge fund." John then proceeded to entertain the group with contemplations of what an appropriate "Bogle Rule" might entail, and shared his recollections of living under "Bogle Rules" growing up.

A Welcome from President William Jefferson Clinton

William Jefferson Clinton

January 30, 2012

Dear Jack:

I'm delighted to join all those gathered at the
Museum of American Finance in celebrating your long-
standing commitment to economic responsibility.

Throughout your celebrated career, you've made it
clear that the origins of financial stability lie
not within partisanship, but within the people. I
continue to be inspired by your common sense
solutions for renewing America's trust with a long-
term economic vision.

As we focus on putting Americans "back to work" and
putting our nation back in the future business, I
send my best wishes to you and all your guests for a
successful and productive event.

Sincerely,

Bill Clinton

REMARKS FROM THE SPEAKERS' DINNER

Tamar Frankel, Professor of Law at Boston University and author of nine books, including *The Ponzi Scheme Puzzle* (2012), made the following remarks:

I raise my glass to John Bogle. Throughout the years he has demonstrated a unique combination of perseverance, inspirational insights, and down-to-earth wisdom. He has taught without preaching, criticized without offending, and dealt with complex ideas simply, without being simplistic. He thus engages the readers in personal conversation at the fireplace, while introducing them to his colleagues. I am proud to be one of them.

Among his teachings, John Bogle has made two important points. One is that notwithstanding the complexity of the environment, the source of all good and evil is people. The second point is that, within the range of freedom, a few principles should not be watered down. Chipping at the block of honesty by interpreting, justifying, rationalizing it away, you end up at the other extreme—dishonesty.

These views represent the balance in a human body. Each cell in our body has an innate drive to propagate. Yet in order to survive, each cell must be limited to its functions and rogue cells must be controlled. The system, I am told, is in charge of controlling rogue cells. But if they succeed in propagating and overcoming the police, these cells grow—we call them cancer—and the body as a whole will die.

The human society is similar to the human body. And John Bogle's ideas reflect the healthy balance. Internal management of mutual funds, indexing, self-limitation of money managers, and controlling costs, among others, are the immune system containing rogue cells. He shows us how the body could maintain health by each cell doing what it ought to do within the range of its capabilities, thus contributing to the whole. John Bogle has been showing this complex balance in a way that draws audiences and followers. His is a truly unique achievement.

So here is to you, John.

And this from William Isaac, Global Head of Financial Institutions for FTI Consulting and chairman of Fifth Third Bancorp, former chairman of the Federal Deposit Insurance Corporation (FDIC), and the author of the 2010 book *Senseless Panic: How Washington Failed America*, with foreword by Paul Volcker:[1]

I have long known and respected Jack Bogle, but always from afar, as I do not believe we have ever met. It would take more time than we have for me to simply list his accomplishments, so I won't even try. Let me just say that Jack Bogle has led a life of innovation, integrity, and public service, exemplified by his creation of The Vanguard Group, the largest mutual fund company in the world with assets under management exceeding $2 trillion.

Both Jack Bogle and the Institute for the Fiduciary Standard demand that "trustees of other people's money act solely in the best interests of their beneficiaries." They espouse six core duties:

· Serve the client's best interest.
· Act in utmost good faith.
· Act prudently—with the care, skill, and judgment of a professional.
· Avoid conflicts of interest.
· Disclose all material facts.
· Control investment expenses.

The past decade has been a period of great turmoil in our nation, and never has there been a more important time to return to these core principles, which I believe can be summed up in the word *trust*. Trust—which I define as "confidence in the honesty, reliability, and fairness of people and things"—is essential to democracy, a free market economy, and the financial system. That trust has been breached in recent years by our government and major private institutions, which has been enormously damaging on many levels.

---

1. The views expressed by Mr. Isaac are his own.

Mopping up the economic damage—a glut of foreclosed properties, millions of lost jobs, trillions of dollars of lost savings—will take time. Restoring trust between the government and the governed and between the captains of industry and the people who invest in their companies and buy their goods and services will be more challenging.

Despite our many challenges, there is nothing wrong with America that we cannot fix if we muster the political courage and will to do it. As bad as things might be today, we have been through worse.

Most Americans place a high value on working hard to create a better life for their families, contributing to their communities and those in need, and behaving with integrity.

We must demand that the leaders of our public and private institutions adhere to those values. These are not Republican or Democratic or Tea Party values; these are American values. These should be the values of both Main Street and Wall Street.

We must hold our public and private leaders to a much higher standard than in recent decades. When leaders in the private and public sectors bring us to the edge of financial ruin, they must be held accountable and, at the very least, be swiftly removed from office.

I believe these are the values Jack Bogle and the Institute stand for. Thank you for all that you have done and are doing.

And from John C. Bogle Jr., founder and president of Bogle Investment Management:

Good evening. My name is John C. Bogle Jr., and I run a hedge fund.

Knut Rostad and the Institute for the Fiduciary Standard, and GenSpring were kind enough to invite me to say a few words about the importance of my dad's legacy to the fund industry and investors, to corporate governance, and to society today.

And I'm really glad because someone had to be here to defend the One-Percenters. I have a feeling we're going to be taking quite a beating over the next 18 hours.

Everyone in this room is aware of the enormity of my dad's impact on the investment industry, particularly on the little guy, the one saving for a child's education, for a comfortable retirement after years of hard work, for a home: the 99-Percenter.

Though let's not kid ourselves; indexing and low costs aren't for just the little guy. There are probably more One-Percenter active fund managers who index than who don't. But not for long—I assume they'll be going after those cost savings next. I can see it now—Paul Krugman's next op-ed—"Do you realize that by investing in index funds, the One-Percenters avoided paying over $5 billion in management fees?"

But my dad's impact goes far beyond the investment world. Through his speeches, interviews, and books, he challenges us, as David Swensen writes about my father's 2008 book, *Enough.*, "to aspire to become better members of our families, our professions, and our communities."

As Arthur Levitt writes, "he gives new meaning to the words 'commitment,' 'accountability,' and 'stewardship.'"

Another: "Unfortunately, there are not enough Jack Bogles around in today's world of instant gratification." High praise, though we'll ignore the fact that this one was submitted by David Sokol. He must not have read the entire book. After his recent dismissal from Berkshire Hathaway, he actually tried to get the publishers to correct the first version to "Unfortunately, there are *too many* Jack Bogles around in my self-absorbed world of instant gratification."

This forum got me thinking—how do you honor someone who has done more for investors than anyone in the history of the business? He has more honorary degrees than he can count, plaques, and certificates. What else is there?

Then it hit me—what he needs, what he deserves, is a Rule!

Your own rule—the new must-have for the titan who has everything!

Now, some rules are already taken:

The Volcker Rule—"Don't screw around with other people's money."

The Buffett Rule—"Raise taxes on every millionaire and billionaire (except me because I'm giving it all away anyhow)."

The Golden Rule—"Give all your money to Goldman Sachs."

Apparently you're nothing these days if you don't have your own rule.

"The Bogle Rule." I like the sound of it. The only problem is defining exactly what the rule should say. I started with "Take all your money away from Goldman Sachs"—probably a good rule, but the Bogle Rule has to encompass more.

The more I thought about it, the more difficult it became, as I realized how many of my dad's beliefs and lessons, how much of his wisdom and character, could provide direction and advice by which to live one's life.

Now, as kids, as my brother, Andrew, who's also here tonight, can attest, we had countless numbers of what we thought of as "Bogle Rules":

Rule 3c. In wintertime, "Never turn the thermostat above 58 degrees.

"Unless there's ice forming on the inside of the windows.

"In which case it's much too warm and should be turned down to 52."

Rule 16b. "Always wear a wool tie in preference to silk, lest you be thought of as being flamboyant.

"Or be mistaken for an active fund manager.

"Or worse: a hedge fund manager."

Rule 400k. "Never turn down an opportunity to be interviewed on TV." Even if it's on HBO with Ali G. "Yo! Check it out! We gots here my main man Mr. John Bogle. Mr. Bogle, how you spend all dat money you save dem investors? You buy many women?" (Might be too much 99-Percenter pop culture for this crowd.)

But truly, as kids, my parents taught us, by word or by example:

To treat everyone you come across, from every walk of life, with respect,
To "press on regardless," not to give up no matter how tough the challenge,
To generously give back through philanthropy to needy causes,

To live your life with integrity,
To always find the time to spend with your children.

The list goes on, but for us it can be pretty well summed up by:

"Be the best Dad you possibly can be."

I hope that we've done well in living up to these and the other principles with which we were raised. We also hope that as parents we have raised our own children to live up to these same principles. I have a 17-year-old son and a 14-year-old daughter. So we're batting 1.000. But I take solace in the fact that, even at .500, if I were an active mutual fund I'd be doing pretty well.

But as for my dad's legacy and its impact on the rest of society, I know that we'll be hearing some great ideas tomorrow. There's an incredible list of speakers and panelists, many of whom are here tonight. And there will be lots of input into where we need to go, what we need to do, to get more individuals to think like and live their lives more like my dad does.

And perhaps, just maybe, we'll get to see the embryonic formation of "The Bogle Rule."

Welcoming Remarks

A few words from David Cowen, president of the Museum of American Finance:

Welcome all to the Museum of American Finance. I am David Cowen, president of the Museum. Our core mission is to preserve, exhibit, and teach about the nation's finances and financial history; we are a Smithsonian Affiliate. We are proud to be a part of this day, which will honor the legacy of one of the giants of the industry, Jack Bogle.

We want to thank our cohosts of Bloomberg, the CFA Institute, and the Institute for the Fiduciary Standard for making this event possible. Jack has an incredible legacy and you will be hearing about that today, but one thing is clear: He has always done the hard right over the easy wrong, to always be a good friend to the small investor, looking out for the little guy.

His legacy also includes being a good friend of this Museum, and among his many accomplishments is that he is a member of our Advisory Board. I'd like to also point out that several other members of our Museum's Advisory Board are here today, including Bill Donaldson and Paul Volcker.

One story we like to share, and it's well known and Jack writes about it is his books, is that he was the fortunate recipient of a heart transplant. So we can be assured that there is at least one Wall Streeter with a heart!

Once again, congratulations to Jack from the Museum.

Opening Remarks by John C. Bogle

John C. Bogle opened the Forum with the following words:

I know of no precedent for Wall Street (as it were) honoring one of its own, marking a legacy of 60 years in the investment profession. (Not so many souls hang around that long!) So I'm greatly honored, truly humbled, and profoundly appreciative that so many industry leaders, financial and academic professionals, friends and colleagues are joining in this wonderful day of celebration.

I've done the best I could to build a better world for investors. Yes, in Philadelphia the press has described me as an entrepreneur, creator, inventor, and citizen, and even compared me—not unfavorably—with Benjamin Franklin. . . . But Walter Isaacson, having completed his biography of Franklin some years back, next turned to Albert Einstein, and then, only a few months ago, to Steve Jobs. I'm not hanging by my thumbs awaiting Mr. Isaacson's phone call (nor his note on my iPad).

Yes, I did start the world's first index mutual fund (though lots of people claim to have thought of it long before I did so). It is now the world's largest equity fund. . . . But the index fund concept represents the essence of simplicity, the triumph of Occam's razor. It required no genius, so I've never won a MacArthur "Genius" grant (and don't deserve one).

Yes, it took determination (and luck, and timing, and the support of a few key directors of the Wellington Fund) to create the first U.S. *mutual* mutual fund organization to be managed, not in the interests of its managers, but in the interests of its fund shareholders. . . . But, despite the name I chose, Vanguard remains a leader with no followers. Even 38 years later, our firm's structure has yet to be copied or even emulated, so low in excitement and acclaim that neither Brad Pitt nor Robert Redford has shown any interest in making a Bogle movie. (*Bogleball*? *Bogle—the Sundance Kid*?)

Yes, I've tried to create a business with character and class, holding human values high. That's a task I've yet to complete. . . . But it's not the only task before me, for I've yet to climb all Seven Summits, host the Oscars, or (despite my Scots heritage) solve the mystery of Loch Ness; nor have I been a candidate to manage the Phillies (or even the Red Sox); and it's too late for me to run for President. (Sorry 'bout that!)

Yes, I'm now writing my tenth book, many of which have been best sellers . . . but only for a little while. After a single week on the *New York Times* best-seller list, *Enough.* was replaced by—I guess it's okay to say it aloud—*Real Sex for Real Women*. "Is this a great country or what?"

Yes, I've been among the strongest advocates in my field for activism in corporate governance. . . . But words aren't the same as deeds, and I've yet to see any tangible results whatsoever. The silence of the funds remains deafening, but I'm not about to give up the mission.

Yes, I've had a few portraits painted. . . . But one sits in my office (it's a long story), not in the Louvre or even the Philadelphia Museum of Art. I confess too that there is a larger-than-life sculpture of me on the Vanguard campus. . . . But its only function seems to be to allow fund industry leaders to describe me (cynically, of course) as "a saint with a statue."

Yes, I think I've played a major role in bringing into the public discourse the importance of long-term investing, of rational expectations for returns in the financial markets, and of the crying need for a fiduciary standard. . . . But there's so much I haven't done: Walk on water, leap tall buildings with a single bound, publish poetry in Russian, make the cover of *Time*, or *Fortune*, or *Forbes*, or *Bloomberg Businessweek*.

Despite my infinite failings, however, I'm simply unable to conceal my pride on this great day of celebration. I'm reminded again of Benjamin Franklin, whose character was central to his dedication to the public interest, so easily observable in his entrepreneurship, in the joy he took from his creations, and in his ingenuity, his energy, and his persistence. That trait of character also found its expression in Franklin's ongoing struggle, not unlike my own, to balance pride with humility—a balance that, in this age of bright lights, celebrity, and money, our society seems to have largely ignored. As Franklin wrote in his autobiography:

> *In reality, there is, perhaps, no one of our natural passions so hard to subdue as pride. Disguise it, struggle with it, beat it down, stifle it, mortify it as much as one pleases, it is still alive, and will every now and then peep out and show itself; you will see it perhaps often in this history; for even if I could conceive that I had completely overcome it, I should probably be proud of my humility.*

In candor, these words serve to remind me that my own pride must be all too evident in the brief history of my career that I've recited here, a career focused on the stewardship of the wealth of our nation's citizens. Too often, I'm sure, my pride has indeed peeped out and shown itself, reminding me that my own humility could doubtless use a little more development.

I must work on that tomorrow. . . .

Thank you again.[2]

CHAPTER 1: FOUR DISTINGUISHED PANELS

The Legacy Forum featured four panel discussions, plus remarks by Gary Gensler, chair of the Commodity Futures Trading Commission (CFTC), and a lively conversation between Paul Volcker and Bogle.

The first panel discussion, on index funds, featured industry luminaries Burton Malkiel, David Swensen, and Gus Sauter. All agreed on the case for indexing, but also mixed it up and expressed differing views on the role of active management in an investor's portfolio, high-frequency trading, and exchange-traded funds (ETFs).

The second panel, on corporate governance, offered candid discussions on board members' responsibilities, conflicts of interest, and executive compensation. Former White House executive pay czar Kenneth Feinberg shared his experiences dealing with fairness in compensation. Former SEC chief accountant Lynn Turner offered insights into the common shortcomings of boards and board membership.

In the third panel, three former chairmen of the Securities and Exchange Commission and the CEO of a Wall Street lobby discuss the issue of fiduciary

---

2. My focus on what I *haven't* done was inspired by Jason Gay's *Wall Street Journal* column of December 1, 2011, on what former Denver Broncos quarterback Tim Tebow, the then-momentary toast of the National Football League, hasn't done.

duty for brokers. Notable was a general deference to different business models when applying fiduciary standards. Former SEC chairman Harvey Pitt suggests that brokers use candid language to convey their conflicts of interest, such as, "My firm puts out its own investments and I may make more money if I recommend those." Chairman Levitt disagreed: "That's where we part ways, Harvey. Having been a broker, I know the reluctance of brokers to be that forthcoming."

Paul Volcker and Jack Bogle then rivet the audience with their friendly banter and candid commentary in a joint interview with Bloomberg's Kathleen Hays. Starting with a question about their "secret" for being "at the top of your game" in their 80s, Bogle answers quickly, "Go to Princeton." In the ensuing wide-ranging discussion, the two giants of finance opine on topics ranging from investor confidence and the Volcker Rule to the bond market and political reform.

The Legacy Forum concluded with a fourth and final panel, moderated by Summit Business Media editor James Green. It featured comments by former Vanguard senior executive Jeremy Duffield and Wall Street strategist Martin Fridson, who provided a lively discussion of Bogle's (then) nine books.

First Panel: Simplicity and Low Cost in Investing: Is the Indexing Model the Way Forward?

American investors poured almost $100 billion into equity mutual funds between 2008 and 2012. But that statistic conceals more than it reveals. In fact, investors pulled some $460 billion out of actively managed equity funds, and invested $560 billion in index funds—a $1 trillion swing in investor preference. This triumph of indexing could not have occurred without the efforts of the pioneers who brought indexing to the investing public. The idea started in academia and spread to pension funds in the late 1960s and early 1970s. But it was John C. Bogle who created the first index mutual fund, finally making indexing available to all investors.

The index fund, founded in 1975, is one of the cornerstones of Bogle's legacy.[3] In celebration of his legacy, four luminaries of investing came together at the Museum of American Finance on Wall Street to discuss the development of indexing:

- Princeton University professor Burton G. Malkiel, who, in the first edition of his classic book *A Random Walk Down Wall Street* (1973), called for "a new investment instrument: a no-load, minimum-management-fee mutual fund that simply buys the hundreds of stocks making up the market averages and does no trading."
- Former Vanguard chief investment officer (CIO) Gus Sauter, who took over the administration of the Vanguard 500 Index Fund in 1987 and has been instrumental in leading the growth of indexing at Vanguard ever since.
- Yale University CIO David F. Swensen, who has managed Yale's endowment since 1985 and is the author of *Unconventional Success: A Fundamental Approach to Personal Investment* (2005), which argues that index funds should play a primary role in the portfolios of most investors.
- Roger G. Ibbotson (moderator), a Yale University professor and chairman and CIO of Zebra Capital Management, whose annual book *Stocks, Bonds, Bills, and Inflation* serves as a standard reference used by capital market participants.

---

3. The other principal cornerstone is his 1974 creation of *a truly mutual* mutual fund structure, in which the fund shareholders actually own the fund management company, which operates on an at-cost basis. Arguably, it was this structure that fostered the new firm's focus on indexing.

Burton Malkiel: The CMH Trumps the EMH

The intellectual foundation of the index fund is the efficient market hypothesis (EMH). The EMH posits that prices set in the capital markets reflect all the information available for a given security; therefore, securities are always fairly priced and asset managers cannot consistently generate excess returns. Yet the debate around the EMH is hardly settled, as Malkiel pointed out.

"We all know that the EMH is very controversial," he said. "Professor Robert Shiller at Yale has called it the most egregious error in the history of economic thought. GMO Co. founder Jeremy Grantham has said, 'The EMH was more or less responsible for the recent financial crisis.'"

But Bogle didn't rely on the EMH to justify index funds. He is a strong proponent of Occam's razor, the fourteenth-century maxim (after the English philosopher Sir William of Occam) that states, "When there are multiple solutions to a problem, pick the simplest one." So Bogle provides a justification for indexing that is both practical and compelling. In Malkiel's words, "The argument that Jack makes justifies indexing whether or not you think markets are efficient. Jack calls his hypothesis the CMH, the 'cost matters' hypothesis. And the argument is really quite simple. We don't live in Lake Wobegon. We can't all be above average. Therefore, portfolio management is going to be a zero-sum game."

Not a Zero-Sum Game

Malkiel explained, "If there are some portfolio managers who are holding the stocks that go up more than average, then it has to be the case that some other portfolio managers are holding the stocks that went up less than average. But in the presence of costs, it's not a zero-sum game; it's a negative-sum game. And the average manager, then, has to underperform the market by the amount of the fees charged."

He continued, "With a very nice empirical study—which I have told Jack was certainly good enough to earn him tenure at a major university if he would like to change careers—he actually showed that performance is strongly related to the fees charged. As Jack puts it, the investor who wants to be in a top-quartile fund should buy one with bottom-quartile explicit expenses and bottom-quartile turnover. As a matter of fact, in the more colorful way that Jack puts it, in this industry the investor doesn't get what he pays for; he gets precisely what he *doesn't* pay for. That is, if he pays *nothing*, he gets *everything*—whatever returns the stock market delivers. And that, of course, leads us inexorably back to index funds, which are the quintessential low-expense, low-turnover funds."

As Malkiel pointed out, the data supporting the CMH are compelling, and additional evidence continues to mount. "The data continued to come in overwhelmingly in support of indexing as an optimal strategy for individual investors. For example, 2011 was a particularly good year for indexing: 83 percent of large cap managers were outperformed by the S&P 500; 82 percent of bond managers were outperformed by Barclays U.S. Aggregate Bond Index. Similar kinds of numbers were recorded for managers of European funds, emerging market equities, small cap equities, whatever asset class you want.

"Now, 2011 was an unusual year. No one—no supporter of indexing, and there isn't a bigger supporter than me—is going to tell you that 80 percent of active managers are going to be beaten each year. The longer-run figures suggest that in the typical year, two-thirds of active managers are generally beaten by the benchmark indexes, and the one-third that win in one year aren't the same as the one-third who win in the next year."

Awarding Tenure

Malkiel continued, "Moreover, the degree to which the typical active manager underperforms the benchmark is well approximated by the difference in costs between the average actively managed fund and the index fund. So, the Bogle CMH continues to be overwhelmingly supported by the data. And when you think of ideas in finance that are supported by the data, I don't know of one that's better supported by the data than Bogle's CMH, which is why I want to award him tenure right off the bat."

While the index fund has been, in Bogle's phrase, "both an artistic and a commercial success," he has improved the prospects for investors in many other ways as well. Malkiel said, "Jack's contributions to the welfare of individual investors go far beyond simply indexing. The active funds managed by Vanguard have rock-bottom expenses and low portfolio turnover. Jack built his values into the Vanguard organization, such as his insistence that the sole criterion for the success of the organization was that it be run for the exclusive benefit of the investor. These values will, I believe, endure indefinitely.

"I think perhaps the best way to describe Jack is to quote from one of the many, many published articles singing his praises. 'John Bogle is the greatest investor advocate ever to grace the fund industry. The profound changes he brought to the realm of personal finance will be felt for years to come.'

"And my favorite quote about Jack comes from the dedication of an investment book that was published by the Bogleheads, which is a group of acolytes dedicated to disseminating Jack's ideas. The dedication reads, and I'll quote, 'While some mutual fund founders chose to make billions, he chose to make a difference.'"

Gus Sauter: The Index Fund Builder Who Followed the Architect's Designs

Bogle's investment philosophy of simplicity, low costs, and proper asset allocation is enduring. In Bogle's words, it is appropriate "no matter how high a greedy stock market flies, nor how low a frightened market plunges." So it should come as no surprise that his commitment to indexing did not waver in the aftermath of the Black Monday market crash in 1987, which occurred just weeks after Bogle hired Gus Sauter. If Bogle is the architect of indexing, he chose a great builder to execute his design.

Very few people have been as central to the growth of indexing as Sauter has been. Early on in his tenure, he developed trading strategies to help Vanguard's index funds track their benchmarks as closely as possible, and he wrote the computer code to implement those strategies. He has long been a respected leader in market structure policy, has helped index providers optimize the structure of their benchmarks, and is trusted by policy makers in Washington for his commitment to the best interests of clients and efficiency in the market.

Gus opened his remarks with an anecdote: "I'm thinking back to the first time that I met Jack. It was August of 1987. I was interviewing for a job at Vanguard and, if you recall, back at that point in time the stock market was up 45 percent in the first eight months of that year. I was interviewing for this job to manage the equity index fund—*one fund*—and I was a little nervous that the market had just spiked up and it might turn down. So I asked Jack, 'I'm the last guy in the door here. If the market tanks, am I the first guy out the door?' And he assured me, 'No, no. We're very committed to indexing. We're going to make a go of this.' And sure enough, I started on October 5 of 1987; two weeks later the market crashed. Our index fund went from $1.2 billion to $800 million overnight. I apologized to the board of directors a month later, but I still contend it wasn't my fault."

"Someday Indexing Is Going to Be Really Big"

Sauter recalled, "When I first started, the assets of our single S&P 500 index fund (another index fund was on the drawing board) totaled $1 billion—just 3 percent of our assets. The other 97 percent were actively managed assets at Vanguard—Vanguard started as an active firm. And I remember Jack coming into my office, probably about 1990, and saying, 'Gus, you just wait. Someday indexing is going to be really big. We'll have $10 billion someday.' And I thought, 'Wow.' As I look back now, we've got about $1 trillion at Vanguard in indexed assets, and I'm thinking Jack's not typically prone to understatement.

"Indexing really has grown quite a bit," said Sauter. "It just absolutely took off in the middle part of the 1990s and throughout the past 10 years as well. It's a low-cost way to gain exposure to the market. And if you can get that low-cost way of gaining exposure to the broadly diversified market, you're going to outperform a majority of investors. There are no guarantees in this industry, but one thing that you can have a great deal of certainty about in advance is that with index funds, you will be among the better performers or usually above average, and you just don't know that with active management.

"Indexing now represents about 30 percent of the equity fund industry. It has absolutely exploded in size. Of that, about 11 percent of mutual fund assets are in conventional index funds and the other 14 percent or so would be in ETFs [exchange-traded funds], which are, by and large, index mutual funds. We offer ETFs right alongside our conventional index funds, and we look at them as just another way to distribute the index fund."

A Difference of Opinion?

The rise of ETFs is one development on which Bogle and Sauter don't exactly see eye to eye. However, their differences are more in emphasis and tone than substance. While Bogle appreciates the low cost, low turnover, and tax efficiency of ETFs (attributes they share with traditional index funds [TIFs]), he worries that the very structure of ETFs, which can be traded "all day long, in real time" (as an early ETF advertisement claimed), implicitly encourages investors to churn their portfolios rather than maintaining a disciplined, long-term strategy. Sauter prefers to focus on the positive aspects of ETFs that are shared with TIFs. As he put it, "I think there's been some confusion in the industry about ETFs, and that's somewhat unfortunate. They were originally promoted as a new product, better than indexed mutual funds. And I kept thinking, 'Well, wait a minute. They *are* indexed mutual funds.' And so we got off to kind of an unusual start there."

But Bogle and Sauter share concerns about the many fringe investment products that have polluted the ETF space. Sauter pointed out, "There are some unusual products that are confusing to investors, and that fly in the face of what the benefits of indexing really are. There are some of these levered products that really require a keen understanding of what's going on. There are many investors who didn't understand what they were getting into. There are some commodity ETFs, and I think that commodities are a very appropriate investment, but a lot of investors don't necessarily understand what they're getting into with a commodity ETF. They don't necessarily get the return of the underlying asset. There was an article in *BusinessWeek* a couple of years ago about an ETF in energy. Crude oil had doubled in price, yet the ETF only went up about 45 percent. It was because the markets were in what is called contango.[4] So it requires a sophisticated understanding of what's going on to really figure this out. And that does fly in the face of what indexing really is all about."

"One problem about ETFs would be the democratization of all of these arcane types of strategies," Sauter said. "The good news is that in the ETF world, most of the assets are in the big, broadly diversified index portfolios, and we think that's where the assets should go. At the same time, individual investors can get exposure to more trouble than you can imagine if they don't know what they're getting into in the ETF space. I think a lot of these ETF strategies can be used effectively by professionals with high skill. But all of a sudden, these types of portfolios are being made available to some investors who really don't know what they're getting into. I think the levered products were an example of that."

With respect to the basics of simple, low-cost, long-term investing, any differences between the philosophies of Bogle and Sauter disappear. "We think of

<hr />

*"Some Investors . . .
Don't Know What
They're Getting Into"*

<hr />

4. Contango is essentially a situation where the price on futures for a commodity exceeds the actual expected price. So as futures contracts are rolled over, contango puts downward pressure on the value of futures contracts as the price inevitably declines to meet the actual market price of the commodity.

indexing as a very simple way, a very effective way, a cost-effective way, to gain exposure to the market," said Sauter. "And we think that most investors should pursue a balanced portfolio, should be broadly diversified, and, by and large, keep things kind of simple. Jack's always talked about stocks, bonds, and cash. Get your asset allocation right. There's so much work that indicates if you get your asset allocation right you'll be in pretty good shape. But too many people spend too much time trying to figure out what the next hot stock will be, and too little time trying to figure out what their asset allocation should be."

David Swensen: A Great Money Manager Endorses Indexing

For decades, Bogle has worked to ensure that fund managers act in accordance with their role as fiduciaries. He has railed against the rise of "managers' capitalism" (see *The Battle for the Soul of Capitalism*, 2005) and described the "double-agency society" and the "happy conspiracy" between corporate manager/agents and money manager/agents (see *The Clash of the Cultures*, 2012) in which corporate and financial intermediaries divert wealth away from the owners of corporate America to themselves.

In his quest to build a new fiduciary society, he has found a kindred spirit in David Swensen, the CIO of Yale University. Since he took the reins in 1985, Swensen has delivered extraordinary returns for Yale's endowment. His investment strategy has come to be known as the Yale model of investing, with an emphasis on alternative and illiquid assets. Swensen has also been an outspoken critic of the financial industry who shares many of Bogle's concerns with high costs and low standards of many investment managers.

"I think Jack Bogle is absolutely correct, as he usually is, when he says that fiduciary responsibility is the fundamental issue for the fund management industry," said Swensen. "Unfortunately for mutual fund investors, the profit motive of fund managers conflicts with their fiduciary responsibility to fund shareholders.

Profit seekers charge high fees, gather unreasonable amounts of assets, and pursue volatile investment strategies. In contrast, fiduciaries charge low fees, limit assets under management to reasonable levels, and pursue stable investment returns."

Supported Overwhelmingly by the Evidence

Echoing Malkiel's point about how the case for indexing is supported overwhelmingly by the evidence, Swensen cited a study conducted by Rob Arnott, student of investment theory and prolific writer on the financial markets. "He looked at 20 years' worth of mutual fund returns and compared them not to a peer group median, which I think is a huge cheat, but rather to the results of the Vanguard 500 Index Fund. And over 20 years, 80 percent of the funds failed to match the pretax return and fell short by an average of 2.1 percent per year. On an after-tax basis, 85 percent of the funds failed to match the returns and failed by 2.8 percent per annum. And the striking thing about these results is that they don't account for survivorship bias and they don't account for loads or other broker-related charges. So if you factor in the broker-related charges and take into account the survivor bias—a huge portion of funds disappear over time—there's almost no chance that you're going to pick an active fund that's going to beat the index over a 20-year period."

The damage inflicted on investors by the mutual fund industry isn't limited to high fees. Swensen argued that a combination of volatile investment strategies and misleading marketing by fund managers leads to poor investor outcomes. "Many people are familiar with the behavioral studies that show that investors tend to chase performance. They buy funds that have performed well and sell funds that have performed poorly. So these terrible results that you get from for-profit active managers are exacerbated by the individual's tendencies to buy high and sell low—to buy after something has done well and sell after it's done poorly. And the greater the volatility in the fund results, the greater the problem."

Fund *Investor* Returns Lag Fund *Reported* Returns

Swensen continued, "In 2005, Morningstar did a study in which they looked at all 17 categories of their equity mutual funds and compared dollar-weighted returns (the returns actually received by investors) to time-weighted returns (reported by the funds). In every single instance in the 10-year performance histories of these categories of funds, the dollar-weighted returns were lower than the time-weighted returns, meaning that individuals went in after they had performed well and sold after they performed poorly. And the greater the volatility, the greater the difference. In the technology fund, the difference between dollar-weighted and time-weighted returns was 13.4 percent per annum. It's stunning. People got into the hot tech stocks after they did well, sold after they did poorly, and damaged their returns enormously.

"A fiduciary would offer low-volatility funds and encourage investors to stay the course, which is exactly what Jack Bogle's Vanguard does with its broad-based index funds and with its valiant attempts to educate investors. But the for-profit mutual fund industry benefits by offering high-volatility funds. It plays the cynical game of selling four- and five-star funds, which are funds that *have* performed well, not funds that *will* perform well, and encourage people to sell their one- and two-star funds, which are funds that have not performed well but will not necessarily perform poorly in the future. And this allows brokers to churn investor portfolios. It allows investors to pretend that they're adding value to their clients by switching them out of the low-rated funds and into the high-rated funds."

The solution to these problems, Swensen observed, is already here. "Of course, Jack Bogle provided a solution to this problem of the conflict between profit motive and fiduciary responsibility. The Vanguard funds operate not on a basis of generating profits for the owners of the funds; rather, they allow the investors in the funds to, in essence, own the management companies and provide these not-for-profit vehicles that offer low-cost index funds. Jack Bogle has given us the tools that we need as investors to succeed. Thank you, Jack."

Roundtable Discussion

The panel transitioned to a roundtable discussion, which began with moderator Ibbotson asking how active and index funds fit together in an investment portfolio. Professor Malkiel started by addressing whether he is disappointed that equity index funds have only a 25 percent market share after being on the market for over 35 years. "If you think of an idea that started in the academy and that was so difficult to get started and has had that much traction," said Malkiel, "I don't see the glass as half empty or two-thirds empty. It see it as one-third full. So I'm actually delighted that indexing has done as well as it has, and I think you ain't seen nothing yet. I think you're going to see indexing continue to grow over time."

While no one disputes the evidence in support of indexing, Sauter pointed out that there still may be a supporting role for active management in an investor's portfolio. Despite "how difficult it is in active management to outperform because of the cost matters hypothesis, it doesn't rule out the fact that an actively managed portfolio can outperform, even over the long term," said Sauter. "I would note I did a study about six or seven years ago, trying to actually quantify this: What percentage should investors have indexed versus what percentage invested actively? I won't go into it in great detail, but I created an efficient frontier and some utility curves and all that sort of stuff.

"Basically what I found was if you have no skill in selecting managers—and, quite honestly, most people don't have skill in selecting managers—then you actually should be 100 percent in index funds. If you have an extreme amount of skill, beyond what anybody's capabilities actually are, I would argue, you should still have 22 percent of your assets indexed. So index funds should be, in many cases, the one investment you have. In some cases, it's a great foundation to build the rest of your portfolio on if you actually have skill in picking some active managers."

"If You're in the Middle, You're Dead"

For Swensen, the difference in pursuing either active or passive strategies is even more black and white. "I think that there are two sensible approaches to take in investing—either 100 percent active or 100 percent passive. I think, unfortunately, most people end up in the middle. For most things in life, the right solution is usually in the middle. But when it comes to investing, if you're in the middle, you're dead. So you should either be all in, 100 percent active, or all in, 100 percent passive. Who should manage their assets actively? I think the only sensible way to structure an active management program is to have a group of incredibly highly qualified professionals who devote their entire careers to trying to find managers or investment strategies that can beat the market."

Another development that Bogle laments is the rise of short-termism in the financial world. Over the six-plus decades that his career spans, he has seen trading volumes and turnover rates soar while investors focus on ever shorter time horizons. The fact that short-termism is detrimental to investors is built into Vanguard's foundation, as Sauter pointed out. "One of Jack's many sayings is, 'Stay the course,' and so Vanguard has always promoted long-term investing. The reason is we think that maximizes an investor's chance of achieving his or her investment goals. If we felt investors could time markets, we'd suggest that they go out and time markets. But we don't think we can do it. We think that most investors get caught up in behavioral problems; they're chasing last year's returns. So it's too often a buy high and sell low strategy. We think investors are best served by figuring out the proper asset allocation and then really just sticking with it over time, realizing that, yes, you're going to go through some volatile periods, but in the long run just getting the market rate of return is going to be a pretty good thing."

Malkiel expanded on the behavioral problems that plague many investors, including professional investors. "More money went into equity mutual funds in the first quarter of 2000 than ever before. And it didn't go into broad mutual funds; it went into the high tech funds because that was what was hot. At the height of the financial crisis in 2008, money poured out of the market. And you might say, 'Well, that's just dumb individuals.' But when you look at the cash positions of professional investors, which I have done, you find exactly the same thing. Professionals tend to have more cash at the bottom of the market and the least amount of cash at the top of the market."

High-Frequency Trading — "A Tax on the Rest of Us"

The panel had some disagreement about the role of high-frequency trading in the markets. High-frequency trading has grown substantially in recent years, with studies suggesting that these high-speed algorithms account for anywhere from 50 percent to 70 percent or more of daily trading volume. The utility of these lightning-fast traders is still up for debate. "There's obviously a lot of volume in the marketplace that is not long-term, but I don't think it's necessarily market timing," said Sauter. "I think a large part of high-frequency trading—which tends to be a lightning rod out there—really is playing micro-inefficiencies in the marketplace and closing those inefficiencies."

Swensen was surprised by Sauter's view. "I always viewed high-frequency trading as a tax on the rest of us," he said, "a bunch of smart people taking advantage of order execution rules as opposed to doing something good for the marketplace."

But for Sauter, the proof is in the pudding. "We've measured our transaction costs over time, and 15 years ago, our transaction costs would have been in the 1 percent range or more, and that actually was good back then. What we've seen over the past 15 years is our transaction costs have declined precipitously. There have been lots of reasons for that. There were changes in the order handling rules, and the proliferation of ECNs [electronic communication networks]; there was decimalization, but also high-frequency traders, which, I think, are kind of the glue that makes all of that happen. We have so many different venues to trade on now; you need somebody to bring those venues back together again, and I view that as the role that the high-frequency traders are playing."

Malkiel pointed out another useful role played by high-frequency traders. "If I'd buy an S&P 500 ETF, it's the high-frequency traders that ensure that the ETF is going to be appropriately priced, because if it was at a premium over the price of the 500 stocks in the market, a high-frequency trader/arbitrager is going to short the thing that's overpriced and buy the stocks and create the unit to cover the short. So I'm not saying that everything that is done by high-frequency trading is correct, but there is certainly an appropriate role for it that doesn't hurt the individual investor. You could even argue that it helps the individual investor."

Individual Investors Need the Tools to Make Intelligent Financial Decisions

One member of the audience asked that if it is time for a concerted effort to better educate investors, given all the evidence that individuals often make poor investment decisions. "I think one of the big problems that we're creating for ourselves and society," observed Swensen, "is we're putting more and more responsibility for retirement savings on the individual without giving the individual the tools that are necessary to make intelligent financial decisions. We've talked about the for-profit mutual fund industry, how they're actually doing things that are adverse to the interests of their investors. And then you've got this firm, Vanguard, operating on a not-for-profit basis, that doesn't have this conflict, that works to educate investors; but it's only one firm."

Sauter pointed out some of the things Vanguard does to ensure investors are well educated. "Jack set up Vanguard to be an advocate for investors. We don't view our role as solely being a 'product' manager providing index funds. We also think that education is a very important part of what we do. So we have an education series or 'plain talk' discussions on the website. At the same time, we have created products that are designed to simplify investing for individual investors. We have our target retirement funds. If you can figure out when you're going to turn 65, you can figure out which fund is going to be right for you. We've created other products that are designed as being kind of advice inside of a product, so we have a spectrum requiring different levels of investment knowledge."

SECOND PANEL: EXECUTIVE COMPENSATION AND GOOD CORPORATE GOVERNANCE

Institutional money managers own some 70 percent of the stocks in the U.S. equity market. Mutual funds alone own more than 30 percent of all equity shares. This voting power gives institutional investors, and mutual funds in particular, virtually complete control over corporate America. With this enormous power, one might expect institutional investors to actively watch over corporate America, working with management to maximize the value of their investments. In reality, nothing could be further from the truth. As John Bogle bluntly states in *The Clash of the Cultures*, "most mutual funds have failed to exercise the rights and responsibilities of corporate citizenship."

Our financial system is plagued by a fundamental conflict of interest: Institutional money managers have the responsibility and means to serve as a watchdog over corporate America, yet they are also seeking the business of those same corporations for retirement plan administration and asset management. As an anonymous money manager once said, "There are only two kinds of clients we can't afford to offend: actual and potential." Perhaps because of this obvious conflict of interest, institutional investors have largely failed in their duty to require that the leaders of corporate America place the interests of their shareholder/owners ahead of their own interests. Yet, in Bogle's grim assessment, "while the managers of most large fund groups carefully review and consider corporate proxies, with few major exceptions, they overwhelmingly endorse the proposals of corporate managements. When they vote, they usually do just as they are asked; they support management's recommendations. This practice is a far cry, not only from activism and advocacy, but from the very process of corporate governance."

The John C. Bogle Legacy Forum brought together an expert panel on corporate governance and executive compensation issues:

- Kenneth Feinberg, founder and managing partner of Feinberg Rozen, LLP, served as Special Master for TARP Executive Compensation, the U.S. Treasury Department's so-called pay czar, responsible for setting compensation for top executives at several firms that received Troubled Asset Relief Program (TARP) money, and as Special Master of the September 11th Victim Compensation Fund. Feinberg has a unique perspective on the process of determining appropriate compensation.
- Lynn E. Turner, chief accountant of the U.S. Securities and Exchange Commission from 1998 to 2001, and a managing director at LitiNomics. His government service and long experience as a CPA give him a firsthand view of the issues facing the accounting profession today. An all-around expert on corporate governance issues, Turner was heavily involved in the shaping of the Sarbanes-Oxley Act.
- Alan S. Blinder (moderator), the Gordon S. Rentschler Memorial Professor of Economics and Public Affairs at Princeton University, served as a member

on President Clinton's Council of Economic Advisers and as vice chairman of the Board of Governors of the Federal Reserve System; he is the author of numerous books, academic articles, and newspaper and magazine essays, and a regular columnist for the *Wall Street Journal*.

Kenneth Feinberg

The Need "to Do Something Symbolic"

In the wake of the financial crisis and the bailout of numerous firms through TARP, political pressure mounted on Congress to do something about executive compensation at the firms receiving taxpayer money. (Taxpayers find something distasteful about massive bonuses for executives at firms relying on government bailouts for their very existence!) So the Treasury Department brought in Kenneth Feinberg as Special Master for TARP Executive Compensation. "Congress passed a law in the wake of the TARP bailout, and Congress decided populism means street revenge," said Feinberg. "Congress wanted to do something symbolic— *symbolic*—so it passed a law that said that the government—the Treasury—will fix the pay of the top 25 corporate officials in only those seven companies that took the most TARP assistance. Citigroup, AIG [American International Group], Bank of America, General Motors, GMAC, Chrysler, and Chrysler Financial. Only for those seven will government set the pay—not the prescriptions, the actual calculation. It had never been done before as far as I know—actually adding up what somebody ought to make in the private sector. But if that's the law of the land, then that's the law of the land, so I agreed to do it.

"Over 16 months, we set pay for the top 25 people. Now, nobody suggested that that authority be expanded. Nobody in Congress or the administration ever suggested, 'Why not do it for everybody in the private sector?' So we invited the seven companies in. They were under my jurisdiction only as long as they owed the taxpayers those loans. Once they repaid, they were out from under my jurisdiction. Four of the companies borrowed money to get out from under my jurisdiction, and they're gone. Citigroup, Bank of America, Chrysler, Chrysler Financial—they're no longer part of this. GM, Ally, and AIG—AIG will be under the jurisdiction of the Treasury forever.

"We asked, 'What do you think we ought to pay you?' Everybody in the seven companies made the same argument: 'This person is irreplaceable. If we lose this person and we don't pay her enough, she will go to a competitor. She's going to go work in China. Everybody's going to work in China if they look for a job, and the company will founder. This person is irreplaceable.' I said, 'The graveyard is filled with irreplaceable people, right?' People aren't irreplaceable. These people stayed at these jobs, and we fixed the pay, and the American people were riveted by this."

"The Graveyard Is Filled with Irreplaceable People"

"The Gap Between Wall Street and Main Street"—Executive Pay Captures the Public's Attention

Feinberg believes that people aren't interested in a public debate about economic incentives; rather, they just want to know the bottom line. "They're really interested in two aspects of this. Much more important is how much people are going to make. Forget all this highfalutin discussion about incentives. What rivets the American people is the gap between Wall Street and Main Street pay. That's what people outside, walking down the street, find interesting."

Despite the fact that he describes the exercise as primarily symbolic, Feinberg thinks there is the possibility of some lasting effect. "The incentives that we promulgated included much less up-front guaranteed cash, and much more compensation tied to company stock performance over the long term, which cannot be redeemed for two, three, four years. I think the prescriptions that we promulgated while I was at Treasury will (hopefully) have some impact."

However, Feinberg points out that there are several other forces at work in setting executive compensation. "I think there are three much more important influences on pay. One is Adam Smith—the marketplace. I think the marketplace is self-correcting in a lot of respects. I think if you look at the marketplace, that's had more impact on pay than anything we've done. Two, the Volcker Rule and liquidity rules have had an impact indirectly on pay because big companies can't invest in excessively risky ventures the way they did. It's more difficult to do so in light of liquidity requirements and the Volcker Rule. And three, more interest among federal agencies: the SEC with its transparency rules on pay, FDIC and Sheila Bair's work with the banks, the Federal Reserve, and the G-20 with Secretary [Timothy] Geithner. I think those three reasons—Adam Smith, Dodd-Frank, and more agency interest—are, relatively speaking, more important than anything we're doing or I did with these few people and these few companies."

Lynn Turner

Lynn Turner is a respected voice on corporate governance issues. His career in accounting, auditing, and beyond has been dedicated to improving transparency in order to maximize value for shareholders. He shares many of Jack Bogle's concerns with the erosion of fiduciary standards evident in corporate America today, and he places much of the blame at the feet of the boards of directors. "In medieval England, the common use of the word *stewardship* meant the responsible use of a congregation's resources in the faithful service of God. In the corporate sense, the word has come to mean the use of an enterprise's resources in faithful service to its owners, but somehow the system has let us down. Boards of directors far too often turned over to the companies' managers the virtually unfettered power to place their own interests first. Both the word and the concept of stewardship became conspicuous by their absence from corporate America's values."

Standards for a Successful Board

Turner described what he sees as the requirements for a successful board. "In my opinion, if we're going to have a good board, we've got to have a number of standards that those boards meet. First of all, they've got to be a very knowledgeable board. We want people who understand the business, know what it's about, and can get in and dig in and figure out if it's on the right track or not. I look for a board that has the diversity and knowledge that we also look for in the CEO—those same critical success factors that the CEO has to have as far as knowledge of operations, marketing, and running the R&D projects are concerned. You've got to have those same qualities on the board if you're going to have a successful board.

"We want a diverse board so that if the CEO needs advice, he can call them anytime and get their input," Turner continued. "I've found that when you have a troubled CEO you also have a troubled board—they go hand in hand. We've seen some examples in the past few years, like HP [Hewlett-Packard] and others that I think spell that out in spades."

It has become common in recent years for boards to seek consensus and speak with a single voice. But Turner does not necessarily think that is progress. "It's got to be an independent board, one that is willing to speak up and have good communication. Often I've sat on boards where some people say, 'Oh, we've got to have a unanimous vote all the time. We can never have a "no" vote.' That's not a truly independent board. There's nothing wrong with having a 'no' vote in the boardroom. In fact, that is probably an indication that you've got a good board and people are really kicking the issues around as they should. Once you've had the 'no' vote, though, you need to move on. You need to have a group that works together as a solid group, and once the 'no' vote is taken, regardless of whether you win or lose, you've got to move on."

A critical factor for a successful board is engagement, and the board cannot be properly engaged if its members do not have adequate time to devote to the company. "You've got to have time to spend on the board," Turner asserted. "These boards take a lot of time, and too often I see board members show up and they're just popping open the board book as they arrive. That just doesn't get it done.

"There's Nothing Wrong With Having a 'No' Vote"

You have to spend enough time on the floor—what I would call 'on the concrete,' where things actually happen—compared to time 'on the carpet,' where you just don't see what's going on in the nuts and bolts of the company."

"I remember being on one board where I went out and visited manufacturing plants," Turner recalled. "During one of the meetings, I was sitting with all the managers at the plant and they told me about this banana report. I said, 'Well, what do you mean by a banana report?' I had never heard about it in the boardroom. As it turned out, that was the single most important report that the management team used to run what was a huge Fortune 500 size company. That report had never made it into the boardroom, yet it was accurate almost to the dime as to how that company was going to perform. You've got to be able to go out there and get that type of information."

Turner relayed another anecdote about a director who overextended himself. "When I was running the Glass Lewis proxy voting service, I received a call from a director whom we had voted against in the past because we thought he served on too many boards. He served on seven boards of public companies at the time. He called me and said, 'Lynn, I wonder if you would mind if I serve on one more.' I said, 'Well, tell me what you do. You've got six or seven boards you're already serving on. Do you do anything outside of the boards?' He said, 'Well, I serve on a couple of not-for-profit boards as well.' I said, 'Okay, so you're on six or seven public boards and a couple not for profit. Is there anything else you do?'

"He said, 'Well, I do serve as the executive director of a not-for-profit foundation in New York City.' And I said, 'Well, how much time do you spend on that?' 'Oh, about half my year.' And I said, 'You've got no time. You're on that for half the year. These boards [should] take 200, 300 hours. You're on six or seven already and you're asking me if you've got enough time to serve on another board?'

I mean, just common sense would tell you what the answer was and that phone call shouldn't have been made. So you've got to have time."

Losing Elections but Winning Board Seats

Turner then moved on to some of the most significant corporate governance issues that he sees, starting with the issue of majority voting. Until recently, the default in many cases was the plurality voting standard, in which the director with the most "for" votes is elected to the board. The controversial implication of plurality voting is that, in the common case of uncontested elections, merely a single "for" vote ensures that a director is successfully elected.

Turner described his concerns: "One thing that indicates to me that the board is not working is when the board refuses to have majority voting. Capitalism and democracy go hand in hand. You can't have one without having the other. To have a boardroom where you don't have democracy, where a director can get reseated with just one vote from a shareholder, as it is today, is flat-out wrong. When the majority of large companies have already gone with majority voting, the rest need to get on that ship. In fact, we've had 200 to 300 corporate directors who have not received a majority of the vote; they have been voted off of the board and yet almost every single one of them has chosen to remain on the board, and the board has let them. It doesn't look as though those boards are working for the shareholders."

Turner then turned his attention to forum shopping and the corporate-friendly laws in Delaware. "The next thing that gets under my skin is forum shopping. This is where companies, with the approval of their board, look to move all their litigation to the state of Delaware, which doesn't speak highly for the Delaware courts. I dislike it when shareholders try to move litigation to a particular county in Mississippi or Indiana or wherever. Likewise, I really dislike it when companies try to do the same to me and go forum shopping. I also dislike it when they try to take my right away—that I think is in the Constitution—that says I have the right to the U.S. judicial system. We're seeing people propose that I, as a shareholder, do not have the right to the U.S. court system. I get forced into an arbitration system that, quite frankly, has turned out to be very costly and is clearly tilted against me."

Turner pulled no punches when describing his animus toward the Supreme Court's decision in the *Citizens United* case. "I hate the political contribution issue, the *Citizens United* case. I think we've got to find a way to get transparency around that. Research has shown that companies that get highly involved with political contributions often damage the value of my investment. Making political contributions is their right—the court has said that—but we certainly need transparency around it."

Roundtable Discussion —"CEOs Became Kings and Queens"

Moderator Alan Blinder posed a question to the panel dealing with the change in the role of corporate executives over the years. "When I was a youngster, a long, long time ago, CEOs of major corporations were the top employee of that corporation. That was their attitude. That was the attitude people had toward them. Sometime between now and then, and some years ago, CEOs became kings and queens and princes and princesses, and I would like your thoughts about how that happened, and whether it's been harmful or good for that matter. And if it's harmful, what, if anything, can be done about it?"

Kenneth Feinberg replied with a sort of libertarian approach to the issue of executive compensation. "I'm not sure there's much you can do about it. What I've learned in the brief time I had that job of fixing pay is that unless you're going to attack the problem with sort of a shotgun, every company is different. Everybody's compensation culture is different, and there are limitations in a free society on what you can really legislate or promulgate. Now, as you point out, Professor, I see in my work abuses. But I worry whether the solutions shouldn't be left to the marketplace or whether the solutions imposed are worse than the problem. That's a roundabout way of saying yes, I'm troubled by the growing gap between CEOs and energy traders and line employees, but that's the easy part. When you're trying to figure out what to do about it, that's where you get into some deep water I think."

Lynn Turner, in contrast, sees the possibility that improved corporate governance can play a role in reining in unchecked executive power. "I'd probably differ with Ken on this. I think that to say we can't solve the problem is to say you're going to accept the status quo. And I think that's unacceptable. I think this is starting to tear this country apart, and I think it's tearing at the very social fabric. So, I don't think you can say you can't fix it. I think you've got to go find a fix."

Government Is Not the Answer

"I don't think that the fix lies in the government," Turner continued. "I don't put a whole lot of faith there. I think that what you've got to do is you've got to put in a system that holds these people accountable, one that requires a great deal of transparency so people can see what's going on. When you give shareholders a vote on compensation and you give them the right to replace directors and you give them majority voting, you are starting to create such a system."

Turner didn't limit the role of corporate governance to having a say on pay, however. "The other piece of it that we don't have, though, is a higher fiduciary standard for the asset managers. We often call these people institutional investors, and that's a grave misnomer. They are asset managers that collect assets and charge fees for it—that's how they make their money and that's their business.

"If we create the type of fiduciary standard that Jack Bogle has talked about in his book *Don't Count on It!* (2011), where those asset managers actually have to vote their shares in the best interest of their investors, then I think you'll have a workable system in the marketplace. To Ken's point, it's not government-driven; it's built around transparency. You've got to give me all the clear details about compensation. You've got to put it to a vote. And if it's a negative vote, the people are held accountable. In this past year, quite frankly, in most of the say-on-pay votes they [compensation rates] were accepted. But there were some where they weren't. I think that type of marketplace mechanism will work and work great. We're part of the way there, but we've got to go the rest of the way, and we've got to get a fiduciary standard or it will not work."

Questions and Answers

An audience member asked about the importance of separating the roles of CEO and chairman of the board. "The board has a fiduciary obligation that I think is critically important," responded Turner. "By separating the roles of CEO and chairman I think you get the board more focused on that obligation to the shareholders, and I think that's a very positive thing.

"What is interesting about it is that 20 years down the road we will be there. We will have separation in most public companies. If you look at the progress of governance in this country, we are extremely slow. We'll be there on proxy access. We'll be there on separation of CEO and board chairman. We'll be there on majority voting. We're getting very close on majority voting, but it takes us forever and it takes us a lot of stumbles to get there. It would be nice if we can just get there and get to a more efficient system that would actually result in higher returns for our businesses, which I'm convinced will occur. So I think the separation is very important. It will happen. It will turn out to be very good, but we'll go through a very painful process in getting there."

Citizens United— "A Horrible Decision"

The topic of the *Citizens United* decision was raised again by a member of the audience. "There is research out there that clearly shows that companies that tend to lobby more aggressively have had negative impacts from that on their shareholder values," said Turner. "So from a shareholder perspective, that obviously concerns me.

"I personally have never had a corporation stand up and have a discussion with me, and I've seen no one tell me when the point of conception is with a corporation, so I'm not sure I understand why they're deemed to be a person. I think that was one of the most outlandish decisions by the Supreme Court that we've ever seen. I think it takes the Supreme Court back to the days of the 1850s and the Dred-Scott-type days. I think it's just a horrendous decision.

"I think companies need to be running a business and need to be serving all their constituents—their employees, their management team, their shareholders, and the community; and I think when you get into the type of political financing that we've got from corporations you get away from those goals. It gets into people's personal ideologies and that doesn't serve me as an investor in any way, fashion, shape, or form."

Feinberg wholeheartedly agreed with Turner's sentiments on *Citizens United*. "*Horrible* decision. A horrible decision that's had a very negative impact. Forget corporate America; it's had a very negative impact, I personally believe, on the entire political discourse in this country.

"You'll need either a Constitutional amendment to change it or over time a change in the personalities on the Supreme Court. Those are the only two solutions. If the existing court finds a First Amendment right to contribute whatever you want, I don't see a short-term solution. Never mind the amount of money being spent by corporate America lobbying in Washington and creating a cottage industry in Washington; the impact of it on the overall political dialogue in this country I think is very, very, very negative. It's very unfortunate."

Reflections by John Bogle   John Bogle is so passionate about corporate governance that he simply had to join in the conversation. Continuing the discussion about *Citizens United* and corporate political contributions, Bogle added, "We don't need a Supreme Court decision. We don't need a Constitutional amendment. We need the shareholders to stand up for their rights. Financial institutions own 70 percent of every publicly held corporation in America, and they do nothing. So they have to be aroused. They must exercise the rights and honor the responsibilities of stock ownership.

"In particular I think there ought to be a shareholder vote—and I sent this proposal to the SEC—on political contributions. Disclosure is fine as a second step, but as a first step let us ask the shareholders of the company, the owners of the company, whether the corporation should make any political contributions whatsoever. And I suggested they would have to have a 75 percent majority of the vote to be able to give those corporate assets away.

"My second point is regarding the failure of our accountants. They have a terrible conflict of interest. Lynn and I were on the Independence Standards Board, created by Chairman Levitt. It's just unbelievable what goes on in the accounting world. Our large CPA firms (the final four) are the captives of management. They represent management and not shareholders."

The "Marketplace" for Executive Compensation

"Finally, we can't rely on the 'marketplace' to ensure reasonable executive compensation," Bogle concluded. "The marketplace for executive compensation is set by a word that we haven't heard up here. The management goes to the compensation consultants, and I can't imagine that there has ever been a compensation consultant that's stayed in business by saying to a chief executive, 'You deserve less money.' When we focus on the compensation of peers rather than corporate performance—the creation of intrinsic value—we have the ratchet effect, and every year compensation goes up, up, up." (In *The Clash of the Cultures*, Bogle noted that problems created by such a "consultopoly" parallel those created by a monopoly or an oligopoly.)

Feinberg agreed with Bogle's point about executive compensation consultants. "At Treasury I decided that I ought to go out and retain the services of an independent compensation consultant to help us. But we couldn't find an independent compensation consultant. We looked. We finally had to go to academia to find a couple of independent compensation consultants. Commercially, for the reasons you say, there was either a direct conflict or a perceived conflict, and it made our job tougher."

THIRD PANEL: FIDUCIARY DUTY: WHAT IS THE FUTURE?

"A Double-Agency Society Engaged in a Happy Conspiracy"

"The managers of other people's money [rarely] watch over it with the same anxious vigilance with which . . . they watch over their own. Like the stewards of a rich man, they very easily give themselves a dispensation. Negligence and profusion therefore must always prevail." These words, written by the great Scottish moral and economic philosopher Adam Smith, succinctly describe the problem of agency. Manager/agents play a central role in the management of both today's giant multinational corporations and the massive pools of investor capital that fund them. As John Bogle puts it, these agents are the dominant participants in a "double-agency society" engaged in a "happy conspiracy." Together, they control nearly all of the public companies in the United States. The traditional values of trusteeship have been "eroded by the same temptations that have challenged agent/principal relationships since the beginning of time: the natural temptation for agents to enrich themselves at the expense of their principals."

Rather than giving primacy to their roles as fiduciaries, today's manager/agents, in Bogle's words, "came to an apparent, if tacit, understanding that the principal focus of corporate accomplishment is 'creating shareholder value.' That's a fine goal, of course, but their shared definition of value has focused on the short-term, evanescent, emotion-driven price of the stock, rather than the long-term, solid, reality-driven intrinsic value of the corporation." Managers trade stocks at the highest turnover levels in history, often trading them for periods measured in days or weeks or even seconds. This short-termism is one of the primary factors driving the change away from the wisdom of long-term investment toward the folly of short-term speculation. To make matters worse, our manager/agents have captured the corporate and financial systems and installed a "heads I win, tails you lose" culture that rewards those at the top no matter the outcome. Golden parachutes for failed corporate executives and excessive fees for underperforming asset managers are today's norm.

A Common-Law System of Fiduciary Duty

Hundreds of years ago, English common law developed a way to mitigate some of these agency issues: a common-law standard of fiduciary duty—the requirement that agents place the interests of their principals first. To the detriment of investors today, we have drifted too far from that lofty standard. But there is a growing chorus of voices calling for a return to the fiduciary standard, John Bogle's being one of the strongest. Bogle has long been an advocate for a federal statutory standard of fiduciary duty, one that not only ensures that money managers act with prudence, but that also demands good corporate governance, with conflicts of interest resolved in favor of shareholder/principals. Such a standard would require all fiduciaries to act solely in the long-term interest of their beneficiaries.

So how do we get there? That question was posed to several individuals who have seen this battle fought from the inside. The panel on fiduciary duty at the John C. Bogle Legacy Forum featured individuals who have seen this fight play out from the inside. The panelists included three former SEC Chairmen:

- Harvey L. Pitt, chairman of the U.S. Securities and Exchange Commission (2001–2003); CEO of Kalorama Partners.
- David R. Ruder, chairman of the U.S. Securities and Exchange Commission (1987–1989); William W. Gurley Memorial Professor of Law, Emeritus, Northwestern University School of Law.

- Arthur Levitt Jr. (moderator), chairman of the U.S. Securities and Exchange Commission (1993–2001); operating executive at the Carlyle Group.
- T. Timothy Ryan Jr., Global Head of Regulatory Strategy and Policy at JPMorgan; former president and CEO of the Securities Industry and Financial Markets Association (SIFMA).

Arthur Levitt set the tone for the panel. While all of the panelists want investors to be well served, he expects that there will be subtle differences in their approaches to applying the fiduciary standard to stock brokers, who now operate under the "suitability" standard. "I'm sure that there'll be a lot of agreement that we all favor the same thing. But if you listen carefully, I think you'll find that all of the panelists do not favor precisely the same outcome. I think we'd all agree that investor protection is critical, but this issue of how to protect that investor and how to sidestep the different interests that the adviser and the broker may have that are apart from those of the investor is the topic that we will discuss."

T. Timothy Ryan

John Bogle has long been an outspoken advocate for the fiduciary standard. But it should not be surprising that the financial industry, in general, does not share Bogle's enthusiasm. T. Timothy Ryan Jr., speaking as the then head of SIFMA, one of Wall Street's chief lobbying organizations, does not embrace the role of the fiduciary standard with open arms. Many of his constituents in the industry would prefer to continue to operate under suitability standards similar to those in existence today. In addition to fee-based independent financial advisers, the retail side of the financial industry includes broker/dealers, underwriters, and distributors who feel that the fiduciary standard does not make sense for their business models.

David Ruder

David Ruder approaches the issue from a different angle. As a longtime academic and former SEC chairman, Ruder observed that the issue is nuanced. "I think that there is a movement to try to impose upon broker/dealers the same fiduciary obligations that investment advisers have. But I've been an academic all my life, a law professor, and I don't see things in black and white. So just that statement alone is not enough. The standard that is being proposed is the standard for broker/dealers that will apply when providing personalized investment advice about securities to a retail customer.

"What is the standard?" asked Ruder. "The standard in the Dodd-Frank Act is to act in the best interests of the customer without regard to the financial interests of the broker/dealer or investment adviser providing the service. So the idea is that the standard should be the same for both broker/dealers and investment advisers. But there are questions about whether that's appropriate.

Brokers and Advisers—The Same Standard?

"For instance, should a dealer acting as dealer in selling a security to the public be required to have this fiduciary duty to say to the public, 'There's something wrong with what I'm selling you'? Or should the dealer be allowed to proceed as an independent person dealing in an arm's-length manner? I know the industry has concerns about that. It's something that they say will affect the way the industry operates.

"The second question that I really have difficulty with is that the Dodd-Frank Act says that it might be possible for investors to have the ability to acknowledge the conflict of interest and waive their right to the fiduciary standard. So I see there are details in the way the industry operates that will purvey the operation of the new law. I do think that it is important for the retail investor to see that he has one kind of duty owed either by the broker or by the investment adviser. But it's going to be a very difficult problem in getting to that result."

Harvey Pitt

"Most People Don't Understand the Differences."

Former SEC chairman Harvey Pitt thinks the key to the fiduciary standard issue is how actual investors are impacted. "I look at this whole question from a very different perspective. And that is pragmatics. What really happens out in the marketplace when people are besieged by either brokers or independent financial analysts or the like? Because in essence, I think the touch point has to be what people think they are getting. And even where a broker may not be giving personalized investment advice, the broker may be looked upon by customers as someone who is putting his client's interests first.

"I started at the Commission in 1968, and we had a lot of broker/dealer cases back in those days. And all of the cases were about concerns that certain brokers hadn't really represented the interests of their clients. If you look at it from that perspective, I'm not persuaded that many people know the difference between the obligations of the suitability rule, the know-your-customer rule, or fiduciary duty. Most people don't understand the differences. Even if they are sophisticated, they're sophisticated about companies where they would like to invest, but they all start with the presumption that the professional who is working with them and to whom they entrust their capital is looking out for their best interests. So as I see it, one really has to start from that model as opposed to trying to decide, first, whether we should have a uniform standard.

"Second, does it have to be applicable across the board in all circumstances? If a broker is doing nothing more than executing trades directed by his or her customers, I don't really perceive that kind of service as requiring a fiduciary standard. If the customer is undertaking to make his or her own decisions, doing his or her own research, I don't see that as warranting the imposition of a fiduciary standard. But if the customer is relying on the professional to provide the kind of assistance and advice that most of us rely on securities professionals for, I think the law has done a poor job of keeping up with the realities of the marketplace.

I think it's not so much that we have to have a uniform standard as it is that we ought to make the reality comport with what people think they're getting. And if they're not getting that, have the professionals totally disclaim whether or not they are offering anything other than, say, a bare execution service.

"It may be far better simply to say we are obligating broker/dealers and investment advisers and financial analysts and the like to act in the best interests of their customers, and to the extent that they are not providing services, to make sure that those services are clearly excluded. Some people have a question as to whether, for example, you can carve out certain services.

Disclose the Conflicts?

"I think if people are sophisticated enough to invest in the markets, and if brokers and investment advisers don't use boilerplate but genuinely tell their customers, 'You should understand you're the one who's going to be making the selections, but if I recommend something to you, I may have a potential conflict. I'm obligated to tell you what my conflict is so you know that there are other alternatives out there.' I don't see why that's such a hard position for the professionals to achieve."

Roundtable Discussion

Chairman Levitt crystallized the argument in favor of a uniform fiduciary standard suggested by Chairman Pitt. "The advisory industry is basing their argument essentially on an unlevel playing field. Brokers are free of the obligations that are imposed upon advisers. What you're suggesting, as I understand it, is a rule that would apply across the board to both brokers and advisers to follow the same standards, the same rules, the same obligations."

"Yes," replied Chairman Pitt, "subject to the ability to make it clear that, as a broker, 'I'm not going to provide you with any investment ideas. That's not what our relationship is. Or if I am going to provide you with investment ideas, you should know that my firm puts out its own investments and I may make more money if I recommend those, and I'll tell you about that. But you have to understand going in that that's what I'm going to do.'"

Chairman Levitt did not feel that this position would work in practice. "That's where we part ways, Harvey. Having been a broker, I know the reluctance of brokers to be that forthcoming. It's very unusual when a broker takes an order and he doesn't have some question, some comment, some observation. David, would you accept the Dodd-Frank version of fiduciary responsibility and go with that as it is?"

"I think the standard is fine," replied Chairman Ruder. "But if there's going to be rule making, there are all kinds of questions that need to be asked."

Chairman Pitt acknowledged that there are practical concerns with a universal fiduciary standard, but didn't think those concerns should stand in the way of the optimal solution for investors. "Let me just say I thought Arthur raised a very good point as to what you can expect from people who are being paid on a commission basis, how forthcoming they will be. Obviously, there will always be people who look to cut corners. But I don't think that should dictate what the proper standards are. I think that means there just needs to be effective enforcement if people go off the reservation. I think the SEC right now cannot win a regulatory case in the D.C. Circuit [Court of Appeals], and thus if any lawyer filed a suit in any other circuit it would probably be prima facie malpractice because the D.C. Circuit does not like the SEC right now. But both the SEC and the CFTC are trying to regulate the derivatives and swaps markets for the first time; they have to adopt hundreds of rules and they have no real experience doing the kinds of cost-benefit analyses that the Court of Appeals seems to be requiring."

Many observers have argued that the SEC's cost-benefit analysis requirement has allowed those skeptical of financial regulation to obstruct the rule-making

"The D.C. Circuit Court Does Not Like the SEC Right Now"

process. Chairman Levitt asked the panel their thoughts on the issue. "Is there any way, Harvey, of really fulfilling the request for cost-benefit analysis?" asked Levitt. "It seems to me this area is so complex that there will always be a way to challenge whatever cost-benefit analysis is set forth by the agency."

"I think there is," answered Chairman Pitt. "And the first thing that really has to be done is that the agencies have to stop using lawyers to do their cost-benefit analysis."

Better Statistical Analysis for the SEC Is Needed

Chairman Ruder also believes it is possible for the SEC to effectively enact new rules despite the cost-benefit analysis requirement. "I think that the Commission needs to present a good case that there are benefits that can't be quantified because we're looking to the future. And it seems to me that's a persuasive argument. I think the argument would get further in the Second Circuit than it would in the D.C. Circuit. And the other thing to note is that the SEC has turned toward having a better statistical analysis, a better set of economists, and needs to be quite careful."

Chairman Pitt believes that the political environment that exists today is much different than when he started at the SEC in 1968. "When Ray Garrett was chairman (and I was privileged to be his executive assistant from 1972 to 1974), a scandal erupted because the equity funding problem had been brought to the Commission's Los Angeles office, and people did not see the problem. So the fellow who raised it took it to the *Wall Street Journal*. They saw it, ran with it, and then the Commission had to spend a great deal of time explaining how equity funding could have come about with all of these regulatory protections.

"The difference was it was a genuine inquiry. People were trying to figure out how this happened instead of figuring out who they could blame for it. It happened. People do screw up. So you get over that and you say, 'Okay, how do we fix this now so that there's less likelihood something like this will happen?' instead of saying, 'Who can we pillory because they missed something like this?'

"That, to me, is what's making work at the current Commission very difficult. And the one thing I would tell those of you here who deal with entities that are regulated is that a fearful, attacked, uncertain regulator is much worse than the most aggressive and vehement regulator. I'd much rather have regulators who believe in what they're doing and are not afraid to go after what they see, and if they overstep their bounds they get pushed back. But we have a Commission now that's—and I agree with you, Arthur, I think they are doing a terrific job—but we have a Commission now where the staff sits in fear that whatever decisions they make will be turned against them for one reason or another. And nobody can regulate in that kind of environment."

"Blood Sport" in the Nation's Capital

Chairman Levitt agreed. "I testified before Congress on an average once every three and a half weeks. Every time I testified it took two days of staff preparation to get me up there. That's an outrageous waste. What happened during our years, certainly during Harvey's and mine, was the business community, instead of making the SEC the first stop, made it the second stop after they had seen congressional staff and congressional members. And the job of those congressional members, particularly of the opposing party, was to make the Commission look inept and stupid and was enormously time consuming. And still is. What is happening in Washington today is a blood sport, and that's not good for investors. It's not good for regulators."

There still remains an unsettled issue in that investment advisers and broker/dealers have, in some cases, different roles in the financial industry. While it is reasonable to expect investment advisers to behave as fiduciaries at all times, some would argue that broker/dealers, in at least some of their capacities, can reasonably operate at arm's length with clients. Chairman Ruder elaborated: "I think it's too easy to say there should be a single fiduciary standard, because businesses are different. The one piece of it that is clear to me is that the dealer is acting in an arm's-length manner and is selling securities that the dealer is buying and selling. And in that case, it may be that you don't want to have a solid fiduciary duty. But when the broker is providing investment advice to the retail client, then I think there needs to be a standard the broker can be held to, and that is that the broker must put the best interests of the client first."

Chairman Pitt agreed with Chairman Ruder. "The goal, I think, is that if I'm doing something more than just being an order taker, I am supposed to put the interests of my clients first. That, it seems to me, is a place where everybody ought to be able to agree. And although the devil will be in the details, I don't think you have to fuss with separate definitions to separate conduct. That is what they do for a living. And I have high confidence that they'll be able to do it and be able to do it well. I'm sure we'll have comments. Others will have comments. And they'll look at them and figure out the answers to those questions."

Chairman Levitt closed the discussion by reiterating his concerns about the cost-benefit analysis requirement. "I probably differ from the others at this table. I really believe the cost-benefit issue is a very, very slippery slope and used by the Congress to thwart regulation. I take from my colleagues' observations that they feel that there is a way of defining sensible cost-benefit obligations."

Put the Interests of Clients First —"A Place Where Everybody Ought to Be Able to Agree"

Reflections by John Bogle—The Fiduciary Standard Should Also Apply to Institutional Money Managers

While the distinguished panel focused on a requirement that registered investment advisers and stockbrokers (wealth managers or account executives) are held to a standard of fiduciary duty to their clients, Bogle added, "I believe that such a standard should also be demanded of institutional money managers—now managing some $13 trillion of other people's money—agents for mutual fund investors, for beneficiaries of private and public pension plans, and for college endowment funds and beneficiaries of trust accounts supervised by banks. These institutional investors now hold more than 70 percent of all U.S. stocks, up from only 8 percent in 1951 when my long career in the mutual fund industry began."

Surely, Bogle added, such a fiduciary standard is *implicit* in the management of assets for clients. Indeed, in the Investment Company Act of 1940, regulating mutual funds, it is blunt and *explicit*: Mutual funds must be "organized, operated, and managed" in the interests of their shareholders rather than in the interests of "investment advisers and underwriters" (fund distributors).[5] Nothing could be much clearer than that mandate. But that noble standard appears in the preamble to the 1940 Act, followed by no explicit standards, nor any means for its enforcement. According to Bogle, "the watchdog has been given no teeth."

Powerful interest groups already resist imposing the fiduciary standard on registered advisers, but the tide seems to be moving in that direction, with the Institute for the Fiduciary Standard relentlessly pushing the ideas from noble principle to business conduct. Despite its clear mandate to institutional investing, that advance will be a tougher slog. But using Chairman Pitt's closing words: "[E]verybody ought to be able to agree. . . . And I have high confidence that [the industry and the regulators will] be able to do it and be able to do it well."

"Mutual Funds Must Be Organized, Operated, and Managed in the Interests of their Shareholders"

FOURTH PANEL: JACK BOGLE, THE COMMUNICATOR

Ten books; 575 speeches; 14 academic articles; 750 annual reports; more than a dozen op-eds in the *New York Times* and the *Wall Street Journal*; countless television and radio appearances; volumes of correspondence with Vanguard shareholders.

---

5. Investment Company Act of 1940.

Bogle "Informs, Educates, Entertains, Challenges..."

Effective communication has been one of the secrets to Jack Bogle's success. But he is not merely an effective communicator; he simultaneously informs, educates, entertains, challenges, and ultimately, improves the understanding of those with whom he communicates. Bogle communicates in a straightforward yet sophisticated manner. Whether you're a financial novice turning on CNBC and seeing him speak for the first time or you're an experienced industry professional reading about the latest developments in an academic financial journal, you are sure to be enlightened by Jack Bogle. The final panel discussion of the John C. Bogle Legacy Forum brought together two experts on Bogle's oeuvre. The panelists for this final conversation were:

- Martin Fridson, Global Credit Strategist, BNP Paribas Asset Management, Inc.; writer of reviews for several of Bogle's books.
- Jeremy Duffield, chairman, Australian Centre for Financial Studies (ACFS); director, McNamee Lawrence & Co. LLC (MLC); former chairman and Founding Managing Director, Vanguard Investments Australia.
- James Green (moderator), Group Editorial Director, Investment Advisor Group, Summit Business Media.

James Green: Setting the Stage

Moderator James Green began the discussion:

> We're here to talk about John Bogle's books, nine so far, with a tenth due for publication later this year, but while we do that, we'll also attempt to assess Mr. Bogle's influence—not just his written word, but also his communication style and his communications approach that runs throughout all his public work. My role as editorial overseer of *Investment Advisor* magazine, of *Research* magazine, and of Advisorone.com is to ensure that these publications serve those professionals who provide investment and wealth management advice to individuals.

We've long recognized the contributions of Mr. Bogle, both to professionals and to clients. In fact, at the time of our 30th anniversary of *Investment Advisor*, we named Mr. Bogle the most influential person in the investment adviser space over those 30 years. He's also been very generous with his time with our reporters, and with the media in general over his long career.

Mr. Bogle never speaks down to the end client. But he does always speak up to professionals, appealing to their better natures, both because it's the right thing to do and because it's the right thing to do for their clients. He speaks simply and bluntly, but also has long used his bully pulpit to call professionals to a higher calling. Professionals have listened, both in this country and throughout the world, as I think we'll agree. He's also a contrarian of sorts, and I think that contrariness is part of his contribution to the public debate about investing.

Martin Fridson: Reflections on Bogle's Books

"A Genuine Benefit to the Investor"

Martin Fridson then took a moment to reflect on Bogle's impact as an author:

Jack Bogle is best known for spreading the gospel of indexing. We've heard quite a bit about that today, and I mean that in the most positive sense. It is something he believes in very strongly, and it has a genuine benefit to the investor, which comes across very strongly in his book. But this is not merely something that he advocates because of a belief in it; he supports this with very powerful, and very rigorous, and intensive research. And that research is accessible to the nonprofessional investor. It does not rely on elaborate quantitative methods that would be very esoteric.

In fact, both he and I have served on the advisory council for the *Financial Analysts Journal*. He has commented from time to time that we need to make sure that, in addition to articles with a lot of research that is very quantitative in nature, we must have articles accessible to the general investor as well. I think the power in the research is not through the massive weight of very advanced research methods, but really the power is knowing the right question to ask and then going out and finding an answer to that and communicating it effectively.

While indexing is a major theme throughout the books that I've reviewed, he goes beyond that, and covers such things as the shortcomings of security analysis, some constructive criticism of institutional money management, corporate governance, executive pay, and how economic statistics are reported. He's mentioned financial reporting by companies and some of the deceptions—that's a topic that's dear to my heart. The government is not totally blameless in that regard, either. He also questions the role of mergers and acquisitions and whether they add value to the economy.

Finally, as for his communications skill, I would say that this goes very directly to the point that he's often made about moral absolutism. I found that having acted in a role as editor on some occasions, the biggest problem is when writers don't really know what they want to say. They feel ambivalent or confused about the message. If they have a clear idea of what they want to say, the writing tends to follow pretty clearly from that.

With Jack Bogle, he lets you know where he stands—he knows where he stands, most importantly—and therefore comes across loud and clear in his writing, and that's why he's such a powerful communicator in that medium.

His story[6] is well known among investment professionals. After writing his Princeton University senior thesis on the fledgling mutual fund industry, he joined Wellington Management, where he rose to chief executive officer. Fired in the wake of the 1972–1974 bear market, Bogle rebounded by founding The Vanguard Group. There, he pioneered and tirelessly championed the index fund, one of the most important financial innovations of the past half century.

"He Lets You Know Where He Stands"

---

6. This section is part of Fridson's review of Bogle's book *The Clash of the Cultures.*

"An Oft-Told Tale"

It is an oft-told tale, yet even Bogle junkies will learn some fascinating new facts from *The Clash of the Cultures: Investment vs. Speculation*. For instance, Bogle recounts that in 2004, he unsuccessfully tried to persuade the chairman of Putnam Investments' funds to convert to the "mutual mutual fund" organizational structure introduced by Vanguard, in which fund shareholders own the management company. In 1994, he purchased 100 shares of T. Rowe Price in order to stay informed about the activities of a Vanguard competitor. His $4,189 investment has grown to $208,960, and the dividend alone now runs $4,325 annually, underscoring the point that investment management has proven far more lucrative than investment.

Readers may also be surprised to learn that Bogle's premise for launching the first index fund was not that markets are invariably efficient; sometimes, he writes, they are "wildly inefficient." Rather, he documented that costs of investment management—particularly those associated with excessive portfolio turnover—had directly reduced the return investors could have earned if a cost-effective means of holding the market portfolio had been available to them. In one study he conducted on this matter, Bogle found that the stocks held by actively managed mutual funds at the start of the year performed better than the funds' actual portfolios 52 percent of the time.

"From a Profession . . . to a Business"

In his tenth book, *The Clash of the Cultures*, Bogle takes up the cudgels on behalf of investors, who he believes have been poorly served by most of the investment industry. He deplores the evolution of money management from a profession—by definition, a group of practitioners who should put their clients' interests ahead of their own—to a business that frequently earns profits at the expense of its clients. Bogle quotes Delaware Court of Chancery chancellor Leo Strine's remark that although legal scholars make much of the agency problem created by the separation of ownership from control of operating companies, they have largely ignored a similar problem in the ownership of investment organizations by public stockholders or financial conglomerates, rather than by the owners of the assets under management. One troubling conflict of interest that Bogle sees in this separation is the extreme reluctance of money managers to vote against corporate management in proxy battles, lest they hurt their chances of winning mandates from the corporations' 401(k) plans. He notes that the California State Teachers' Retirement System, which faces no such conflict, votes against management 23 percent of the time.

Institutional Investors Must Exercise Their Rights as Shareholders

If Bogle had his way, institutional investors would use their voting power to push for essential corporate reforms. For one thing, he would rein in CEOs' compensation, which has grown from 42 times to 320 times the average U.S. salary since 1980 on the premise that the corporate kingpins have created massive shareholder value. In reality, he asserts, the average corporation's real profits have failed to keep pace with GDP growth over the period. Bogle criticizes the profligate use of stock options in executive pay, noting that the modest amount of resulting annual shareholder dilution can cumulate to as much as 25 percent over a decade. Also in the governance area, Bogle wants corporations to refrain from making political contributions unless 75 percent of their shareholders approve of the practice.

Citing John Maynard Keynes, one of Bogle's major themes is the need to distinguish between *investment*—forecasting an asset's yield over its full life—and *speculation*—forecasting the psychology of the market. He sees a place for speculation in a healthy capital market but argues that the balance has shifted too far away from investment. For example, he contends that the exchange-traded fund (ETF) is a sound concept but thinks the financial industry has gone overboard by offering variants that dangle the lure of a quick buck. Some of these innovations have turned out to have severe design flaws. For instance, one ETF designed to triple the return of its associated index worked well enough on a daily basis but not over longer periods. Over the most recent five years, it returned –25 percent, versus 10.5 percent for the S&P 500 Index. Early in 2012, an ETF designed to magnify volatility surged when the sponsor stopped creating new units, then plunged 50 percent over two days in a sideways market.

Diligent Research, with a Few Exceptions

Bogle has been diligent in his research, leaving only minor imperfections in the finished texts. He dutifully credits the originators of the aphorisms he sprinkles throughout *The Clash of the Cultures*, yet in one case he neglects to identify Hillel as the source. Along with countless other authors, Bogle maintains that Keynes said, "When conditions change, I change my mind. What do you do?" There is but thin evidence that the eminent economist ever uttered those words, and it is apparently owing to another eminent economist, Paul Samuelson, that so many people believe he did. Quoting a speech in which Benjamin Graham alluded to the expulsion from Eden, Bogle mentions "Graham's reference to Original Sin." Original Sin is a uniquely Christian doctrine derived from events recounted in the book of Genesis and so presumably was not the intent of the Jewish Graham's allusion.

In *The Clash of the Cultures*, he brings invaluable historical perspective to current issues ranging from high-frequency trading to the looming crisis in the U.S. retirement system to the use of mutual fund investors' money to promote the growth of assets under management. ("There is no evidence whatsoever," he writes, "that advertising benefits fund investors by bringing in an amount of new assets adequate to create economies of scale that offset the amount spent. On the other hand, there is considerable evidence that building assets above a certain size impinges on the manager's ability to create superior performance.") Every thoughtful investor can benefit from John Bogle's wisdom, served up with refreshing modesty by a giant in a field notorious for outsized egos.

Jeremy Duffield: The Right-Hand Man's Perspective

Jeremy Duffield continued the panel discussion:

My first experience with Jack Bogle's communication skills was when I worked in Paul Volcker's Federal Reserve System back in 1979. I came up to give a speech on money market funds just seven days after Chairman Volcker had let interest rates loosen in pursuit of killing off inflation. Jack happened to be in the audience. He came up to introduce himself afterward and invited me to come and see a real-world mutual fund company and find out what it was all about. I had no intention at the time of pursuing anything but an academic career, but within six months I was working for Jack as his assistant, and that was my introduction to Jack's persuasiveness and his communication skills.

Today, I want to talk about my observations of Jack as a communicator. I do this not really to praise Jack, but to help us build on his legacy, because I hope everyone in this room has some part of Jack's legacy that they want to take away and work on in their own lives. To do that, I think you have to be an effective communicator, and I've really enjoyed 32 years of observing Jack's skills as a communicator. I'd like to share a few of my observations with you, and give you some of the secrets of Jack's success as a communicator.

"Absolutely Maniacal and Disciplined"

The first point is that it helps to be compulsive about it—to be absolutely maniacal and disciplined about being a great communicator. And Jack certainly is that. So the first lesson is you've got to work very, very hard at it. Anyone who's watched Jack scrawling with those arthritic hands of his on a yellow pad knows just how hard that work actually is. But Jack's done this, not just with his books (10 books, including his newest book *The Clash of the Cultures*), but with 575 speeches, 14 papers published in the *Journal of Portfolio Management* and the *Financial Analysts Journal*, 100 television appearances, 750 annual reports he wrote to shareholders, and the countless pieces of shareholder correspondence that his longtime assistant Emily Snyder has typed over the years.

Jack takes communication very, very seriously and works very, very hard at it. But even with all that hard work, you're not going to be a great communicator unless you have three things. First, you need great content; next, an ability to impart that content with great impact and style; and finally, great credibility. And those are the secrets, I think, of Jack's success. Sticking with the content, I think Marty's absolutely right to say that Jack has clarity about what he wants.

He has his own North Star, which is definitely about putting the investor's interests first. And having your own North Star really makes a difference. He has all those things Marty talked about—a thorough research approach, real content across a breadth of topics, giving you commonsense guidelines on how to invest, how to act, and how to live. There's a lot of content in this man's life's work.

It's also fun to think about his style and impact. From a style and impact point of view, he's an absolute master. He's a master of the art, and I say this with full intent of meaning he does it without artifice. It's an art. His command of the language is just superb. Superb. He's a master storyteller, and I've never seen anyone who can build on the work that other people have done by abstracting their quotes and using them to great effect. He incorporates quotes both to reflect and respect the originator's work, and to build upon them with his own ideas. He's a real master at that.

But perhaps the secret to Jack's impact is his ability to bring drama into the equation. A lot of that derives from his state of constant agitated moral indignation about the plight of the investor. Most of us today are done with moral indignation; we've had as much as we can take. But Jack has unparalleled reserves of moral indignation. He's a master of high dudgeon. His work brings in a real unique Manichean view of good versus evil, right versus wrong. There's no gray in Jack's thinking. It's moral absolutism.

There are plenty of villains in Jack's stories, but they are rarely individual people. He talks about practices that deserve to be vilified. And if you're doing those practices,

"Agitated Moral Indignation"

you know who he's talking about. And even if you're not doing any of those things, because of the questions he makes you ask yourself, you wonder if in fact you are. You ask yourself, "Am I really living up to Jack Bogle's standards?" And they're hard to live up to. So, Jack does succeed by introducing drama.

All of the factors that I've described bring together Jack's real strength, which is his credibility in the marketplace, which has been built over his 60-year career. There are three elements of that I'd like to discuss. The first is the leadership aspect. Australian Prime Minister Paul Keating defined leadership as imagination and courage. Those are two things that Jack Bogle brings, but he brings a lot more than just imagination and courage. He brings a sense of humility, and a sense of the responsibility that leadership justifies, in a way that really touches us as individuals.

Next, he brings common sense to a world that's largely lacking it. And he breaks through with common sense. If I had to pick any one phrase to describe what I love about Jack Bogle and his communications, it's that common sense aspect. Finally, the third aspect of Jack's communications credibility is that he actually walks the talk, and he's been doing it for as long as he's been talking. So these factors and more about Jack Bogle's style reflect on what a character he is . . . and what character he has. The title of his book, *Character Counts*, sums up both uses of the word.

"Imagination and Courage"

CHAPTER 2: A CONVERSATION WITH PAUL VOLCKER AND JOHN C. BOGLE

The main event of the John C. Bogle Legacy Forum brought together two living legends—both Princeton graduates—for a lively and wide-ranging discussion. The Forum's namesake, Vanguard founder Jack Bogle, and Paul Volcker, the former chairman of the Federal Reserve who tamed runaway U.S. inflation in the late 1970s and early 1980s and remains a formidable voice for the reform of our nation's financial system, were joined onstage by moderator and Bloomberg News journalist Kathleen Hays. Bogle and Volcker entertained and enlightened the crowd with anecdotes and insights from their long careers. The discussion was a memorable one for all those in attendance. Presented here is a lightly edited transcript of this momentous conversation.

KATHLEEN HAYS, BLOOMBERG NEWS: My first question, gentlemen: I need to know the secret. You're both into your 80s. You're both going strong. In many ways, you're at the top of your game. You both went to Princeton. Is there a link? Is there a secret you can share with us?

BOGLE: Yes, go to Princeton.

PAUL A. VOLCKER, 12th chairman of the Board of Governors of the Federal Reserve, and chairman of President Barack H. Obama's Economic Recovery Advisory Board: I thought it would be "get a new heart." Speaking of Princeton, this guy has a unique experience. He's still living off an undergraduate thesis that he wrote at Princeton. He got the thing reprinted, and it sells 50 years later. Now, who else wrote an undergraduate thesis at Princeton and made a career out of it?

BOGLE: Well, never underestimate the power of luck. But I think most people don't know the thesis story. There would be no Vanguard if I hadn't gone to Princeton. There would be no Vanguard if, back in 1949, I hadn't been sitting in the Firestone Library, the big new library we built during my freshman year, and I tried to keep up with the financial news. I was majoring in economics (without particular success at first). I happened to read the December 1949 issue of *Fortune* magazine.

"He's still living off an undergraduate thesis . . . 50 years later."

Up in the reading room of the Firestone Library, I turned to page 116, where I was struck by a story titled, "Big Money in Boston." It was an article about the mutual fund industry. The industry was described as tiny, but contentious. I didn't want to write about Adam Smith or John Maynard Keynes, subjects that had been covered by economics majors time and time again. So here's a tiny but contentious industry, totally untouched by academia or by the press. It was a small industry, but ready to be contentious. So I decided to make the mutual fund industry the subject of my senior thesis. If that fortuitous moment had not happened on that sunny day in Firestone Library, it's fair to say that I would not be here today. We might be here, but we'd be celebrating Mr. Volcker instead of me, which is surely more appropriate.

Why Aren't There More Believers?

VOLCKER: It's quite an innovation you have fostered through the years, and you stuck with it, and I don't know anybody else who could do it so clearly and consistently, and you write with this didactic skill and proved your case over and over again. Why doesn't everybody believe it?

BOGLE: Investors are getting the message more and more. Vanguard's assets are over $1.8 trillion today. We now manage about 17 percent of all of the long-term assets in the mutual fund industry—the highest share in the industry's history. Fidelity reached about 13 percent at its peak. Investors Diversified Services—American Express, as it was later called—peaked at around 13 percent. Massachusetts Financial Services, originally only MIT [Massachusetts Investors Trust], was the first fund company to reach 13 percent. But Vanguard is up to 17 percent, and I don't see this trend slowing down.

But even more significant in terms of momentum is that in the past five years, U.S. investors have added a net $100 billion into equity mutual funds. But $600 billion went into index funds, and $500 billion came out of actively managed funds. I think it was Bob Dylan who said you don't need a weatherman to tell which way the wind is blowing.

HAYS: I want to ask you about that, Jack and Chairman Volcker, because the question we pose here is how to restore investor confidence when it seems to be so broken. Let me ask you, where do we see evidence that investor confidence is broken? In stocks, the Dow is not too far off the recent highs. Bond yields are at record lows. The dollar is still relatively firm. Why do we say investor confidence is broken?

BOGLE: I'd say the data that I just mentioned is a pretty good example. The confidence that active managers can accomplish anything, that they are a panacea to all the investment ills of the average investor, is slowly vanishing, and they're getting used to the idea of owning all of American businesses. That is where returns are created—returns are not created in the stock market. As I said in one of my books, the stock market is a giant distraction to the business of investing. We look at those ephemeral prices every day, but they have little to do with intrinsic value.

So I think investor confidence in active equity management is clearly broken. When you hear someone like BlackRock's Peter Fisher—one of the fine people in this business—say the whole paradigm for bond management is also changing to indexing, the transition is accelerating.

HAYS: Chairman Volcker, what do you see?

VOLCKER: I would add a footnote and maybe a headline to what Jack said. If confidence in the investment markets and financial markets is broken, we face a problem in this country where trust and confidence in the whole country—and its government—are broken. I think this is a very big issue that we are

> "The Stock Market Is a Giant Distraction to the Business of Investing"

struggling with as a country. It's an issue that's going to overshadow and influence financial markets, as well as our destiny.

Shaky Confidence —20 Percent Trust Their Government to Do the Right Thing

HAYS: Are you seeing that confidence is shaky, and that's affecting the markets?

VOLCKER: There is no question it is shaky. For many years, polling agencies have been asking the question "Do you trust your government to do the right thing most of the time?" The answer these days runs about 20 percent. I read someplace they did a recent poll and the answer was 10 percent. It's a little hard to run a strong democracy if only 10 percent of the people or even 20 percent of the people trust the government to do the right thing even half the time.

HAYS: We'll get to that issue, because I know Jack has some very strong feelings about government, taxes, and more. But first, let's go back to the question of restoring investor confidence. Jack, you've said that in order to do that, we need to fix the financial system. So have we fixed the things that caused the financial crisis? Are the ratings agencies fixed? Do we have a grasp on derivatives? Have we corralled the problem of "too big to fail" at the banks? What kind of grade would you give the U.S. financial system?

BOGLE: I'd go with "D." I realize how difficult it is to get anything done in Washington, but I happen to be an advocate of bringing back the Glass-Steagall Act, separating investment banks and commercial banks into distinct institutions. That original act required only 37 pages; it doesn't take 198 pages, as with the Volcker Rule, to explain what bankers can and cannot do. It really is quite simple: If you're in the business of deposit banking, you may not be an investment bank. And if you're in the business of investment banking, you may not take deposits.

VOLCKER: I've been preoccupied with this same question myself. I went back and looked at the legislative language in Glass-Steagall. Glass-Steagall deals with some things that aren't relevant here, but with respect to the trading and powers of banks, there are two sentences at the core of the issue. Together, they say that no bank may handle both functions. Yes, there's a lot of debate about the detailed rules proposed in Dodd-Frank. That's less important to me, frankly, than the end result.

HAYS: I want to ask you two quick, specific questions on this. Bank of Canada governor Mark Carney said that the Volcker rule could damage the government bond market. He's talking about the exemption for government bond trading, which he said will favor the United States and will have unintended consequences. How do you address his criticism?

VOLCKER: Well, that's very strange to me, and I'm a bit startled by it. I saw an article in the paper this morning that was set in the cool confines in the mountainous area of Davos. Foreign governments suddenly discovered this is a big problem. I've not heard that before.

"What Is Not Permitted Is a Proprietary Position"

Under Dodd-Frank, trading is permitted and underwriting is permitted. If a foreign entity wants to engage in underwriting, it gets the assistance of an American bank. What is not permitted is a proprietary position.

What I heard out of European governments repeatedly in the past is they're concerned about all the speculative activity in financial markets by hedge funds and taking proprietary positions and destroying their currencies with speculative activity. Do I now understand that they want more of this speculative activity they used to frown upon in their currencies, and it's suddenly become healthy and wonderful for their currencies? There will be plenty of proprietary trading in securities without the half-dozen or so American banks participating in it.

Hedge Funds and
the Volcker Rule

HAYS: I want to ask you a question about hedge funds. Chairman Volcker, I'm going to start with you, because it comes out of this question about the Volcker Rule. The Volcker Rule is going to constrain proprietary trading at banks. Are you concerned that it's going to migrate into unregulated hedge funds that get a lot of their financing from the regulated banking system?

VOLCKER: I guess my answer to that is no. How many thousands of hedge funds are there now? They like to take speculative positions; that's what they do. They are financed typically with a very high ratio of equity. The destruction of a hedge fund affects their long-term equity investors and typically should not pose a threat to the banking system or a threat to the normal, essential operations of the banking system—making loans, payment system, safety for your deposits. Hedge funds have a different function. It is a speculative function, and they ought to be allowed to fail, as it will not have the same disruptive influence on the financial system that a breakdown of the banking system does. That is the distinction we are trying to make.

HAYS: On this question of hedge funds, Jack, you stand for long-term investment and reduced cost. You're a champion of index funds and the long-term benefits of corporate growth. When you look at the hedge fund industry (the hot new kid on the block), it's the exact opposite—high costs, big risky bets, and short-term strategies. How do you view this competitor that is the antithesis of what you stand for?

BOGLE: First, a significant portion of hedge fund assets—and I don't think people have spent nearly enough time thinking about this—are held by tax-exempt institutions like endowments and pension funds. One thing I would do to deal with that is have a tax on short-term capital gains whether you're a tax-exempt institution or you are not. That may sound communistic or something to you, but Warren Buffett said it about 15 years ago, and stock exchange volume then was probably one-hundredth of what it is today. It would be an attempt to slow down all this crazy trading. Warren says that it was a tongue-in-cheek comment, but I think that it is an idea whose time has come.

VOLCKER: Market liquidity is not just a costless, wonderful thing. There is a danger that the presumption and the actuality of a liquid market contribute to a short-term trading horizon. You're willing to do things you would not otherwise do because you're convinced you can turn around tomorrow and sell it.

But then you have a crisis. If you can't turn around and sell it, all the structural faults in the system are suddenly exposed. Liquidity is partly a state of mind: whether you think you can sell something instantaneously. It is not like holding a Treasury bond. A more prevalent form of liquidity today is the thought that you can sell a bond tomorrow or sell some complicated structured instrument tomorrow.

It's interesting that there is more and more academic analysis of the fact that we want tradable markets. We want markets that have some liquidity, but is there such a thing as too much liquidity? It can lead people into investment behavior that's actually damaging to the economy. The most eloquent person on this—he writes so well and is worth reading—is the head of the FSA [Financial Services Authority] in London, Adair Turner, who wrote a long essay about a year ago on this point. Is there social utility to liquidity? He says yes, up to a point. Can there be too much liquidity? Yes, at some point it becomes socially destructive instead of socially useful.

"Liquidity Is the Last Refuge of the Scoundrel"

BOGLE: I agree with Paul. Let me add some perspective. For inspiration, I go back to London to the days of Samuel Johnson. He had a saying, "Patriotism is the last refuge of the scoundrel." In this new fast-moving market, I'd advance the idea that *liquidity* is the last refuge of the scoundrel.

All this trading creates no value—in fact, it subtracts value. If you want to get some perspective on how our economic and financial systems work, you must go back to the fundamental role of Wall Street: It raises capital. The main function of the financial system is to direct capital to its highest and best uses; to companies with the greatest prospects for future growth; to companies creating the best goods and services at the lowest price. We might ask the question: How much of that actually happens?

We *know* how much of that happens. IPOs—initial public offerings—and secondary offerings have provided about $250 billion per year over the past five years. That's the financial industry's primary economic function. I'll call that investment. Compared to that, how much liquidity or short-term speculation do we have? Over that same span, we've had $33 trillion of annual trading in U.S. securities. There's 130 times as much speculation as there is investment. Or, to put it another way, speculation accounts for 99.2 percent of what Wall Street does, and investment accounts for merely 0.8 percent. That just isn't getting us anywhere. In fact, it diverts returns from Main Street to Wall Street.

HAYS: Does the high level of liquidity have anything to do with global central banks, with very high balance sheets, with zero interest rate policies, et cetera?

"Putting Real Liquidity Into the Market"

VOLCKER: No, they're putting real liquidity into the market. They're putting short-term assets into the market—their own liabilities. Indeed, it is beyond comprehension that they will not be respected. If you have a short-term liability of a central bank, you have true liquidity. That's quite different from having a bond or a complex instrument that you want to sell tomorrow. You want to be able to easily sell that short-term asset; you shouldn't necessarily be able to sell the long-term asset.

Let me return to this business about the government securities market and foreign securities. Here we have European governments that are debating over whether to put a so-called Tobin tax (financial transaction tax) on trading in their own market because they think there's an excess of speculation and liquidity. I read that on page one of the newspaper.

Then I read on page two that they're worried about a loss of liquidity because the United States' banks can't trade Greek bonds—or they can trade them, but they can't hold them in a proprietary position. They can't speculate in them. I wonder how populated Davos is with lobbyists who are explaining to these foreign countries how much they're going to lose from the Volcker Rule. I don't think they're going to lose anything important.

The Financial Transaction Tax

HAYS: The transaction tax is something you both support?

BOGLE: I do support a very modest transaction tax, maybe 0.1 percent of the value traded. I believe it should be paid, not within the financial markets, because I think that would be bad for liquidity, but should be paid by the firms that are trading. The cost of each share that a given mutual fund buys would be 0.1 percent higher than the unit price that's paid.

I think what people don't understand is there has been this incredible reduction in the frictional costs of investing—taxes and trading costs. Decimalization of security prices was a big part of it. Today, it's almost free to trade. I suppose you could argue, as my son does, that if transaction costs were zero, I shouldn't be against it. But they're not zero, because the rate of trading activity has gone up so much faster—at least as fast as the costs have declined. So while the commission cost has gone down, increased volume has driven total costs up. That leaves us with a negative impact on the overall wealth of investors. So I don't see it does anything constructive. The system just doesn't seem to be working in the interest of investors.

HAYS: Chairman Volcker, regarding the Volcker Rule, one of the criticisms is that if foreign banks don't have the Volcker Rule, U.S. banks will be at a competitive disadvantage.

VOLCKER: This argument about competitive disadvantage goes both ways. The American banks have been saying that they are at a competitive disadvantage because of the proposed capital rules, and European banks argue they're at a competitive disadvantage for other reasons. Of course, there are some core issues that you have to decide, as a matter of national sovereignty, regarding what kind of a banking system you want. The United States has a big banking system. It's important internationally. But just because it might put the banks at a disadvantage, I don't think we have to permit proprietary trading. That's not a detriment to the American economy.

The objective of these changes is to have a stronger global banking system, one less vulnerable to crisis, and that will be a plus for the American banking system. If other banks are weaker and more speculative, so be it.

The Bond Market Index— Too Much in Treasurys?

HAYS: Jack, you are one of the pioneers of index funds, and also index bond funds. A large portion of the trillions you manage at Vanguard, some 17 percent or 18 percent of all long-term mutual fund assets, is invested in bonds. I want to ask you a broad question about the bond market. We've got rates at historic lows. We've got the Federal Reserve trying to stimulate the economy. We've even got some Fed officials and policy makers or academics close to the Fed saying we could use some more inflation. You're a long-term bond investor. What is your view on this issue, and what does it mean for bond investors?

BOGLE: For me, the bond market is the essence of simplicity. If you simply take today's yield on a given bond or a given bond portfolio, you have established a very reasonable expectation for returns on bonds over the next decade. For long-term investors, it's not possible to have a bond bubble. After all, people that are holding even those 2 percent 10-year Treasurys have basically agreed to accept 2 percent as their return for the next 10 years. If they don't trade, that's the way it will be. It could be 2.25 percent; it could be 1.75 percent. But it's not going to be 15 percent, and it's not going to be zero. So the bond market is even more basic than the stock market in setting reasonable expectations for future returns.

Defining the Bond Market

Now, I do confess to being a little bit troubled with how we define "the bond market." We started the first bond index fund in 1986. I recently looked at its first annual report and saw that about 72 percent of its holdings were in U.S. Treasurys, agencies, and Treasury-backed mortgages. That number has remained fairly stable; it's about 70 percent today. I think investors in bond market index funds ought to be very conscious of the fact that that index is dominated by U.S. government investments.

The bond market index does have very high quality, and it's also quite short in maturity, because Treasury bills and shorter Treasury notes and bonds are very dominant in the overall Treasury picture. Ginnie Maes are in some ways even shorter because of the buyer's ability to "put" the mortgage back to the lender before it matures.

So I think we should be trying to expand our bond horizon just a bit. I'm not suggesting a portfolio that consists solely of corporate bonds, maybe A-rated, but a portfolio that is maybe 30 percent in U.S. government credits and 70 percent in corporate bonds. That would take the yield up by about 100 basis points, fully 1 percent. So you can't really talk about the bond market without breaking it down into these segments of Treasury and government-related and also maturity.

Low Interest Rates: Great for Borrowers, Terrible for Lenders and Savers

The banks have given us a system where the savers of America are basically being ruined. A three-year CD may yield about 1 percent. In money market funds, most managers—excluding Vanguard because we operate at rock-bottom costs—are subsidizing the yield by waiving their fees. That can't go on forever, and they still have negligible yields.

So our banks, having gotten us into all this trouble, are in Fat City. Everybody says, "Let's have lower interest rates." That's great for borrowers, but terrible for lenders—another reminder that everything we do in the securities business has two sides.

HAYS: I would like Chairman Volcker to weigh in on this, too. Jack Bogle is blaming the banks. But it's the Federal Reserve that has a zero interest rate policy; they're happy with low interest rates. More recently they're implementing policies to lower long-term rates, as well.

VOLCKER: Well, it's an unhappy situation to have such low short-term and long-term rates when you consider the desirability of savings, what it means for defined-benefit pension funds, and what it means for defined-contribution 401(k) plans and IRAs. But interest rates are a symptom, of course, of an economy that's operating way below capacity. The effort to stimulate our economy takes priority over the immediate needs of savers and investors. So let's hope that we'll get back to a more normally operating economy in which investors can earn a positive real return on their savings. In the short run, the Fed can't operate monetary policy on the basis of what's most convenient for investors when we have a major economic crisis on our hands, which we've had.

HAYS: Does it restore investor confidence if the discussion at central banks—like the Federal Reserve—focuses on more inflation, higher nominal GDP, et cetera?

VOLCKER: You're asking *me* whether it's a contribution to confidence to have more inflation?

HAYS: I sure am.

VOLCKER: No, that answer's too predictable. No, the worst thing the Fed can do is, in an already very uncertain situation, raise questions about whether they're going to stimulate inflation. Of course there is some discussion in the Fed about it. But I think those that are casual about inflation risk and actually aim for a higher rate of inflation are simply wrong and potentially destructive.

HAYS: Is there something wrong with the economy that needs to be fixed, Jack? Again, we're talking about restoring investor confidence. Do we have to fix the economy? We've talked about regulation. We have to talk a bit about government. But if the economy were healthier, wouldn't investors be confident again?

Deleveraging Is Necessary in Our Consumer Economy

BOGLE: Of course a stronger economy would help. But it's going to take time. We went through roughly a decade of ever-growing indebtedness—leverage on the part of our homeowners and consumers in America. Something like $4 trillion or $5 trillion was borrowed against people's homes and spent on consumption. So that inflated normal purchasing habits and the consumer share of GDP, and probably helped inflate things. That leverage is now being reversed very slowly.

But deleveraging is necessary in our consumer economy—to say nothing of our government sector—whether we like it or not. It's happening right now. Despite short-term interest rates that are close to zero, the saving rate in the United States is the highest it's been in seven or eight years.

VOLCKER: The rate just went down again, unfortunately.

BOGLE: None of this is easily explicable, except to say that consumers have to get out of this leveraged position and get their balance sheets in order before we restore earlier levels of economic growth.

VOLCKER: The Federal Reserve has just hardened its language about the 2 percent inflation rate. And you can argue whether 2 percent is too high or could be modified. But presumably, they've done that to reinforce to the market that 2 percent and no more is acceptable, even desirable.

HAYS: But the Fed has a dual mandate now. They've got to keep their eye on unemployment.

"2 Percent Inflation Is It"

VOLCKER: Yes, they must consider employment, but they recently came out and said 2 percent inflation is it. They mentioned employment, but they are now to reinforce that regardless of what some governor said; the judgment of the Federal Reserve is that the inflation rate shall not go above 2 percent. Maybe they're wrong, but that's what they're saying.

HAYS: Let's get to government, and I want to open it up to some audience questions, because you started out by saying, Chairman Volcker, that what you see is broken-down confidence in government, and that is one of the big negatives hanging over the financial markets. Jack, I know that you said basically the same thing—that our biggest problem right now has to do with our government.

BOGLE: Yes, it seems as though we've lost the ability to govern ourselves. You don't have to watch those wonderful, enlightening, Lincoln-Douglas-style debates among our presidential candidates (only kidding!) that we see almost every week to believe that our politicians care more about sound bites than about solutions. So our ability to govern ourselves is fading. I'm not sure it's worse than it's ever been, but it's worse than I've ever seen.

And gerrymandering has produced a bad system where there are too many safe seats in our Congress. We have the ridiculously inflated role of money in our elections. The *Citizens United* case opened the door to silent contributors to campaigns. Of course, the campaign itself has "no idea" of what's in those ads; there's no communication at all, if you believe what they say. I don't believe it.

It's a little bit like restoring confidence in the financial markets. We need to have the electorate stand up and be counted. This is a democracy—really a republic with democratic aspects—and we have to have an informed electorate, just as we have to have an informed investor base.

As I look at solving the confidence problem on the investor side—which should be a little easier—we need to give investors the right information about how the markets work and have them focus on the long term, have them focus on low cost, have them focus on diversification, and have them focus on some kind of a reasonable asset allocation. This information is really all that most investors need. If you go much beyond that, it usually confuses the average investor.

The same principle is really true of government. We're getting into these tiny, midget kind of regulations, and we should be looking at the whole system and say, "You know, it's broken." And so I have a pact with Paul, and if we're asked, we will agree to be the co-czars of the entire securities industry, so we can't be second-guessed by Congress.

Would Co-Czars Help Restore Confidence?

VOLCKER: We're going to limit it to the securities industry?

BOGLE: No.

HAYS: These two guys will take over everything.

VOLCKER: There was a comment made this morning that lobbying had become a cottage industry. I think that comment is wrong. It is no longer a cottage industry. It is a big industry. You can't go to Washington, D.C.—where I've been going in and out for 60 years—without recognizing that Washington is a big, prosperous city. Why is it prosperous? It's filled up with lobbying firms that have buildings that cover a whole city block. The amount of wealth in that city is tremendous, and it's in an attempt to influence the government.

BOGLE: The Supreme Court tells us that the Founding Fathers would have loved this. I don't happen to believe that.

HAYS: You guys are in your 80s.

BOGLE: Don't mention that, please.

VOLCKER: What I say all the time is, "Oh, to be 80 again."

HAYS: I hear you. But are you a lost breed? Are there more Paul Volckers and Jack Bogles in the subsequent generations? Are you voices crying in the wilderness?

VOLCKER: Well, I've got a feeling the wilderness is a little less than it used to be. We've gone through this great financial crisis, while in Washington political ideologies still reign. There is more sense now—and Jack is very articulate about this—that something's the matter and something has to be done in a way that was not evident five or six years ago, when everything seemed to be so wonderful with the stock market rising and everybody making a lot of money and taking home tens of millions or a billion or two a year. That was part of a seemingly prosperous, growing economy, and a political system that worked.

It doesn't look like that way now. And I think there are a lot more young people, in my sense, who are reacting by saying, "Yeah, something's the matter,

"There Is More Sense Now . . . That Something's the Matter"

and I want to be part of fixing it," whereas 10 years ago, everybody wanted to go to Goldman Sachs.

Now, a lot of those people are saying, "No, I want to see whether I can do something in government or at least nonprofit institutions and make things better." I think it's a distinct change in attitude, and is promising for what's a very bad situation.

Is Financial Engineering Really "Engineering"?

BOGLE: I do worry about the growing use of complex mathematics, even physics, in our financial system. For example, almost all universities with engineering departments—and certainly at Princeton University, where I have the data—we have moved away from, for example, mechanical engineering, civil engineering, and electrical engineering being the drivers of the engineering department. Now, for four or five years, the fastest-growing and largest major has been financial engineering.

When you're investing other people's money that way, you don't feel the same constraint. As Adam Smith wrote a long time ago, in 1776, one doesn't manage other people's money with the same prudence and care with which one manages one's own. Maybe 25 years ago, investment banks were private partnerships with unlimited liability. They were betting their own money.

Believe me, in those days investment bankers would not have a whole lot of junk on their balance sheets. That's just not the way it works. But when you're investing someone else's money, public shareholders take all the risk and the firm's executives take the annual compensation. It's an agency problem. We have agency problems here in corporate America. We have agency problems in investment America.

In short, we must have a federal standard of fiduciary duty. We need a standard of fiduciary duty for both our investment manager/agents and our corporate manager/agents.

A Question from the Audience

HAYS: Let's take some audience questions.

MICHAEL PENTO, PENTO PORTFOLIO STRATEGIES: I'm very curious about your comment about an impossibility of a bond bubble. If you look at what is happening in Portugal and in Greece, they were borrowing a tremendous amount of money because they had the German balance sheet behind them, and now their yields are skyrocketing.

And likewise, the Federal Reserve has indicated we're going to have a zero interest rate policy for probably about six years, if you go back from when it started until the end of 2014, at a minimum. So I'm very much concerned about an interest rate shock. And why do you feel that we're not going to have a bond bubble here in the United States? Thank you very much.

BOGLE: Well, in part, I stand corrected. When I talked about there not being a bond bubble for long-term investors, I was talking about here in the United States where credit risk is relatively low. (I may be wrong on that.) But obviously in Greece and the other "PIIGS" countries—Portugal, Ireland, Italy, Greece, and Spain—there's clearly a possibility that a bond bubble could burst. Interest payments may not be made.

In the United States, the credit of our corporate sector is strong, and eventually there will be enough sense of reality in Washington to take the steps that will finally strengthen the credit standing of our Treasury. So, when I say that the bond market for long-term investors—not traders—is not a bubble, I mean that investors have entered into a contract that says, "This bond is going to pay me, say, 3 percent interest each year over the next 10 years, and if interest rates rise to 7 percent, I'm still going to get my 3 percent." In fact, if that happens, the investor will probably get 4 percent, because the higher reinvestment rate will increase the total return. So that's my position. I don't think yours is without merit at all. But if you look at it as a contract between a creditworthy borrower and an informed long-term lender, there's no bubble.

VOLCKER: We're still borrowing too much as a country, as others are. I don't know that you'd call it a bubble, but I don't want the lack of a bubble to mean that we're not borrowing much more than is sustainable over a period of time.

BOGLE: I agree with Paul that today's level of government borrowing is not sustainable, so we ought to be thinking about how to slow the growth of debt throughout our system. Should we allow interest to be deductible at the corporate level? It just adds leverage to corporate and consumer balance sheets at the expense of equity. That's the way it works when bond interest is deductible and dividends are not.

HAYS: Chairman Volcker, I just have to ask you, because I've been following your words for a very long time. You used to warn back in the 1980s about excessive borrowing and crowding out in the credit markets. Now you seem to be warning that you see something more akin to a crisis that could occur. Could we have some kind of crisis in the bond market? Maybe that kind of crisis is what Washington needs to get something done on the budget.

Facing Up to Our Long-Term Problems

VOLCKER: Well, we're not close to a real crisis, but we're close enough that we have time to take action to deal with it. But in the political environment that we were both describing earlier, that's the big challenge. Obviously, you don't want to be too aggressive right at the moment when the economy is in the doldrums and recovering—but recovering at a rather slow pace, kind of slog, that appears to be where we will be for some time. But there's no reason why we can't be putting in place legislation to deal with some of our longer-range problems, not only with Social Security and Medicare, but also: How big do we want defense spending to be? How much money should we have left over for discretionary spending, which isn't very big to start with? We ought to be working to resolve these problems.

HAYS: Thank you, Chairman Volcker. Thank you, Jack.

VOLCKER: Thank you, Kathleen.

BOGLE: Thank you, Kathleen. I wanted to close by reminding the audience that my book *Enough. True Measures of Money, Business, and Life* is available, gratis, thanks to our sponsors. I'll be signing copies at the back of the room.

VOLCKER: I will say that it's been terrific being on this program in honor of Jack Bogle, who's stuck with his very sensible comments and disciplines for year after year in a way that just is without precedent. Thank you.

BOGLE: Thank you, sir.

THE VANGUARD VISION

Part II FEATURES several of Bogle's visionary essays on Vanguard, written between 1980 and 2013. Bogle launched the enterprise in 1974 and worked tirelessly to see that it reflected his vision, values, and views of what a *mutual* mutual fund company ought to be. His writings can be understood more as a minister speaking to his flock on enduring ethical principles, and less as a financial executive (a numbers guy) focused on meeting short-term corporate financial goals. He writes boldly of "a company that stands for something": *stewardship*. He then describes what stewardship means to clients (Vanguard shareholders) and to crew members (Vanguard employees) when a firm is dedicated to putting shareholders' interests first.

It is here that Bogle also emphasizes the theme (in 1999), "On Human Beings." He says that "'human beingness' has been one of the keys to our development. . . . Fiduciary values: candor, integrity, trust, and fair dealing" form the basis for the policies guiding how Vanguard deals with the clients whom the funds serve, as well as with the crew members who, together, serve the clients.

Bogle's 1980 speech to the Vanguard crew—"A Time to Dance"—was the first celebration of a Vanguard milestone, in this case the achievement of the $3 billion in assets milestone. Bogle spoke to the crew to celebrate this occasion, and then at the far larger milestones that followed through 1996—31 talks in all. Fast-forward to 2013 when, rounding out this part with his essay "Big Money in Boston," Bogle vividly describes the transformation of the mutual fund industry and the rise of Vanguard during his career.

From the dominant but relatively small, privately held boutique businesses of 1951 to the publicly held corporate conglomerates that now drive the industry, Bogle provides a deft narrative contrasting this new business culture with the professional culture reflected in the Quaker-like simplicity, thrift, and stewardship that he imbued in the creation of Vanguard's truly mutual structure.

CHAPTER 3: *CHARACTER COUNTS—THE INTRODUCTION*[1]

As the autumn of 1974 began, a company named *Vanguard* would shortly come into existence. Just 27 years later, as 2001 drew to a close, that company had become one of the largest financial institutions on the face of the globe.

Beginning with $1.4 billion of investor capital under management, The Vanguard Group of Investment Companies now manages $530 billion for more than 15 million investors, sited largely in the United States but also scattered all over the world. What is more, the 25 percent compound annual growth rate that the firm has achieved has, against all odds, been sustained at a remarkably steady rate—21 percent per year from 1974 through 1984, 29 percent from 1984 through 1994, and even 23 percent since then. While the turbulence in the world

---

1. John C. Bogle, *Character Counts: The Creation and Building of the Vanguard Group* (McGraw-Hill, 2002); this Introduction was written September 12, 2001.

economy, the burst in the stock market bubble as the twentieth century ended, and the staggering impact of the September 11, 2001, terrorist bombings in the United States—vividly exemplified by the utter obliteration of the proud towers of New York's World Trade Center—have markedly slowed the growth rate of the investor capital managed at Vanguard, the firm continues to thrive.

What accounts for this remarkable record of growth? Certainly the great boom in the financial markets that began in 1982—a period that saw the Dow Jones Industrial Average rise from 770 to 11,700 by January 2000, before tumbling to 8,000—played a major role. The impact of that long boom, magnified by the rise to preeminence of stock funds, bond funds, and money market funds, the investments of choice in the $30 trillion of financial assets of American families, has carried the assets of the U.S. mutual fund industry, $36 billion when Vanguard began, to $7 *trillion* today.

In such an environment, to be sure, few asset management firms have failed to prosper. But the industry's growth rate has been but a fraction of Vanguard's. More than one-half of Vanguard's growth has come at the expense of its rivals in the mutual fund industry. With a 1980 market share equal to but 2 percent of mutual fund assets—the tenth largest firm in a dwindling industry—Vanguard now holds an 8.5 percent share, the second largest firm in a vibrant industry, slowly closing on the industry asset leader. [By 2013, Vanguard's share of long-term mutual fund assets had grown to over 17 percent, the largest in the industry.]

But what accounts for Vanguard's growth is something more than booming financial markets and a burgeoning mutual fund industry. We had marched to a different drummer. Our indisputably successful drive to become the world's lowest-cost provider of financial service was the sine qua non. It led to our record of innovation, most notably the creation of the industry's first index funds, structured bond funds, and tax-managed funds. And our unprecedented decision to abandon our dealer distribution network also set us apart from our rivals.

"We Had Marched to a Different Drummer"

But our rise to leadership goes even deeper than that, to the very *character* that undergirded all those business decisions: the ethical standards, the moral values, and the investment principles to which the firm has adhered since its creation. Only you, the reader, can judge how many enterprises you have encountered of which it can be said: *They stand for something*. Something bigger than mere commercial success, something more important than growth at any price.

A company that stands for something. I believe you can say that of Vanguard. What we stand for, if I were to pick a single word, is: *stewardship*. The loyal stewardship of the assets entrusted to us by millions of investors; placing the interests of our fund shareholders paramount; holding long-term investment values and strategies above marketing opportunism and speculation; and assuring that shareholders receive their fair share of the returns earned in the financial markets. *A company that is of the shareholder, by the shareholder, and for the shareholder*.

It is Vanguard's unique *mutualized* structure that accounts for most of our principles and values. Other fund managers operate their mutual funds under contracts that generate substantial management fees, and on which the managers earn generous profits. Vanguard is owned by its shareholders and operates at cost. Other fund groups view their shareholders as *customers*, there to buy their *products*. Vanguard views its shareholders as *owners*, there to receive our *services*. Vanguard, then, is an enterprise with a singular character, reflected in the particular moral qualities, ethical standards, and principles that drive the conduct of our affairs.

Character counts. That is the message I seek to convey in this book. The way I will convey this message is *not* in the form of conventional corporate history, in a chronological, step-by-step, event-by-event fashion. For I fear such an approach would *describe*, rather than *explain*, Vanguard's growth. The march of events would overwhelm the underlying character that shaped those events. What is more, I fear

*"Two Separate Journeys
Through the Wilderness
of Wall Street"*

WORDS FROM THOSE WHO KNOW BOGLE BEST

William H. Donaldson, 27th chairman, U.S. Securities and Exchange Commission; former chairman and CEO, New York Stock Exchange; founder, Yale School of Management; cofounder, Donaldson, Lufkin & Jenrette

It is hard to believe that roughly 30 years have passed since a couple of young whippersnappers named Bogle and Donaldson initiated their separate journeys through the wilderness of Wall Street. And now the senior of those lads, by virtue of a two-year birth head start, is about to celebrate the historic occasion of his 80th birthday!

Jack, you really have had an amazing career in so many ways that I now hasten to salute your lifetime of achievement, physical courage, and public service. At a time when so many in the financial world have slipped their ethical and moral moorings, you have continued to show the way as a living example of a life well spent. Although the title of your most recent literary effort, *Enough.*, is a marvelous testimony to the Bogle way of life—a clever summary of lessons learned along the way—those of us who have known you and admired you are united in saying no—not enough! We want more Bogle bon mots.

May 2009

that my retrospective reconciliation of the events of our history might, however inadvertently, alter their original reality. *So, I shall tell most of the story when it happened, as it happened.*

It is easy to tell the Vanguard story in this way. For over the past quarter-century, I have spoken regularly to our crew about our mission—first at our asset milestone celebrations, each billion-dollar increase at the outset, then larger thresholds; then each midyear and at each year's end; and finally at our 25th Anniversary and at the 50-year mark of my career in the mutual fund industry. All told, 42 speeches are included in this book.

I gave those speeches primarily for four purposes:

1. *To celebrate*—savoring what we had accomplished, for just a moment in a day that was always busy and sometimes chaotic, and expressing appreciation to the members of our crew for their work in the greater good for Vanguard and our clients.

2. *To inculcate*—pounding home the importance of a solid system of human and ethical values in the modern business enterprise: integrity, continuity, discipline, honesty, quality, ambition, competition, creativity, innovation, cooperation, even a sense of humor—in all, the *character* of our company. These values may well be more important measures of success than such conventional business standards as our billions of assets, our market share, or our productivity.

3. *To communicate*—presenting a chronicle of The Vanguard Group's history and traditions, going all the way back to the founding of Wellington Fund—the first fund in what would come to be called The Vanguard Group—in 1928; commenting about the march of events at Vanguard, in the financial markets, in the marketing of financial services, and in the mutual fund industry, always attempting to highlight the important differences between the way we do business and the way so many of our rivals do. Since any company is a continuum, in which the response to each future challenge grows out of the totality of its past, my intention was to convey both *a sense of history and a sense of who we are.*

4. *To elevate*—raising the context of our mission by seasoning my talks with quotations from some of the great (and less great) persons of history: John

Maynard Keynes, Grantland Rice, Marcus Aurelius, Lord Horatio Nelson, Thomas Paine, Longfellow, Tennyson, Shakespeare, Archimedes, Frank Sinatra, Carl Sandburg, Queen Victoria, Robert Frost, Rudyard Kipling, Joseph Schumpeter, even Isaiah and Ecclesiastes. As we considered the worthy mission that Vanguard had set for itself, I wanted to elevate our mundane work with a grand—not, I hope, grandiose—perspective.

"A Stern Set of Values and Standards"

Publishing these speeches today has some wonderful benefits. First, now they are, well, *published*—preserved not only for our crew members and our owners, but for future generations. Second, they represent history, not in neat retrospect, but in the messy way in which history is actually experienced; truly, *a living history*. And third—although this may prove to be a vain hope—the speeches and accompanying text may inspire those idealists out there who believe (or persuade those who can be persuaded to believe) that it is possible to create a firm that can succeed in a competitive, dog-eat-dog business, all the while holding to a stern set of values and standards. To build, as it were, a firm that is both a *commercial* and an *artistic* success. To validate, finally, this one great premise about creating a company and building it to a position of industry leadership in the right way: *Character counts*.

CHAPTER 4: A TIME TO DANCE[2]

Ecclesiastes tells us that there is "a time to mourn and a time to dance, a time to keep silence and a time to speak." This occasion is a time to dance, and, I hope, an appropriate time to speak about what we have together accomplished.

---

2. This speech titled "A Time to Dance" was given to the Vanguard crew on September 19, 1980.

On September 17, 1980, total assets of The Vanguard Group of Investment Companies crossed the $3 billion mark. This truly awesome sum, of course, simply represents in dollar terms the huge responsibility that has been entrusted to our stewardship by nearly four hundred thousand individual and institutional investors. The achievement of this milestone can stand some historical perspective. It took 31 years—from 1928 to 1959—for Wellington Fund, the first Vanguard Fund, to reach $1 billion. It took only six years more for the assets of the Vanguard Funds in the aggregate to reach $2 billion, in 1965. But we then fell back below that mark, finally crossing $2 billion for good in March of 1979.

It has therefore taken us either 15 years—or, more ebulliently, just 18 months—to get from the $2 billion mark to the $3 billion mark. It may be for good, or we may go above and below it from time to time. Just remember that we crossed the $2 billion mark, not only in 1965 and 1979, but also in 1970, 1976, and 1978.

Can We Not Control Our Circumstances?

What this brief perspective makes clear is that we are in a business of challenge, economic sensitivity, market (both stock and bond) volatility, and extraordinary competitiveness. In short, we must not lose sight of the fact that we are in a cyclical business, well described, though that was not his intention, by the poet Robinson Jeffers:

> All these tidal gatherings, growth and decay
> Shining and darkening, are forever
> Renewed, and the whole cycle, impenitently
> Revolves, and all the past is future.

Are we, then, just victims of fate? Can we not control any of the circumstances that confront us? Of course we can! With skill in what we do, imagination in what we create, integrity in what we produce, judgment in the goals we set for ourselves, courage in times of peril, good humor in adversity, we *can* continue to build this enterprise in the future, as we have in days and years past.

We have been through a lot together. And I thank each of your personally for all you have done to give us the success that $3 billion of responsibility represents. Without our people, we are nothing. And I wish each of you every personal success as we work together in what we try to make a good environment, one that challenges your abilities, one that will give you the rewards that you seek.

So, the first $3 billion is behind us—at least for now. It is, in that sense, past. And we must turn to future milestones, however measured, and whatever they may be. The poet Jeffers had some words on this subject too, and let me close by reading them to you:

> Lend me the stone strength of the past
> And I will lend you
> The wings of the future.

*"Lend Me the Stone
Strength of the Past"*

CHAPTER 5: THE POWER OF AN IDEA: REFLECTIONS ON OUR 25TH ANNIVERSARY[3]

Remember ye not the former things, neither consider the things of old. Behold. I will do a new thing; now it shall spring forth; shall ye not know it? I will maketh a way in the sea, a path in the mighty waters, and the army and the power shall lie down together and they shall not rise: they are quenched; they are extinct.

3. A speech given to the Vanguard crew on the occasion of Vanguard's 25th Anniversary, September 24, 1999.

These words attributed to the Lord by the prophet Isaiah strike me as eerily prophetic of the success Vanguard has enjoyed since our birth 25 years ago.[4] We did a new thing, and it sprang forth. HMS *Vanguard* made her way in the sea; many of the industry powers then opposing us have been quenched and, despite the extraordinary growth of this industry, a few are even extinct.

Perhaps even more to the point, the passage from Isaiah poses an interesting paradox: Even at the pinnacle of our success today, should we now forget our things of old? Before we look ahead to the next 25 years, let's look back to the time of our founding for some perspective.

Like the phoenix, Vanguard sprang from the ashes of its predecessor. Just as that mythical bird of gorgeous plumage burned itself to ashes when it grew old, only to reemerge with renewed youth, so Vanguard was created out of the shift of the responsibility for the operations of the then-Wellington funds from Wellington Management Company to this new, untried enterprise. At the outset, only the administrative activities—not the investment or the marketing activities—were transferred.

Put the Shareholder in the Driver's Seat

In 1974, the proposition that mutual funds would administer their own affairs was a novel idea. Our objective: to put the fund shareholder in the driver's seat, in effect moving the management company to the rear. In order to suggest that our idea would be in the forefront of an important new trend, I chose the name *Vanguard*, hardly unaware that in the glorious sea battle at the Nile in 1798, Lord Nelson's victorious flagship was named HMS *Vanguard*. And so, with the naming of the new firm on September 24, 1974, our nautical tradition, too, began.

---

4. I confess that I modified the passage from Isaiah 43:15 in my ordering of the phrases, the better to focus on their relevance to Vanguard.

To get where we wanted to be—to manage all of the activities of the now-Vanguard funds—it was obvious that we needed to control both our investment management and our share distribution activities. But at the outset, these responsibilities had been declared the sole responsibility of Wellington Management Company. Since they were off-limits for Vanguard, they put a roadblock in the way of our ability to control our destiny. Overcoming that obstacle came with remarkable speed. In less than a year, I proposed that Vanguard introduce a new and hitherto unheard-of approach to mutual fund investing: the market index fund. In a contentious Board meeting, the day was carried only when, reaching for a straw that would justify this apparent breach of our limited mandate, I pointed out that such a fund required no active management. And when the world's first index mutual fund was incorporated on December 31, 1975, we had assumed our first important responsibilities.

*The Argument that
"May Have Stretched the
Board's Credulity"*

Less than eight months later, we turned our attention to distribution. Sales commissions and stockbrokers had been used by Wellington throughout its 50-year history, but the future seemed to call for making funds available to investors on a no-load basis through the direct marketing channel. Thus, I took a deep breath and recommended that we abandon our historical dealer network and terminate Wellington's services as distributor. No, we were not becoming a distributor (or so I argued in order to justify another departure from the Board's initial mandate). Rather we were obviating the very need for a distributor. While that argument, like the index argument, may have stretched the Board's credulity, the plan to go the no-load route was approved by the narrow vote of 8 to 5, and sales charges on all of the funds were eliminated on February 9, 1977. In little more than two years from our founding, we had put into place the essential structure under which we operate today: a full-line mutual fund complex providing administrative, investment, and marketing services.

Stewardship—The One Great Idea

Stewardship: the one great idea that explains what Vanguard is, who we are, and what we do. Serving the shareholder first; acting as trustee, in a fiduciary capacity. *Mutual funds of the investor, by the investor, for the investor.*

If you reflect on this concept, you quickly come to realize that it is from this one great idea that everything else flows. ***Our mutual structure:*** Funds owned and controlled by their shareholder-owners. ***Low costs:*** Eliminating the huge profits extracted by fund managers, and then holding operating expenses to the lowest level possible, together ensuring that the maximum portion of each fund's investment returns flows through to its owners. ***Market index funds:*** Relying on minimal cost to effectively guarantee that investors receive some 98 percent of the annual returns earned by a given financial asset category. (The facts are that few fund managers can ever reach 100 percent consistently, and that the typical mutual fund has provided some 75 percent.) ***Long-term investment policies:*** Holding portfolio turnover, and hence the attendant costs and taxes, to rock-bottom levels, and allowing a seemingly modest annual cost advantage to compound the aggregate growth of an investment account at a rate that can easily *double* the wealth accumulations of a fund's long-term shareholders. ***Fixed-income funds:*** Giving low cost its optimal leverage in providing extra returns to investors by clearly defining maturity ranges, maintaining peerless quality, and providing skilled professional management.

I hope you will forgive me repeating this litany of things you already know about Vanguard. But I have presented them in order to drive home the point that it is that one great idea—*stewardship*, as I have defined it—that explains so very much of our success. These simple policies I have described may not seem very imaginative. Indeed they are not. Not only are they unremarkable, but they are trite; they are dull; and they are obvious. In fact, they are startlingly close to the formula for fund success that I described in my Princeton senior thesis, which I began to write nearly 50 years ago this December: *Mutual funds should be run in the most honest, efficient, and economical way possible.* And it works.

Why Did the Job Fall to Vanguard?

Anyone else in this business could easily have thought of these policies and implemented them long before I started Vanguard. Why they *didn't* and why we *did* is a question that is surprisingly easy to answer: If a fund manager were interested in maximizing *its own* profits—inevitably at the expense of the owners of the mutual funds it manages—it would charge the *highest* fees that traffic would bear, unless it was absolutely forced to charge lower fees, either by the marketplace or by government regulation. But if the firm's goal were to maximize the profits of its *fund shareholders*, it would charge the *lowest* fees possible, and minimizing fund costs would be its highest and most obvious priority.

In the direct, dollar-for-dollar trade-off between the returns earned by fund shareholders and the returns earned by fund managers, the manager who takes the least delivers the most. No matter whether it is a stock fund or a bond fund or a money market fund, the syllogism holds. This trade-off is not only self-evident, it is borne out by the record: Low-cost funds as a group consistently outpace their high-cost counterparts. In some cases it takes a while; in others it is immediate— money market funds and index funds, for example. That's one reason why index funds are so unpopular with managers, and why they are so popular with investors.

Twenty-Five Years Later—Tangible Results

Twenty-five years later, the tangible results of our one great idea are all around us. Our assets, $1 billion at the outset, are $500 billion today. With a compound annual growth rate of 27 percent, our assets have doubled every three years, and with remarkable regularity. At the outset, we were an also-ran in a stagnant industry with aggregate assets in 1974 of but $40 billion, and ranked 12th among mutual fund firms. The Dow Jones Industrial Average was then at 650, right at the bottom of a horrendous bear market that had slashed stock prices by 50 percent. (Never forget that it *can* happen again.) But within a year, the industry's resurgence began.

Today, the Dow stands above 10,000; the assets of the mutual fund industry exceeded $5.6 trillion; and we are one of the industry's two leaders in assets under management. What is more, we are *the* leader in cash inflow, and by a compelling margin. Vanguard alone accounts for a truly remarkable 31 percent share of the market for long-term funds: One dollar of every three that flows into mutual funds presently comes through the door of the house we built all those years ago.

But it is not the tangible reflections of our leadership that rate highest with me. It is the great intangible: the leadership of our philosophies and values. And, even if ever so slowly, they are beginning to spread. *Even one company can make a difference.* The most obvious example is the index fund. We formed the Vanguard 500 Index Fund in 1975, and almost a decade passed before a single competitor entered the fray. But today there are 341 index funds out there, 108 modeled on the Standard & Poor's 500 Index. We remain the leader by far, with 63 percent of the industry's index fund assets, including not only our two 500 funds, but index funds keyed to the total U.S. stock market, mid-cap and small-cap stocks, growth and value, international, bond and balanced, virtually all Vanguard firsts.

Index funds today represent nearly $200 billion of our $500 billion asset base, and their importance is soaring. So far this year, they represent 88 percent of our stock fund cash flow, 97 percent of our balanced fund cash flow, and 40 percent of our taxable bond fund cash flow. The initial theoretical appeal of indexing has proven itself through pragmatic experience, providing superior performance relative to active professional managers.

Tax-managed funds are another example. While I'm proud of the early timing of our first index funds, I'm embarrassed by being so late to start our tax-managed funds. Not until mid-1994 did we form these funds, probably at least five years after their need became obvious. Yet, once again, our series of tax-managed funds was another Vanguard first. And the list hardly stops there. Our bond funds totally dominate the direct marketing arena. Only 33 of 1,200 such bond funds have topped $2 billion of assets, and 10 of them are Vanguard funds.

Many of our rivals have aped our pioneering defined-maturity strategy, but, alas for their success, without copying our quality rigor and our low costs. Our money market funds are among the very highest-yielding and, hardly surprising, therefore among the largest in the field. And while the excessive costs that burden the returns of these bond and money market funds have declined but little, most observers credit our competitive posture with helping to put a ceiling on expense ratios of the funds of our peers.

Making a Difference in the Marketplace

These examples are enough to make the point: In the areas that mean the most to investors, we are the leaders in investment policy and strategy. *We have made a difference in the marketplace*. But, most important of all to me, we have built a name and reputation that are second to none in serving investors—*stewardship* in the truest sense. And stewardship means far more than the mere mechanisms through which we deliver our services. Yes, it means funds with sound investment policies and clear investment strategies. Yes, surely, it means providing services that result in record-keeping precision, financial controls second to none, and the communication of information, accurate to a fault, that approaches the instantaneous.

But stewardship means even more than that. The human beings we serve—honest-to-God, down-to-earth human beings—have been at the very epicenter of every business decision we have made. Vanguard does *not* represent a throng of 14 million investors; Vanguard represents 14 million souls, *each* with *their own* hopes and fears, *their own* financial objectives, and *their own* trust in us. And we have never let them down. This philosophy was hardly invented here. We see some of it, for example, in the film classic *It's a Wonderful Life*, now 55 years old. Mr. Potter (a grouchy Lionel Barrymore) tells George Bailey (integrity-laden Jimmy Stewart) that Bailey's father, who founded the local building and loan society, was no businessman. "He was a man of huge ideas . . . a starry-eyed dreamer who gave people impossible ideas" about owning their own homes. Bailey responds, "People were human beings to him, Mr. Potter, but to you, you warped, frustrated old man, they're cattle." To which a growling Potter snarls, "Sentimental hogwash."

Well, it's *not* sentimental hogwash. Even in this age of instantaneous communication, electronic commerce, and computerized investment advice—all at our fingertips and in real time—it is human beings that must be at the core of any enterprise worth its salt. And this focus on human values is one of the "former

---

"It Is Human Beings that Must Be at the Core of Any Enterprise Worth Its Salt"

WORDS FROM THOSE WHO KNOW BOGLE BEST

Clifford S. Asness, Managing and Founding Principal, AQR Capital Management

You are often called Saint Jack. I think you'd agree that nobody is a saint. Everyone does right and wrong. But some rare few do a lot more right than they do wrong. Some rare few speak the truth without fear or favor. Some rare few think of their clients or investors or customers first and trust that if they do that, rewards will follow. Some rare few have the courage to do what's right when the world of entrenched interests and ignorance tells them they're crazy. These rare people "press on regardless" and ultimately they win.

I keep saying "rare" and it's not an exaggeration. After carefully considering each criterion, I've pretty much narrowed my list of people who do it right down to you! This is why you were my hero before I met you. This is why my feelings have only grown stronger after the wonderful experience of getting to know you.

April 2009

things" that, contrary to Isaiah's warning at the outset, we must remember. This grand intangible would, however, serve little use if it represented good intentions but flawed investment policies. So we must also remember the investment policies that are fundamental to almost all that we have built—our mutual structure, our dedication to low costs, our fixed-income policies, our index funds, and our implementation of long-term investment strategies for long-term investors. Truly, we need *both* our human values *and* our investment philosophy if we are to retain our leadership as stewards of the assets of investors in the future.

What, then, should we forget? Certainly any investment approach that no longer works; any organizational qualities that have proven flawed; any corporate strategies that have become inconsistent with common sense in the new world in which we exist today. That said, sometimes the changes in the world—to say nothing of the changes in the financial markets—are transitory, so we must hold the line against fads and fashions and adhere to our bedrock principles, no matter how painful in the short run. Sound investment principles and decent human values have proved to be the bedrock underlying Vanguard's foundation 25 years ago. They are the *right* principles and the *right* values, not only enduring, but eternal.

Hold Fast to That Which Is Good

What then do we make of Isaiah's words? Doing the new thing he described in the Holy Bible has surely sprung forth the Judeo-Christian ethic that has marked its way in the sea, its path in the mighty waters of our world. So, I don't imagine that now, centuries later, old Isaiah would be looking for *another* new thing. So it is with Vanguard. Our new thing, too—albeit a pale reflection of what Isaiah was talking about—has sprung forth, and we all know it and recognize it every day. The world of investing is beginning to know it too. Our version of the great flagship HMS *Vanguard* has made its way in the sea, its path in the mighty waters of the world's financial system. Yes, we must be ever alert for fundamental change, but our watchword for the next quarter century and beyond must be, as the Bible entreats us: *Hold fast to that which is good.*

So as this anniversary day ends, I thank each of you who serve so ably on our remarkable crew, now 10,000 strong, for helping to make that vision of 1974 come to pass. Our investment ideas and human values are necessary to all we have done, but without your dedication and loyalty, your enthusiasm and spirit, and your teamwork, Vanguard today would be a mere shadow of what we have become.

Chapter 6: On Human Beings: Clients and Crew[5]

My account of Vanguard's founding, our persistence through the struggles of 1974 to 1981, and the qualities of leadership that seem to have been required is a story that is part tragedy and part triumph. Each crushing disappointment was eventually followed by serendipitous success. Not until 1981, when the modern Vanguard was fully formed, did we begin to sail on an even keel. But even in the rough seas of the early years, when the horizon dissolved in darkness and our very survival was in doubt, I retained my conception of those who would serve within our ranks and those whom we would strive to serve: human beings.

If simplicity was to be the focus of our investment principles, human beings would be the focus of our management principles. Over the years, I have come to love and respect the term *human beings* to describe both our clients and our crew members. In December 1997, I gave a talk at Harvard Business School on how our focus on human beings had enabled Vanguard to become what at Harvard

---

5. From Chapter 22 of *Common Sense on Mutual Funds*, originally published in 1999, revised 10th anniversary edition published 2009.

"I Challenged the Students to Find the Term 'Human Beings' in Any Book They Had Read on Corporate Strategy"

is called a "service breakthrough company." I challenged the students to find the term *human beings* in any book they had read on corporate strategy. As far as I know, none could meet the challenge. But *human beingness* has been one of the keys to our development.

How often I have said, over these long years, that those whom we serve must be treated as "honest-to-God, down-to-earth human beings, each with their own individual hopes and fears and financial goals." This credo says nothing about aggregate billions of dollars of assets; nor millions of investors; nor, Lord forbid, market share; nor even corporate strategy; nor the need for financial controls, technological support, and focused marketing, although all of them are, to one degree or another, necessary. They are secondary to our primary goal: to serve, to the best of our ability, the human beings who are our clients. To serve them with candor, with integrity, and with fair dealing. To be the stewards of the assets they have entrusted to us. To treat them as we would like the stewards of our own assets to treat us. This mission is not very complicated, but anyone who *preaches* it had better *live* it, every single day.

It should go without saying that the concept of human beingness should also apply to those who serve on our Vanguard crew. Those of us who earn our livelihood at Vanguard should treat one another in the way we would like to be treated. The keys are: respect for the individual; recognition that even one person can make a difference; and financial incentives to each and every crew member, based on how the rewards we earn for our fund shareholders compare to those earned by our peers. Our crew has made me look good for almost 25 years, and that is the least that I owe to them.

In this final chapter, I offer some thoughts on what it means to treat those we serve, and those with whom we serve, as honest-to-God, down-to-earth human beings. The idea is not very complicated, but it has a profound impact on the institution's relationship with its investors and with its crew. When you treat the investor as a human being, you must necessarily pursue a fiduciary relationship with a client, as opposed to a business relationship with a customer. And when you treat those who work for the institution as human beings, rather than as soldiers of fortune paid to execute a certain task in a certain period, policies and practices that respect individuals and reward their contributions necessarily follow. In short, a focus on human beings must be manifest in every action of the enterprise.

The Rise of the Bogleheads

When the previous edition of *Common Sense on Mutual Funds* was published back in 1999, any number of persons asked me, "Why on earth would you include a chapter on human beings in a book about investing?" To which I responded, likely with a bit of a snap, "Who do you think we are investing all that money *for*?" In any event, I have no regrets about my focus on human beings, which has found its way—in one manner or another—into every book I've written.

I've come to know and love hundreds, perhaps thousands, of these humble souls, these good citizens who exemplify the millions of investors who have followed the sound investment principles described in this book, and have been well served by doing so.

Shortly after the 1999 publication of the original edition of *Common Sense on Mutual Funds*, my conviction that human beings represent the heart and soul of any sound investment process was confirmed—and then some. For on March 10, 2000, at a speaking engagement at "The Money Show" in Orlando, Florida, I first met Taylor Larimore—an army veteran who served with America's "Greatest Generation"—then as now considered the unofficial leader of a growing group of community-minded, largely self-taught, integrity-laden investors who would soon become firmly established as the "Bogleheads" (originally known as "Vanguard Diehards"). Taylor and I struck up a friendship that, a decade later, is stronger than ever.

Individually and collectively, the Bogleheads have come to believe passionately in Vanguard's mission of investment simplicity—economy, efficiency, asset allocation, widely diversified portfolios of high quality and low cost, and, above all, a commonsense focus on the wisdom of long-term investing and the folly of short-term speculation. They also share a confidence in Vanguard's philosophy of trusteeship, holding the interests of our shareholders above those of all others.

The Bogleheads' Guide to Investing—Accolades from Readers

After congregating for several years at a dedicated website on Morningstar.com, the Bogleheads launched their own website (Bogleheads.org) in 2007, and word of their mission spread like wildfire. The Bogleheads website now attracts some 9,000 unique visitors daily. Each month, more than 100,000 investors visit the site, more than 300,000 times in all, collectively poring over the one million pages of text. The forum is a treasure trove of information, as its contributors and visitors alike help one another, with no ax to grind, on all manner of topics that essentially cover the entire field of investing.

In 2006, three of the Bogleheads (Taylor Larimore, Mel Lindauer, and Michael LeBoeuf) got together to write a marvelous self-help book for investors, *The Bogleheads' Guide to Investing*, which quickly became a best seller. In 2009, two of the original authors (Taylor Larimore and Mel Lindauer) were joined by fellow Bogleheads Richard Ferri and Laura Dogu in publishing a sequel, *The Bogleheads' Guide to Retirement Planning*, already winning the accolades of readers. The Bogleheads' story is one of a community of successful investors who have joined together to spread the wisdom of their simple investment philosophy, and share their own personal investment experiences.

Beginning with a wonderful dinner prepared by Taylor's wife Pat in their Miami condominium, when I met with some 20 Bogleheads in 2000 for the first time ("Bogleheads I"), these committed believers in Vanguard's principles have gathered together each year thereafter—for example, in Denver in 2004, in Las Vegas in 2006, in San Diego in 2008, and most recently in Dallas in 2009 ("Bogleheads VIII"). There, once again, this diverse band of wise and happy investment warriors convened to share their investment wisdom, their experiences, and the stories of their lives and careers.

I've attended every one of these gatherings except 2009's, when illness precluded my traveling. Being with these "real, honest-to-God, down-to-earth human beings, each with their own hopes, fears, and financial goals" (a phrase I've used to describe Vanguard investors, well, forever) has been one of the brightest highlights of my long career. Yes, investing is all about human beings.

"When Human Beings Are the Focus of an Enterprise, Certain Practices Follow Naturally"

When human beings are the focus of an enterprise, certain practices follow naturally. The primary goal is to help clients succeed in the activity of investing, an all-too-human pursuit in which reaching one's goals seems to depend as much upon emotions as economics. Success in investing, in turn, allows clients to achieve human goals such as purchasing a home, paying for a child's education, or enjoying a comfortable retirement. Failure means that these basic human goals will not be met. In this long bull market, the mutual fund industry seems to have lost sight of these realities. Instead of helping people to develop prudent, long-term investment plans, fund firms have mounted aggressive marketing campaigns that suggest that they have found the holy grail of investment superiority. Too many funds have followed imprudent policies, and, despite the long bull market, their shareholders have paid a heavy price. When investment returns eventually revert to more normal levels, even more funds will disappoint their shareholders. Firms that focus on human beings, on the other hand, act as fiduciaries, not as aggressive asset gatherers. They strive to uphold fiduciary values: candor, integrity, trust, and fair dealing. Such firms should be far more likely to weather any storms that may come to the financial markets.

How do these values shape Vanguard's dealings with clients? *Candor* means that, in communicating with our shareholders, we must follow a policy of full disclosure: tell the whole truth and nothing but the truth. This policy seems unremarkable. But candor is conspicuous by its absence from the mutual fund industry's promotional materials and shareholder communications. Long-term returns of the stock market are presented without adjustment for the costs of owning stocks through mutual funds. Fund advertisements trumpet past performance that will not be repeated in the future. Fund prospectuses fail to describe the importance of costs. And, too often, mutual fund annual reports neglect to discuss the risks inherent in particular investment strategies. When we see investors as human beings rather than target markets, however, we realize that, if they are to invest successfully, our clients need straight talk and common sense: frank discussions about risk and return, an honest accounting of a fund's success (or failure) in matching the returns of its benchmark and its peers, a review of the rudiments of a sensible program of balanced investing, and attention to the critical role that costs play in shaping long-term investment returns.

The Essentials: Integrity and Fair Dealing

Candor reinforces a second element in the relationship between fiduciary and client: *integrity*. Integrity comes down to the ability to *trust* that, when the self-interest of the institution's managers comes in conflict with the interests of the institution's clients, the interests of the clients will be held paramount. Vanguard's unique corporate structure, in which the financial benefits of our success accrue to the fund shareholder rather than to the management company, has eliminated many potential conflicts of interest between a financial institution and its clients. Yet, integrity demands additional practices not necessarily dictated by corporate structure. Integrity means putting the client first in all aspects of the relationship, investing prudently with the sole purpose of meeting a particular investment objective, and operating strictly under generally accepted principles of business conduct. Such practices arise, not from an organizational structure or policy manual, but from a recognition that our clients are human beings who deserve the highest standards of respect.

Closely related to integrity is the final element of the fiduciary relationship, a commitment to *fair dealing*. We pledge to serve all clients to the best of our abilities, making sure that their investment costs remain low and their investment returns remain as high as possible relative to the asset classes or market segments in which they invest. Not infrequently, conflicts may arise between the business interests and the fiduciary duties of an organization, and the organization that serves human beings must ensure that fiduciary duties remain paramount. Consider this example of a potential conflict. In 1996, an institutional client attempted to invest $40 million in a Vanguard short-term fixed-income fund, a sum that amounted to 10 percent of the fund's assets. To satisfy a prior financial commitment, he intended to redeem his holding within two months. In the client's view, the arrangement would benefit both parties: For Vanguard, we would have a new shareholder with substantial assets. For the client, he would earn an attractive return on a substantial sum of money, and the purchase and liquidation of his investment portfolio would carry no transaction costs whatsoever.

Turning Down New Business Can Show a Firm's Values

No organization dedicated to the best interests of its clients—rather than to profits, assets, or market share—would be interested in such a transient shareholder. A short-term transaction of that size would have imposed *on the remaining shareholders of the fund* unnecessary transaction costs in purchasing and then selling the portfolio investments. We refused to accept the order. Irate, the investor informed us that he would advise his colleagues "never to do business with Vanguard again." What is more, he took his story to the press, and it wound up on the front page of the Money & Investing section of the *Wall Street Journal*, which duly reported that the client "would no doubt find many eager takers at other mutual fund companies, especially since an investment that size . . . could earn the fund company roughly $30,000 in management fees." To accept the investment and earn the fees, however, would have placed the fund organization's business interests above its fiduciary obligation to the fund's remaining shareholders. In response to the article describing our rejection of this $40 million order, the scores of letters I received from our shareholders, 100 percent of which supported Vanguard's position, were so favorable that I felt obliged to write to the *Journal*'s editor that I was "a bit embarrassed that such favorable public notice arose from the simple act of choosing the path that was honorable and ethical."

A Fiduciary Society

When in the earlier edition I included *integrity* as one of the key fiduciary values, I was reluctant to do so for two reasons: (1) important as integrity is, bragging about it seemed a little too self-serving, and (2) while 100 percent of the leaders I've known or read about describe integrity as the principal quality of leadership, less than 100 percent of them actually deliver on that promise in their business and personal lives. But include it I did, along with candor, trust, and fair dealing. During the passage of a decade, however, the observance of these traditional fiduciary values in our financial system has seriously deteriorated.

So my latest crusade is to demand that our money managers be required to measure up to the traditional standards of fiduciary duty that have existed for centuries under English common law. A *fiduciary society* would guarantee those last-line owners—largely the mutual fund shareholders and pension fund beneficiaries who have committed their capital to equity ownership and whose savings are at stake—their rights as investment principals, rights that their money-manager/ agents have failed to adequately honor.

It will take federal government action to foster the creation of this new fiduciary society that I envision. Above all else, it must be unmistakable that government intends, and is capable of enforcing, standards of trusteeship and fiduciary duty under which money managers operate with the *sole* and *exclusive* purpose of serving the interests of their beneficiaries—in short, allowing "no man to serve two masters."

Shareholders Respond— In Droves

Everyone wants to be treated as a human being. No one wants to be part of a target market. I believe that Vanguard's development in recent years is in part the result of public recognition that Vanguard treats the investor as a valued individual, not a dollar sign. In the many letters I receive from shareholders, a common theme is their appreciation of our efforts to deal with them candidly, fairly, and with integrity, to help them achieve important investment goals. Consider these excerpts from some recent letters. The first is from a shareholder who read the *Wall Street Journal* article noted earlier:

> I always knew you talked the talk. Now I know you walk the walk, too.
>
> My wife and I, now in our fifties, find we are now worth better than $1 million, have no debts, and paid off the house. Not bad considering that we have never earned much more than $40,000 a year each, that I came to this country at 30 with almost nothing, and spent my first four years in college. I hope you know the impact you have on individuals such as us to enable us to reach our own American dream.
>
> One reason why I invest with Vanguard is that it has been guided by Mr. Bogle's Old Testament patriarch image . . . it is not ludicrous to liken old Bogle to Moses bringing the law down off Sinai amidst thunder, lightning, and a thick cloud: simplify, simplify, simplify. . . . I would like to see Vanguard stick to its roots. I'm sure Bogle is a hard man

to work for. People like that always are. I know. We have one in our family and the fact that he's been dead for 53 years hasn't lessened his influence much. But people like this strike a chord in the public because they stand for something good and pure and true.

The shock waves you have unleashed will not soon be quelled by those in the industry who should really be embarrassed by many of their actions, but, instead, will reverberate throughout for a long time to come. I gleefully say "Thank you!"

You "recognize the obvious, follow powerful ideas with prompt action, and press on regardless" . . . words of wisdom for steering a true course regardless of the seas you sail. I am in your debt.

You are a throwback to an age when a businessman's handshake was worth more than a contract. Thank you for resisting many of the current popular trends that focus on high fees rather than quality performance and service. From all the working stiffs of America one more time: Thank you!

In style and substance you remind me of my dad, who also talked often of the wisdom of low costs, mistake avoidance, and a long-term buy-and-hold philosophy. It rewarded him well. Please continue to spread the message of commonsense investing. You have been an important, clear voice of reason in an industry increasingly dominated by quacks.

More Shareholder Responses

While I haven't run Vanguard for many years, I'm still in my office on our campus pretty much all day, every day. And, almost daily, I still get wonderful letters from clients. Here are just a few examples. The first one is from a shareholder whom I met on a flight to California en route to Bogleheads VII.

I thought you'd be riding first class, but to my surprise you rode in coach. That tickled my heart because you were one of us, with us. Thanks for having the fortitude of character to do the right thing and to leave us a legacy to follow.

I'm indebted to you for convincing me of the wisdom of index funds and (conservative) asset allocation. I've seen my nest egg grow to unimaginable size, and am relatively unfazed by the recent market gyrations. I sleep well at night. It's all so simple. Thanks.

Thanks for giving the wisdom of the ages, sprinkled throughout your books. I can't even imagine the forces within you that have driven you. Despite overwhelming obstacles, you never slackened in your struggle to bring a chance for financial well-being to individual investors.

Shareholder Loyalty to Mutual Funds—"An Astonishing Measure of General Dissatisfaction"

Do these few anecdotes accurately portray how millions of investors perceive Vanguard? The answer seems to be "Yes, they do." A recent study by Cogent Research concluded that "Vanguard Group generates substantially more loyalty than any other fund company . . . and outshines all its peers." The Cogent methodology is based on a poll of fund clients that asks whether they would "definitely recommend" or "definitely *not* recommend" their mutual funds to friends and family, scaling the result from 10 (best) to 1 (worst).

Cogent then subtracted the percentage of fund "detractors" (ratings of 1 to 5) from fund "supporters" (ratings of 9 or 10), to arrive at "net client loyalty." With a rating of +44, Vanguard was virtually peerless; the next three firms had scores around +25, and the 11th ranked firm (among 38) had a score of +1, barely positive. The remaining 27 firms all had negative loyalty scores, ranging all the way down to –54 (!). For the funds as a group, excluding Vanguard, the average loyalty score was –13, an astonishing measure of general dissatisfaction with mutual funds that so far seems to be ignored by the industry. But it cannot be ignored forever.

The Vanguard Crew

These letters are a tribute not only to the fiduciary values of candor, integrity, and fair dealing, but also to the human beings who uphold these values: the Vanguard crew. When we began operations in 1975, the choice of the word *crew* may have seemed a bit trite and corny. But it is well accepted now, suggesting, as it does, the nautical heritage of our HMS *Vanguard* symbol—the crew of a warship, working together in partnership, fighting for each knot of progress on a sea voyage in which even one member's failure to perform can sink the ship, doing our best to ensure a voyage that is safe and sound, and sailing purposefully and on course through calm and rough waters alike.

It almost goes without saying that any enterprise that aspires to measure up to the symbolism of a fighting ship must rely on the loyalty of its crew. And there are few leaders who do not invoke the need for loyalty—whether through a shared mission or through compensation programs or, for that matter, even through a climate of fear. But however loyalty may be built into a firm's values and character, the one message that must come through is: Loyalty is not a one-way street. No enterprise, no matter what endeavor it pursues, has any right to ask for loyalty from those who do the hard work required for its success, without a reciprocal commitment that the enterprise will offer its own loyalty in return. If an institution is to care for its clients, it must care too about the human beings who assume the responsibility for serving them. The members of the crew are the heart and soul of the enterprise; without their care and effort, the enterprise will fail.

Caring about the Institutions That Touch Our Lives

In my frequent speeches to our crew, I have, on several occasions, cited this marvelous quotation from Dean Howard M. Johnson, former chairman of the Massachusetts Institute of Technology, on the need for individual human beings to care for the institutions of which each of us is a part:

> We need people who care about the institution. In an increasingly impersonal world, I have come to believe that a deep sense of caring for the institution is requisite for its success.

The institution must be the object of intense human care and cultivation: even when it errs and stumbles, it must be cared for, by all who own it, all who serve it, all who are served by it, all who govern it.

Caring, we know, is an exacting and demanding business. It requires not only interest and compassion and concern; it demands self-sacrifice, wisdom and tough-mindedness, and discipline. Every responsible person must care, and care deeply, about the institutions that touch his life.

If we ask those who work at Vanguard to treat the institution with care, to ensure that it meets the needs of the human beings we serve as clients, we must in turn care for our crew. We manifest our regard for the human beings who work here by treating each individual, from the highest to the humblest, with respect. We simply won't tolerate a "big shot" demeaning one of the "working stiffs." (If I learn of it, I'm tempted to have the former do the latter's work for a day—if he or she is able to do it!) This policy carries over to a "no perquisite" rule—no leased cars, no reserved parking places, no first-class flying, no officers' dining room. One of the greatest treats of each of my workdays is to have lunch in our galley and chat with some of the crew members who are doing the work of serving our sharehold-ers. And we trust our crew members. For years, I told our crew that we had just one rule of business conduct: "Do what's right. If you're not sure, ask your boss."

In addition to this list of values, we have established formal rituals to cel-ebrate the efforts of our crew. The most important are the Award for Excellence and the Vanguard Partnership Plan. The former recognizes the achievements of a single outstanding individual; the latter rewards the collective efforts of our crew. Together, the Award for Excellence and the Partnership Plan recognize that to provide valuable services for our clients, we need the human beings who serve on our crew to uphold our values, corporate character, and spirit.

A Single Rule: "Do What's Right. If You're Not Sure, Ask Your Boss."

The Award for Excellence: "Even One Person Can Make a Difference"

When I created the Award for Excellence in 1984, my purpose was to honor those crew members who embody "the Vanguard spirit." Since then, more than 350 crew members have received the award, which is presented in each quarter of the year to five to 10 individuals who demonstrate particular excellence in the performance of their duties. What makes these awards especially meaningful is that the recipients are nominated by their peers. At an award luncheon, we quote from the nominations submitted by fellow crew members, commending those who "give 110 percent," demonstrate "speed, determination, energy, and smarts," or are "unflappable, dependable, responsible, and indefatigable" (to cite a representative set of comments). In an organization that serves, and is served by, human beings, the ceremony is an opportunity to reaffirm our core value of respect for the individual.

In this increasingly impersonal era, when bureaucracy and technology threaten to obscure the contributions of individual human beings, the Award for Excellence is a tribute to individual effort. Each winner receives a plaque inscribed with a phrase I have used throughout my career to recognize the potential of a single human being: *I believe that even one person can make a difference.* And so one person can, and does, at Vanguard. Even as we have grown, we continue to recognize that our crew is a group of individual human beings, and that, no matter the size of our fleet, even one person can make a difference.

Partnership: Sharing the Fruits of Our Labors

If the Award for Excellence celebrates individual effort, then Vanguard's Partnership Plan recognizes the collective efforts of our crew in creating value for our shareholders. Each Vanguard crew member is made a partner in Vanguard on the first day on the job, and, without investing one cent of capital in the organization, shares in The Vanguard Group's earnings. Because Vanguard is effectively owned by the shareholders of its mutual funds, rather than third-party stockholders, earnings are defined as a combination of the value added to our shareholders' returns by

*Recognizing the Crew
Members' "Contributions
to the Value Created for
Our Shareholders"*

(1) the difference between Vanguard's expenses and the expenses that would prevail if our average expense ratio equaled those of our largest competitors, and (2) the extra returns (net of any return shortfalls) earned for shareholders by the investment strategies of our funds and the portfolio supervision skills of our managers. In 1998 alone, based on our assets then under management, more than $3 billion of value was added to our clients' returns. I have no doubt that the few percentage points of these annual savings that are shared among the crew members, in recognition of their contributions to the value created for our shareholders, are repaid manyfold by our operational effectiveness, efficiency, and productivity.

Since the firm's founding, we have consistently reduced our average expense ratio. That achievement is the result of our unique mutual structure and the energy and initiative of the thousands of crew members who work tirelessly to better serve our owners. The crew is continually finding ways to offer enhanced services and to save our shareholders additional millions of dollars: the introduction of cost-saving services on the World Wide Web, the development of more useful account statements, the elimination of duplicate mailings, and more informative tax reporting, to name just a few. The Partnership Plan helps to reward these collective efforts.

Each spring, we distribute the partnership checks at the Vanguard Partnership Picnic. The checks can amount to as much as 30 percent of a crew member's annual compensation, leaving little reason to wonder why thousands of crew members seem so enthusiastic about gathering under a huge tent in our Valley Forge parking lot and listening to some informative and, it is hoped, inspirational comments (mine have been called "sermons," but I'm not sure that word is used in a complimentary sense!) about Vanguard's corporate values. Over the years, I have regularly reminded the crew that we're engaged in an important pursuit, serving our shareholder-owners, and that the efforts of each individual human being who serves on the HMS *Vanguard* crew make a difference. That sense of participating in a worthy human enterprise is evident in the hundreds of letters I have received from current and former crew members.[6]

A Golden Rule: "Treat Those Whom You Serve As Stewards As You Would Like Your Stewards to Treat You"

The Vanguard story has been a unique combination of the unforeseen circumstances and unusual ideas on entrepreneurship and leadership recounted in *Common Sense on Mutual Funds*. As much as any of these odd twists of fate and flashes of inspiration, however, I believe that our decision to put human beings at the center of our enterprise has been key to everything that Vanguard has become. Like much of the wisdom presented in this book, the idea of treating people as human beings is common sense. It is a simplified, if dual, version of the Golden Rule: "Treat those whom you serve as stewards as you would like your stewards to treat you, and treat those with whom you serve as you would like them to treat you." Once a firm puts these ideas at the heart of its organizational values, treating both clients and crew members as honest-to-God, down-to-earth human beings with their own hopes, fears, and aspirations, the result shapes everything the firm accomplishes.

Many will regard this vision as utopian. And even I am not foolish enough to think that every firm in the mutual fund industry is prepared to operate as a demanding, disciplined financial service organization that relies largely on simplicity as the cornerstone of its investment strategy and on the Golden Rule as the cornerstone of its service strategy, placing its future in the hands of all-too-fallible human beings and retaining the goodwill of its clients through rough and calm seas alike. However, as Christopher Hitchens, columnist for the *Nation*, has recently noted, "Man cannot live on Utopias alone. But as Oscar Wilde so shrewdly remarked, a map of the world that does not include Utopia is not even worth glancing at." Thomas Paine, with his innate common sense, would surely have agreed.

---

6. Some of those letters are reproduced in Chapter 6.

Still a Utopian Vision

A lot can happen in a decade! And surely the past decade has been filled with surprises, some delightful and some horrendous, many of which are destined to find their way into the history books. But, as I write in 2009, the utopian vision with which I concluded the 1999 edition of *Common Sense on Mutual Funds* remains serene and undisturbed, a beacon of wisdom and hope for years to come, not yet to be realized. But my mission to build a better industry for mutual fund investors continues unabated.

Chapter 7: "Big Money in Boston" . . . The Commercialization of the "Mutual" Fund Industry[7]

This is a story about the radical change in the culture of the "mutual" fund industry. For more than 63 years, I have not only witnessed it, I have been an active part of it for almost that long. During that span, the fund culture has moved in a direction that has ill-served its mutual fund shareholders. It's time to recognize that change, and understand how it all happened.

The story begins a long time ago in December 1949. Almost halfway through my junior year at Princeton University, in the newly built Firestone Library, I was striving to keep up with current developments in economics, my major course of study, reading the December issue of *Fortune* magazine. When I turned to page 116, there was an article entitled "Big Money in Boston." That serendipitous moment would shape my entire career and life.

"Big Money in Boston"

The boldfaced type beneath the story's headline explained what was to follow: "But money isn't everything, according to the Massachusetts Investors Trust, which has

7. Scheduled for publication in the *Journal of Portfolio Management*, Fall 2013.

prospered by selling the small investor peace of mind. It's invention: the open-end fund. The future: wide open."

In the 10 fact-filled pages that followed, "Big Money . . ." described the history, policies, and practices of Massachusetts Investors Trust. M.I.T. was the first and by far the largest "open-end fund,"[8] founded in 1924, a quarter-century earlier. In its discussion of the embryonic industry's future, *Fortune* was optimistic that this tiny industry—"pretty small change . . . rapidly expanding and somewhat contentious, could become immensely influential . . . the ideal champion of the small stockholder in controversies with . . . corporate management."[9]

In those ancient days, the term *mutual fund* had not yet come into general use, perhaps because "mutual" funds, with one notable exception, are *not* mutual. In fact, contrary to the principles spelled out in the Investment Company Act of 1940,[10] they were "organized, operated, and managed" in the interests of the management companies that control them, rather in the interests of their share owners.[11] So *Fortune* relied largely on terms such as *investment companies*, *trusts*, and *funds*.

> ## "A Tiny Industry That Could Become Immensely Influential, the Ideal Champion of the Small Stockholder."

---

8. M.I.T. was an "open-end" fund, one that redeemed its shares on demand. The "closed-end" fund has a fixed number of nonredeemable shares outstanding.

9. *Fortune*'s optimism arose from the fact that in the late 1940s, funds played a role in a number of corporate management changes. Today, however, that promise has yet to be fulfilled. Despite holding virtual control over corporate America—mutual funds now collectively own more than one-third of U.S. stocks—they lack the spirit and the will to perform this central role in corporate governance.

10. Section 1(b)(2): Mutual funds must be "organized, operated, and managed" in the interests of their shareholders rather than in "the interests of directors, officers, investment advisers, . . . underwriters, brokers, or dealers."

11. At the 1968 Federal Bar Conference on Mutual Funds, former SEC Chairman Manuel Cohen gave a speech entitled "The 'Mutual' Fund," putting quotation marks around the word *mutual*, since "its salient characteristics raise the serious question whether the word 'mutual' is an appropriate description."

The Princeton Thesis

That article was the springboard for my decision—made on the spot—to write my thesis on the history and future prospects of open-end investment companies, with the title simplified: "The Economic Role of the Investment Company." After an intense analysis of the industry, I reached some clear conclusions:

> Investment companies should be operated in the most efficient, honest, and economical way possible. . . . Future growth can be maximized by reducing sales charges and management fees. . . . Funds can make no claim to superiority over the market averages [indexes]. . . the principal function of investment companies is the management of [their] investment portfolios. Everything else is incidental. . . . The principal role of the investment company should be to serve its shareholders.

Such idealism is typical of a young scholar. But, as you'll see in this paper, despite the passage of more than 63 years since I read that *Fortune* article, my idealism has hardly diminished. Indeed, likely *because* of my lifelong experience in the field, that idealism is even more passionate and unyielding today.

Walter Morgan, "My Mentor, the Great Hero of My Long Career, and the Founder of Wellington Fund"

Following my graduation in 1951, Walter L. Morgan, Princeton Class of 1920, read my thesis. Mr. Morgan—my mentor, the great hero of my long career, and the founder of industry pioneer Wellington Fund, offered me a job. I decided to join his small but growing firm—then managing but a single fund, with assets of $150 million. "Largely as a result of this thesis," he wrote to our staff, "we have added Mr. Bogle to our Wellington organization." Although I wasn't so sure at the time, it was the opportunity of a lifetime.

When I joined the fund industry in 1951, there were but 125 mutual funds, with aggregate assets of $3 billion. As can be seen in Exhibit 2.1, the field was dominated by 10 large (for those days) firms, accounting for almost three-fourths of industry assets. With assets of $438 million—a market share equal to 15 percent of

Exhibit 2.1 Mutual Fund Industry Assets, 1951

Rank	Fund Name	Total Assets* (million)	Notable Smaller Funds	Total Assets* (million)
1	M.I.T.	$ 472	Eaton & Howard	$ 90
2	Investors Mutual	365	National Securities	85
3	Keystone Funds	213	United Funds	71
4	Tri-Continental	209	Fidelity	64
5	Affiliated Funds	209	Group Securities	60
6	Wellington Fund	194	Putnam	52
7	Dividend Shares	186	Scudder Stevens & Clark	39
8	Fundamental Investors	179	American	26
9	State Street Investment	106	Franklin	25
10	Boston Fund	106	Loomis Sayles	23
			T. Rowe Price	1
			Dreyfus	0.8
	Total	$2,239	Total	$537
	Percentage of Industry**	72%	Percentage of Industry	17%

*Includes associated funds.
**Total industry assets: $3.1 billion.

What the "Tiny but Contentious" Industry Looked Like in 1951

industry assets—M.I.T. was overpoweringly dominant, by far the industry's largest fund, and by far the lowest-cost provider (expense ratio 0.42 percent). Indeed while "Big Money in Boston" focused on M.I.T., Boston itself was the center of the fund universe. The funds operated in that fair city dwarfed their peers—22 of the 50 largest funds, managing 46 percent of the largest firms' assets. (For the record, New York funds then represented 27 percent of those assets; Minneapolis, 13 percent; and Philadelphia, only 7 percent.)[12] (See Exhibit 2.2.)

12. Minneapolis is the headquarters of the giant Ameriprise/Columbia Funds (originally named Investors Diversified Services, formed in 1894). In 1951, as in 2012, the firm accounted for virtually all of the fund assets located there.

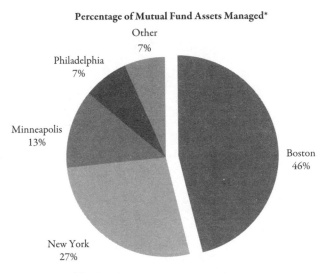

Percentage of Mutual Fund Assets Managed*

Other
7%

Philadelphia
7%

Minneapolis
13%

Boston
46%

New York
27%

*By location of firm headquarters.

Exhibit 2.2 "Big Money in Boston," 1951

Most firms, including Wellington, managed but a single fund, or a second fund as well that was usually tiny. For example, the five M.I.T. trustees also managed Massachusetts Investors Second Fund (hardly a name that would appeal to today's mutual fund marketers!) with assets of just $34 million, only a tiny fraction of M.I.T.'s $438 million.[13]

---

13. Five smaller fund managers of that era operated multiple funds, each providing a wide selection of investment objectives and specialized portfolios—often 20 or more—focused on a variety of single industries. Designed for market timing, at first they grew with the burgeoning industry. All had their moment in the sun during the 1960s, but not one remains today.

The Old Model— Stewardship . . . the New Model—Salesmanship

The idea of trusteeship—indeed, the so-called Boston trustee—dominated the industry's image, as a photo of the five M.I.T. trustees in the *Fortune* story suggested. Chairman Merrill Griswold, unsmiling, seated in the center, dark suits with vests, serious in demeanor, all looking, well, "trustworthy." The original operating model of the fund industry was much like that of M.I.T.: professional investors who owned their own small firms, often relying on unaffiliated distributors to sell their shares. (In those days distribution was a profitable business.) "Puritan" seems an apt description of those Boston managers of yore.

But the industry culture was soon to change, and change radically. In 1951— and in the years that immediately followed—the fund industry that I read about in *Fortune* was a *profession* with elements of a *business*, but would soon begin its journey to becoming a *business* with elements of a *profession* (and, I would argue, not enough of those latter elements). The old notion of fiduciary duty and *stewardship* was crowded out by an overbearing focus on *salesmanship*, as *management* played second fiddle to *marketing*—gathering assets to manage. That is the industry that exists today.

What explains this profound change in the culture of mutual funds?[14] I'd argue that there were four major factors: (1) gargantuan growth and new lines of business; (2) widespread use of aggressive, higher-risk strategies, leading to less focus on long-term investment and more focus on short-term speculation; (3) the rise of "product proliferation" with thousands of new funds formed each year, embracing aggressive share distribution as integral to the manager's interest in gathering assets and increasing fee revenues; (4) the conglomeratization of the industry—ownership of fund managers by publicly owned financial intermediaries— a development that served the monetary interests of mutual fund *managers* but was

---

14. This subject is one of the major themes of my 2012 book *The Clash of the Cultures: Investment vs. Speculation*.

a disservice to the interests of mutual fund *shareholders*. But a fifth factor emerged that has the potential to take our industry back toward its Puritan heritage: the triumph of the index fund, which did precisely the opposite; shareholders served first, managers only second. Let's review each of these changes.

The Stunning Growth of Mutual Fund Assets—1951 $3 Billion; 2013 $13 Trillion

When I joined the industry in 1951, fund assets totaled just $3 billion.[15] Today, assets total $13 *trillion*, a remarkable 15 percent annual growth rate. When a small industry—dare I say a cottage industry?—becomes something like a behemoth, almost everything changes. Big business, as hard experience teaches us, represents not just a difference in degree from small business—simply more numbers to the left of the decimal point—but a difference in kind: more process, less human judgment; more conformity, less tolerance of dissent; more business values, fewer professional values.

For almost the entire first half-century of industry history that followed the founding of M.I.T. in 1924, equity funds were the industry's backbone—some 95 percent of total assets. Equity fund assets topped $56 billion in 1972, and then, after a great bear market, tumbled to $31 billion by 1974, an unpleasant reminder of stock market risk and investor sensitivity to market declines. Recovering with the long bull market that followed, equity assets soared to $4 trillion by 1999. Despite two subsequent bear markets (off some 50 percent, twice), equity fund assets have now reached the $6 trillion level, still the engine that drives the industry. (See Exhibit 2.3.) The growth of balanced funds is sort of spasmodic; suffice it to say that their important role in the industry dwindled with the coming of the "Go-Go" era during the mid-1960s and then, following the 1973–1974 bear market, was overwhelmed by the boom in bond funds. But in recent years, the

---

15. $3 billion in 1951 is equivalent to $28 billion in 2013 dollars.

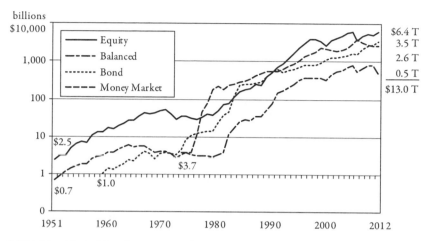

billions

	$6.4 T
	3.5 T
	2.6 T
	0.5 T
	$13.0 T

— Equity
- - - Balanced
.... Bond
- - - Money Market

$2.5

$3.7

$0.7 $1.0

1951   1960   1970   1980   1990   2000   2012

Exhibit 2.3   Mutual Fund Asset Growth, 1951–2012

importance of balanced funds has grown, and at the end of 2012, assets reached $500 billion.

Bond Funds Wax and Wane, and Wax Again

During the 1950s, assets of bond funds seemed stuck at around $500 million, with little growth during the next two decades. But in 1975, bond funds began to assert themselves. As the financial markets changed, so did investors' needs. Income became a high priority. After that earlier unpleasantness in the stock market, bond fund assets grew nicely, reaching $250 billion in 1987, actually exceeding the $175 billion total for equity funds. Bond funds then retreated to a less significant role during the 1990s. But today, following years of generous interest rates that were to tumble in recent years, bond fund assets have risen to $3.4 trillion, 26 percent of the industry total.

In the decade following the stock market crash of 1973–1974, the dominance of equity funds waned. Money market funds—the fund industry's great innovation of the mid-1970s—bailed out the industry, compensating for the shrunken equity fund base. (See Exhibit 2.4.) They quickly replaced stock funds as the industry's prime driver. By 1981, money market fund assets of $186 billion represented fully 77 percent (!) of industry assets. While that share has declined to 20 percent today, it remains a formidable business line, with $2.6 trillion of assets. But given today's pathetic yields and the possibility of a new business model for money market funds (one that would require that the rounded $1.00 net asset value now reported by money market funds reflect the fact that their net asset values vary each day in accordance with interest rate charges and credit quality), it won't be easy.

With the rise of bond funds and money market funds, nearly all of the major fund managers—which for a half-century had primarily operated as professional *investment* managers for one or two equity funds—became *business* managers,

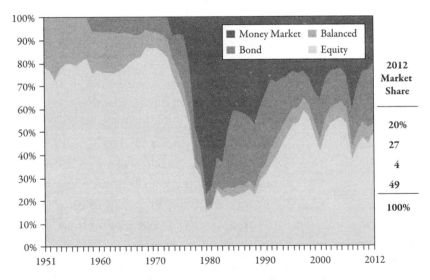

Exhibit 2.4   Mutual Fund Industry Share by Asset Class, 1951–2012

offering a smorgasbord of investment options, "financial department stores" that focus heavily on administration, marketing, and, in this current age of information, shareholder services.

The Sea Change in Equity Fund Management— Investment Committees to Portfolio Managers

In addition to the growth and changing composition of the mutual fund asset base, a second force in changing this industry culture developed: a sea change in the industry's investment operations. The modus operandi of our equity funds, once largely supervised by conservative investment committees with a long-term focus and a culture of prudent investment—that original approach of the Boston trustees—gradually gave way to individual portfolio managers, often operating with a short-term focus and a more speculative culture of aggressive investing.

This change from a group approach to an individual approach has fostered a surge in portfolio turnover. The turnover rate of actively managed funds has leaped from the 30 percent rate of the 1950s and early 1960s to the 150 percent rate of the past few decades.[16] While most fund managers were once investors, most now seem to be speculators. A new financial culture of ever higher trading activity in stocks was embraced by investors of all types. These institutional traders, of course, were simply swapping shares with one another, with no net gain for their clients as a group, indeed a guaranteed loss relative to the return of the stock market after accounting for transaction costs.

Equity Fund Risks Rise Sharply

What's more, the traditional equity fund model of blue-chip stocks in market-like portfolios—and commensurately market-like performance (before costs, of course)—evolved into a new, more aggressive model. The relative volatility of

---

16. The turnover measure that I'm using represents the total portfolio purchases plus the total sales of equity funds each year as a percentage of assets, not today's conventional—if inexplicable—formula: the lesser of purchases and sales as a percentage of assets.

Exhibit 2.5 Relative Volatility of Equity Mutual Funds

Relative Volatility*	1950–1956	2008–2011**	Difference
Over 1.11	0%	38%	+38%
0.95–1.11	34	38	+4
0.85–0.94	30	10	−20
0.70–0.84	36	6	−30
Below 0.70	0	9	+9

*S&P 500 = 1.00.
**Largest 200 Equity Funds.

individual funds increased, as measured in the modern era by "beta," the volatility of a fund's asset value relative to the stock market as a whole. This increase in riskiness is easily measured. The volatility of returns among actively managed equity funds increased sharply, from an average of 0.90 during the 1950s (10 percent *less* volatile than the market) to 1.11 during recent years (11 percent *more* volatile). That's a 30 percent increase in the relative volatility of the average fund. In the earlier era, *no* equity fund had volatility above 1.11; during recent years, 38 percent of equity funds exceeded that level. (See Exhibit 2.5.)

That shift toward higher volatility began during the "Go-Go" years of the late 1960s, when hot managers were treated like Hollywood stars and marketed in the same fashion. It has largely continued ever since. (The creation of index funds was a rare and notable exception. An all-market index fund, by definition, has a beta of 1.00.) But as the inevitable reversion to the mean in fund performance came into play, these aggressive manager *stars*—who focused on changes in short-term corporate earnings expectations, stock price momentum, and other quantitative measures—proved more akin to *comets*, speculators who too often seemed to soar into the sky and then flame out. Too often, the managers forgot about prudence, due diligence, research, balance sheet analysis, and other old-fashioned notions of intrinsic value and investing for the long term.

With all the publicity focused on the success of these momentary stars, and the accompanying publicity about "the best" funds for the year or even the quarter, along with the huge fees and compensation paid to fund management companies, accompanied by the huge compensation paid to fund portfolio managers of the hot funds, of course the manager culture changed, too. But even a short-term failing in performance became a career risk, so it was deemed smart to be agile and flexible, and for managers to watch over their portfolios in, as they say, "real time."

Large numbers of aggressive funds were formed and equity fund assets soared. Steady and deliberate decision making was no longer the watchword. As managers tried to earn their keep through feverish trading activity, portfolio turnover leaped upward, never mind that it seemed to improve fund performance only randomly, and—because of advisory fees and trading costs—couldn't work for all managers as a group. The tautology that for each winner there is a loser remains intact.

The Rise of Product Proliferation

Closely linked to the change in the investment culture was the turn toward product proliferation. Such proliferation reflects in part a marketing strategy for fund management companies that, in essence, says, "We want to run enough different funds so that at least *one* will always do well." An industry that used to sell what we made became an industry that makes what will sell. And in the mutual fund industry, what will sell—the latest investment fad, the hottest subsector—is too often exactly what investors should avoid. This problem began to take hold during the "Go-Go" years, but soared as the great bull market of 1982–2000 created ever higher investment expectations—especially in the late 1990s as technology stocks blossomed (before they wilted). The number of funds exploded upward.

When I entered the industry in 1951, there were but 125 mutual funds, dominated by a few leaders. Today, the total number of equity funds comes to a staggering 5,091. Add to that another 2,262 bond funds and 595 money market funds, and there is now a mind-boggling total of 7,948 traditional mutual funds, plus another 1,446 exchange-traded index funds (which are generally themselves mutual funds). If you have difficulty choosing from such a staggering number of investment options, just throw a dart! It remains to be seen whether this quantum increase in investment options—ranging from the simple and prudent to the complex and absurd—will serve the interests of fund investors. I have my doubts, and so far the facts seem to back me up.

The Good News . . . the Bad News

The good news is that many of those new funds were bond funds and money market funds, potentially offering investors a new range of sound investment options. The bad news is that in the equity fund sector of the industry, the massive proliferation of so many untested strategies (and often untested managers) has resulted in confusion for investors. "If you want to win, just pick the right fund or manager" seems to be the desideratum. But how could investors or their advisers possibly know *in advance* which funds or managers will win? How many advisers stoked the expectations that it would be easy to succeed and difficult to fail?

The proliferation of fund products was followed (unsurprisingly!) by nearly all of today's largest fund groups, resulting in a quantum increase in the number of funds offered. In 1951, industry leaders offered an average of 1.7 funds. Today, these firms offer an average of 117 funds. Fidelity once managed just a single fund; the firm now manages 294 funds. Similarly, Vanguard also began the period with a single fund (Wellington), and is now responsible for 140 funds. (See Exhibit 2.6.) Shareholders can only trust that each member of the board of directors of the funds whose shares they hold takes seriously his or her fiduciary duty to know

Exhibit 2.6 Number of Funds, 1951 and Today
Major Mutual Fund Groups

Original Name	1951		Current Name	2013	
	Total Assets (million)	No. of Funds Managed		Total Assets (billion)	No. of Funds Managed
M.I.T.	$ 472	2	MFS	$ 128	80
Investors Mutual	365	3	Columbia	162	116
Affiliated	209	3	Lord Abbett	97	38
Wellington	194	1	Vanguard	2,136	140
Eaton & Howard	90	2	Eaton Vance	107	139
Fidelity	64	1	Fidelity	1,372	294
Putnam	52	1	Putnam	59	76
American	27	2	American	994	33
T. Rowe Price	1	1	T. Rowe Price	375	106
Dreyfus	0.8	1	Dreyfus	228	152
Total/Average	$1,475	1.7	Total/Average	$5,658	117

Note: In 1951, 12 of today's 20 largest firms did not exist (or did not manage mutual funds), including BlackRock, PIMCO, State Street Global, and JP Morgan.

In 1951, Less Than 2 Funds Per Manager; Now, 117 Funds.

"Too Many Funds Seem Born to Die"

and to evaluate all of the relevant data for those funds and for the scores of other funds under the board's aegis.

With the rise of all of that product proliferation, the fund industry has come to suffer a rate of fund failures without precedent. Back in the 1960s, about 1 percent of funds disappeared each year, about 10 percent over the decade. By 2001–2012, however, the failure rate of funds had soared sevenfold to 7 percent per year; over that entire period, to 90 percent—too many funds seem born to die. With some 6,500 mutual funds in existence during that time, 5,500 have been liquidated or merged into other funds, almost always into members of the same fund family (with more imposing past records!). Assuming (as I do) that such a failure rate will persist over the coming decade, by 2023 some 3,500 of today's 5,000 equity funds will no longer exist—the death of more than one fund on every business day. While the mutual fund industry proudly posits that its mutual funds are designed for *long-term* investors, how can one invest for the *long term* in funds that may exist only for the *short term*?

Soaring Costs for Fund Investors . . . Almost Without Exception

Another result of proliferation is the soaring (and, again, truly absurd) rise in fund costs. Despite the quantum 5,000-fold growth in mutual fund assets—bringing with it enormous economies of scale—expense ratios (annual fund expenses as a percentage of fund assets) leaped upward. Just consider eight of the major fund managers of 1951 that survive today, each operating under the conventional industry model, each actively managing its fund portfolio. (Five of these management companies are owned by public shareholders, with only three remaining privately held by firm insiders.) From 1951 to 2012, the expense ratios of the funds managed by these eight giants have soared by 84 percent—from an average of 0.62 percent of assets to 1.15 percent. (See Exhibit 2.7.) The four largest fee increases came in firms that were publicly owned. By contrast, the only mutually owned firm (Vanguard, which adopted that model at its inception in 1974) actually drove expenses *down* from 0.55 percent to 0.17 percent, a drop in unit costs of fully 69 percent. When the expense ratios of funds that operate under the original industry business model *rise* by 84 percent, and the expense ratio of the one fund group that operates under a new business model *falls* by 69 percent, it is at least possible that there's a message there.

The data in the chart reflect the average *expense ratios* of funds offered by each manager, unweighted by assets. While asset-weighted ratios can only be approximated, one can conclude that the *aggregate dollar fees* paid to these eight firms rose from $58 *million* in 1951 (measured in 2012 dollars) to $26 *billion* in 2013—a

Exhibit 2.7 Mutual Fund Expense Ratios, 1951 and 2012

Conventional Industry Model	1951	2012	Change
M.I.T./MFS (C)	0.42%	1.33%	+220%
Investors Mutual/Columbia (C)	0.56	1.23	+121
Eaton & Howard/Eaton Vance (SH)	0.64	1.32	+108
Putnam (C)	0.66	1.31	+98
Fidelity (P)	0.63	1.04	+65
T. Rowe Price (SH)	0.50	0.81	+62
Affiliated/Lord Abbett (P)	0.75	1.14	+53
American (P)	0.84	0.98	+17
Average	0.62%	1.15%	+84%
New Industry Model			
Wellington/Vanguard (M)	0.55%	0.17%	−69%

Ownership type: (C) conglomerate; (SH) public shareholders; (P) private; (M) mutual.

Fund Managers: 400 Times As Much Money to Spend, But No *Brute Evidence* That It Helps Fund Returns

400-fold jump (!) in the fees that investors pay to fund managers. *Expense ratios* seem small. *Actual expenses* are another story. One might have hoped that with that staggering increase in the resources available to improve the quality of their stock selection, their price discovery, and their portfolio strategy, the returns earned by fund managers for their shareholders relative to the stock market index would have improved. Alas, there is no "brute evidence" whatsoever that such has been the case.[17] None.

---

17. In his 1974 paper "Challenge to Judgment," published in the first issue of the *Journal of Portfolio Management*, Nobel laureate Paul Samuelson noted that academics had not been able to systematically identify superior active fund managers, and said that the burden of proof belonged to the proponents of active management to produce "brute evidence to the contrary."

The Conglomeratization of the Fund Industry: "A Date Which Will Live in Infamy," Part I: April 7, 1958

In my opinion, the coming of public ownership of management companies played a major role—perhaps *the* major role—in changing the nature and structure of our industry. This baneful development began with an unfortunate decision by the U.S. Court of Appeals, Ninth Circuit (San Francisco) that affirmed the right of a fund adviser, Insurance Securities Incorporated (ISI), to sell a controlling interest in its stock at a premium to its book value. The Securities and Exchange Commission (SEC) argued that the transaction was a sale of the responsibilities of trusteeship, and hence a violation of fiduciary duty. The date of that decision, April 7, 1958, was therefore a date that will live in infamy for mutual fund shareholders. That seminal event, now long forgotten, changed the rules of the game.[18] It opened the floodgates to public ownership of management companies, providing the huge potential rewards of entrepreneurship for fund managers, inevitably at the expense of fund shareholders.

From 1924 through the 1950s, as I recall, all but one[19] of the industry's 50 largest fund management companies was operated primarily by investment professionals, through either a partnership or a closely held corporation. But within a decade after the Circuit Court's decision, scores of mutual fund management companies would go public, selling their shares (but with their managers usually retaining voting control). It was only a matter of time until U.S. and international financial conglomerates acquired most of these newly publicly owned firms, and many of the industry's privately owned firms as well. These acquiring firms, obviously (one could even concede appropriately), are in business to earn a high return on *their* capital, and they looked at the burgeoning fund industry as a gold mine for managers. (It was!) But that high return came at the expense of the return on the capital *entrusted to them* by the mutual fund investors whom they were duty-bound to serve.

---

18. Ironically, ISI went out of business decades ago, its records lost in the dustbin of history.

19. IDS (which today is Ameriprise/Columbia) was the lone exception. See footnote 12 for additional detail.

Conglomerates and the Public Control 40 of the 50 Largest Fund Managers

As can be seen in Exhibit 2.8, the dimension of that change has been extraordinary. Among today's 50 largest mutual fund complexes, only nine remain private. Forty are publicly held, including 30 owned by financial conglomerates. The only different ownership model is the sole *mutual* mutual fund structure at Vanguard, where the fund management company is owned by the fund shareholders. All of the public fund management companies have external owners, and these owners face an obvious potential conflict of interest that has deeply concerned me for at least four decades. As I wrote to Wellington's officers in 1971 (when our firm was owned largely by public shareholders):

> I reveal an ancient prejudice of mine: All things considered . . . it is undesirable for professional enterprises to have public stockholders. . . . The pressure for earnings and earnings growth engendered by public ownership is antithetical to the responsible operation of a professional organization.

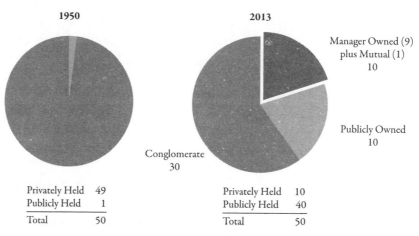

Exhibit 2.8   Ownership of 50 Largest Mutual Fund Management Companies, 1950 and 2013

Despite the far-reaching consequences of its unfortunate birth, "conglomeratization" has been the least recognized of all of the changes that have beset the mutual fund industry. Ownership by financial conglomerates has now become the dominant industry model. In 1951, there was, as far as I can tell, only a single conglomerate owner. After all, assets of most funds then totaled $1,000,000 or even less, hardly enough to whet the appetites of hungry acquisitors. But not all of today's giant firms have heeded the call of the conglomerateurs. All three of today's largest fund complexes—Vanguard, Fidelity, and American Funds—have remained independent. These three firms alone manage $4.4 trillion, or some 30 percent of all mutual fund assets.

While most of the private firms have grown organically, many of the public firms have grown by acquisition, a pattern hardly unfamiliar to the business behemoths of corporate America. For example, Ameriprise Financial (manager of the Ameriprise/Columbia Funds) has acquired fully 12 previously independent fund managers. BlackRock obtained substantially its entire fund asset base through its acquisition of Barclays Global Investors in 2009, Merrill Lynch Asset Management in 2006, and State Street Management and Research Corporation in 2005, previously owned by MetLife. (That acquisition was followed by the liquidation of the industry's second-oldest fund, State Street Investment Corporation. I still mourn its demise as a death in the family.) Franklin Resources, another huge firm, is the product of the 1992 merger of giant Franklin Group and the giant Templeton Group. And so on.

"Trafficking" in Management Contracts

So, yes, opening the doors to public ownership produced exactly what the SEC was concerned about a half-century ago in the ISI case: "trafficking" in management contracts, and the likelihood that it would dramatically erode the sense of fiduciary duty that largely characterized the industry during its early era. And product proliferation hardly helped. So I reiterate: How can an independent fund director feel a fiduciary duty to each one of the hundred or more fund boards on which he or she serves?

What's the problem? It's summarized in Matthew 6:24: *No man can serve two masters*. Yet when a management firm is owned by a giant conglomerate (or even by public owners), the conflict of interest is palpable. Even when a conglomerate builds internally a fund management company, the conglomerate's goal is to earn the highest possible return on its invested capital. That's the American way! The idea: maximize fees by gathering assets and creating new products, and resist reductions in fee rates that would enable fund shareholders to benefit from the economies of scale.

The Conflicting Fiduciary Duties of Directors

Fund shareholders, of course, have precisely the opposite interests. They benefit from lower fee rates, which would increase their returns dollar for dollar. Think of it this way: the officers and directors of financial conglomerates have a *fiduciary duty* to increase the returns earned by their corporate shareholders. Yet they also have a *fiduciary duty* to maximize returns earned by their mutual fund shareholders. As Matthew suggested, this obvious conflict in serving two masters will cause them "to love the one and hate the other," and it seems obvious that the manager is the master who gets the love. There can be only one resolution to this profound conflict: a federal statute that prohibits the ownership of fund managers by holding companies.[20]

---

20. The Investment Company Institute (ICI) still appears not to understand this distinction. It recently defended the industry by acknowledging that "both fund advisors and fund board directors are fiduciaries and therefore must act in the best interests of a fund and its shareholders." But it ignores the obvious conflict that advisers and boards also have fiduciary duties to management company shareholders that directly conflict with the duties they owe to mutual fund shareholders.

The Triumph of Indexing: "A Date Which Will Live in Infamy," Part II: December 31, 1975

If April 7, 1958, is a date that will live in infamy for mutual fund *shareholders*, then surely December 31, 1975, is a date that will live in infamy for mutual fund *managers*. That is the date that Vanguard—a tiny, brand-new mutual fund firm that had begun operations only seven months earlier—filed with the State of Delaware the Declaration of Trust for a new mutual fund that promised *not* to engage in the practice of active management. Originally named First Index Investment Trust, it was the world's first *index mutual fund*.

Its birth was, curiously, the product of a divorce. (Now, there's a paradox!) In 1966, as head of the long-established Wellington Management Company, I bet the firm's future on, yes, a merger. We joined with a small Boston firm, Thorndike, Doran, Paine, and Lewis, run by four aggressive equity managers. The firm operated a hot "Go-Go" fund named Ivest, managed a growing pension business, and had investment talent that, I believed, could more effectively manage the portfolio of our faltering Wellington Fund.

Yes, I was young and foolish, and (even worse!) I was wrong. For a time, the merged firm prospered, but only until the "Go-Go" era came to its inevitable end. As 1973 began, the stock market began its terrible 50 percent crash, even worse for Ivest Fund, which never did recover. (Ivest failed, and two of its Boston sister funds also failed.) Worse, Wellington Fund's performance continued to deteriorate. Indeed, it was a disaster—the worst performer among *all* balanced mutual funds from 1967 to 1977. Our new business model faltered, and then it failed. In the merger, I had ceded substantial voting power to the new managers, and it was *they* who fired *me* as the leader of Wellington Management. On January 24, 1974, I was replaced by their leader, Robert W. Doran.

I leave it to wiser heads than mine to explain the perverse logic involved in that outcome. But I know that it was the most heartbreaking moment—actually, up until then, the *only* such moment—of my entire career. I decided to fight back.

Fired by Wellington Management Company—actually "fired with enthusiasm"—I continued in my role as chairman of the board of Wellington Fund and its 11 sister funds. There was a considerable overlap in board membership between the funds and the manager (this is the mutual fund industry!), but the funds, as required by law, had a majority of independent directors. As far as I know, such a power struggle, if you will, had never before occurred in our industry. I doubt that its counterpart will ever occur again.

The Mysterious Question Mark Reflects the Uncertainty of the Outcome

That's too long and complex a story for this paper. (For more detail, it's chronicled in *The Clash of the Cultures*.) But the outcome was a mighty near thing. Even the *New York Times* couldn't figure out what was happening. In the early edition of the newspaper on March 14, 1974, the *Times* headline read "Ex-Fund Chief to Come Back." In the late edition, the story and the photo of me were unchanged. But the original headline now ended with a giant question mark. A few excerpts:

> John C. Bogle, who was forced out of his $100,000-a-year job as president and chief executive officer of the Wellington Management Company in late January, is expected by his associates to try to fight his way back at the next board meeting, scheduled to be held within a week.
>
> Mr. Bogle is understood to believe that this may be the appropriate time for the funds to "mutualize," or take over, their investment advisers.

But the haunting "?" silently described the struggle that was going on.

Six months later, the fund board, King Solomon–like, made its decision: cut the baby in half (more or less). "Boston" would continue as investment adviser to and distributor of the funds. "Philadelphia," under my direction, took on the responsibility of running the funds' administrative, accounting, record-keeping, and compliance activities, as well as the responsibility for evaluating the performance of our adviser and distributor (then, of course, Wellington Management Company). So for the first time in industry history, mutual funds would be independent of their management company, free to operate solely in the interests of their own shareholders.

Vanguard Is Born as a Mutual Mutual Fund Company

The fund board accepted my recommendation to operate as a truly mutual organization, with the new firm owned by the funds themselves, providing its services to shareholders on an at-cost basis. In yet another contentious vote during the long process of making our decision, the board also approved my choice of a name for the new firm: Vanguard. The Vanguard Group of Investment Companies was born on September 24, 1974.[21] As I took on my new job, I was "fired with enthusiasm" for the second time within eight months. (Think about that!)

As I considered Vanguard's priorities in the years ahead—we were then overseeing just $1.4 billion in fund assets—I recalled the analysis of the fund industry that I had presented in my senior thesis. I decided to buttress my conclusion that mutual funds can "make no claim to superiority over the market averages." With my hand calculator and my slide rule, I documented the failure of mutual fund managers generally to outpace the market (using the Standard & Poor's 500 Index) during the previous three decades. It clearly demonstrated the continued superiority of the index fund strategy. Equally important, I was inspired by powerful encouragement from Nobel laureate Paul Samuelson, expressed in his previously mentioned essay "Challenge to Judgment." Result: Vanguard formed the world's first index mutual fund.

---

21. One could easily argue that the date that will live in infamy for fund managers was Vanguard's precedent-breaking formation on September 24, 1974. For it replaced the industry's business model with a truly mutual model, a model that was virtually essential in the creation of our index fund. More about that later.

Despite the persuasive data, our board was skeptical, for its mandate to the warring partners precluded Vanguard from providing investment advisory services to the funds. But when I explained that an index fund required no adviser, the board reluctantly acceded to my recommendation. That day of infamy for mutual fund managers "changed a basic industry in the optimal direction," as Professor Samuelson wrote in his 1993 foreword to my first book.[22] It was indeed the beginning of a far better direction, one aimed at placing front and center the interests of the mutual fund shareholders.

"INDEX FUNDS ARE UN-AMERICAN!"

The initial public offering (IPO) for the First Index Investment Trust index fund took place on August 31, 1976. It was a flop. The underwriters raised initial assets of only $11 million, despite a target of $150 million. The fund barely grew for years, and industry leaders scorned it publicly. ("You wouldn't settle for an 'average' brain surgeon, so why would you settle for an 'average' mutual fund?")[23] A Midwest brokerage firm flooded Wall Street with posters, illustrated by an angry Uncle Sam using a large rubber stamp to cancel the index fund's stock certificates. Its headline screamed, "Help Stamp Out Index Funds/INDEX FUNDS ARE UN-AMERICAN!"

To make matters worse, during First Index's early years it appeared to lag the returns of the average fund manager, largely because of flaws in the data. The fund attracted few additional assets. Even with the acquisition of a $40 million actively managed Vanguard fund, First Index didn't cross the $100 million mark until 1982.[24] Indeed, it wasn't until 1984 that a second index mutual fund joined the industry. By 1990, total assets of, by then, five index funds had reached $4.5

---

22. *Bogle on Mutual Funds* (John Wiley & Sons, 1993).

23. Fidelity's chairman, Edward C. Johnson III, doubted Fidelity would follow Vanguard's lead. "I can't believe," he told the press, "that the great mass of investors are [*sic*] going to be satisfied with just receiving average returns. The name of the game is to be the best." Today Fidelity oversees some $140 billion of index fund assets.

24. In 1980, the name of First Index Investment Trust was changed to Vanguard 500 Index Fund.

billion, only about 2 percent of equity fund assets. The experiment in indexing was stumbling.

The Triumph of Indexing

But, as Thomas Paine reminded us all those years ago, "the harder the conflict, the more glorious the triumph." And just as Paul Samuelson predicted, indexing changed the fund industry in the optimal direction. Index fund assets leaped to $100 billion by 1996, and to $1 trillion by 2006, and to about $2 trillion today. (See Exhibit 2.9.) So, no, I don't think that the word *triumph* in the title of this section is hyperbolic. Consider that during the past five years, investors have liquidated some $386 billion of their actively managed equity funds and poured $667 billion into passively managed index equity funds—a *$1 trillion-plus* shift in investor preferences. Today, assets of passively managed equity index funds are equal to almost 40 percent of the assets of their actively managed peers, their

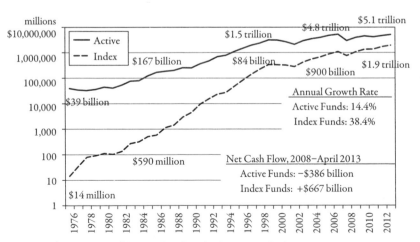

Exhibit 2.9   Growth in Assets of Equity Funds—Active versus Index

superiority confirmed by scores—perhaps hundreds—of independent academic studies, *and denied by none*. Index fund growth seems certain to continue, and likely even accelerate, from today's massive total.

The Moral History of U.S. Business

Those two days of infamy—one in 1958 and one in 1975—were polar opposites. Conglomeratization placed a heavy burden of costs on the returns earned by mutual fund investors; indexing, with its minuscule costs, provided an automatic boost in the returns that, as a group, fund investors earn. Here we have two subtle lessons for fund investors and their managers. The first reflects a diminution of the power of the fiduciary; the second reflects a clear buttressing of the concept of fiduciary duty. Could there be a lesson here about financial ethics and stewardship? Is the moral culture of our financial system involved? Will our society demand that business success be harmonized with social purpose? Ironically, that provocative question was raised in that very same December 1949 issue of *Fortune* in which "Big Money in Boston" appeared.

The lengthy essay was entitled "The Moral History of U.S. Business." American business leaders, the article noted, "do not work for money alone. A dozen nonprofit motives lie behind their labors: love of power or prestige, altruism, pugnacity, patriotism, the hope of being remembered through a product or institution, etc. American business leaders in general have offered few pure specimens of economic man. . . . It is relevant to ask," *Fortune* added, "what are the leader's *moral* credentials for the social power he wields."

The essay presented a brief history of the values of U.S. business leaders, beginning in Colonial America. Here we meet Benjamin Franklin,[25] who looked

---

25. Ironically (in light of what will soon follow), Franklin began his life in Boston, but in his youth moved to Philadelphia and spent his entire career there.

WORDS FROM THOSE WHO KNOW BOGLE BEST

Dr. Bernard Lown, world-renowned cardiologist; inventor of the defibrillator; founder, Physicians for Social Responsibility; cofounder, International Physicians for the Prevention of Nuclear War

At some moments it is worth looking back. Forty-two years ago, when we first met, medical experience taught that a sick heart like yours afforded a life span measured in months, not years. Even a 40th birthday seemed beyond the horizon of hope.

You have not merely held on to life, you have enriched it for multitudes. A few years ago, *Time* magazine anointed you among the "Leaders and Revolutionaries, Builders and Titans" as one of the world's most influential people. Several weeks ago, the *New York Times*, searching out "a bit of wisdom from a moral authority," turned to you as one of the "few voices of reason and integrity left in this upside-down world."

Already, decades ago, you intoned fearlessly, like some ancient Hebraic prophet, exposing what ails "the soul of capitalism." You inveighed against the abuses of morality for many on Wall Street. You predicted a breakdown of a system wherein self-enrichment, whatever the means, was the sole litmus of success. You did not merely speak out against a culture of greed. You launched a new model of investing. You put back the "mutual" in "mutual funds" and forged ahead single-mindedly against the major currents of narrow economic self-interest.

How were your major achievements possible with a heart struggling for the next uncertain pulse, for the next hesitating contraction? I marveled at your iron will and still do. The advances in medical science certainly added years to your life. Yet science alone does not account for the miracle of John Bogle.

You taught me a deeper truth that surviving against great odds demands intangibles not readily measured by the metrics of science—above all the might of the human

"Like Some Hebraic Prophet"

spirit that defines our self-awareness. It includes a commitment to serving others, a fearless sense of transience, and a joy in making a difference. Such a self-image enabled you to cultivate a web of devoted family and intimate friends, to bond with the future even when it was merely a shimmer of possibility. Thereby you gained a hold on a meaningful life.

You taught me also that living a moral life can impart divinity on flawed human beings. You offered this as an antidote to the dread of our transience. So thanks, ever thanks. While I was privileged to be your doctor, I profited from even a greater privilege of having you as my consummate teacher.

May you continue to enrich our lives for years to come.

May 2009

upon his business as the foundation of all else he did. He set himself a course of conduct, using his favorite words, "industry and frugality," which he described as "the means of producing wealth, and thereby securing virtue."

Fortune also cited:

"A Mind to Improve, a Heart to Cultivate, a Character to Form"

. . . the generic features of the businessman of that era, as described in *Lives of American Merchants* in 1844. Speaking of William Parsons, a New Yorker of probity, the book declared: "the good merchant is not in haste to be rich. . . . He recollects that he is not merely a merchant, but a man, and that he has a mind to improve, a heart to cultivate,[26] a character to form. The good merchant, though an enterprising man and

---

26. As some readers may know, I was the beneficiary of a heart transplant in 1996, so I've been cultivating a new heart for the past 17 years.

willing to run some risks, yet is not willing to risk everything, nor put all on the hazard of a single throw. . . . Above all, he makes it a matter of conscience not to risk in hazardous enterprises the property of others entrusted to his keeping. . . . He is careful to indulge in no extravagance, and to live within his means. . . . Simple in his manner and unostentatious in his habits of life, he abstains from all frivolities and foolish expenditures. . . .

The spirit of character, of prudence, and of rectitude—described in a book written in 1844, more than 150 years ago—is worthy of careful consideration by today's mutual fund officers and directors. It is that spirit that must come to animate the values and conduct of the professional investors and financial institutions that now dominate the field of money management.

"Puritan Boston and Quaker Philadelphia"[27]

Yes, today—six-plus decades after I read that *Fortune* article—there's still "Big Money in Boston." While no longer the center of the industry, Boston firms manage about $2.2 trillion of industry assets or 18 percent, well down from that 1951 peak of a dominant 46 percent. Almost one-half of that loss has been offset by Philadelphia's gain—from 7 percent to 18 percent. (See Exhibit 2.10.) Whether we like it or not, there have been some significant changes, not only in the center of the industry's geographic core, but in the business model of many firms.

How did Boston lose so much and Philadelphia gain so much? Largely because M.I.T. abandoned its, well, Puritan model even as Vanguard adopted its new Quaker-like model. In both cases, it came down to choices about the business model and strategy of the firm. The fund industry now has

---

27. *Puritan Boston and Quaker Philadelphia* is the title of a book by E. Digby Baltzell (Free Press, 1979), describing the contrasting cultures of the two cities.

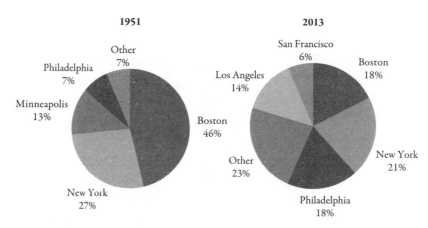

Percentage of mutual fund assets by location of firm headquarters.

Exhibit 2.10   Big Money in Boston—Still Huge, but No Longer Dominant

The Importance of Industry Structure

four business models—mutual, private ownership, public ownership, and conglomerate ownership—and those structures play an important role in shaping a firm's investment strategy (notably active money management versus passive indexing). In his foreword to my 1999 book *Common Sense on Mutual Funds*, economist and famed author Peter L. Bernstein clearly articulated this distinction.

. . . [W]hat happens to the wealth of individual investors cannot be separated from the structure of the industry that manages those assets. Bogle's insight into what the structure means to the fortunes of the individuals whose welfare concerns him so deeply is what makes this book most rewarding.

In 1969, M.I.T. abandoned its highly successful original business model, with its sharp focus on prudent trusteeship and low costs. It became the nucleus of a new, privately owned, profit-seeking firm owned by its trustees, Massachusetts Financial Services (MFS), that managed the funds' affairs and distributed their shares. In 1976, MFS was sold by its relatively new owners (at a healthy profit) to a publicly owned Canadian insurance company, Sun Life.[28] The firm's once rock-bottom costs have soared from a low of 0.17 percent in 1961 to 1.33 percent for the MFS funds in 2012, an astounding increase of 700 percent—and are now among the highest in the industry. Its once-record market share of 15 percent of industry assets in 1949 has tumbled to just 1 percent. (MFS has yet to offer investors an index fund.) Nonetheless, it has been a gold mine for the financial conglomerate that acquired it. Since 1995 alone, Sun Life has earned almost $4 billion of profits from its ownership of MFS. Readers can decide whether or not the SEC conclusion about the implications of trafficking in the management contracts—trafficking in fiduciary duty, if you will—was justified.

Quaker Thrift and Simplicity

The change in the business model of M.I.T.—that former exemplar of Puritan Boston—left a void that shortly would be filled by Vanguard in Quaker Philadelphia.[29] With a bow to the legendary Quaker thrift and simplicity, Vanguard's new mutual structure engendered rock-bottom costs—the firm's expense ratio of 0.17 percent (less than one-fifth of 1 percent) in 2012 is but one-eighth of the unit costs of MFS. The fortuitous creation of Vanguard's index fund—which simply

28. Similarly, staunch old Putnam Management Company was bought from its manager/trustees by U.S. insurance giant Marsh and McLennan in 1970, and resold in 2008, for almost $4 billion, to yet another Canadian conglomerate. Its fund assets have stumbled from $250 billion in 1999 to $60 billion today.

29. While I believe profoundly in Quaker principles, I'm not a card-carrying member of the Society of Friends.

buys and holds the 500 stocks of the Standard & Poor's 500 Index and delivers their returns to investors at rock-bottom costs—has been the prime force in the firm's rise to the industry's leadership.

Now overseeing $2.2 trillion of assets, Vanguard's remarkable growth is a reflection of the triumph of indexing; offering middle-of-the-road stock, bond, and money market funds; and the pervasive realization by investors that lower fund costs lead to higher fund returns. In 2012, Vanguard's share of assets of stock and bond mutual funds set an all-time industry high of 17 percent. Continued growth in market share seems likely, for the firm has accounted for more than 70 percent of industry cash flows since 2010. It seems only a matter of time until a serious challenger emerges. The challenge is *simple*: operate at far lower costs, manage more index funds, tone down the emphasis on (and costs of) marketing, and run the funds with the interests of shareholders as the highest priority. But, given the priority of building earnings for the public stockholders that characterizes the business models of so many management companies, it won't be *easy*.

A Final Word from Adam Smith: "The Interest of the Consumer ... [Must Be] the Ultimate End and Object ..."

So the issue is joined. Which should be the higher priority for a fund manager: the interests of its fund shareholders or the interests of its management company owners? In *The Wealth of Nations*, Adam Smith gave us an unequivocal answer:

> . . . [T]he interest of the producer ought to be attended to, only so far as it may be necessary for promoting that of the consumer. The maxim is so perfectly self-evident, that it would be absurd to attempt to prove it. . . . [T]**he interest of the consumer . . . [must be] the ultimate end and object of all industry and commerce. [Emphasis added.]**

Even as I wish our fund peers well—especially those in Boston, the industry's birthplace—the challenges facing the industry's present business model are enormous. The Vanguard way, of course, is not the only way. But whichever way others may choose, I believe that there is a central principle involved that has informed my long career. It all began with the incredible good luck—against all odds—of stumbling upon that 1949 story that began on page 116 in *Fortune* magazine, "Big Money in Boston," that inspired my Princeton thesis. There I concluded, in words similar to those cited by Adam Smith in 1776, "The principal role of the investment company should be to serve its shareholders." In the years ahead, that principle must become the watchword of our industry.

THE INDEX FUND VISION

FOR MANY INVESTORS, Jack Bogle and the index fund are one and the same. In Part III, the discussion of the index fund starts with an introduction by Morningstar CEO Joe Mansueto, "The Index Fund Revolution." Mansueto highlights the origins, struggles, and eventual dominance of index funds. He concludes simply, "The index fund is the revolution that Jack brought."

Bogle's 2004 essay comes next: the Gary M. Brinson Distinguished Lecture at Washington State University, "As the Index Fund Moves from Heresy to Dogma... What More Do We Need to Know?" Here he discusses the early "revolutionary" years of indexing and the initial scowls from industry leaders, including a charge that index funds are "un-American." Bogle also offers a commentary on the "big idea" of active management, and concludes, unsurprisingly, that "there *is* no big idea."

Part III concludes with excerpts from a recent special edition of the *Journal of Indexes*, where its editor, Jim Wiandt, pays tribute to the "marvelous, brutally honest, and passionately sensible Jack Bogle." Then, a number of investment luminaries address Bogle's contributions, offer candid commentary, and include answers to the question, "What do you think Jack Bogle has gotten wrong?"

A roundtable with Professor Burton Malkiel of Princeton University, Vanguard's Gus Sauter, Morningstar's Don Phillips, author and financial adviser William Bernstein, investment manager Ted Aronson, and others is followed by a tribute from Standard & Poor's David Blitzer, who credits Bogle with making "whole-market investing a reality for investors."

THE INDEX FUND REVOLUTION

Joe Mansueto, Founder and CEO, Morningstar

Of all Jack Bogle's accomplishments—among them, establishing the company that would become the world's largest mutual fund provider, leading by example in stewardship by asset managers, and making available by far the lowest-cost funds that ordinary investors could own—perhaps his greatest was bringing the index fund to market.

Mind you, it took some patience on Bogle's part to do so. The index mutual fund was anything but an overnight success. Five years after its launch, the world's first and only index mutual fund, Vanguard 500 Index Fund, was still the world's first and only index mutual fund. Five years after that, it had gained competitors but few assets; while several younger funds had leapfrogged from nothing to $10 billion in assets, the decade-old Vanguard index fund was operating in relative obscurity, still looking to crack the $1 billion mark.

It took the fund another full decade, until the mid-1990s, to crack the $10 billion mark itself and become one of the nation's largest funds. But even then, all index funds combined held only 1 percent of industry monies. Index funds remained for specialized tastes, offered by only a handful of fund companies and purchased by a small group of investors. They were the equivalent of a cult film.

Flash forward to today. There are more than 1,000 index mutual funds, offered by virtually every major fund company in the country. Collectively they boast $1.5 trillion in assets—15 percent of the U.S. mutual fund marketplace. What's more, the existence of the index fund made possible the invention of exchange-traded funds (ETFs), which have boomed over the past decade. The U.S. ETF market now contains $1.1 trillion in index funds.

Increasingly, the indexing movement is global. As a thoroughly American invention, indexing was even slower to spread internationally than it was to spread at home. Eventually, however, the strategy's domestic success began to attract the attention of global fund companies and investors. First mutual funds and later exchange-traded funds popped up around the world.

The numbers are starting to add up. At $250 billion, index funds are a modest 2 percent of non-U.S. mutual fund assets—but that's still double the market share that they enjoyed in the United States in the 1990s. Overseas ETFs contribute another $650 billion into the coffer, putting the grand total for global index funds, both conventional and exchange-traded, at $3.5 trillion. To put the matter another way, there is now more than $10,000 invested in global index mutual funds for every man, woman, and child in the United States.

The Man Who Started It All

The man who started it all is Jack Bogle. In a very real sense, Bogle had spent his entire adult life preparing for the moment. As a Princeton undergraduate, he had studied mutual fund returns when preparing his senior thesis. Bogle discovered, surely to his adviser's surprise, that most of the professionally managed funds in his study had trailed the performance of an unmanaged index, the S&P 500.

This finding didn't directly lead to the concept of the index mutual fund, but it set the stage. Over the next 15 years, finance professors and leading institutional investors saw the same data that Bogle has assembled and they formed a theory: The stock market was not a turkey shoot as portrayed and viewed by professional investment managers. It was instead a ruthlessly competitive field—an efficient market, in their phrase—wherein millions of buyers and sellers, bringing billions of data points to their collective analyses, set prices that were as close to being objectively "correct" as any expert could say.

If this theory is reality, then buying winning mutual funds becomes a fools' game. Funds that were successful in the past were so because they were lucky—no more and no less. Have 1,000 people each roll five dice, and one of those people will likely roll a Yahtzee (that is, all five dice land on the same number). That doesn't make the person who rolled those particular dice skilled at the task. It just happened. Similarly, by the efficient markets theory, funds leading the charts just happen.

From such logic sprang the argument for the index fund. If managers are lucky rather than good, and skill cannot be identified, then fund investors should instead seek what they can control: cost and diversification. Find a fund that operates on the cheap and that owns an entire market rather than only a segment of the market—so that the fund achieves the highest possible level of diversification, and does not miss the biggest winners. That is, find an index fund.

Bogle Was Ready

Jack Bogle was ready. Through his Princeton research, he saw no reason to believe that the average portfolio manager was any better than, well, average. And since an average portfolio manager would produce average results before expenses, the results would be distinctly less than average after taking into account a fund's official expense ratio and its unofficial trading costs. Thus, when Bogle saw the first articles emerging in the 1970s arguing the case of index funds, the answer was obvious to him.

It wasn't very obvious to others in the investment industry, however. Few besides Bogle paid attention to the new theories. The papers arguing for index funds had too many equations and seemingly too few insights for practical investment managers. Plus, who in their right mind would be content to buy an entire market's worth of securities without doing any further research?

Jack Bogle would, that's who. All he needed was the chance—and in 1974, he got just that. That year, Bogle assumed control of a new fund company, The Vanguard Group. Quickly, he filed the papers to launch the world's first index mutual fund, which was released in early 1976. When the First Index Investment Trust (renamed the Vanguard 500 Index Fund in 1980) was launched, there were a few indexed investments that were sold to institutions, but no publicly available mutual funds that could be owned by ordinary investors.

Off to a Bad Start

The fund had an inauspicious debut. Not only was the concept un-American, as one critic stated to Bogle's cackling delight, but the timing of the fund's launch couldn't have been worse for showcasing its strategy. Almost immediately after the fund began operations, small-company U.S. stocks waged a furious rally, easily beating the shares of larger companies. Many mutual funds held stock in these smaller companies. However, Vanguard's index fund did not. The critics chuckled as the index fund trailed most of its competitors.

Their pleasure was short-lived. By the early 1980s, larger-company shares started to catch up with the smaller companies' stocks, and the Vanguard 500 Index Fund began to show its merits. In 1984, the fund outperformed most of its competitors. It did so again in 1985, and then in 1986, and in 1987, and in 1988, and in 1989, and in 1990, and in 1991, and in 1992. Nine straight years of above-average results put an end to the jibes.

The gains were steady rather than spectacular, index funds being built to harvest modest, ongoing advantages, rather than to score big and sudden victories.

The index fund is the house at the casino. Those on the other side of the table will have their winning nights, and will enjoy the thrill of the chase. There's nothing like the excitement that comes from beating the odds. But inexorably, funds with their lower costs will grind out victory. The house's advantage confers inevitability.

The Proof Is in the Numbers

The proof can be seen in the numbers. Over the near term, index funds perform very similarly to other funds. For example, over a recent time period the average low-cost index mutual fund (*low-cost* being defined as index funds with annual expense ratios of less than 0.50 percent) finished in the 47th percentile for performance for the trailing one month, compared to peers. For the trailing one year, index funds improved to the 43rd percentile. For the trailing 10 years, they moved up to the 37th percentile among surviving funds, and into the top quartile of all funds, when the failures that were merged or liquidated out of existence are considered.

Bogle's own funds fared even better. Recent Morningstar research has reaffirmed what the academic community has long maintained, that cost is the strongest and most reliable factor predicting future mutual fund performance. As Vanguard's index funds have historically carried the lowest expense ratios in the industry, they have been good performers even as index funds go.

The 1976 launch of what became the Vanguard 500 Index Fund proved to be a tripartite triumph—for Vanguard, for investors, and for the legacy of Jack Bogle. Introduced to yawns, 37 years later the index mutual fund has grown to command $2.6 trillion in the United States and $3.5 trillion globally. Index funds now make up more than 20 percent of the total U.S. funds marketplace (that is, counting ETFs as well as mutual funds). The index fund is the revolution that Jack brought.

CHAPTER 8: AS THE INDEX FUND MOVES FROM HERESY TO DOGMA, WHAT MORE DO WE NEED TO KNOW?[1]

December 2005, a little more than a year from now, will mark the 30th anniversary of the creation of the first index mutual fund. That fund—originally, and proudly, named First Index Investment Trust—is now, as Vanguard 500 Index Fund, one of the largest equity mutual funds in the world. (The other, at about the same size, is the Vanguard Total Stock Market Index Fund.) But that is only one indication of the success of index investing. For the *heresy* that was indexing—passive portfolio management that invaded a kingdom ruled, indeed populated solely by, active portfolio managers—has now become *dogma*, part of the academic canon, taught almost universally in college finance courses and in business schools, and part of the daily discourse of investors.

The evidence on the triumph of indexing is overwhelming. In the mutual fund industry, total assets of equity index funds, barely $1 billion in 1990, now total over $1.9 trillion, almost 30 percent of all equity fund assets. While that first index fund of 1975 wasn't copied until 1984, nearly a decade later, there are now almost 1,100 equity index funds, and over 200 bond index funds. In the pension world, where the idea of indexing took hold several years earlier than in the fund field, the indexed assets of corporate and state and local retirement plans, $900 billion in 1990, now total some $2 *trillion*.

Combined indexed assets—linked to U.S. and international stock and bond indexes—of mutual funds and retirement plans now exceed $6 trillion. Indeed,

---

1. These are excerpts from the Gary M. Brinson Distinguished Lecture, delivered by Bogle at Washington State University on April 13, 2004. This edited version of the lecture was published as Chapter 16 of *Don't Count on It!* (2011).

America's three largest money managers (BlackRock, State Street Global Advisors, and Vanguard, all overseeing from $2 trillion to $3.5 trillion in assets) have reached this pinnacle largely on the basis of their emphasis on index strategies.

But the impact of indexing has gone far beyond the trillions of dollars of assets that rely on pure index strategies. Closet index funds that closely track the Standard & Poor's 500 Index, for example, are rife, seeking to add value by making relatively modest variations in index stock weightings, all the while engaging in tight risk control by maintaining a high correlation with the movements in the market index itself. And rare is the active buy-side institutional portfolio manager who, seeking to minimize what has come to be called "benchmark risk," fails to compare the weights of his portfolio holdings with those in the index. The icing on the cake of indexing: Wall Street's sell-side analysts no longer recommend "buy, sell, or hold." Today, "overweight, underweight, and equal-weight" stocks relative to a firm's share of the market's total capitalization have become the profession's words of art, itself a sort of closet indexing approach.

There can be no question that index-matching strategies—simple and broadly diversified, heavily weighted by stocks with large capitalizations, with low fees and low portfolio turnover—have changed the landscape of our financial markets, and set a new standard in the way we both measure and enjoy our investment returns. Yes, our focus has turned away from absolute return and toward relative performance—beating or falling short of the index benchmark. Of course, absolute performance is what investors can actually spend, but, to state the obvious, the fund that has the best *relative* performance is also the *absolute* champion.

The Intellectual Basis for Indexing

While the clear triumph of indexing can hardly have surprised thoughtful observers of the financial scene, few commentators have recognized that two separate and distinct intellectual ideas form the foundation for passive

"The Icing on the Cake"

investment strategies. Academics and sophisticated students of the markets rely on the *efficient market hypothesis* (EMH), which suggests that by reflecting the informed opinion of the mass of investors, stocks are continuously valued at prices that accurately reflect the totality of investor knowledge, and are thus fairly valued.

But we don't need to accept the EMH to be index believers. For there is a second reason for the triumph of indexing, and it is not only more compelling but unarguably universal. I call it the CMH—the *cost matters hypothesis*—and not only is it all that is needed to explain why indexing must and does work, but it in fact enables us to quantify with some precision *how well* it works. *Whether or not the markets are efficient, the explanatory power of the CMH holds.*

More than a century has passed since Louis Bachelier, in his PhD thesis at the Sorbonne in 1900, wrote: "Past, present, and even discounted future events are [all] reflected in market price." Nearly half a century later, when Nobel laureate Paul Samuelson discovered the long-forgotten thesis, he confessed that he "oscillated . . . between regarding it as trivially obvious (and almost trivially vacuous), and regarding it as remarkably sweeping." In essence, Bachelier was, as far as he went, right: "The mathematical expectation of the speculator is zero." By 1965, University of Chicago professor Eugene F. Fama had performed enough analysis of the ever-increasing volume of stock price data to validate this "random walk" hypothesis, rechristened as the efficient market hypothesis. Today, the intellectual arguments against general thrust of the EMH religion are few. While it would seem extreme to argue that *all* stocks are efficiently priced *all* of the time, it would seem equally extreme to deny that *most* stocks are efficiently priced *most* of the time.

But whatever the consensus on the EMH, I know of no serious academic, professional money manager, trained security analyst, or intelligent individual

---

"*The Cost Matters Hypothesis . . . Is All That Is Needed to Explain Why Indexing Must and Does Work*" investor who would disagree with the thrust of EMH: *The stock market itself is a demanding taskmaster.* It sets a high hurdle that few investors can leap. While the apostles of the new so-called behavioral theory present ample evidence of how often human beings make irrational financial decisions, it remains to be seen whether these decisions lead to predictable errors that create systematic mispricings upon which rational investors can readily (and economically) capitalize.

The Mathematical Expectation of the Speculator Is Less than Zero

But while the precise validity of the EMH may be debatable, there can be *no* debate about the validity of the CMH. It posits a conclusion that is also, using Dr. Samuelson's formulation, both "trivially obvious and remarkably sweeping," and it confirms that Bachelier's argument had to be taken one step further. The mathematical expectation of the speculator is not zero; *it is a loss equal to the amount of transaction costs incurred.*

So, too, the mathematical expectation of the long-term investor also is a shortfall to whatever returns our financial markets are generous enough to provide. Indeed the shortfall can be described as precisely equal to the costs of our system of financial intermediation—the sum total of all those advisory fees, marketing expenditures, sales loads, brokerage commissions, transaction costs, custody and legal fees, and securities processing expenses. Intermediation costs in the U.S. equity market may well total as much as $250 billion a year or more. If today's $13 trillion stock market were to provide, say, a 7 percent annual return ($910 billion), costs would consume more than a quarter of it, leaving less than three-quarters of the return for the investors—those who put up 100 percent of the capital. We don't need the EMH to explain the dire odds that investors face in their quest to beat the stock market. We need only the CMH. *Whether markets are efficient or inefficient, investors as a group must fall short of the market return by the amount of the costs they incur.*

Nominal Dollars versus Real Dollars

Now for the *really* bad news. Investors pay their investment costs each year in nominal *current* dollars, but they measure their long-run investment success in *real* dollars, almost inevitably eroded in value by inflation. The *nominal* long-term returns of about 10 percent on stocks that the financial intermediation system waves before the eyes of the naive investing public turn out to be about 6.5 percent in *real* terms. When we realize that in the mutual fund industry intermediation costs total at least 2.5 percentage points annually, *they confiscate nearly 40 percent of the historical real rate of return on equities*. And when we subtract the cost of taxes (paid by taxable investors in current, nominal dollars), the confiscation of real return rises to nearly 75 percent. In a coming era in which returns may well fall below historical norms, we must look at potential investment accumulations in a new and harsh light.

The academic and financial communities have dedicated enormous intellectual and financial resources to studying past returns on stocks, to regression analysis, to modern portfolio theory (MPT), to behaviorism, and to the EMH. It's high time we turn more of our attention to the CMH. We need to know just how much our system of financial intermediation has come to cost, to know the extent to which high turnover may reduce returns, and to understand the *real* net returns that managers deliver to investors.

Two Schools of Indexing— Quantitative and Pragmatic

All these years later, the distinctly different intellectual approaches of the EMH and the CMH illuminate the history of indexing. The *quantitative school*, led by masters of mathematics such as Harry Markowitz, William Fouse, John McQuown, Eugene Fama, and William F. Sharpe, did complex equations and conducted exhaustive research on the financial markets to reach the conclusions that led to the EMH. In essence, the modern portfolio theory (MPT) developed by the quantitative school showed that a fully diversified, unmanaged equity portfolio was the surest route to investment success, a conclusion that led to the formation of the first index *pension* account (for the Samsonite Corporation), formed by Wells Fargo Bank in 1971. That tiny $6 million account was invested in an equal-weighted index of New York Stock Exchange equities. Alas, its implementation proved to be a nightmare, and in 1976 it was replaced with the market-capitalization-weighted Standard & Poor's 500 Common Stock Price Index, which remains the principal standard for pension fund indexing to this day.

While the quantitative school developed its profound theories, what I'll call the *pragmatic school* simply looked at the evidence. In 1974, the *Journal of Portfolio Management* published an article by Dr. Samuelson entitled "Challenge to Judgment." It noted that academics had been unable to identify any consistently excellent investment managers, challenged those who disagreed to produce "brute evidence to the contrary," and pleaded for someone, somewhere to start an index fund. A year later, in an article entitled "The Loser's Game,"[2] Charles D. Ellis argued that, because of fees and transaction costs, 85 percent of pension accounts had underperformed the stock market. "If you can't beat the market, you should certainly consider joining it," Ellis concluded. "An index fund is one way."[3]

Doing the Math

In mid-1975, I was both blissfully unaware of the work the quants were doing and profoundly inspired by the pragmatism of Samuelson and Ellis. I had just started a

2. "The Loser's Game," Financial Analysts Journal, Vol. 31, No. 4, July/August 1975, 19–26.
3. I should note that one of the earliest calls for indexing came from a book that I did not read until many years later: *A Random Walk Down Wall Street*, by Princeton University professor Burton S. Malkiel (W.W. Norton, 1973). Dr. Malkiel suggested, "A New Investment Instrument: A no-load, minimum-management-fee mutual fund that simply buys the hundreds of stocks making up the market averages and does no trading [of securities]. . . . Fund spokesmen are quick to point out, 'you can't buy the averages.' It's about time the public could." He urged that the New York Stock Exchange sponsor such a fund and run it on a nonprofit basis, but if it "is not willing to do it, I hope some other institution will." In 1977, four years after he wrote those words, he joined the board of directors of First Index Investment Trust and the other Vanguard funds, positions in which he has served with distinction ever since.

tiny company called Vanguard, and was determined to start the first index mutual fund. It was then that I pulled out all of my annual *Weisenberger Investment Companies* manuals, calculated by hand the average annual returns earned by equity mutual funds over the previous 30 years, and compared them to the returns of the Standard & Poor's 500 Stock Index. Result: annual returns, 1945–1975, S&P Index 10.1 percent; average equity fund, 8.7 percent.

As I mused about the reasons for the difference, the obvious occurred to me. The index was cost-free, and its 1.4 percent annual advantage in returns roughly approximated the total costs then incurred by the average fund—the expense ratio plus the hidden costs of portfolio turnover. To illustrate the enormous impact of that seemingly small percentage difference, I calculated that a hypothetical initial investment of $1,000,000 in 1945 would by 1975 have grown to $18,000,000 in the S&P Index versus $12,000,000 in the average fund. In September 1975, using those data and the Samuelson and Ellis articles, I urged a dubious Vanguard board of directors to approve our creation of the first index mutual fund. They agreed.

How Vanguard Came to Start the First Index Mutual Fund

The idea of an index fund was hardly anathema to me. Way back in 1951, the anecdotal evidence that I had assembled in my Princeton University senior thesis on the then-minuscule mutual fund industry led me to warn against the "expectations of miracles from mutual fund management," and shaped my conclusion that funds "can make no claim to superiority to the market averages." When the newly formed Vanguard began operations in May 1975, I had realized my dream of establishing the first truly *mutual* mutual fund complex, and the idea of an index fund was at the top of my agenda.

Why? Because while the idea of an index fund would hardly have appealed to a high-cost fund manager whose very business depended on the false conviction that, whatever his past record, he could outpace the market in the future, indexing would be a natural for us. We were organized as a shareholder-owned, truly *mutual*, mutual fund group, with low costs as our mantra. So while our rivals had the same opportunity to create the first index mutual fund, only Vanguard, like the prime suspect in a criminal investigation, had both the opportunity *and* the motive.

Our introduction of First Index Investment Trust was greeted by the investment community with derision. It was dubbed "Bogle's folly," and described as un-American, inspiring a widely circulated poster showing Uncle Sam calling on the world to "Help Stamp Out Index Funds." Fidelity chairman Edward C. Johnson led the skeptics, assuring the world that Fidelity had no intention of following Vanguard's lead: "I can't believe that the great mass of investors are going to be satisfied with just receiving average returns. The name of the game is to be the best." (Fidelity now runs some $125 billion in indexed assets.)

The early enthusiasm of the investing public for the novel idea of an unmanaged index fund designed to track the S&P 500 Index was as subdued as the admiration of our detractors. Its initial public offering in the summer of 1976 raised a puny $11 million, and early growth was slow. Assets of First Index didn't top $100 million until six years later (in 1980 it was renamed Vanguard 500 Index Fund), and only because we merged another Vanguard (actively managed) fund with it. But the coming of the great bull market that began in mid-1982 started the momentum, and the fund's assets crossed the $500 million mark in 1986.

"Bogle's Folly"

In 1975, the 500 Index; In 1991, the Total Stock Market Index

From the outset, I realized that the Vanguard 500 Index Fund, by owning large-cap stocks that represented 75 percent to 80 percent of the value of total U.S. market, would closely parallel, but not precisely match, the stock market's return, since the 500 Index excluded mid-cap and small-cap stocks. So in 1987, we started a fund called the Extended Market Fund, indexed to those smaller companies. If used in harness with the 500 Index Fund, it would provide a *total* market exposure. By year-end, combined assets of the two funds were nearly $1 billion. In 1990, we added another fund, the Institutional 500 Fund designed for pension plans, and in 1991, a Total Stock Market Index Fund, modeled on the Wilshire 5000 Total (U.S.) Market Index, bringing total assets of these essentially all-market index funds to $6 billion.

Strong Returns Lead to Accelerating Asset Growth

During 1994–1999, as the bull market continued, and as our index funds continued to outpace the overwhelming majority—upwards of 80 percent!—of actively managed funds, asset growth accelerated—$16 billion in 1993, $60 billion in 1996, and $227 billion in 1999. Much of this success, as I warned our index share owners, "should under no circumstances be regarded either as repeatable or as sustainable." *It wasn't.* But even in the ensuing bear market, the index funds outpaced more than 50 percent of their actively managed peers, and solid growth continued. Assets of our four all-market index funds now total some $560 billion, with our other 69 index funds bringing our total indexed assets to $1.3 trillion today.[4]

So indexing has enjoyed a considerable commercial success, drawing huge assets to Vanguard, and even larger amounts to other managers and pension funds. It has enjoyed that success, not only because of the sound and pragmatic foundation on which indexing relies, but because it has, over three decades now, worked effectively in providing superior returns. This is to say, indexing has not been merely a *commercial* success. It has been an *artistic* success. *Indexing worked!*

Brute Facts

How *well* did it work? Thirty years ago in "Challenge to Judgment," Dr. Samuelson wrote: "When [respected] investigators look to identify those minority groups endowed with superior investment process, they are quite unable to find them. . . . [Even] a loose version of the 'efficient market' or 'random walk' hypothesis accords with the facts of life . . . any jury that reviews the evidence must at least come out with the Scottish verdict: Superior performance is unproved." And so he issued his challenge: "The ball is in the court of those who doubt the random walk hypothesis.

---

4. This figure includes our specialty index funds (small-cap, growth, value, Europe, Pacific, etc.), as well as a series of bond index funds and enhanced index funds. Their rationale and development, however, are stories for another day.

They can dispose of that uncomfortable brute fact in the only way that any fact is disposed of—by producing brute evidence to the contrary."

So today, three decades later, let's examine some brute evidence. Let's go back to the era in which the Samuelson article was published, and see what lessons we can learn by examining the evidence on the ability of mutual fund managers to provide market-beating returns. In 1970, there were 355 equity mutual funds, and we have now had more than three decades over which to measure their success. We're first confronted with an astonishing—and important—revelation: *Only 147 funds survived the period.* Fully 208 of those funds vanished from the scene, an astonishing 60 percent failure rate.

Now let's look at the records of the survivors—doubtless the superior funds of the initial group. Yet fully 104 of them fell short of the 11.3 percent average annual return achieved by the unmanaged S&P 500 Index. Just 43 funds exceeded the index return. If, reasonably enough, we describe a return that comes within plus or minus a single percentage point of the market as statistical noise, 52 of the surviving funds provided a return roughly equivalent to that of the market. A total of 72 funds, then, were clear losers (i.e., by more than a percentage point), with only 23 clear winners above that threshold.

1970–2000: Only 2 Percent of All Equity Funds Top the Index

If we widen the noise threshold to plus or minus *two* percentage points, we find that 43 of the 50 funds outside that range were inferior and only seven superior—a tiny 2 percent of the 355 funds that began the period, and an astonishing piece of the brute evidence that Dr. Samuelson demanded. The verdict, then, is here, and it is clear. The jury has spoken. But its verdict is not "unproved." It is "guilty." *Fund managers are systematically guilty of the failure to add shareholder value.*

But I believe the evidence actually *over*rates the long-term achievements of the seven putatively successful funds. Is the obvious *creditability* of those superior records in fact *credible*? I'm not so sure. Those winning funds have much in common. First, each was relatively unknown (and relatively *unowned* by investors) at the start of the period. Their assets were *tiny*, with the smallest at $1.9 million, the median at $9.8 million, and the largest at $59 million. Second, their best returns were achieved during their first decade, and resulted in enormous asset growth, typically from those little widows' mites at the start of the period to $5 billion or so at the peak, before performance started to deteriorate. (One fund actually peaked at $105 billion!) Third, despite their glowing early records, most have lagged the market fairly consistently during the past decade, sometimes by a substantial amount. The pattern for five of the seven funds is remarkably consistent: a peak in relative return in the early 1990s, followed by annual returns of the next decade that lagged the market's return by about three percentage points per year—roughly, S&P 500 +12 percent, mutual fund +9 percent.

"Nothing Fails Like Success"

In the field of fund management, it seems apparent that nothing *fails* like success—the reverse of the threadbare convention that nothing *succeeds* like success. For the vicious circle of investing—good past performance draws large dollars of inflow, and having large dollars to manage crimps the very ingredients that were largely responsible for the good performance—is almost inevitable in any winning fund. So even if an investor was smart enough or lucky enough to have selected one of the few winning funds at the outset, selecting such funds by hindsight—after their early success—was also largely a loser's game. Whatever the case, the brute evidence of the past three decades makes a powerful case against the quest to find the needle in the haystack. *Investors would clearly be better served by simply owning, through an index fund, the market haystack itself.*

More Brute Facts

In the field of investment management, relying on past performance simply *has not worked*. The past has *not* been prologue, for there is little persistence in fund

Dr. Sharpe: "...A Student of Yours As Well As One of Your Greatest Admirers"

WORDS FROM THOSE WHO KNOW BOGLE BEST

William F. Sharpe, Nobel laureate in economic sciences; STANCO 25 Professor of Finance, Graduate School of Business, Stanford University

It seems like only yesterday—yet here you are, celebrating 50 years in the mutual fund industry! As you know, I have followed your career almost from the start. What a career it has been—and still is.

As I have said before on many occasions, you are one of my investment heroes (and the list is not long). When the accounts are settled to see who have truly helped individual investors, your name will be there in lights.

I consider myself a student of yours as well as one of your greatest admirers. Your current research and publications are, as always, profound yet simple, provocative yet relevant, and unsettling to those mired in the status quo. I look forward to more of the same in the future.

April 2001

performance. A recent study of equity mutual fund risk-adjusted returns during 1983–2003 reflected a randomness in performance that is virtually perfect. A comparison of fund returns in the first half to the second half of the *first* decade, in the first half to the second half of the *second* decade, and in the first full decade to the second full decade makes the point clear. Averaging the three periods shows that 25 percent of the top-quartile funds in the first period found themselves in the top quartile in the second—*precisely* what chance would dictate. Almost the same number of top-quartile funds—23 percent—tumbled to the bottom quartile, again a close-to-random outcome. In the bottom quartile, 28 percent of the funds mired there during the first half remained there in the second, while slightly more—29 percent—had actually jumped to the top quartile.

Perfect randomness would distribute the funds in each performance quartile randomly in the succeeding period—16 blocks, each with a 25 percent entry. As the matrix shows, the reality comes close to perfection. In no case was there less than a 20 percent persistence or more than a 29 percent persistence. Simply picking the top-performing funds of the past fails to be a winning strategy. What is more, even when funds succeed in outpacing their peers, they still have a way to go to match the return of the stock market index itself.

High Returns Attract Large Dollars

Yet both investors and their brokers and advisers hold to the conviction that they can identify winning fund managers. One popular way is through the *star* system espoused by the Morningstar rating service. Indeed, over the past decade, fully 98 percent (!) of all investment dollars flowing in equity mutual funds in the nine Morningstar style boxes was invested in funds awarded five stars or four stars, the firm's two highest ratings. (The ratings are heavily weighted by absolute fund performance, so we can hardly blame—or even credit—Morningstar for primarily being responsible for these huge capital inflows. Stars or not, high returns attract large dollars.)

But as Morningstar is first to acknowledge, its star ratings have little predictive value. The record bears out its caution. Academic studies show that the positive risk-adjusted returns ("alpha") that distinguish the four- and five-star funds *before* they gain the ratings typically turn negative *afterward*, and by a correlative amount. Data from *Hulbert's Financial Digest* confirm this conclusion. *Following* their selection, the funds in the top-ranked Morningstar categories typically lag the stock market return by a wide margin. Over the subsequent decade, for example, the average return of these star funds came to 6.9 percent per year, fully 4.1 percentage points behind the 11.0 percent return on the S&P 500 Index. What is more, that 37 percent shortfall in annual return came hand in hand with a risk (standard deviation) that was 4 percent *higher*. Even for the experts, picking winning mutual funds is hazardous duty.

What Is the Intellectual Foundation for Active Management?

Let me summarize what I see as the intellectual basis for indexing: Even if the EMH is weak, the CMH remains a tautology—all the more important in the mutual fund arena where costs are so confiscatory. The brute evidence on the rarity of superior management goes far beyond the relatively few examples I've cited today. And the vicious circle of superiority generating growth, generating inferior returns—with few managers courageous and disciplined enough to defy it—has become a truism. That the typical fund portfolio manager holds his post for less than five years, furthermore, means that a long-term investor has to identify not only a superior manager, but bet on his longevity. And the astonishing fund failure rate that, at current rates, implies a 50–50 survival rate over the coming decade is the icing on the cake of the case for indexing.

What, then, is the intellectual foundation for active management? While I've seen some evidence that managers have provided returns that are superior to the returns of the stock market *before costs*, I've *never* seen it argued that managers as a group can outperform the market *after* the costs of their services are deducted, nor that any *class* of manager (e.g., mutual fund managers) can do so. What do the proponents of active management point to? Themselves! "We can do it better." "We have done it better." "Just buy the (inevitably superior-performing) funds that we advertise." It turns out, then, that the big idea that defines active management is that there *is* no big idea. Its proponents offer only a few good anecdotes of the past and heady promises for the future.

"In the Fund Business, You Don't Get What You Pay For. You Get What You Don't Pay For!"

Alas, it turns out that there is in fact one big idea that can be generalized without contradiction. *Cost* is the single statistical construct that is highly correlated with future investment success. The higher the cost, the lower the return. Equity fund expense ratios have a *negative* correlation coefficient of -0.61 with equity fund returns. In the fund business, you don't get what you pay for. You get what you *don't* pay for!

If we simply aggregate funds by quartile, this correlation jumps right out at us. During the decade ended March 31, 2013, the lowest-cost quartile of large-cap funds provided an average annual return of 8.74 percent; the second-lowest, 8.53 percent; the second-highest, 8.28 percent; and the highest quartile, 8.10 percent. The difference of 64 basis points per year between the highest and lowest quartiles is equal to an 8 percent increase in annual return! The same pattern holds irrespective of the time period, and essentially irrespective of manager style or market capitalization. But of course, with index funds carrying by far the lowest costs in the industry, there are few, if any, promotions by active managers of the undeniable relationship between cost and value.

Changing Times and Circumstances

So it is the crystal-clear record of the past, an understanding of the present, and the realization that even the future returns of today's successful managers are unpredictable that together seem to make the search for the holy grail of market-beating returns a fruitless quest. It is the recognition of this reality that has carried indexing to its remarkable eminence and growth. But please don't imagine that I am sitting back and reveling in where indexing stands today. I press on in my mission as an apostle of indexing, not only because complacency doesn't seem a very healthy attitude and resting on one's laurels is too often the precursor of failure, but for three other reasons: first, because indexing has not yet adequately fulfilled its promise; second, because we have subverted the idea of indexing, adding to its role as the consummate vehicle for long-term investing ("basic indexing") a new role as a vehicle for short-term speculation ("peripheral indexing"); and third, because not nearly enough individual investors have yet come to accept the extraordinary value that indexing offers.

The initial promise of indexing was reflected in an article that appeared in *Fortune* magazine in June 1976, smack in the middle of the launch of our First Index Investment Trust. Written by journalist A. F. Ehrbar, it was entitled "Index Funds—An Idea Whose Time Is Coming," and concluded that "index funds now threaten to reshape the entire world of money management." Yet nearly three decades later, while the influence of indexing has clearly been powerful, it has failed to reshape that world. This failure has been most abject in the mutual fund field, where active managers have largely ignored the lessons they should have learned from the success of indexing.

"An Idea Whose Time Is Coming"

The Essence of Simplicity

The reasons for that success are the essence of simplicity: (1) the broadest possible diversification, often subsuming the entire U.S. stock market; (2) a focus on the long term, with minimal, indeed nominal, portfolio turnover (say, 3 percent to 5 percent annually); and (3) rock-bottom cost, with neither advisory fees nor sales loads, and with minimal operating expenses. Rather than being inspired to emulate these winning attributes, however, the fund industry has largely turned its back on them.

Consider that only about 500 of the 3,700 equity funds that exist today can be considered highly diversified and oriented to the broad market, bought to be *held*. The remaining 3,200 funds focus on relatively narrow styles, or specialized market sectors, or international markets, or single countries, all too likely bought to be sold on one future day. Portfolio turnover, at what I thought was an astonishingly high 37 percent in 1975 when the first index fund was introduced, now runs in the range of 100 percent, year after year.

While fund costs essentially represent the difference between success and failure for investors who seek to accumulate assets, they have gone *up* as index fees have come *down*. The initial expense ratio of our 500 Index Funds was 0.43 percent, compared to 1.40 percent for the average equity fund. Today, it is 0.17 percent or less, while the ratio for the average equity fund has risen to 1.43 percent. Add in turnover costs and sales commissions and the all-in cost of the average equity fund is *at least* 2.5 percent, suggesting a future annual index fund advantage at least 2.3 percent per year.

Vanguard's Actively Managed Funds Follow Index Principles

Pointedly, however, Vanguard's actively managed funds *have* learned from the success of our index funds. Indeed, with low advisory fees paid to their external managers, relatively low portfolio turnover, and our reasonable, if sometimes erratic, success in selecting managers, these funds, according to a study in the *Journal of Portfolio Management*,[5] have actually outpaced our index fund since its inception. (However, if *after-tax* returns had been considered, or if the base date of the study had been 1989 rather than 1976, the index fund would have had the superior record.) While I cannot agree with the authors' suggestion that I should take "*more* joy" in our active funds than in our index funds, be assured that I take great joy in the application of the principles that underlie the success of our index funds and managed funds alike.

A Great Idea Gone Awry

My second concern is that the original idea of the index fund—own the entire U.S. stock market, own it at low cost, hang on to it forever—has been, to put

---

5. Kenneth S. Reinker and Edward Tower, "Index Fundamentalism Revisited," *Journal of Portfolio Management*, Summer 2004.

it bluntly, bastardized. The core idea of relying on the wisdom of long-term investing is being eroded by the folly of short-term speculation. And index funds are one of the principle instruments for this erosion. Why? Because the term *index fund*, like the term *hedge fund*, now means pretty much whatever we want it to mean.

In addition to 116 index funds now linked to a relative handful of *broad* market indexes (S&P 500, Wilshire Total Market, Russell 3000), there are a staggering 1,239 index funds linked to *narrow* market indexes—small-cap/growth stocks, technology stocks, even South Korean stocks—funds that seem to be bought to be sold. (I confess that, for better or worse, I did my share in the creation of market segment index funds—growth, value, and small-cap, for example. But today's segmented index funds are far narrower in scope.)

Much of the expansion of the index fund marketplace has taken the form of exchange-traded funds (ETFs), essentially mutual funds that are designed to be traded in the stock market, often day after day, even minute by minute. The assets of ETF index equity funds now total $885 billion, about 85 percent of the index mutual fund total of $1.05 trillion. It seems logical, as far as it goes, to actively trade specialty funds, and 1,082 of them have come in ETF form, with assets of some $60 billion. But, to my amazement and disappointment, the dominant form of ETF is not these narrow segment funds, but the broad market index funds, including the S&P 500 "Spiders" and iShares, the NASDAQ "Qubes," and the Dow Jones "Diamonds." It is these ETFs that dominate the field, representing some $90 billion of assets currently—index funds originally bought to be held, now bought to be sold.

"Bought to be sold" is hardly hyperbole. ETFs turn over at rates I could never have imagined. Each day, about $8 billion (!) of Spiders and Qubes change hands, an annualized portfolio turnover rate of 3,000 percent, representing an

"Bought To Be Sold"

average holding period of just 12 days! (Turnover of *regular* mutual funds by their shareholders now runs in the 40 percent range, itself an excessive rate that smacks of speculation.) The extraordinary ETF turnover should hardly be surprising, however. The sponsor of the Spiders regularly advertises this product with these words: "Now, you can trade the S&P 500 Index all day long, in real time." (To which I would ask, "What kind of a nut would do *that*?")

"What Have They Done to My Song, Mom?"

So, "What have they done to my song, Mom?" The simple broad market index fund of yore, which I believe is the greatest medium for *long-term investing* ever designed by the mind of man, has now been engineered for use in *short-term speculation*. What is more, it has also been joined by far less diversified index funds clearly designed for rapid speculation. Please don't mistake me: the ETF *is* an efficient way to speculate, trading opportunistically in the entire market or its segments, and using them for such a purpose is surely more sensible (and less risky) than short-term speculation in individual stocks. But what's the point of speculating—costly, tax-inefficient, and counterproductive as it is—an almost certain loser's game? Mark me down as one whose absolute conviction is that long-term investing is the consummate winning strategy.

The lyrics of the song that I cited conclude: "They've tied it up in a plastic bag and turned it upside down, Mom. That's what they've done to my song." That's far too dire a conclusion for what's happening in indexing, for traditional indexing continues to grow, and to serve investors efficiently and economically. But pay attention to the song's message, the better to be sure that it could never happen to indexing.

What More Do We Need to Know?

My third concern is that, for all of the inroads made by indexing, it has achieved only a small fraction of the success that its clear investment merits deserve. *If heresy*

WORDS FROM THOSE WHO KNOW BOGLE BEST

Mario M. Cuomo, 52nd governor of New York; partner, Wilkie Farr, & Gallagher, LLP

I'm close enough to you in age to be aware that at this stage of your life you've spent considerable time looking back on what you have done with the years that have so swiftly passed. Very few of us will ever be able to come away from that kind of reverie with the degree of satisfaction—and disappointment—you are entitled to.

For more than half a century no one has done more to protect shareholders, businesses, and America from the damage done by greedy and negligent CEOs, directors, money managers, and politicians. No one did more to warn us of the perils that lay ahead and to instruct us on how to avoid them.

It must be painful for you to realize how right you were and how shortsighted our leaders have been. But, you have a consolation: There is a long way for you still to go and maybe the economic calamity that has shaken the financial systems of the world will finally alert people to the value of truths you have already offered them and will continue to offer in the days ahead.

Happy 80th birthday! Don't spend too much time celebrating—you have a lot of work still to do.

May 2009

"No One Did More to Warn Us of the Perils that Lay Ahead"

has turned to dogma, why hasn't indexing become an even more important part of the financial scene? Yes, the assets of index mutual funds now total over $1.9 trillion, representing nearly 30 percent of equity fund assets. Yes, investors have invested $650 billion in index funds over the past five years, compared to $400 billion in outflows for actively managed equity funds—a swing of over $1 trillion in investor preference.

But no, American families now hold some $10.0 trillion of equities, meaning that nearly $8 trillion is *not* indexed. Indexing has achieved a far smaller share of individual equity investments than in the pension field. And yet its cost advantage is much larger in the highly priced fund marketplace than in the competitively priced pension marketplace. If we as a nation are going to rely even more heavily on individual retirement and thrift plans than on corporate pension plans and Social Security, the retirement savings of our citizens are going to be far less robust. *What more do we need to know in order to accept the superiority of index funds so that they earn the acceptance they clearly deserve?*

I, for one, don't think we need more information. But the problem will not be easy to solve. The fund industry, like the insurance industry, is a marketing business, and in both cases the high costs of marketing represent a deadweight loss on the net returns that investors receive. The problem faced by low-cost, no-load index funds is that, as I have often observed, "(almost) all the darn money goes to the investor!" The more money that goes to the investor, of course, the less that goes to the manager and marketers, the brokers and advertisers, the marketing system that drives the world of financial intermediation. So we need to work, day after day, to get across the message of indexing to the "serious money" investors who, truth be told, need it the most.

Don't Forget Occam's Razor

There are lots of lessons to be learned from the issues I've discussed today. Broadly, I've suggested that, while innovation cannot be separated from luck, it can't be separated from intellectual discipline and determination, either. I've also suggested that simple ideas can hold their own—or more—with complex concepts. When you get out in the business world, *Occam's razor*—"when confronted with multiple solutions to a problem, choose the simplest one"—is worth keeping in mind.

I hope you also take note that it is indeed possible to gild to excess a sound innovation—in this case, the lovely lily of all-market indexing, which needs no gilding—noting as well the powerful forces that would like nothing better than to stop indexing in its tracks before it strikes at their wallets. Their only weapon is to use the records of their successful funds during their flowering periods and imply that such success will persist—and you now know how rarely that happens. Most of all, of course, I hope I've not only explained the universal mathematical logic of indexing—*gross return minus intermediation costs equals net return*—but also presented an overwhelming array of brute evidence that ought to persuade even the most skeptical among you of its worth as an investment strategy.

Now think of this in personal terms. What difference would an index fund make in your own retirement plan over, say, 40 years? Well, let's postulate a future long-term annual return of 8 percent on stocks. If we assume that mutual fund costs continue at their present level of at least 2.5 percent a year, an average mutual fund might return 5.5 percent. Extending this tax deferred compounding out in time on your investment of $3,000 each year over 40 years, and investment in the stock market itself would grow to $840,000, with the market index fund not far behind. Your actively managed mutual fund would produce $430,000—only a little more than one-half as much.

Accumulating 52 Percent of Your Potential Wealth: A Fair Shake?

Looked at from a different perspective, your retirement plan has earned a value of $840,000 before costs, and donated $410,000 of that total to the mutual fund industry. You have kept the remainder—$430,000. *The financial system has consumed 48 percent of the return, and you have achieved but 52 percent of your earning potential.* Yet it was you who provided 100 percent of the initial capital; the industry provided none. Confronted by the issue in this way, would an intelligent investor consider this split to represent a fair shake? Merely to ask the question is to answer it: "No."

So when investors consider the nest egg that they'll need 40 or 50 years from now when they retire, I shamelessly commend using an all-market index fund—the lower the cost, the better—as the centerpiece of the savings they allocate to equities. If you do, as Dr. Samuelson has written, you will become "the envy of your suburban neighbors, while at the same time sleeping well in these eventful times."

Finally, a word for those who seek careers in investment management. Please don't be intimidated by the obvious odds against beating the market. Rather, learn, as so few fund managers seem to have done, from the reasons for the success of the index fund. It is long-term focus, broad diversification, and low cost that have been the keys to the kingdom in the past; active managers who learn both from the disciples of EMH and the apostles of CMH will have the best chance of winning the loser's game, or at least providing respectable long-term returns for their clients in the future. So whatever you do in your investment career—indeed whatever you do in *any* endeavor to which you may be called—*never fail to put your client first*. Placing service to others before service to self is not only an essential part of whatever success may be; it is the golden rule for a life well lived.

CHAPTER 9: "THE BOGLE ISSUE" OF THE *JOURNAL OF INDEXES*

In its spring issue of 2012, to commemorate the occasion of John Bogle's six full decades in the mutual fund industry, the *Journal of Indexes* published a special "Bogle Issue." It began with an accolade by editor Jim Wiandt, followed by an extensive interview with Bogle, and appraisals of his career by some of the financial field's most thoughtful participants.

The Editor's Note: "Tipping Our Hats"[6]

If one person can be credited with making the existence of this publication possible, it would be John Bogle. Yes, indexes have been around for over a century, but it wasn't until Mr. Bogle launched the Vanguard 500 and kick-started an entire investment phenomenon that they were viewed as anything other than measures of the market. So some 35 years after the advent of the first index fund, it makes sense to pay tribute to the man who started it all.

We begin with our recent interview with the man himself: Find out what Jack Bogle *really* thinks about our current investment environment, taxes, politics, and his accomplishments. Next is a roundtable that asks Bogle's friends and colleagues about his impact on them and the investing public. Gus Sauter, Burton Malkiel, William Bernstein, Rob Arnott, Don Phillips, David Blitzer, and others offer their personal impressions and thoughts.

Let's all raise our glasses to the marvelous, brutally honest, and passionately sensible Jack Bogle!

The Bogle Interview: Big Picture, Big Challenges— Vanguard's Founder Talks about the Current Market Environment

The editors of the *Journal of Indexes*—Jim Wiandt, founder and CEO, IndexUniverse, and Matt Hougan, president of ETF Analytics, IndexUniverse—sat down for a chat with Vanguard founder John Bogle to discuss his long career and his views on the current market.

MATT HOUGAN, PRESIDENT OF ETF ANALYTICS, INDEXUNIVERSE:
What key advice would you provide to investors who are worried about

6. Written March/April 2012.

today's markets? What would you tell them to do, drawing on all your experience?

BOGLE: Well, I'm an optimistic conservative—so I'd be careful. As I look ahead, I think reasonable expectations are for about a 7 percent return on stocks, and about a 3.5 percent return on bonds, counting longer maturities and a greater weighting toward corporates, which are only 25 percent of the bond market index.

Over a Decade, a 7 Percent Annual Return Doubles the Value of an Investment

That means you'll double your money in stocks over the next decade and make 50 percent on bonds if those expectations are realized. I wouldn't write off stocks, despite all the scare talk. But it's going to be a bumpy ride. Everybody should be fully aware of that. They should be investing for a decade.

Anyone that's buying stocks thinking about what's going to happen next year is a fool, to be quite blunt about it. Buying stocks—owning stocks—is a lifetime endeavor. And as Mr. Buffett says—and I feel particularly strongly about this in the context of an index fund—my favorite holding period is "forever."

HOUGAN: Do you think a traditional broad-based bond index has enough weight in corporates?

BOGLE: I don't think it does. I mean, obviously it does for all investors because that's the bond market. All those bonds are owned by U.S. investors. It's approximately 70 percent Treasurys, agencies, and Treasury-backed mortgage bonds and 30 percent corporate. And that ratio is not that different from what it was when I started the bond index fund in 1986. It's (surprisingly) lower today, but not much.

A Treasury is now, according to somebody, rated AA. I don't believe that, by the way. But even so, the yields are low: The spread between Treasuries and corporates is 2 to 2.5 percent. It's hard for me to believe the default rate on Treasuries versus corporates is that wide. And so, as long as the default rate is less than that, you're making a better choice in corporates.

I think we ought to be thinking more about corporates in a very low-interest environment than we should about the total bond market. I love the Total Bond Market Index Fund. I started it. But it's not the answer to all things for everybody. If people are pinched for yield, I'd recommend they have a higher weighting in a corporate bond index fund.

JIM WIANDT, FOUNDER AND CEO, INDEXUNIVERSE: Burton Malkiel sees a very bad environment for bonds in the United States right now, particularly Treasuries. People are effectively going to be, he thinks, earning less yield than inflation, which is kind of where the government is aiming things right now. What are your thoughts on that?

Low Yields Mean Low Decade-Long Returns

BOGLE: In the bond market, today's yield is the best predictor we have for the returns over the next 10 years. Certainly the 10-year Treasury doesn't look like a very good deal—and yet it seems to do better and better every time there's an international crisis. It's the first place people run. That, however, is not going to go on forever.

I agree with [Malkiel] up to a point. You can probably get a 3.5 percent yield on higher-yielding equities, but you can also get 3.5 percent on a diversified bond market portfolio.

[Are high-yielding equities] a better strategy? Only time will tell. But if everybody is doing it, look out.

They're not stupid choices. But I still would not abandon a bond position for a stock position, even with higher yield.

Challenge to Bogle's Asset Allocation Strategy

WIANDT: Burton Malkiel's commentary is interesting, because he is saying that we should look at the market to some degree, and bonds are not only going nowhere, they're probably going backward in terms of yield. The traditional asset allocation says to buy the total bond market equivalent to how old you are. So when you're 65 years old, you should be 65 percent bonds, et cetera. And he's really been saying you should adjust that a little bit because the environment for bonds is very bad.

BOGLE: I think that's a correct analysis. None of us *know*. He is, I'm sure, confident about that being the case. But think about it this way: When you've got a 6 percent government market and an 8 percent corporate market, the premium is 33 percent. When you've got a 2 percent government market and a 4 percent corporate market, the premium is 100 percent. These spreads haven't changed much over time. I would just be very cautious about telling people not to take too much risk.

I think I don't need to get into a debate with Burt about this, because one of us will be right, but probably not by a lot, and one of us will be wrong, but probably not by a lot.

HOUGAN: Do you think international bond exposure is going to become part of the core that every investor should have exposure to?

BOGLE: I think for the typical investor it is not necessary. If you look back at the record of international bonds, I for one don't see much to write home about. I don't like the credit risk. I don't like the currency risk.

WIANDT: You don't like the Greek bond market?

BOGLE: I don't like the Greek bond market. And I don't like the Italian bond market. And I don't like the Brazilian bond market. And I don't like the Portuguese bond market. And I don't like the Irish bond market. Shall I continue? I'm not even sure about the French bond market. I feel pretty good about the German bond market. But what's the point of guessing? The yields probably take all that into account. The bond markets are fairly efficient, or have been in the past—and I believe they will continue to be efficient in the future. They are very good arbitrageurs between the present and the future.

That's also the way I feel, as you probably know, about international stocks. If they're efficiently priced, I just don't see why they would give you a higher return in the future than they're giving you today.

And let me say this about a better diversifier: Better diversification is the last refuge of the scoundrel. What were we talking about five years ago as a good diversifier? Well, I can't remember, but it wasn't gold. And when gold does well, as it certainly has, then someone says it's a great diversifier. And when international bonds get a little ahead of U.S. bonds—not before, but after—then someone says it's a great diversifier. Anything that's done well recently is considered a great diversifier.

Gold—The Ultimate Speculation?

WIANDT: What do you think about gold?

BOGLE: What people don't get about gold and commodities in general is that they have no internal rate of return. I can tell you about stocks with a 2 percent yield and earnings growing with the economy, let's call it 5 percent nominal, and say these are underlying strengths to deliver a 7 percent return. And I can talk about bonds and say there is a 3.5 percent interest coupon today, and that's probably 91 percent of the future return of a bond. When you get to a commodity, there is no coupon, there is no dividend, and there are no earnings.

When we buy gold, we're buying gold because we think we can sell it to somebody else at a higher price. If that isn't the ultimate in speculation, I would not know what is. It may be a good speculation—I don't make that argument—but I would full well doubt it.

A Nation-by-Nation Analysis

HOUGAN: You've said most U.S. investors don't need exposure to international equities, that U.S. stocks at this point are international firms with 50 percent of their revenues overseas.

BOGLE: This is another one of my pet peeves. If you go through developed international nations, your largest investment is Britain. And I think they're in deep trouble. Everybody knows they're putting on heavy austerity. They've got terrible financial problems. I think Keynes was right—economies around the world ought to be stimulating, rather than cutting back. So if you want 22 percent of your money in Britain, just understand that's what you're getting.

The next one is Japan, at 21 percent of your portfolio. What's so good about Japan? They've got a structured society. They've had a lot of innovation in the past. Will that continue? I don't know.

And then you go to France, who's next in size, believe it or not. They don't seem to work very hard over there. Next are Switzerland, Australia, and Germany. They all look pretty good.

The three largest countries, accounting for almost half of the international index, are countries that have significant problems. But when you put them in a single package of international, you don't think about that. You *ought* to think about that.

HOUGAN: What do you think about the future of the United States? Are you as pessimistic there as you are about Britain and Italy and France? Or do you think we're a different case?

BOGLE: We are headed toward a catastrophe—unless we do something. We simply can't be the kind of nation we have been until we knock some sense into our elected officials. But that's going to take some common sense on the part of those who elect them. In politics, we get the politicians we deserve. And I hope we deserve better than the politicians I have seen on television night after night. I call them the seven dwarves plus Jon Huntsman.

*"We Get the Politicians
We Deserve"*

    I'm deeply worried about the political system. I'm worried about the monied interests in our political system. I'm worried about the *Citizens United* case and the disgraceful decision by the Supreme Court.

HOUGAN: What would give you more confidence? What's the single thing you think we need to fix or control most? How would we turn it around?

BOGLE: Well, it's not easy to do. All these redistrictings that all these states are doing, it makes Elbridge Gerry, from whom the word *gerrymander* comes, look like a piker. Really not a good situation at all, the way seats are locked in. And it's not good for the nation that extremist parties get entrenched, as with the Tea Party, which, to me, is thoughtless. It's not a national asset.

    The role of money, particularly these special PACs [political action committees] that are out there, is simply a disgrace to a civilized nation.

    There must be better ways to get big money out of the system without violating the precious First Amendment—we could just decide that corporations aren't persons. For example, we know that corporations can't commit crimes, and they can't go to jail. It's a big project in which we need to engage our best citizens in trying to fix the system. And Congress has to, whether it likes it or not, do intelligent things to address the budget deficit.

Taxing Income by Its Source

    I happen to believe the president is maybe a little off target in his focus on taxing the rich. That sounds a little bit—and I'm talking more about image than anything else—not quite American. If only someone could tell him to tax the sources of income differently. Just think about a society that rewards those who collect capital gains during the day with a lower tax rate than people who run out of the house every morning, work hard all day, by the sweat of their brow, the sweat of their brain, and come home. That's insane. That's socially wrong, and it's economically wrong.

I say tax capital gains at least at the same rate as earned income. Tax dividends at least at the same rate as earned income.

People talk about double taxation as dividends. Seventy percent of all stocks are owned by institutions that are largely tax-free—so we can think about it a little bit differently.

I would say let the investor who's focusing on his retirement have—just for the purpose of argument—the first $25,000 of dividend income and capital gains each year with no tax. I don't see anything the matter with that.

And then I'd say increase capital gains taxes at least to the ordinary income rate. Maybe there's somewhere we can carve out an exception and divide capital gains into two groups: One group is those who start companies that create value for society, and the other group is those who are gambling in the stock market and subtracting value from society. I'd like to be able to intellectually separate those two and tax the one who's a waste for society and give a more favorable tax treatment to those who are a benefit.

WIANDT: Even in the indexing industry, we have people reluctant to talk about politics. I'm of the mind-set that enough is enough. Why aren't we working in the interest of the country here?

BOGLE: I'm happy to make some suggestions. My tax suggestion, for example; I feel very strongly about that. I'm engaged in this battle over *Citizens United*. And I've recommended to the SEC that each corporation be presented with a resolution to present to its shareholders, saying, "Resolved, that this corporation shall make no political contributions without the approval of 75 percent of its shareholders." Why should corporations be able to give money away, to make gifts without approval by a majority of shareholders? And a majority is not enough for me. Actually, a Delaware law, no longer in force, said corporations may make no gifts of their assets without approval of 100 percent of their shareholders.

Investors Must Stand Up and Be Counted

One thing we badly need in our society is for investors to stand up and be counted and not let corporations run amok in the interest of their own agents. Executive compensation is a mess. Mergers are made just to make companies bigger or to fix the accounting mess they're in, or whatever it might be—just simply to be larger and justify more compensation. Shareholders should get a vote on every one of those issues.

WIANDT: Some people might say that indexing is partly responsible for that state of affairs, since almost by definition, in indexing, you're buying the market, so you have a lot of very large institutional investors that really aren't holding accountable the companies that they're investing in, just because it's a massive task to read all the minutes of all 500 companies in the S&P 500, or whatever your index is. How would you respond to that?

BOGLE: The old so-called "Wall Street Rule" is that if you don't like the management, sell the stock. Index funds cannot sell a stock, so their rule has to be that if you don't like the management, change the management. And index funds indeed do have an obligation to stand up and be counted.

[The problem is that] people don't organize mutual funds for their shareholders. They organize mutual funds because they think they can sell them. It's quite clear in the record that we used to be an industry that sold what we made, and now we're an industry that makes what will sell. And there is no finer example of this than the exchange-traded fund business.

HOUGAN: You've definitely expressed concern about ETFs. Is that because they've become the venue for hot, new, thematic ideas? Is there anything wrong with ETFs? Can ETFs be used appropriately?

BOGLE: There's nothing the matter with certain ETFs, properly used. So start off with the S&P 500, the SPDR. I tell the story in my book about the day Nate Most—the ETF visionary—stopped into my office, and he tried to sell me on the idea. I found flaws in what he showed me, and then I said even if he can fix the flaws, it's not for Vanguard. Index funds are designed for long-term investors, not for short-term speculators.

So we didn't do anything with them. Nate fixed the flaws, and then he went to State Street, and they did it. And there's nothing the matter with [SPY], except it turned over last year at 7,700 percent. It's a trading fund, mostly for institutional trading. In a way, it's failed to live up to its promise.

I see nothing the matter with an investor who wants to buy and hold a broad market index fund. It's a sound way to participate.

Fundamental Indexing Still Must Prove Itself

But there's a lot of marketing. I think Jeremy Siegel [of WisdomTree] and Rob Arnott [of Research Affiliates] had what were perfectly reasonable ideas, and that is to give you an index fund that was slightly, only slightly, different from the regular market-value-weighted index. The so-called fundamental value products don't seem to be doing so well, now giving you roughly the same return over their history—it's five years now—as the total stock market index, although the Arnott one has quite a bit higher volatility.

The Jeremy Siegel idea of weighting by dividends I kind of thought was good because I could understand it. But you look at WisdomTree, and their dividend fund is $300 million of their $25 billion total assets. Nobody wants it. They want rupees and—I don't know—bahts, yen, renminbi; God knows what WisdomTree is offering in the way of currency.

The main problem with ETFs, it seems to me, is the narrow subdivision of the markets, which makes it almost like picking stocks. If you look at the year-end *Wall Street Journal*, in tiny type, it's a page and a third of ETFs, 1,617 of them. It's like stock picking, and that seems ridiculous and offensive. Risk is concentrated in individual countries and individual industries and subindustries, and sub-subindustries. And it's not enough to speculate whether the market will go up or down; now you've got to have three times leverage. And that's going to hurt investors.

The original paradigm for the index fund was to buy the stock market and hold it forever. That is the paradigm for only 1 percent of the ETF market—or be generous and call it 5 to 10 percent.

The ETF is certainly the greatest marketing innovation so far in the twenty-first century. Whether it's the greatest investment innovation or best innovation for shareholders is totally in doubt.

What I don't understand, and I will never understand, is why the ETF is an attractive vehicle for an actively managed fund. It's bad enough to guess each minute whether an index is going up or down. But to guess each minute whether a manager is doing a little bit worse or a little bit better than the market strikes me as kind of crazy.

The Massive Tilt toward Passive Investing Is Rational

HOUGAN: For the past couple of years, there's been a massive tilt toward passive indexes and away from active. Is there an element of investors coming to their senses? Do you think this pattern will continue? Or do you think this is a short-term phenomenon and that active funds will be back?

BOGLE: It's only the beginning for passive investing. Index funds are now around 25 percent of equity fund assets. They're going to be bigger with all these target retirement funds. They're going to be bigger on the bond side. According to our data, in the past five years, $349 billion has flowed into equity funds. That's $564 billion into index funds and $214 billion out of active equity funds. That's a pretty dramatic swing.

And the numbers aren't getting any better for the active managers. I think people are waking up. How many Bill Millers (Legg Mason Value Fund) do investors have to observe? How many Bruce Berkowitzes (Fairholme Fund) do investors have to observe?

The average mutual fund manager lasts for about six years. And 50 percent of mutual funds themselves go out of business every decade. How the heck do you invest for the long term if your fund doesn't live for the long term? Some people say new managers do better; some people say they do worse. All my instincts would say new managers do the same as old if you just spread it across an industry. But who knows, really?

When we trade shares, we're trading with each other. And who wins when we trade with each other? Not the investors as a group. The croupiers of Wall Street win. There's no way around that, is there? Not that I know.

WIANDT: What's your view on the current state of the global markets? How should investors be looking at the market?

BOGLE: My rule is: Don't peek. There's so much noise in the markets, so much volatility, and if you get captivated by that, you're thinking like a speculator and not an investor. What you want to do is be prepared. You're going to put away $500 a month for the rest of your life, or whatever it might be—maybe it increases with your earnings. And every five years expect a 20 percent drop in the market—sometimes even more. We know it's coming, but we never

---

"The Croupiers of Wall Street Win"

know when. What happens is, we put money in before the crash—and the mutual fund record is crystal clear here—and take it out at the bottom. In the late 1990s, we created hundreds of technology funds. When? When the technology boom was at its peak.

An "Absolute Mathematical Tautology"

We have to get marketing out of the equation and put management in. I call it the wisdom of long-term investing versus the folly of short-term speculation. That's in the math—that is not my opinion.

Assume that every company on the S&P 500 has half of its shares held by long-term investors who don't trade, and half of its shares held by short-term speculators who do. We know that those long-term investors as a group will capture the exact return of the S&P 500. And we know those speculative traders will capture the exact same return because they own the same stocks. But by trading among one another, they will underperform the market by the amount of their trading costs.

So speculation is, by absolute mathematical tautology, a loser's game—losing to the market. And investment is, by absolute mathematical tautology, a winner's game—capturing the market return, or almost 100 percent of it.

WIANDT: What single accomplishment are you proudest of?

BOGLE: It's a little early to think about that. But the obvious thing is that everybody else claims to have created the index fund, but we actually did it. And we created a mutual structure that is yet to be emulated in our industry. We gave substance to the no-load market. All these steps—Vanguard, the index funds, and the no-load decision, as well as the first multitiered bond funds. Put them all in one lump and say we created a better world for mutual fund investors.

The Bogle Impact: A Roundtable— Colleagues and Friends Offer Their Thoughts

In his long career, John Bogle has influenced countless financial professionals and investors. The *Journal of Indexes* reached out to some of his best-known colleagues, rivals, and friends to ask them about how his advocacy has affected them and its lasting impact on how Americans invest.

JoI: What impact has John Bogle had on you as an investor and a financial professional?

GUS SAUTER, CHIEF INVESTMENT OFFICER, VANGUARD GROUP: I entered the industry with a more theoretical approach to investing, and Jack helped me understand the practical side. Indexing works, not because markets are efficient, but because it doesn't have the high cost burden of active management.

JoI: What is your current long-term market outlook? Do you think traditional buy-and-hold index-based investing has a place in that market scenario?

SAUTER: There's always a possibility for just about anything to happen, but the stock market has reasonable valuations, and so historical rates of return are quite possible over the long term. Bond yields are extremely low, so the longer-term prospect for bonds is likely to be less than historical returns.

JoI: What do you think John Bogle has gotten wrong?

SAUTER: Jack and I agree on many things, but we also disagree about certain topics, including the use of ETFs. I believe they can be used as a very effective way for many advisers and direct investors to gain low-cost, indexed exposure to the market. Let's just say Jack disagrees with that view.

JoI: What do you think John Bogle's lasting impact will be on investing and investors?

SAUTER: Not only did Jack create a company solely dedicated to the interests of investors, but he also created indexing in the mutual fund industry. Many, many investors are much better off today because of Jack's contributions.

JoI: What impact has John Bogle had on you as an investor and a financial professional?

WILLIAM BERNSTEIN, PRINCIPAL, EFFICIENT FRONTIER ADVISORS LLC: Two big things. First, he has taught me the importance of institutional structure and culture.

His Deeds Are Even More Powerful Than His Words

He did that not so much through his words, which are powerful enough, but through his deeds. His biggest deed was of course his donation—there's no other word for it—of Vanguard itself to its fund investors. It's almost as if Ford or Procter & Gamble issued shares to the people who bought their cars and soap, or if Bill Gates had given away a piece of Microsoft to each purchaser of Windows. Vanguard's culture is thus entirely different from that of any major corporation, and especially from any financial corporation. The typical bank, brokerage, or mutual fund company would have you believe that the best interests of its customers and the owners are the same. If we have learned anything during the recent financial crisis, it is that this is a fiction.

Second, he's shown me that you never stop moving, never stop striving. Most people in his position would have long since gone to the beach, done the odd charity gig. He's still learning, still trying to improve the world, still making a difference, still reaching out and helping people with an almost superhuman vigor.

JoI: What is your current long-term market outlook? Do you think traditional buy-and-hold index-based investing has a place in that market scenario?

*"The Bogle Modification
of the Gordon Equation"*

BERNSTEIN: I only know what Jack taught me, which is what I call "the Bogle modification of the Gordon equation," that long-term return is simply the sum of what Jack calls the "fundamental return," which is the sum of dividend payout and dividend growth, and what he calls the "speculative return," which is the change in the dividend or earnings multiple. What that tells me is that the expected return of stocks is perhaps 7 to 8 percent, which assumes that stocks are fairly valued at the moment.

Whenever the market does poorly, people trumpet "the death of buy-and-hold." What they forget is that it's not "buy and hold," but rather "buy, hold, and rebalance." That last operation mandated that investors purchase some equities after the declines of 1987, 1990, 2000–2002, and 2007–2009, and sell some equities when the sun shone in between. Add to that benefit the long-run surefire above-average performance and lower risk of deploying stock assets in broad market indexes. Why would you ever want to screw that up by chasing last year's best active manager or listening to this year's lucky talking head?

JoI: What do you think John Bogle has gotten wrong?

BERNSTEIN: I can't answer that for certain, since I only know what we disagree about, and I could be the one who is wrong. And given Jack's track record, the latter could easily be the case. Where we're a few degrees apart is on the existence of the value and small premiums, and on the variability of the equity premium itself with valuation. Actually, on that last point, he understood earlier than most that valuation matters. He just differs on what to do about it—I say adjust your equity allocation up or down a small amount opposite big changes in valuation; he says do nothing. I also think that U.S. investors should expose themselves to more foreign assets than he recommends.

JoI: What do you think John Bogle's lasting impact will be on investing and investors?

BERNSTEIN: I had dinner the other night with a friend who, like many well-to-do individuals, has a stockbroker. In addition, he has a low-cost 401(k) plan that is heavily index oriented. When the broker heard that my friend had retired, he asked him to move his 401(k) plan to his brokerage firm. My friend wondered aloud to me, "Why would I want to do that? My employee plan's expenses are one-quarter of my broker's."

I'm not sure whether he'd heard of Jack, and I'm pretty sure he's never read him, but he sure as heck was channeling him. That will be Jack's legacy: For the first time, large numbers of ordinary investors are thinking about investment expenses; that's a very big thing.

JoI: What impact has John Bogle had on you as an investor and a financial professional?

"Jack Made Indexing Possible"

BURTON MALKIEL, CHEMICAL BANK CHAIRMAN'S PROFESSOR OF ECONOMICS EMERITUS AND SENIOR ECONOMIST, PRINCETON UNIVERSITY: As a believer in indexing before such funds were available, I am delighted now to be able to recommend specific vehicles to the investing public. Jack has made that possible.

JoI: What is your current long-term market outlook? Do you think traditional buy-and-hold index-based investing has a place in that market scenario?

MALKIEL: We are likely to be in an age of financial repression, such as the period following World War II. Interest rates are now artificially low, and high-quality bond portfolios are unlikely to produce positive real returns. But even though investment returns may be low for all asset classes, I believe a substantial equity risk premium does exist. Broadly diversified equity portfolios (including stocks from the rapidly growing emerging markets) will, I believe, serve investors well over the long term. I do not believe in market timing. No one can do it consistently, and when we try, individuals as well as professionals are more likely to get it wrong rather than right, as our emotions tend to get the best of us. Buy-and-hold index-based investing is still the best course. But techniques such as dollar-cost averaging and rebalancing can reduce risk.

JoI: What do you think John Bogle has gotten wrong?

Too Negative on ETFs?

MALKIEL: Jack has been too negative on the ETF revolution. To be sure, his criticism that they are too often used for speculation rather than investment is absolutely correct. But because they can be even lower-cost vehicles than mutual funds (and because they can have potential tax advantages), they can be very valuable instruments for longer-term investors. Buying an ETF at 11 A.M. and selling it at 2 P.M. is speculation rather than investing. But some people will want to do this, however foolish that may be, and trading in and out of mutual funds can create costs for long-term investors in the fund.

JoI: What do you think John Bogle's lasting impact will be on investing and investors?

MALKIEL: Jack Bogle has made two major contributions with a lasting impact, in particular. First, Bogle created a unique mutual fund company in Vanguard—owned by its fund investors and providing the lowest-cost investment vehicles publicly available. Vanguard is truly a "mutual" investment services company.

Second, Bogle created the first publicly available U.S. equity index fund, followed by a family of index funds covering a variety of investment markets. By doing so he made an indexing revolution possible.

JoI: What impact has John Bogle had on you as an investor and a financial professional?

DON PHILLIPS, PRESIDENT OF FUND RESEARCH, MORNINGSTAR, INC.: Jack is an inspiration. His willingness to fight tirelessly for his cause and his alignment of his interests so closely with investors' is a model of entrepreneurial spirit and ethical behavior. There is no one in the industry whom I admire more.

JoI: What is your current long-term market outlook? Do you think traditional buy-and-hold index-based investing has a place in that market scenario?

PHILLIPS: I think there's a reasonable case to be made for modest returns from equities and a poor case for bonds over the next decade. I think that buy-and-hold index-based investing makes great sense in this, or any, time. Remember, however, that rebalancing is an important part of a buy-and-hold strategy. Given the extreme success of bonds and the poor returns of equities over the past decade, many investors may need to rebalance their portfolios to get back on track.

JoI: What do you think John Bogle has gotten wrong?

PHILLIPS: Not much. He may overstate his case at times—don't we all?—but directionally, he has an amazing track record. Time is on the side of his argument.

JoI: What do you think John Bogle's lasting impact will be on investing and investors?

PHILLIPS: Fifty years from now, when all of the current fund leaders and CEOs have been forgotten, Jack Bogle will still be remembered. He's raised the bar for the industry, and investors are the better for it. Fees nearly everywhere are

"Time Is on the Side of His Argument"

lower because of him. Investors are, and will continue to be, more demanding because Jack showed them the way.

JoI: What impact has John Bogle had on you as an investor and a financial professional?

ROB ARNOTT, founder and chairman, Research Affiliates LLC: We all need mentors or heroes to help inspire us if we want to accomplish important things. Jack ranks as one of my heroes, alongside Peter Bernstein, Marty Leibowitz, Bob Lovell, and Harry Markowitz. His decision to launch Vanguard Group in his late 40s was a contributing factor in my decision to launch Research Affiliates in my late 40s. His missionary zeal for cap-weighted indexation helped inspire my missionary zeal for the Fundamental Index. His single-minded focus on helping the end customer to win—in his case, by cutting implementation slippage and costs to the bone—reminds us all that we can do well by doing good. In my case, the quest for low-cost alpha trumps the quest for rock-bottom pricing, but it's fair to say that neither of us is a big fan of high-fee random-alpha products.

JoI: What is your current long-term market outlook? Do you think traditional buy-and-hold index-based investing has a place in that market scenario?

ARNOTT: True buy-and-hold investing is a myth, as is true passive indexing. Is there a single investor on the planet who has never made a trade, has never rebalanced their portfolio, or reconstituted their index investments to reflect

"Jack Ranks as One of My Heroes"

"*A Darker View of the Future*"

corporate actions? Of course not. But the basic idea of buy-and-hold index-based investing has a very important place in the investing pantheon: In the absence of a strong conviction to the contrary, it should be our default choice.

I think it's fair to say that I have a darker view of the future than Jack, or indeed most of the investing community. I think that a low-yield environment means lower prospective future returns. I think that an aging population means slower GDP growth. I think that an addiction to debt-financed consumption throughout the developed world crowds out the private-sector capital markets, and eventually crushes healthy entrepreneurial capitalism.

I think that stocks are like any other investment: Buy them when they're cheap and we don't have to wait for the long run to enjoy ample profits; buy them when they're expensive and we may have a very, very long run to wait before we can be happy.

In short, I believe that broad diversification into a wide array of alternative markets, often at higher yields, trumps the classic 60/40 buy-and-hold mantra. And while I love indexing, I don't love the fact that conventional cap-weighted indexing puts most of our eggs in the most expensive baskets, which is not the ideal way to earn good long-term returns.

JoI: What do you think John Bogle has gotten wrong?

ARNOTT: Like a lot of visionary leaders, Jack is a bit rigid about other points of view. His visceral distaste for ETFs—"giving kerosene to arsonists," as he describes them—ignores the fact that investors can make grievous errors in their daily liquidity with mutual funds, almost as easily as with ETFs. Witness Russel Kinnel's study "Mind the Gap," in which he showed that the time-weighted returns for mutual funds exceed their dollar-weighted returns by over two and a half percentage points a year. Jack's vocal criticism of the Fundamental

He Shaped the
Indexing World

Index ignores the fact that we're both on the side of the angels in terms of vastly lower fees, vastly lower turnover, vastly broader diversification, and vast capacity, when compared with most active managers and funds.

One of the things I like about Jack is that we can remain friends when we disagree; it clearly helps that we're in agreement on 80 percent of the things we think matter. He's a bit like the wise and curmudgeonly uncle, usually right and always insightful; we may find we occasionally differ, to the consternation of the uncle, but we would be fools to dismiss his insights without careful reflection.

JoI: What do you think John Bogle's lasting impact will be on investing and investors?

ARNOTT: Jack has shaped the indexing world more than anyone else. He has put the well-being of the end customer squarely at the top of the food chain—no investment professionals should prosper unless their customers are doing well. More broadly, he has correctly challenged the notion that active management is anything more than a zero-sum game—indeed, a negative-sum game net of costs. If we depart from cap-weighted indexation, we do well to recognize that we can beat the market only if someone on the other side of our trades is a willing loser. We do well to ask who are losing, and why they are willing to lose. Without a satisfying answer to that question, we shouldn't stray from the buy-and-hold index-based investing that Jack pioneered.

JoI: What impact has John Bogle had on you as an investor and a financial professional?

STEVE GALBRAITH, FORMER MARKET STRATEGIST, MORGAN STANLEY, AND FOUNDER, HERRING CREEK CAPITAL: We have a Harold-and-Maude relationship—he is probably my best friend in the business despite the fact he is my father's peer and I (like his son!) practice active management.

JoI: What is your current long-term market outlook? Do you think traditional buy-and-hold index-based investing has a place in that market scenario?

GALBRAITH: I actually do not necessarily totally equate index investing with buy-and-hold; to me, it is more about the fee structure (witness the crazy trading in index ETFs). As to markets, the relative expected returns to stocks have not been better in the past 30 years. This may be damning with faint praise, given alternatives are near nil, but after 13-plus years of zero returns for stocks, it is getting interesting again.

JoI: What do you think John Bogle has gotten wrong?

GALBRAITH: Well, Yale and Tufts are clearly superior to Princeton, but not a lot beyond that.

JoI: What do you think John Bogle's lasting impact will be on investing and investors?

GALBRAITH: He has democratized investing. There is no question he is the most important investment figure of the past century.

"A Harold-and-Maude Relationship"

JoI: What impact has John Bogle had on you as an investor and a financial professional?

TED ARONSON, MANAGING PRINCIPAL, ARONSON JOHNSON ORTIZ: Jack Bogle single-handedly democratized investing by making capital market returns achievable to the entire investing public. His impact on the investing world cannot be overstated.

Jack's other influence is as a clear and articulate voice of reason, balance, prudence, and sensible investing. He will go down in history as one of the architects of modern finance.

Successful investing hinges on three things: taking risk intelligently, diversifying, and keeping costs to a minimum. The Vanguard Group, Jack's creation, provides the opportunity to achieve all three. As such, he drowns out the cacophony that is Wall Street's self-serving, costly drivel.

JoI: What is your current long-term market outlook? Do you think traditional buy-and-hold index-based investing has a place in that market scenario?

ARONSON: My current long-term investment outlook calls for premium returns from emerging markets (after all, the operative word is *emerging*), below-historical returns from developed equities (after all, *developed* is in the past tense), and disastrously bad returns from long Treasuries.

Buy-and-hold index-based investing holds a dominant position in all environments!

JoI: What do you think John Bogle has gotten wrong?

ARONSON: My only criticism of Jack Bogle's investment philosophy is a historical bias against international diversification. It is dangerous to disagree with Jack, but on this topic, I would allocate more to the international arena. (This criticism might seem akin to inside baseball, because our disagreements are a matter of degree.)

JoI: What impact has John Bogle had on you as an investor and a financial professional?

STEPHEN DAVIS, EXECUTIVE DIRECTOR, MILLSTEIN CENTER FOR CORPORATE GOVERNANCE AND PERFORMANCE, YALE SCHOOL OF MANAGEMENT: While I have a hat as an investor, I'm really more a sort of governance expert, as it were, in the field. But I also have a hat on as a nonexecutive director at Hermès in London.

I think what Bogle has done is . . . give the world an insider view as to how the mutual fund industry really operates. In many ways, it has operated—as Bogle himself would argue—to the benefit of many investors, but not without risks and without negative factors. Very few people outside the industry would have been so perceptive, insightful, and knowledgeable in giving a clear, unvarnished picture of what this industry amounts to.

JoI: What is your current long-term market outlook? Do you think traditional buy-and-hold index-based investing has a place in that market scenario?

DAVIS: [Market outlooks are] not my thing. I run a corporate governance center at Yale—I'm not running money. [But . . .] I think that the way the industry has evolved is increasingly diverging from the norms that we expect within market institutions in terms of governance and transparency. We have a system where most people know very little about their mutual funds other than some performance figures that may or may not be accurate. But they have very little say, for example, in who the boards are, in who the directors—who represent their interests as opposed to the shareholders in the mutual fund companies themselves—are. They don't really know that. There are occasional votes for those boards, but there's very little attention paid to who's on those boards and what they are meant to do. How do they really represent grassroots investors? I think that's a problem.

"Very Few People . . . Would Have Been So Perceptive, Insightful, and Knowledgeable"

Funds Must Be Responsible
Owners of Stocks

From the point of view of systemic risk, we have a big problem in that mutual funds have only reluctantly acted as owners. They tend to turn stocks, for one thing, much too quickly. And as a result, they don't own shares for all that much time. But when they do, they tend as owners to almost reflexively support management in many cases. It's less true today than it was before votes were made public. . . . But they need to do a lot more. They need to demonstrate a lot more that they are responsible owners, that their ownership responsibilities are really and truly in line with the interests of their grassroots investors, and that those votes are integrated fully in the investment process rather than simply a rote compliance exercise.

"The Agents of Mutual
Funds Act As If They're
Very Short-Term"

The people who invest in mutual funds are not quite as long-term as [a Warren Buffett]. But they are for the most part long-term. The problem is that the agents of the mutual funds act as if they're very short-term. There's a misalignment between the time horizons of the ultimate beneficiaries or ultimate investors and their mutual fund agents.

JoI: What do you think John Bogle has gotten wrong?

DAVIS: That's a tough one, because I think I almost always agree with him. This isn't what he's gotten wrong, but I think his argument that there should be a fiduciary duty standard set out in a clear way has taken a *long* time to take hold. And I don't entirely know why that is, but I think it would benefit investors if it were perhaps fleshed out more, and if there were a way in which to really galvanize the grassroots shareholders of the United States. He's done more than almost anybody to mobilize grassroots investors, so I'm very loath to criticize in this regard. But somehow we still have a situation where there are tens of millions of Americans who invest through the stock market, many of them through mutual funds, and they're still not a political force. As a result, they lose when the issues come up in Congress, for instance, or before regulators.

This isn't a criticism of what he's done; it's really a question and a challenge for those who agree with him to turn those views into political power.

JoI: What do you think John Bogle's lasting impact will be on investing and investors?

DAVIS: There's almost no one who can give a clear, independent view of the mutual fund industry as well as Jack Bogle. I think he's opened a lot of eyes to the drawbacks within this field, and I think that has a lasting impact. If he hadn't been out there throwing light on various practices, then I think lots of people would still have their eyes closed and they'd be losing more money than they are.

"A Clear, Independent View of the Mutual Fund Industry"

JoI: What impact has John Bogle had on you as an investor and a financial professional?

ED HALDEMAN, FORMER CEO, PUTNAM MANAGEMENT; CEO, FREDDIE MAC: Jack has impacted me in many ways. As an investor, he has obviously made me more aware of the significance of fees and trading expenses on long-term performance. In addition, he has provided a simple and useful framework to allow me to think about the long-term expected return from equities (yield plus expected earnings growth plus change in P/E ratio). But more importantly, Jack has impacted me by challenging me on the inherent conflict between serving as a fiduciary and being an owner of an asset management enterprise. Finally, through his book *Enough.*, he has impacted me by causing me to reevaluate my personal value system.

JoI: What is your current long-term market outlook? Do you think traditional buy-and-hold index-based investing has a place in that market scenario?

HALDEMAN: My long-term market outlook is for U.S. equities to return 7 percent per year, non-U.S. equities to return 8 to 9 percent per year, and diversified bond portfolios to return 4 percent. I definitely think traditional buy-and-hold should play a major role in any portfolio. Some might argue that the extreme volatility and low returns of the past five years mean that a buy-and-hold strategy doesn't work any longer. I don't agree with that view. There is a difference between getting the opportunity to time markets and being successful in timing markets. We know that the extreme volatility of the markets provided a huge opportunity to time the market, but this does not mean that investors in aggregate who practiced market timing outperformed the buy-and-hold strategy.

Challenges to Bogle's Philosophy

JoI: What do you think John Bogle has gotten wrong?

HALDEMAN: I am not so bold as to say Jack Bogle has gotten something wrong. I will offer three areas where I have had conversations with Jack in which I challenged his views. First, I have questioned him on his long-held view that non-U.S. equities should be only a small weighting in the portfolio of a U.S. investor. To me, holding less than a market-cap weighting in non-U.S. securities is logically inconsistent. It is akin to holding less than a market-cap weighting of financial stocks in an S&P 500 Index fund.

Second, I don't think it is morally wrong to seek to outperform the market. The possibility of outperformance may be a low-probability event, but if an investor wants to hire a fund manager in the hope that he might be one of the few outperformers, I don't think either the investor or the fund manager has an ethical or moral problem. Sometimes Jack's language suggests he sees a moral problem.

Third, I have questioned Jack on why he focuses exclusively on fees, when I believe investors in funds are hurt much more by the gap between a fund's return and the average investor's return in the fund. The differential in fees costs the typical investor about 75 basis points per year. However, some of the things funds do to encourage investors to mistime their flows in and out of funds cost investors 300 to 500 basis points per year.

JoI: What do you think John Bogle's lasting impact will be on investing and investors?

"His Impact Goes Much Beyond Vanguard"

HALDEMAN: Jack Bogle will have many lasting impacts that are incredibly significant. Certainly, Vanguard and the benefits it brings to investors because of its focus on low costs and passive management will have a lasting impact. But his impact goes much beyond Vanguard. What would be the market share of passively managed money without Jack Bogle? What would be the average fee level of actively managed money without Jack Bogle? Think how much more net worth savers have because of the popularity of index funds and the pressure on actively managed fees because of index funds. The legacy of Jack Bogle will endure and benefit millions of investors.

JoI: When did the science of financial economics begin?

DAVID BLITZER, MANAGING DIRECTOR AND CHAIRMAN, STANDARD & POOR'S INDEX COMMITTEE:[7] Essentially, it began with the publication of Harry Markowitz's "Portfolio Selection" paper in the *Journal of Finance* in 1952. This practice of investment has borrowed heavily from theoretical advances published in academic journals. The theoreticians have returned the favor by expanding the ideas that seek to explain how financial markets work. But at times investment practice has become too enraptured with the mathematical complexity and pyrotechnics of finance while the fundamentals are forgotten.

JoI: What was Jack Bogle's contribution to the history of modern finance?

BLITZER: As the theoretical idea of investing in the whole market began to attract interest in the 1960s, it was Jack Bogle who made whole-market investing a reality for investors with the introduction of the first index mutual fund in 1975. Among his many contributions to modern investing, the other that stands out is the founding of The Vanguard Group. These two achievements alone are enough to establish him among the leading investors of the past half-century.

JoI: Where does the efficient markets hypothesis (EMH) fit in?

BLITZER: Among the many practitioners mining financial theory and economic science for investment ideas, Jack Bogle and a few others kept their feet on the ground and avoided many of the recent manias. The EMH—which posits that markets are informationally efficient and therefore investors cannot consistently beat the market—underlies many of the ideas about how stocks are valued, priced, and traded. Many believers in index investing

---

"It Was Jack Bogle Who Made Whole-Market Investing a Reality"

---

7 Format altered from original commentary.

argue that the EMH is why indexing works. Lately, the theory has been the subject of much debate caused by bear markets and suggestions that prices aren't always as random or unpredictable as the EMH seems to hold. However, as Jack Bogle has pointed out, the success of index investing does not depend on the EMH, but rather on his own alternative hypothesis—the cost matters hypothesis (CMH). Simply put, CMH holds that indexing is cheap and index investors keep more of their own money than investors who use active managers. The proof is in the low-fee index funds pioneered under Bogle's leadership.

JoI: How do index funds fit into a prudent investment strategy?

BLITZER: Keeping the cost of investing down depends on more than just using indexes. Investors who rush into the newest "perfect" strategy by abandoning their last "sure bet" end up spending too much on trading and taxes (if there were any gains to be taxed) while keeping far too little. Bogle's answer was to suggest buying a total market index fund and never selling. This approach should keep the transaction costs of investing down.

JoI: What about those who argue that buy-and-hold is dead?

BLITZER: No one ever promised that investing with indexes guaranteed outsized or even merely positive returns. Indeed, the only claim by those espousing index investing was that the costs would probably be lower and the diversification would probably be greater with index investing than by attempting to buy only the stocks that are supposed to rise. The idea behind indexing as an investment strategy is that over the long run, the market rises as the economy grows and the costs of participating in economic growth can be quite modest. Does buy-and-hold *always* work? No. No investment strategy always works. Although there are promises of strategies that can be replicated

---

"Keeping the Cost of Investing Down"

and that consistently outperform buy-and-hold, few if any have succeeded. In investing (and in so many other pursuits), there are no sure things.

JoI: What impact did Jack's creation have on S&P?

BLITZER: I can't talk about Jack Bogle without acknowledging a debt to Jack's daring idea to launch an index mutual fund and basing the fund on the S&P 500. Since the S&P 500 took its current form in 1957, it has been part of many investing innovations, including index mutual funds, ETFs, and index futures and options. The Vanguard mutual fund stands out among investment and financial history as one of the first and most successful examples of borrowing from financial science for investing results.

"A Debt to Jack's Daring Idea"

PART IV

THE CORPORATE GOVERNANCE VISION

B OGLE'S LASERLIKE FOCUS on mutual fund shareholders inevitably puts corporate shareholders (largely the mutual funds themselves) and governance issues in his line of sight. Corporate governance expert Nell Minow introduces this chapter by noting Bogle's blunt (and sometimes unflattering) commentary on financial executives, followed by his "four key insights" regarding shareholders and corporate governance.

Following Minow's essay, Bogle writes lucidly about the topic in two sections. First, in "The Silence of the Funds," he discusses why mutual fund companies seem so reluctant to represent their shareholders' interests in proxy votes, and then why it is so important that they do. To the first point, he accepts as the explanation of one anonymous money manager, "There are only two kinds of clients we can't afford to offend: actual and potential." As to the second point, Bogle underscores the central issue, articulated by governance policy veteran Robert A. G. Monks, that "capitalism without owners will fail." Or in Bogle's words, "Only if managers are focused on creating long-term value for their owners . . . can corporate America be the prime engine of the nation's growth and prosperity."

Then, in "What Went Wrong in Corporate America?," Bogle broadens his analysis of commerce and finance through a review of the tenets of capitalism. He describes shortcomings in recent business or financial practices and the failures of different players in both the private and public sectors. He then offers evidence of progress being made and remedies for specific ills. Underlying his faith in reforming capitalism in the twenty-first century are the wise words of the "patron saint of capitalism," Adam Smith, and the words of the observer of nineteenth-century America, Alexis de Tocqueville, as relevant now as then.

Four Key Insights

Nell Minow[1]

When John Bogle turned the financial services industry upside down, most people admired—and envied—him for his business vision. But his creation of an entirely new industry was almost incidental to his realization that individual investors were entitled to better treatment from the financial services industry.

Bogle was the first to realize that individual investors should have the opportunity to invest in index funds, which would give them better value and less risk over the long run than managed funds. His focus on what is essentially a permanent capital infrastructure for public companies led him to a profound understanding of the importance of corporate governance. Before Bogle, it was understood that individual and institutional shareholders would follow the Wall Street rule: If you

---

1. Nell Minow is the editor of The Corporate Library and author of more than 200 articles on corporate governance.

don't like the management, sell the stock. Bogle recognized that index funds do not have that luxury. If they are not happy with the performance of a portfolio company, they can watch it sink until it falls off the index, or they can do something about it.

He is not afraid to use strong terms to describe his colleagues in the financial services industry, calling their diversion of revenues from investors to managers a "betrayal." In *The Battle for the Soul of Capitalism*, he describes

> the remarkable erosion that has taken place over the past two decades in the conduct and values of our business leaders, our investment bankers, and our money managers. . . . Over the past century, a gradual move from *owners' capitalism*—providing the lion's share of the rewards of investment to those who put up the money and risk their own capital—has culminated in an extreme version of *managers' capitalism*—providing vastly disproportionate rewards to those whom we have trusted to manage our enterprises in the interest of their owners.[2]

Bogle has four key insights, especially with regard to the role of the shareholder. They are not just critical to the understanding and practice of corporate governance but to the protection of our system of capitalism from those who would distort and subvert it for their own short-term gain.

Investors Have an Inalienable Right to Proxy Access

It is up to shareholders to address "the ugly deviations from fair play"[3] and "the ascendancy of capitalism that benefits managers at the expense of the owners."[4]

Bogle recommends that investors meet their responsibilities as corporate citizens, voting their proxies thoughtfully and communicating their views to corporate

---

2. *The Battle for the Soul of Capitalism*, xvi–xvii.

3. Ibid., 31.

4. Ibid., 47.

managers and directors constructively. But they need to be able to do more. Bogle supports giving investors "proxy access" to nominate their own candidates for the board[5] and to submit proposals on matters like executive compensation.

The Failure of Money Managers to Act in the Interest of Clients

The failure of money managers to act in the best interest of their customers in exercising shareholder rights is due to intractable conflicts of interest. First are the perverse incentives of commercial relationships. Money managers, including index fund managers, do not want to vote their shares in a manner that can offend clients who are executives at portfolio companies and who make decisions about which money manager gets the 401(k) or pension business. And, as Bogle often quotes, "There are only two kinds of clients we can't afford to offend: actual and potential."

The second conflict is the collective choice conundrum resulting from the small fractional individual holdings. Even the largest institutional investor rarely holds as much as 1 percent of a company's stock. So any investor who wants to spend the additional resources to research, much less oppose, a company's proxy proposal or submit a proposal of his or her own will put in 100 percent of the expenses for only a pro rata share of any possible returns.

Excessive Executive Compensation

One key problem of conflicts of interest is excessive executive compensation. Bogle points out that compensation is tied to measures that can be too easily "massaged," while more important measures like the cost of capital are seldom factors.

---

5. "Proxy access" was included in the post–financial meltdown Dodd-Frank legislation. [*Note:* Although a provision directing the Securities and Exchange Commission to promulgate rules for proxy access was included in Dodd-Frank and the SEC did issue the rule, it was thrown out by the District of Columbia Circuit Court of Appeals as insufficiently supported by economic analysis.]

Furthermore, "It is now obvious that CEO compensation should have a contingent component, and a durable one."[6] As long as the executives' incentive compensation rewards actions that are contrary to the creation of long-term, sustainable growth, the executives will not be committed to investor interests.

Citizens United Puts the Onus on Corporate Shareholders

The *Citizens United* decision creates the most severe conflicts of interest and potential for abuse—with one small hope for increased accountability and transparency. Bogle wrote in the *New York Times*:

> For all its faults, the *Citizens United* ruling upheld the disclosure requirements of the campaign financing law, and I had hoped full disclosure might limit corporate contributions. But in fact, corporations are able to exploit provisions in the law governing nonprofit groups to make lavish political contributions without disclosure, making it easier than ever for cash to subvert our political system. Action to limit contributions at the corporate level is therefore urgent.
>
> Indeed, the Supreme Court itself put the onus on shareholders to control corporate political giving. In his opinion for the majority in *Citizens United*, Justice Anthony M. Kennedy predicated the First Amendment right of free speech on the ability of shareholders to ensure that the speech reflects their views rather than diverting corporate assets for the benefit of executives. He suggested that any abuse could be corrected by shareholders "through the procedures of corporate democracy."

Bogle once again calls on institutional shareholders. "America's institutional investors must stand up to the Supreme Court's misguided decision and bring

---

6. *The Clash of the Cultures*, p. 95. Bogle recommends clawbacks beyond those mandated by the Sarbanes-Oxley Act of 2002. He points out that the law does not require them for performance, only in the case of "misconduct," and that even for misconduct "the SEC has yet to pursue a single case."

democracy to corporate governance, recognize conflicts that arise from the inter-locking interests of our corporate and financial systems, and take that first step along the road to reducing the dominant role that big money plays in our political system."

What makes Bogle unique in his industry is that his success is based on what is best for the individual investor—not on what is best for the industry or its top executives. What makes him a statesman is his insistence on what is best for all of us.

CHAPTER 10: THE SILENCE OF THE FUNDS: WHY MUTUAL FUNDS MUST SPEAK OUT ON THE GOVERNANCE OF OUR NATION'S CORPORATIONS[7]

> *The good shepherd lays down his life for the sheep. He who is a hired hand and not a shep-herd, who does not own the sheep, sees the wolf coming and leaves the sheep and flees, and the wolf snatches them and scatters them. He flees because he is a hired hand and cares nothing for the sheep.*
>
> —JOHN 10:11–13

> *There are only two kinds of clients we can't afford to offend: actual and potential.*
>
> —ANONYMOUS MONEY MANAGER

My 1951 thesis on the mutual fund industry also explored the role of mutual funds in corporate governance. In those ancient days, funds were quite hesitant to make their votes count. The common refrain was, "If you don't like the management, sell the stock." I was, however, able to find a number of examples of fund activism. The most notable was the Montgomery Ward case of 1949, in which mutual funds

---

7. Excerpts from Chapter 3 of *The Clash of the Cultures: Investment vs. Speculation* (2012).

joined in the effort to remove Chairman Sewell L. Avery from his job. Avery was a controversial character—a few years earlier, in 1944, a pair of soldiers removed him from his office while he was seated in his desk chair, a moment that was immortalized in a famous photo. The negative votes cast by the funds were based on his notorious reluctance to spend money on future growth, fearing a postwar depression that would never come to pass.

The Funds' Duties As Corporate Citizens

My thesis reflected my then, as now, idealism. I predicted that it was only a matter of time until mutual funds exercised their duties as corporate citizens:

> . . . *basing their investments on enterprise rather than speculation* . . . and exerting influence on corporate policy, often in a decisive manner, and in the best interest of investment company shareholders. Since they possess not only a greater knowledge of finance and management than the average stockholder, but also the financial means to make their influence effective, the mutual funds seem destined to fulfill this crucial segment of their economic role.

My words echoed the position of the Securities and Exchange Commission. In its 1940 report to Congress, the SEC called on funds to serve ". . . the useful role of representatives of the great number of inarticulate and ineffective individual investors in industrial corporations in which investment companies are also interested." In 1951, when I cited those words in my thesis, mutual funds owned less than 3 percent of the shares of U.S. corporations, and I expected their voice would strengthen in tandem with their muscle.

A Flawed Prediction of Fund Activism

Alas, I was wrong. So was the SEC. Now, more than 60 years later, mutual funds have become the largest investors in U.S. stocks, owning fully 30 percent of all shares. Mutual fund managers, who typically provide investment management services to pension plans and other institutions, control more than 60 percent. Together these institutional money managers are by far the most potent force in corporate America, and their power is highly concentrated—the largest 25 managers alone own $6 trillion of U.S. equities, about three-quarters of the institutional total. But the strong voice I expected to hear is barely a whisper. Switching metaphors and putting a reverse twist on the saying that "the spirit is willing, but the flesh is weak," the mutual fund flesh is strong, but the spirit is unwilling. The silence of the funds is deafening.

As far as I can tell, while the managers of most large fund groups doubtless review and consider corporate proxies, they overwhelmingly endorse, with few major exceptions, the proposals of corporate management. When they vote, they usually do just as they are asked; they support management's recommendations. This practice is a far cry, not only from activism and advocacy, but from the very process of corporate governance. Most mutual funds have failed to live up to their responsibilities of corporate citizenship.

Thanks to Congress and the SEC, there has been halting movement to give stock owners some access to participation in corporate proxies. In the 2012 "proxy season" (usually the spring), a wide range of proposals by shareholders are appearing on a variety of issues, including the issues of executive pay and corporate political contributions. Increasingly, the proposals are included in corporate proxies. Now the financial institutions that hold absolute control over corporate America will have to stand up and be counted, unless, of course, they choose to abstain.

Why Mutual Funds Are Passive Participants in Corporate Governance

The reasons for this passivity by institutional investors are not hard to fathom. First, as other chapters of this book discuss, funds are often essentially short-term holders of stocks, moving away from investment and toward speculation. We've moved, as I've often said, from an "own-a-stock" industry to a "rent-a-stock" industry. Simply put, renters all too rarely handle their property with the same care as they would if they were owners.[8] As the late Columbia Law School professor Louis Lowenstein has said, fund managers "exhibit a persistent emphasis on momentary stock prices. The subtleties and nuances of a particular business utterly escape them." Pure and simple, most mutual fund managers, while they seem to care about corporate governance, shun active participation in the proxy voting process.

A second obstacle to mutual fund activism is the commercial nature of the mutual fund business. We've become primarily a marketing business rather than a management business, a business in which salesmanship has come to overwhelm stewardship. When a fund manager takes a position on controversial proxy issues, it generates unwanted publicity. Better, it seems, to keep a low profile and avoid the risk. Perhaps even more significantly, our giant investment managers seek giant corporate clients, for managing their retirement plans is where the big money is . . . and where the big profits lie for the managers.

"Salesmanship Has Come to Overwhelm Stewardship"

Since the mid-1990s, corporate 401(k) thrift plans have been among the driving forces in generating new mutual fund assets. Corporate pension funds—absent the need for all of that complex and costly subaccounting—are also considered plums by institutional money managers. Given the drive to attract corporate clients, the reluctance of fund managers to risk the opprobrium of potential clients by leaping enthusiastically into the controversial areas of corporate governance is discouraging, but hardly astonishing. One manager hit the nail on the head with this (perhaps apocryphal) comment: "There are only two kinds of clients we can't afford to offend: actual and potential."

---

8. As former Treasury Secretary Lawrence Summers plaintively asked, "When was the last time someone washed a rental car?"

A third obstacle to activism, or so it has been alleged by the fund industry, is that corporate activism would be expensive for the funds to undertake. In a sense, it would be. Yet TIAA-CREF, whose investment portfolio totals some $500 billion, is unique in this industry in taking on the responsibilities of corporate activism. Several years ago, it spent an amount said to exceed $2 million per year on the implementation of its splendid—and productive—corporate governance program.[9] This expenditure, however, would amount to but 0.003 percent (3/1,000ths of 1 percent) of its present invested assets. But the benefits generated for TIAA-CREF's academic community participants are said to have been well worth the modest costs.

The (Evanescent) Federation of Long-Term Investors

While small fund managers could hardly spend the resources necessary for a broad-gauge program, they could at least engage their security analysts in some kind of serious review of the governance of their major corporate holdings. And there is nothing that prevents fund managers from banding together and joining forces. Given the fund industry's now $6.3 trillion worth of stock holdings, an industry-wide governance effort that entailed just 1/1,000th of 1 percent of expenses (relative to fund assets) would produce an annual budget of $60 million for an active corporate governance program—far in excess of what such a program would require.

Even that huge sum of money, however, would be but a drop in the bucket relative to today's roughly $100 billion that funds spend each year on administrative, investment management, marketing, and operating costs. I tried to form such a coalition—"The Federation of Long-Term Investors"—in 2002. My effort was applauded by Warren Buffett, who offered to support the effort if other large fund managers joined the effort. Alas, my proposal failed abjectly to attract a single

---

9. It may be significant that TIAA-CREF does not manage retirement plans for corporations, and therefore has no such clients to offend.

one of the 10 largest mutual fund groups, and the proposed federation never got under way.[10]

A fourth and final obstacle might be described as the "people who live in glass houses" syndrome. The mutual fund governance system itself has come under severe and well-deserved criticism. The problem is that it has enabled external managers, paid under contract, to essentially control the affairs of the mutual fund industry that they work for. These firms with relatively small capitalization (say, $1 billion) actually control the huge capital of the giant mutual funds (say, $100 billion) that they contract to serve.[11]

The Mutual Fund—A Corporate Shell

How can that happen? Largely because the manager holds the nexus of control over the funds, usually solely responsible for as much as 100 percent of the administrative, accounting, shareholder record-keeping, legal, investment management, and marketing and distribution services required to run the mutual fund complex. The manager usually provides the funds' officers, and plays an influential role in selecting the funds' directors. Yes, the funds' manager typically does all of those things, and the fund itself is little more than a corporate shell.

Where else in corporate America is there a parallel to the control of a series of giant publicly held corporations (the mutual funds themselves) by a relatively small outside firm (the management company)—with its own separate group of shareholders—whose principal business is providing those giant corporations with

---

10. Importantly, such a federation would have represented the participation of some 60 percent of mutual fund equity holdings, and would have largely responded to the "free-riding" issue—that is, the concern that if a fund owning 1 percent of the shares of a corporation spent its resources to make a proxy proposal that was implemented, the benefits would be shared by the shareholders of the other 99 percent who contributed nothing to the effort.
11. Janus Capital Group, for example, manages some $89 billion in mutual fund assets, but itself has a market capitalization of only $1.6 billion, a ratio of more than 55 to 1.

all of the services required to conduct their affairs? As far as I can tell, nowhere else in the corporate world does such a perverse and counterintuitive structure exist. Looking at this peculiar fund structure a few steps removed, it's hard to imagine why it exists. But it is easier to understand than to accept the reluctance of fund managers to become corporate activists, daring to throw stones from their own glass houses at the managements of the corporations whose shares the funds own.

Throwing Stones from Glass Houses?

One fund executive who dared to throw stones—at corporate directors in general— is the CEO of Fidelity Management Company. In 1994, in an extremely rare public speech, Edward C. Johnson III, CEO of Fidelity Management Company and CEO of each of the now-280 mutual funds managed by Fidelity, demanded that corporations (without naming them) put their owners first. The quotations

"Physician, Heal Thyself"

Excerpts from comments by Edward C. Johnson III

"We want directors who will mind the store for us, making sure management's doing a good job. . . . Their final responsibility is to the shareholders. Too often they represent their own interests or the Chief Executive Officer's. . . . [Managers must be] the best available. If not, [the board of directors] has to fire, rehire, and pay new managers . . . diligently spotting issues where the interests of managers and shareholders may conflict and then taking the initiative to deal with them. . . . [When the chairman sets the directors' pay], he can influence their loyalty. . . . When it comes to an issue where shareholders' interests diverge from management's, which way will this person vote? . . . We should have intelligent national laws that spell out directors' accountability to shareholders. . . . [We must] ensure better boardrooms—boardrooms that are responsible to shareholder interests and not passive rubber stamps for the chairman's agenda."

in the box are excerpts from that speech. He was speaking about the responsibilities of the directors of the corporations in which the Fidelity fund owns shares.

Passive Rubber Stamps for the Chairman's Agenda?

Mr. Johnson was calling on corporate directors to challenge their CEOs, and if necessary, get rid of underperforming managers. Similarly, one would expect mutual fund directors also to challenge their own CEOs and replace failed managers. So it is ironic that these totally appropriate demands were directed to the directors of the giant corporations that make up the Fortune 500. Mr. Johnson seemed to ignore the obvious fact that his demands should also have been directed to independent directors of mutual funds, specifically including the independent directors of the Fidelity funds.

Yet those directors have never fired Fidelity Management from its position as manager of any Fidelity fund, nor—even when a fund's performance turned miserable—ever hired a new firm as manager. The failure of Magellan Fund, once by far the industry's largest fund, is a case in point. Its once outstanding early investment performance faded away in the early 1990s, replaced by mediocrity ever since. Fund shareholders left in droves, leading to a drop of almost 90 percent in its assets—from $103 billion to $15 billion. Yet Fidelity's lucrative contract to run the fund continues.

Further, so far as we know, Johnson has never lobbied Congress to pass "intelligent national laws that spell out directors' accountability to shareholders . . . boardrooms that are responsible to shareholder interests." "Passive rubber stamps" continue to dominate the roles both of corporate directors and of mutual fund directors, even though, as a legal matter, their responsibilities are identical. Neither group should be allowed to shirk the solemn responsibilities that Johnson appropriately urged on them back in 1994. But he has yet to break the long silence that began when his speech ended.

The Picture Begins to Change

Mutual funds have been the epitome of nonactivism in the governance of the corporations in their portfolios. This silence has been the dominant standard of conduct ever since the beginning of the fund industry's history in 1924. Up until the 1980s, however, the industry had limited resources, fund voting power was but a tiny fraction of what it is today, and the issues presented to shareholders were rare. It's no wonder the industry was timid. (The Montgomery Ward case described earlier was a rare exception.)

Corporate Responsibility Issues

But corporate policy issues that rightfully concerned many fund managers gradually began to loom large. Beginning in the mid-1980s, societal issues came to the fore; for example, apartheid in the Republic of South Africa. Many institutional shareholders—especially university endowment funds—demanded that corporations doing business in South Africa shut down their operations and pull out. Other so-called corporate responsibility issues also arose in that era, notably regarding munitions makers, tobacco manufacturers, and protection of the environment. Mutual funds, like other shareholders, had to take a stand, pro or con, or abstain. But we have no way to know which course they chose, for at the time there was no requirement that their proxy votes be disclosed.

"The Power to Wield the Big Stick"

By the mid-1990s, more substantive issues arose that affected corporate performance: executive compensation, including option issuance; corporate restructuring; dividend policy; staggered board terms for corporate directors; and anti-takeover defenses such as "poison pills" and the like. These issues were far more likely to be raised by relatively small investors with little clout (such as religious organizations and labor unions) than by the major mutual funds and pension funds that had the power to wield the big stick and ultimately impose their will on the corporations involved. Did they vote their proxies for or against these resolutions? We just don't know. For there remained a giant information gap on how or even whether institutional investors voted the proxies they controlled. Were they indeed serving the interests of the fund shareholders and pension beneficiaries whom they were duty bound to serve? Again, we had no way of knowing.

Reporting Proxy Votes— The *New York Times* Op-Ed, December 2002

Finally, the Securities and Exchange Commission decided to shine the spotlight of full disclosure on the proxy voting practices of mutual funds. The Commission, however, took no position on voting by pension funds, labor unions, endowment funds, trust companies, and insurance companies—perhaps because only their mandate to regulate mutual funds was beyond challenge or perhaps because of the ascendance of mutual funds as the dominant ownership institution. In any event, in September 2002, the SEC released a proposal that would require mutual funds to report their voting decisions, company by company, to their share owners. Given that there were tens of millions of fund share owners, this was essentially the public at large. (Today, access to information on proxy votes by funds is generally available on the website of each fund complex, and from the SEC.)

In my opinion, the SEC position was conceptually correct—agents have a duty to report to their principals, for heaven's sake. It was also the right direction for public policy to take in serving the interests of fund shareholders and in serving the national interest. I hoped—and expected—that proxy vote disclosure would force funds to reexamine their heretofore passive approach to governance in favor of a more active approach. The single overriding goal: *to force our giant publicly held business corporations to place the interests of their own stockholders first, ahead of the interests of their managers.* Soon after it was issued, I applauded the SEC proposal. My op-ed piece in the *New York Times* on December 14, 2002, explained the logic of my support.

The *Wall Street Journal* Op-Ed, February 2003

It did not take long for the opponents of the proposal to respond. Just two months later, on February 14, 2003, in an op-ed in the *Wall Street Journal*, John Brennan, my successor as CEO of Vanguard, and Edward C. Johnson III, CEO of Fidelity, spoke out in opposition. In my *Times* op-ed, "I cast my lot in opposition to the industry that I've been part of for my entire career." My position was simple. "In

WORDS FROM THOSE WHO KNOW BOGLE BEST

Jonathan Clements, former *Wall Street Journal* columnist, "Getting Going"; Director of Financial Guidance, myFi

Five or six years ago, when I was still with the *Wall Street Journal* in New York, Jack called to say he was in the World Financial Center, he had a few minutes to spare, and would it be okay if he stopped by. Soon enough, he was striding across the tenth-floor newsroom, slightly stooped, to be sure, but—like Cassius—he had that "lean and hungry look. He thinks too much: such men are dangerous."

Giants of corporate America occasionally made their way through the *Journal*'s news-room, but they typically moved quickly, lest lingering too long might invite awkward questions. Not Jack. He snagged a cubicle, commandeered a phone, and, before long, had the ear of those around him. On display was the charisma and principles that built Vanguard. That I expected.

On that day, however, I saw another side of Jack Bogle. Here he was, conversing easily with my fellow ink-stained wretches, a motley crew of skeptical, disaffected ankle biters, who all believed themselves engaged in an important endeavor but would never dream of admitting as much. And Jack fit right in. It was as if one of us had made good and now was returning to the old neighborhood for a visit. This man might be a corporate visionary, but underneath he had the sensibilities of a newspaper reporter. It was at that moment that I realized why journalists loved Jack.

March 2009

"Conversing Easily with My Fellow Ink-Stained Wretches"

the mutual fund director's world, the fund's officers and managers are agents for their principals, the fund shareholders. It is management's responsibility to act solely on their behalf. It would thus seem self-evident that mutual fund shareholders should have the right to know how the shares of the corporations the funds own in their portfolios are voted. Such shareholders are partial owners of these stocks, and to deny them that information would stand on its head the common understanding of the principal-agency relationship."

In the *Wall Street Journal* op-ed, those who opposed disclosure said, "Our fiduciary duty (to our mutual fund stockholders) brings our two companies together to oppose the SEC's disclosure proposal. If the SEC's proposed rule (to require disclosure of votes) goes into effect, one—and only one—group of investors will be singled out to lose this right: mutual funds. Pension funds, insurance companies, foundations, bank-trust departments, and other investors would retain their rights of confidentiality. The effect would be to make mutual funds the prime pressure point for veiled threats from every activist group with a political or social ax to grind with corporate America."

On January 23, 2003, the SEC approved the proxy disclosure requirement by a unanimous vote. (A senior Commission official told me that my *New York Times* op-ed had played an important role in their decision.) As a result, ever since 2004, funds have had to disclose their proxy votes, without, as far as I know, veiled threats or mass protests from any "activist group with a political or social ax to grind."

Proxy Voting Disclosure Would Make "Mutual Funds the Prime Pressure Point for Veiled Threats From Every Activist Group with a Political or Social Ax to Grind"

Mobilizing Institutional Investors

The requirement that mutual funds disclose their proxy votes to their owners has created a new and powerful motivation for funds to exercise their rights as corporate citizens. We ought to require similar disclosure on the part of all fiduciaries to their constituencies, including traditional corporate pension funds; pension funds of federal, state, and local governments; trust companies and insurance companies;

and endowment funds. With 100 million fund shareholders, of course, this disclosure is equivalent to public disclosure. But with rights come responsibilities, and we need to develop standards so that all of those with trusteeship responsibilities—including those of university endowment funds, where political and economic judgments have been known to overshadow other factors in voting—will also be held to high standards of fiduciary duty.

"Institutional Investors Should Be Given the Tools to Do What's Right"

With voting disclosure providing the motivation to do what's right, institutional investors should be given the tools to do what's right, with clear access to the corporate proxy statement. Corporations, however, allow such access only grudgingly. A 2003 SEC proposal to facilitate access only left the door ajar. This complex proposal would have allowed large shareholders to nominate one to three directors depending on the board's size, but only after certain triggering events take place—namely, a 5 percent combined ownership position for at least three years. The Commission, I thought, should have gone further, and opened that door wide enough to permit much greater freedom of collective investor action. But at least its proposal would give institutional investors a seat at the table, so to speak, by potentially playing a role in the selection of directors for corporate boards.

When the SEC issued that proposal in 2003 to facilitate access to corporate proxy proposals, it asked for comments. But I saw not one single response by a large institutional manager demanding even more access. Indeed, rather than seeking greater access, institutional investors seemed to seek even less. Some commentators sought to make a weak access proposal even weaker, suggesting even higher ownership thresholds. Nowhere did I see a hue and cry to encourage—or even allow—fiduciaries to behave as active owners.

"Dragged Kicking and Screaming into the Fray"

As far as I could determine, most of the industry's biggest guns— Dreyfus, Fidelity, Janus, MFS, Putnam, Vanguard—didn't even respond to the SEC proposal. Neither did Citibank, Goldman Sachs, Merrill Lynch, or Morgan Stanley respond, despite their control of giant fund empires. And other institutions—Schwab, Prudential, Northern Trust, and JPMorgan Chase, all with large institutional investment and mutual fund units—actually opposed the SEC's modest thrust toward corporate democracy.[12] If we are to return to true owners' capitalism, investment America apparently will have to be dragged kicking and screaming into the fray.

In the face of such opposition by corporations, and the demonstrated lack of interest by their institutional owners, the SEC proposal was ultimately dropped. (When the corporations are organized and determined to win and the managers are unorganized and don't care, such an outcome is less than astonishing!) Since then, sad to say, we've actually moved backward. For in 2006, the U.S. Court for the Second Circuit ruled essentially that the proposed limits on proxy access were illegal, requiring the SEC to amend its proposal to virtually eliminate proxy access by shareholders. The Commission subsequently abandoned its effort for reform.

In a new proposal in 2009, the Commission tried again, formally adopting new rules for granting access by shareholders in 2010. But the Business Roundtable and the U.S. Chamber of Commerce went to court in opposition, and the D.C. Circuit Court struck down the new rule, stating that the SEC "acted arbitrarily and capriciously for having failed once again adequately to assess the economic effects of a new rule."

The court's decision was based on the Congressional requirement for a cost-benefit analysis of any new regulation. As noted earlier, the costs of a new rule can be easily measured in tangible dollar terms and the benefits are often largely

> *"Corporations Are Organized and Determined to Win. The Managers Are Unorganized and Don't Care."*

---

12. It is significant that, except for Fidelity and Vanguard, each of these corporations was either publicly held or owned by public corporations. In effect, they could be affected by the proposal in one way as the owners and another way as the owned—an obvious conflict.

intangible. How does one measure the potential shareholder value added by the active participation of stockholders in the governance of the corporations whose shares they own? One can only agree that the federal government, as the court said, should "tailor regulations to impose the least burdens on society," as its statement reads, and should "achieve the common good . . . ensuring that benefits outweigh costs." But when that noble principle is ignored in the quest for mathematical purity in its implementation, it is our society that is the loser. In any event, the SEC chose not to appeal the court's wrong-headed ruling, and there the matter rests today.

The Rights and Responsibilities of Ownership

The judiciary has failed to give the owners of stocks—and the agents of those owners—the full power to execute all of the rights that would seem implicit in such ownership. Yet there is still much that our institutional money managers can do. The first task is to demand that these financial intermediaries that dominate investment America put the interests of those they serve as their first and overriding priority. We must strengthen the traditional fiduciary law, now only loosely administered by the states in which corporations are chartered. We ought to impose a federal statute of fiduciary duty, as well as consider whether federal chartering of corporations—something that was debated at the Constitutional Convention in 1787—would be wise.

All those years ago, James Madison argued that the new federal government should be authorized to charter corporations. But as author Roger Lowenstein describes it, "federal charters smacked of royal perquisites, [so] it was left to the states to write the rules. Delaware, through its utter permissiveness, became the corporate residence of choice, much as the Cayman Islands is a paper domicile for secrecy-minded bankers. To this day, more than half of America's largest companies are incorporated in its second-smallest state. Delaware laws are so lax they don't even require publishing an annual report."

What is essential, finally, is that the last-line owners—the investors them-selves—demand high standards of trusteeship from those who represent their owner-ship interests. In mutual funds, those 100 million direct owners have no individual power, but awesome collective power. These fund investors need to understand what investing and trusteeship are all about, and, by voting with their feet, gradually gravitate to fund organizations that are serious about putting their interests first.

Acting Like Owners— Five Standards

In retirement plans, while the contributors to the thrift plans and the beneficiaries of pension plans presently have no mechanism for bringing about the same result, they surely deserve some formal legal voice. They could establish standards of conduct for the trustees of the assets that have been set aside to fund their retirements. State law is clear that retirement plan fiduciaries have the traditional duties of loyalty and prudence. Now we need a federal statute that goes even further, one that codifies that the agents of those institutions entrusted with the responsibilities for managing other people's money have a fiduciary duty to the principals whom they serve. Such a duty would be broad and far-reaching. It would include five points:

1. A requirement that all fiduciaries must act solely in the long-term inter-ests of their beneficiaries.
2. An affirmation by government that an effective shareholder presence in all public companies is in the national interest.
3. A demand that all institutional money managers should be accountable for the compulsory exercise of their votes in the sole interest of their shareholders.
4. A recognition of the right of shareholders to nominate directors and make proxy proposals, subject to appropriate limits.
5. A demand that any ownership structure of managers that entails conflicts of interest be eliminated.

"Capitalism without Owners Will Fail"

That five-point list is not my own. Rather, I'm citing—with enthusiasm—the ideas of Robert A. G. Monks, author, founder of International Shareholder Services (ISS), cofounder of The Corporate Library, and former federal government official with responsibility for the U.S. pension system. The title of Monks's monograph (with Allen Sykes)—*Capitalism without Owners Will Fail*—is no overstatement. Corporate managers must be focused on creating long-term value for their owners rather than focusing on short-term stock prices for their renters. Monks speaks with a passion and intensity that few others can equal. He presents the issue clearly. "American corporations today are like the great European monarchies of yore: They have the power to control the rules under which they function and to direct the allocation of public resources. This is a simple statement of the present state of affairs. Corporations have effectively captured the United States: its judiciary, its political system, and its national wealth, without assuming any of the responsibilities of domination."

The fact is that, yes, *capitalism without owners will fail*. Only if managers are focused on creating long-term value for their owners rather than on short-term stock prices for the renters of their stock can corporate America be the prime engine of the nation's growth and prosperity and a major source of innovation and experimentation. To the extent that corporate managers sit unchecked in the driver's seat, feathering their own nests at the expense of their own stock shareholders, and rent-a-stock shareholders focus solely on momentary, ephemeral prices, capitalism cannot flourish.

The giant institutions of investment America are obviously hesitant to take the lead in accomplishing these goals. But who else can lead the effort? These money managers not only hold more than 70 percent of all shares, but they have the staffs to pore over corporate financial statements and proxies; the professional expertise to evaluate CEO performance, pay, and perquisites; and (now that full disclosure of all proxy votes by mutual funds is mandatory), they have the incentive to vote in the manner that their beneficiaries have every right to expect. As they move away from today's culture of short-term speculation and return to their traditional focus on long-term investing, these institutional owners must fight for the access to the levers of control over the corporations they own. These are powerful levers that are both appropriate for their ownership position and a reflection of their willingness to accept both the rights and the responsibilities of corporate citizenship.

Accomplishing these goals forces us to consider some ideas about corporate democracy that are rarely mentioned. What about allowing longer-term owners greater voting rights? Or even requiring a specific holding period (say, three years) before shares can be voted? What about a premium dividend payment on a new class of stock available only to those same long-term owners? Surely a little imagination could provide even more encouragement to owners of stocks who care about good governance vis-à-vis renters of stocks who don't seem to care.

"Where Is the Proof of the Pudding"

So far, however, our money managers seem far more inclined to shun those rights and responsibilities than to embrace them. If "the proof of the pudding is in the eating," the SEC regulation that required mutual funds to report their proxy votes seems to have had no more than a modest positive influence on mutual fund voting practices. So far, I've seen no academic articles whatsoever that have examined mutual fund proxy voting patterns. But an exhaustive analysis of fund voting practices has been undertaken by the giant American Federation of State, County, and Municipal Employees (AFSCME) and produced annually over the past five years.

The union's report for the year ended June 30, 2011, focused on the differences between the voting profiles for funds that are the dominant providers of retirement plan services to corporate retirement plans, a $4 trillion business for the fund industry. The AFSCME data showed that the four largest providers (Fidelity, Vanguard, American Funds, and BlackRock) "exhibited the most corporate-management-friendly voting patterns," generally supporting directors' elections, approving management proposals, and opposing shareholder proposals. To reach that conclusion, AFSCME examined the votes cast by the 26 largest mutual fund managers, ascertaining how often they supported three broad types of proposals:

1. Selection of specific directors of S&P 500 companies where 30 percent or more of shares were withheld from or voted against one or more directors for reasons related to concern over executive pay and where proxy advisory services specifically recommended voting against the selected directors.
2. Company management proposals affirming compensation-related proxy proposals made by company management, such as equity compensation plans, bonus plan performance criteria, management advisory vote on executive compensation, or "say on pay" proposals and option issuance.
3. Shareholder proposals relating largely to limiting executive compensation.

A Report on the Voting Practices of the 26 Largest Fund Managers of Retirement Plans

The report ranked the voting practices of these 26 fund families from the most supportive of efforts to tie executive pay to company performance (and in turn, to shareholder value) to the least supportive of those efforts. AFSCME chose categories of shareholder proposals on executive pay that the union believed to be most likely to enhance shareholder value. They dubbed the fund families that most consistently supported measures to rein in pay the "pay constrainers" and those that voted least often for such measures the "pay enablers," with the lowest scores going to them. The data for 2011 were roughly consistent with the data for the prior year. Here's what the study found:

The four largest defined contribution (DC) retirement plan managers were Fidelity, Vanguard, BlackRock, and American Funds, which together supervised nearly one-half of all DC plan assets held in funds that were reviewed in the report. The other 22 fund families controlled the remainder. Plan assets supervised by all 26 families totaled $3.1 trillion.

- The largest plan providers exhibited the most management-friendly voting patterns on the shareholder proposals and director-voting categories.
- While these firms apparently do apply a higher level of scrutiny to management proposals than the majority of fund families, they rank among the bottom five fund managers in favoring shareholder proposals.

"Their Singling Out of Vanguard as the Least Shareholder-Friendly Manager . . . Hardly Gladdens My Heart"

Unfair as such a broad generalization may be, their singling out of Vanguard as the least shareholder-friendly manager—the firm ranked #26 on the list of 26—hardly gladdens my heart. But the AFSCME numbers, however interpreted, are not inconsistent with the data used by Vanguard in its public report: 94 percent in favor of directors, 89 percent in favor of management proposals, and 13 percent in favor of shareholder proposals.

I do not presume to know how Fidelity or BlackRock or American Funds would respond to the question of whether their fiduciary duty to vote proxies in the interests of mutual fund shareholders is compromised by the managers' desire for more revenue and profits, or simply reflects their competitive instincts to prevail in that huge marketplace. Vanguard management flatly denies any such connection. In the firm's policy statement describing its proxy voting policies, Vanguard states, in effect, that the actual number of votes cast is less relevant than the "significant amount of time spent in engaging—whether in writing, conference calls, or face-to-face meetings—with management and board members of portfolio companies regarding potential governance and compensation issues. . . . In some cases, company officials acknowledged our concerns and pledged responsive actions. . . . (If not) we voted against."

Index Funds Should Be Active in Their Voting Decisions

I take at face value Vanguard's statement, and have no information that would contradict its position. But what surprised me—and, I confess, disappointed me—was that the two index fund providers among the Big Four—Vanguard and BlackRock—were both notably passive in their voting policies. After all, if an index fund isn't happy with a corporation's management, it can't sell the stock. So logic would suggest that it should work to change the management. In a 2010 *Wall Street Journal* op-ed, John Brennan, former Vanguard CEO, seemed to agree that index funds should be active in their voting decisions: "As one of the largest index providers in the world, Vanguard hardly takes a passive approach to corporate governance. As permanent shareholders of a corporation, [we have] a shared interest in maximizing long-term value and in meeting short-term goals." Yet Dimensional Fund Advisors—also a major index manager (but one with a relatively small $15 billion in defined contribution plan assets under management) ranked #1 in shareholder activism in the ACFSME study, supporting a remarkable 99 percent of shareholder proposals.

While the voting data and the policy statement are not necessarily inconsistent, the issue is whether the giant managers of defined contribution plans are honoring their responsibility to serve the interests of their own shareholders rather than protecting their dominant position in serving the retirement plans of corporate America—and protecting their ability to attract more business from other corporations. You'll recall the idea that money managers want to offend neither

The Announcement of the John C. Bogle Legacy Forum, January 31, 2012

INSTITUTE FOR THE FIDUCIARY STANDARD

Bloomberg
LINK

The
JOHN C. BOGLE
LEGACY FORUM

TUESDAY, JANUARY 31, 2012

RESTORING INVESTOR TRUST IN FINANCIAL MARKETS:
DOES JACK BOGLE OFFER A PRESCRIPTION?

Jack Bogle's legacy is rooted in the concept that investing should be conducted solely in the interest of shareholders and investors. Bogle's single mindedness on fiduciary stewardship finds its meaning in the company he founded, the (low cost and simple) product strategies and corporate governance reforms he champions, and the nine books he wrote.

This program explores whether Bogle offers a prescription that can help restore trust.

HOST COMMITTEE
Paul Volcker and Arthur Levitt, Co-Chairs
Sheila Bair, John Biggs, Alan Blinder, William Donaldson,
Peter Fitzgerald, Andrew Golden, Roger Ibbotson,
Burton Malkiel, David Swensen

EVENT ORGANIZERS
Institute for the Fiduciary Standard, CFA Institute,
and the Museum of American Finance

EVENT SPONSOR
Bloomberg Link

Leaders of the successful effort to hold the Forum, with their honoree.

From left, top row: Roger Ibbotson, Professor, Yale University; John Biggs, Former Chairman and CEO, TIAA-CREF; Arthur Levitt, Chairman, U.S. Securities and Exchange Commission (1993–2001), Burton Malkiel, Professor, Princeton University. Bottom row: Alan Blinder, Professor, Princeton University; John Bogle, Founder, The Vanguard Group; Paul Volcker, Chairman, Federal Reserve (1979–1987).

The Speakers Dinner

Tamar Frankel, Professor of Law, Boston University

William Isaac, Global Head of Financial Institutions, FTI Consulting

John C. Bogle, Jr., Founder and President, Bogle Investment Management

Theodore Aronson, Founder and Managing Principal, AJO

The Speakers Dinner (continued)

John Bogle; Paul Volcker; Maria Elena Lagomasino, CEO, WE Family Offices; Vartan Gregorian, President, Carnegie Corporation of New York

Knut Rostad, President, Institute for the Fiduciary Standard

Bogle and Volcker

Volcker and John Biggs

The Forum Begins

David Cowen, President, Museum of American Finance

Knut Rostad

John Bogle

Bogle

Panel One: Indexing

Roger Ibbotson; Burton Malkiel; Gus Sauter, former Chief Investment Officer, The Vanguard Group; David Swensen, Chief Investment Officer, Yale University

Sauter and Swensen

Malkiel

Sauter

Panel Two: Corporate Governance

Alan Blinder; Lynn Turner, Chief Accountant, SEC (1998–2001); Kenneth Feinberg, Founder and Managing Partner, Feinberg Rozen

Blinder

Feinberg

Turner

Panel Three: The Fiduciary Standard

Arthur Levitt; Timothy Ryan, Former President and CEO, SIFMA; David Ruder, Chairman, U.S. SEC (1987–1989); Harvey Pitt, Chairman, U.S. SEC (2001–2003)

Levitt

Pitt

Ruder

Panel Four: Bogle the Communicator

James Green, Editorial Director, Summit Business Media; Martin Fridson, Founder and CEO, FridsonVision; Jeremy Duffield, former Vanguard Executive

Green

Fridson

Duffield

John Bogle and Paul Volcker

A Conversation with John Bogle and Paul Volcker

Kathleen Hays, Journalist, Bloomberg News; Paul Volcker, John Bogle

Volcker

Bogle

Bogle Signs Copies of *Enough.* for the Attendees

John Bogle and David Swensen

Bogle

Bogle

Anne Sherrerd (Bogle's niece) and her son-in-law
Schuyler Laird

The Crowd Gathers; Notables Meet

John C. Bogle Legacy Forum Attendees

John C. Bogle Legacy Forum Attendees

Andrew Golden, President, Princeton University Investment Company; John Bogle

Golden; Roger Ibbotson; Daniel Kahneman, Nobel Laureate in Economic Sciences (2002)

Among the Guests

Kevin Laughlin, Bogle's Staff Assistant for 11 years

Rick Ferri, Author, Investment Advisor

Allan Roth, Author, Investment Advisor

Jason Zweig, Columnist, *The Wall Street Journal*; Charles Ganoe, Princeton '51

Chan Hardwick, Headmaster, Blair Academy (1989–2013) and his wife, Monie

Gary Gensler, Chiarman, CFTC

John Bogle's Sons Andrew and John, Jr.

A Family Affair

Bill Bogle, John Bogle's Brother

Father and Sons

Members of The Bogle Family in Attendance

"The Bogle Issue" of the *Journal of Indexes*, **March/April 2012**

Journal of Indexes

www.journalofindexes.com

the bogle issue

March / April 2012

The Economic Role Of The Investment Company
John Bogle

The Bogle Impact: A Roundtable
Featuring Gus Sauter, William Bernstein, Burton Malkiel, Don Phillips, Ted Aronson and more!

Lessons From SPIVA
Srikant Dash

The Case For Indexing
Christopher Philips

Plus an excerpt from Bogle's forthcoming book and an interview with the man himself,
as well as thoughts on indexes and investing from Agather and Blitzer

actual nor potential clients—that is, all of the large corporations with either defined contribution plans or defined benefit plans, or both.

Only time will tell if Vanguard and the other large institutional money managers—whether or not they manage retirement plans—will take a higher profile in their activism in the governance of our nation's publicly held corporations. Perhaps they will decide to have more discussions with management; perhaps they will support more aggressive shareholder-friendly proxy votes; perhaps one day they will even make their own proxy proposals that demand increased management focus on shareholder interests of all kinds.

So far, however, most proxy proposals have come from individuals and small institutions. Few, if any, have been made by these giants. The variety and number of shareholder proposals are substantial. In recent years, proposals have increasingly focused on environmental and social issues, and demand for proxy access to elect directors is growing. In 2012, two of the major thrusts are "say on pay" proposals and corporate political contributions, both of which are worthy of special discussion.

Executive Compensation Has "Gotten Totally Out of Hand"

In the case of executive compensation, our giant institutional manager/agents seem particularly reluctant to take on this issue. By failing to do so, they must assume at least partial responsibility for the extraordinarily high salaries, bonuses, deferred compensation, stock options, and other compensation to corporate CEOs and their highest-ranking fellow officers. Compensation has simply flown "off the wheels" in the recent era, and the numbers, it seems to me, have gotten totally out of hand.

How high are these compensation levels and wealth levels for CEOs? We can thank the *New York Times* for its annual survey of the compensation of chief executives of 200 companies with at least $5 billion of revenue, published in April 2012. The median compensation of the 15 highest paid CEOs was $30 million.

The next 15 CEOs all received compensation in the $18 million to $22 million range, and the lowest among the top 50 received $11 million. The median compensation for the 100 highest-paid CEOs was $14.4 million, 320 times the average American salary of $45,230. Ironically, if CEOs are able to increase profits by holding the lid on the compensation of their workers, they win and their millions of employees who produce what the company makes and sells are the losers.

That 320:1 ratio of the compensation of CEOs relative to the average worker's pay in 2011 contrasts with a ratio of just 42:1 in 1980. Over that 30-year span, CEO compensation measured in nominal dollars rose nearly 16 times over that of the average worker, while the compensation of the average worker slightly more than doubled. Measured in real 1980 dollars, CEO compensation rose at a rate of 6.5 percent annually, increasing by more than 560 percent in real terms during the period. In comparison, the compensation of the average worker increased by only 0.7 percent per year, leading to an insignificant cumulative increase (compounded over 30 years, an increase of only 14 percent) in family living standards. I find this change shocking, and virtually inexplicable.

"Were CEOs Actually Creating Value Commensurate with This Huge Increase in Compensation?"

The rationale of today's ratio is that these executives had "created wealth" for their shareholders. But were CEOs actually creating value commensurate with this huge increase in compensation? Certainly the average CEO was not. During the past 24 years, corporations had projected their earnings growth at an average annual rate of 11.5 percent. But they actually delivered growth of 6 percent per year—only half of their goal, and even less than the 6.2 percent nominal growth rate of the economy. In real terms, profits grew at an annual rate of just 2.9 percent, compared to 3.1 percent for our nation's economy, as represented by the gross domestic product. How that somewhat dispiriting lag can drive average CEO compensation to a cool $9.8 million in 2004, and then to $11.4 million in 2010, is one of the great anomalies of the age.

Executive Stock Options—"Heads I Win, Tails You Lose"

Much of the corporate executive compensation and wealth has been created by the "heads I win, tails you lose" nature of stock options. The share dilution by these options is often kept within seemingly reasonable limits, within 2 percent to 3 percent of shares outstanding each year, often offset by the company's repurchase of a number of shares equal to those issued to executives. But limited attention seems to be paid to cumulative dilution over the years, which comes to staggering levels—perhaps as much as 25 percent or more over a decade. However, I have been unable to find a single governance study or academic paper on the overpowering significance of such dilution over time.

Another explanation given for soaring CEO compensation is that it merely reflects the enormous (and increasingly public) compensation paid to star athletes, entertainment personalities, and movie stars. Such comparisons are irrelevant and absurd. These celebrities are essentially paid by their fans, or the owners of teams or networks, out of their own pockets. But CEOs are paid by directors, not out of their own pockets but with other people's money. Corporate directors are the agents of the shareholders, but whether they are acting in shareholders' best interests is another matter. This agency problem—yet another agency problem—permeates corporate governance, and bears a major responsibility for the rise in CEO compensation.

Compensation Consultants and the Ratchet Effect

The rise of the executive compensation consultant is also heavily responsible for our flawed system of CEO compensation. First, consider what those in the business of recommending executive compensation must do to stay in business: lots of good analysis, yes; handsome presentations, yes; persuasiveness, of course. But above all, never recommend lower pay or tougher standards for CEO compensation, not if you want to be in business for long. To make matters worse, the well-known methodology of consultants—grouping CEOs into peer groups measured in quartiles—inevitably leads to a ratchet effect.

Here's how it works: When a board finds that its own CEO's pay reposes in the fourth quartile, it is all too likely to raise his or her compensation to bring it into, say, the second quartile. (Directors rarely seem to jump it all the way to the first quartile.) This leap, of course, drops another CEO into the fourth quartile. Eventually, he'll be moved to a higher quartile, too. And so the cycle repeats, onward and upward over the years, almost always with the encouragement of an ostensibly impartial overseer retained by the board of directors, who is at least tacitly endorsed by the CEO. So the so-called free market that sets CEO compensation doesn't exist. Rather, it is a controlled market that is essentially created by compensation consultants.[13]

A Fundamentally Flawed Methodology

Such a methodology is fundamentally flawed, and has the obvious effect: The figures in these compensation grids almost always go up for the group, and almost never go down. Again, Warren Buffett pointedly describes the typical consulting firm by naming it, tongue in cheek, "Ratchet, Ratchet, and Bingo." This name calls attention to the lottery that executives cannot lose when they receive stock options: Stock up, exercise the option; stock down, forget it. Until we pay CEOs on the basis of corporate performance rather than on the basis of corporate peer groups, CEO pay will, almost inevitably, continue on its upward path.[14]

---

13. There ought to be a word for such a perverse market anomaly. Not a monopoly, not an oligopoly, but perhaps "consultopoly" would do the job.

14. An idea for improvement: Require that the quartiles into which CEOs fall are consistent with the quartiles in which the success of their firms is measured. (Performance would be measured not by stock price performance, but by return on the firm's total capital.) Perhaps such a comparison would help to halt the perpetual motion machine that executive compensation has become.

I must add that one reason that our very highly paid institutional managers have basically been inert in challenging the astounding compensation of our also very highly paid corporate managers may well be that these money managers themselves are so highly paid. Finally, most of these large money management firms are in fact owned and controlled by other publicly held corporations. ("If the CEO of the parent of my money manager is up there at the top, how can I vote against similar compensation for one of the corporations in my portfolio?") The obvious conflict involved in this circular ownership pattern in which one hand washes the other ought to hold a high priority among the emerging issues of the coming decade.

What's to Be Done About Executive Compensation?

What's to be done? First, CEO compensation should be based on the building of long-term and enduring intrinsic value, which is as real as it is imprecise. (Now there's a paradox!) Yes, stock prices correlate nicely with business results, but only over the very long run. In the short term, the correlation seems random at best. Simply put, stock prices are a flawed measure of corporate performance. Using Lord Keynes's classic formulation, the level of stock prices involves both enterprise—the yield on an investment over the long term—and speculation— betting on the psychology of the market. I argued for the ultimate validity of the triumph of enterprise 60 years ago. Today, I continue to opt for the preeminence of enterprise.

During the 1980s and 1990s, for example, earnings of the corporations in the S&P 500 grew at about 5.9 percent a year, well below their growth rate of 7.7 percent during the previous two decades. Yet stocks performed well during that period, simply because the price-earnings multiple on the S&P 500 soared from 8 times to 32 times, adding about 7.5 percent per year of speculative return to stock prices. Obviously, this outcome was a nonrecurring event that, compounded, dwarfed the actual earnings growth rate. That is, high stock performance generated by higher stock market valuations led to high pay. Short-term emotions-based market madness played a critical role in the "lottery effect" that underlies stock options. It suggests, at the absolute minimum, that options prices should be adjusted to reflect changes in the general level of stock prices, as measured by, say, the S&P 500 Index.

Basing compensation on increasing the intrinsic value of a business would be a far better way of rewarding executives for durable long-term performance. For example, CEO compensation might be based on corporate earnings growth—or even better, corporate cash flow, which is far more difficult to manipulate—and dividend growth, or return on total corporate capital (not only equity capital)—both relative to the company's peers and relative to corporations as a group, say, the S&P 500. Such returns should be measured only over an extended period of time, but only after deducting the corporation's cost of capital.

Consider the Cost of Capital

Yet this return on capital is a concept rarely, if ever, considered in compensation plans. But it must not be ignored. The corporation should set a sort of hurdle rate that takes into account the firm's cost of capital. Even if it is set at a relatively modest annual rate—say, 8 percent— executives should be paid only for returns in excess of that rate. If a corporation has, say, $1 billion of capital, it ought to earn at least an 8 percent return, or $80 million. Until that target is reached, no bonuses and no options. Compensation should be paid only on profits in excess of that return on corporate capital. Of course, these standards are challenging, but meeting tough competitive standards is what real business success is all about.

It is now obvious that CEO compensation should have a contingent component, and a durable one. Incentive pay should be spread out over an extended period of years, and stock options should be phased in as well. For example, say,

50 percent of options should be exercisable on the first exercise date, with 10 percent exercisable annually over the subsequent five years. The acquired holdings would be mandated to be held for a significant time, perhaps until the executive leaves the firm. There should also be claw-back provisions for returning incentive compensation to the company if earnings are restated. (I had understood that Section 304 of the Sarbanes-Oxley Act provided effective claw-back provisions for equity-based executive compensation when restatements occur. However, such claw-backs are limited to restatements resulting from "misconduct," and the SEC has yet to pursue a single case.)

Slight Progress on Reform— The Dodd-Frank Wall Street Reform and Consumer Protection Act of 2010

One important step is now being taken. Significantly, it is not at the behest of our institutional money managers, but by Congress. The Dodd-Frank Wall Street Reform and Consumer Protection Act of 2010 provides a mandate for all public corporations to allow nonbinding shareholder votes on executive compensation. Its implementation costs will be relatively modest, and it will force institutional shareholders to consider compensation issues with greater care—a nice step forward. Anything that draws the institutional owners who now control corporate America into acting as responsible corporate citizens should benefit our society at large.

Yet even though the first proxy season allowing the so-called say-on-pay votes at all public companies took place in the spring of 2011, little seems to have changed. Later that year, in July, the *Wall Street Journal* reported that shareholders rejected their firms' executive compensation plans at only 39 of 2,532 companies. (Proxy adviser Institutional Shareholder Services had recommended votes against executive pay for 298 firms.) Some 71 percent of companies received at least 90 percent of shareholder votes in favor of their executive compensation practices.

Why such an overwhelming agreement? There were two apparent reasons. One, many companies enhanced disclosure in their compensation discussion and analysis statements, providing a clearer view of their compensation philosophy and the metrics used to make compensation decisions, giving shareholders a better understanding of the issues. Two, many companies engaged in dialogue with their largest shareholders to understand the factors institutional shareholders use to evaluate executive compensation, and presumably persuaded them of their fairness.

But it's not at all clear that say-on-pay voting will slow the rise of executive compensation. Robert A. G. Monks was quoted as saying "say-on-pay is at best a diversion and at worst a deception. You only have the appearance of reform, and it's a cruel hoax." Lynn Turner, former chief accountant of the SEC, noted the conflict of interest that mutual funds have as they try to attract corporate 401(k) clients, saying that the big fund companies "won't vote against management proposals on compensation unless they're really bad."[15] Interestingly, the giant California State Teachers Retirement Systems (CalSTRS), which faces no comparable conflict of interest, voted against management compensation fully 23 percent of the time.

Corporate Political Contributions and the Flawed *Citizens United* Decision

Another major emerging issue on corporate governance relates to political contributions. Particularly in the face of the Supreme Court's decision in the landmark 2011 *Citizens United* case that opened the door to virtually unlimited political contributions by our corporations, this may well be the hot issue of the 2012 proxy season. So far, the political contribution question is in the process of being resolved by voluntary corporate disclosure of such contributions, a result of enlightened self-interest by corporate managers and the demand by some institutional investors to make such disclosure mandatory.

---

15. On April 18, 2012, Citigroup shareholders voted to reject the management's pay package proposal, a stinging rebuke that was the first such vote to reject the compensation plan at a once-near-failed financial giant. Some 55 percent of shareholders voted against the nonbinding plan.

"Mere Disclosure May Not Be Enough"

Mere disclosure, however, may not be enough. Investors should be raising the issue of whether any contributions whatsoever should be allowed without the approval of shareholders. Unlike the executive compensation issue, where the standards were established by the SEC early in 2011, the Commission has as yet made no attempt to establish appropriate and uniform standards for voting on disclosure of political contributions. I believe that the SEC must promptly do exactly that.

In November 2011, a coalition of asset managers and investment professionals representing over \$690 billion in assets wrote to the SEC to express their strong support for the proposition that the SEC promulgate rules requiring corporate political transparency. (However, not a single major mutual fund manager joined in this plea.) Since there are significant gaps in the type of spending that is required to be disclosed, they asked the SEC for clear rules on full disclosure by all public companies on their political expenditures. The Council for Institutional Investors seconded the motion:

> Shareowners have a right to know whether and how their company uses its resources for political purposes. Yet the existing regulatory framework creates barriers to this information. Disclosure is either dispersed among several regulatory authorities or entirely absent in cases where political spending is channeled through independent organizations exempt from naming donors.

As one state treasurer added: "It is troubling that many companies are funding political campaigns without their shareholders' consent or even knowledge."

For all its faults, the *Citizens United* ruling upheld the disclosure requirements of the campaign financing law. I had hoped that full disclosure might limit corporate contributions. But in fact, corporations are now able to exploit provisions in the law that enable nonprofit groups to make lavish political contributions without any disclosure. This shocking loophole has made it easier than ever for mountains of cash—spent on lobbying, attack ads, and advocacy ads that are theoretically uncoordinated with a candidate's own campaign—to subvert our political system, and indeed the national interest. Action to limit contributions at the corporate level is therefore urgent.

"The Procedures of Corporate Democracy"

Indeed, the Supreme Court itself put the onus on shareholders to control corporate political giving. In his opinion for the majority in *Citizens United*, Justice Anthony M. Kennedy predicated the First Amendment right of free speech on the ability of shareholders to ensure that corporate speech, as it were, reflects their views, rather than diverting corporate assets for the benefit of executives. He suggested that any abuse could be corrected by shareholders "through the procedures of corporate democracy."

Well, corporate democracy is on the way. The critical battle over political spending by corporations has been joined. For the first time, the financial institutions—not only mutual funds, but pension funds and other large institutional investors—that now hold absolute control over corporate America will have to stand up and be counted. The ballots on mandatory disclosure of corporate political contributions and on shareholder approval of corporate contributions are appearing on the 2012 proxies of many companies. They have passed SEC review, so now our powerful institutional money managers will have to vote yes or no.

It seems logical to me that, if and when institutional investors vote against corporate political contributions, they will have to forswear such contributions by their own firms. Entering the fray "with clean hands" would seem mandatory.[16]

---

16. That will not happen easily. Fidelity, one of the largest mutual fund managers, recently disclosed a total of more than $5 million in political contributions from its organization during 2011.

"Will Agents Put the Interests of Their Principals First?"

Once again, however, given that a huge portion of our largest money management firms are either publicly held or controlled by publicly held financial conglomerates, these clean hands will take a lot of scrubbing. Will these agents put the interests of their principals first? Or will their own interests come first? We shall see.

Since 2004, the SEC has mandated that our nation's mutual fund agents break their silence and disclose to their principals how they have voted. But in terms of being active participants in corporate governance, the silence of nearly all mutual funds remains. The same silence also emanates from pension funds and their managers. With critical issues like executive compensation and political contributions now in the spotlight, it is high time for fund managers to stand up and be counted on the controversial issues of the day. They also must break their long silence and actually make their own proposals, demanding that they be placed in corporate proxies. I see these steps toward greater activism in corporate governance by our giant investor/agents who represent the shareholder/principals as essential to sound long-term investing, to our system of modern capitalism, and to the national interest. The mutual fund industry should be in the, well, vanguard of this movement.

CHAPTER 11: WHAT WENT WRONG IN CORPORATE AMERICA?[17]

As so many of us have read in the gospel of Matthew: "A prophet is not without honor, save in his own country." Yet by your invitation to speak to you this evening you honor me, even as I stand here in my own country! I live right down the road

---

17. Based on my lecture at the Community Forum Distinguished Speaker Series of the Bryn Mawr (Pennsylvania) Presbyterian Church, February 24, 2003. Also published as Chapter 6 of *Don't Count on It!* (2011).

from this great church, and for the better part of a half-century have regularly attended Sunday worship services in the thrall of such extraordinary preachers as David Watermulder and Eugene Bay, who have helped me beyond measure in gaining enlightenment, inspiration, and faith.

"It's Business, Business, Business" in the "Bottom-Line Society"

While my remarks center on what went wrong in corporate America, being in this sanctuary compels me to begin with some words from the teacher Joseph Campbell: "In medieval times, as you approached the city, your eye was taken by the Cathedral. Today, it's the towers of commerce. It's business, business, business."[18] We have become what Campbell calls "a bottom-line society." But our society, I think, is measuring the wrong bottom line: form over substance, prestige over virtue, money over achievement, charisma over character, the ephemeral over the enduring.

I'm sure it does not escape you that Joseph Campbell's analogy proved to be ominous. We have now witnessed the total destruction of the proudest of all America's towers of commerce, at New York's World Trade Center. We have seen a $7 trillion collapse of the aggregate market value of America's corporations—from $17 trillion to $10 trillion, in the worst stock market crash since 1929–1933. And we've seen the reputations of business leaders transmogrified from mighty lions of corporate success to self-serving and less-than-trustworthy executives, with several even doing "perp walks" for the television cameras.

Our bottom-line society has a good bit to answer for. As the United Kingdom's Chief Rabbi Jonathan Sacks put it: "When everything that matters can be bought and sold, when commitments can be broken because they are no longer to our advantage, when shopping becomes salvation and advertising slogans

---

18. Quoted in Warren G. Bennis, "Will the Legacy Live On?" *Harvard Business Review*, February 1, 2002, 95.

become our litany, when our worth is measured by how much we earn and spend, then the market is destroying the very virtues on which in the long run it depends."[19]

So let's think about what went wrong in our capitalistic system, about what's now beginning to go right, and about what investors can do as a part-owner of corporate America. Whether you own a common stock or a share in a mutual fund, or participate in a private retirement plan, you have a personal interest in bringing about reform. Both as shareholders and as citizens, each of us must accept the responsibility to build a better corporate world.

Capitalism—A Brief Review

Capitalism, *Webster's Third International Dictionary* tells us, is "an economic system based on corporate ownership of capital goods, with investment determined by private decision, and with prices, production, and the distribution of goods and services determined mainly in a free market." Importantly, I would add, "a system founded on honesty, decency, and trust," for these attributes, too, have been clearly established in its history.

As the world moved from an agrarian society to an industrial society during the eighteenth and nineteenth centuries, capitalism came to flourish. Local communities became part of national (and then international) commerce, trading expanded, and large accumulations of capital were required to build the factories, transportation systems, and banks on which the new economy would depend. Surprising as it may seem, at the heart of this development, according to an article in *Forbes*'s recent 85th Anniversary issue,[20] were the Quakers. In the 1700s and early 1800s, probably because their legendary simplicity and thrift endowed them with

---

19. Jonathan Sacks, *Morals and Markets*, 1998 Hayek Lecture (London: Institute of Economic Affairs, 1998).
20. James Surowiecki, "A Virtuous Cycle," *Forbes*, December 23, 2002.

the capital to invest, they dominated the British economy, owners of more than half of the country's ironworks and key players in banking, consumer goods, and transatlantic trading. Their emphasis on reliability, absolute honesty, and rigorous record-keeping gave them trust as they dealt with one another, and other observant merchants came to see that being trustworthy went hand in hand with business success. Self-interest, in short, demanded virtue.

Adam Smith's "Invisible Hand"

This evolution, of course, is exactly what the great Scottish economist/philosopher Adam Smith expected. Writing in *The Wealth of Nations* in 1776, he famously said, "The uniform and uninterrupted effort to better his condition, the principle from which (both) public and private opulence is originally derived, is frequently powerful enough to maintain the natural progress of things toward improvement. . . . Each individual neither intends to promote the public interest, nor knows how much he is promoting it . . . [but] by directing his industry in such a matter as its produce may be of the greatest value, *he is led by an invisible hand to promote an end which was no part of his intention.*"

And so it was to be, the *Forbes* essay continued, that "the evolution of capitalism has been in the direction of more trust and transparency and less self-serving behavior. Not coincidentally, this evolution has brought with it greater productivity and economic growth. Not because capitalists are naturally good people, [but] because, the benefits of trust—of being trusting and of being trustworthy—are potentially immense, and because a successful market system teaches people to recognize those benefits . . . a virtuous circle in which an everyday level of trustworthiness breeds an everyday level of trust." The system *works*!

Or at least it *did* work. And then something went wrong. The system changed—"a pathological mutation in capitalism," as an essay in the *International*

Herald Tribune[21] described it. The classic system—owners' capitalism—had been based on a dedication to serving the interests of the corporation's owners in maximizing the return on their capital investment. But a new system developed—managers' capitalism—in which "the corporation came to be run to profit its managers, in complicity if not conspiracy with accountants and the managers of other corporations." Why did it happen? "Because," the author says, "the markets had so diffused corporate ownership *that no responsible owner exists*. This is morally unacceptable, but also a corruption of capitalism itself."

From Virtuous Circle to Vicious Circle?

What caused the mutation from virtuous circle to vicious circle? It's easy to call it a failure of character, a triumph of hubris and greed over honesty and integrity. And it's even easier to lay it all to just a few bad apples. But while only a tiny minority of our business and financial leaders have been implicated in criminal behavior, I'm afraid that the barrel itself—the very structure that holds all those apples— is bad. While that may seem a harsh indictment, I believe it is a fair one. Consider that *Predators and Profits*, a 2003 book by Reuters editor Martin Howell, lists fully 176(!) "red flags," each of which describes a particular shortcoming in our recent business, financial, and investment practices, many of which I've witnessed with my own eyes.

It is now crystal-clear that our capitalistic system—as all systems sometimes do—has experienced a profound failure, a failure with a whole variety of root causes, each interacting and reinforcing the other: the stock market mania, driven by the idea that we were in a New Era; the notion that our corporations were trees that could grow not only to the sky but beyond; the rise of the imperial chief executive

---

21. William Pfaff, September 9, 2002.

"The Great Bull Market Had a Thousand Fathers, but the Great Bear Market Seems To Be an Orphan"

officer; the failure of our gatekeepers—those auditors, regulators, legislators, and boards of directors who forgot to whom they owed their loyalty; the change in our financial institutions from being stock *owners* to being stock *traders*; the hype of Wall Street's stock promoters; the frenzied excitement of the media; and, of course, the eager and sometimes greedy members of the investing public, reveling in the easy wealth that seemed like a cornucopia, at least while it lasted. There is plenty of blame to go around. But even as it drove stock prices up, this happy conspiracy among all of the interested parties drove business standards down. Yes, the victory of investors in the Great Bull Market had a thousand fathers. But the defeat in the Great Bear Market that followed seems to be an orphan.

If we had to name a *single* father of the bubble, we would hardly need a DNA test to do so. *That father is executive compensation, made manifest in the fixed-price stock option.* When executives are paid for raising the price of their company's stock rather than for increasing their company's value, they don't need to be told what to do: Achieve strong, steady earnings growth and tell Wall Street about it. Set "guidance" targets with public pronouncements of your expectations, and then meet your targets—and do it consistently, without fail. First, do it the old-fashioned way, by increasing volumes, cutting costs, raising productivity, bringing in technology, and developing new products and services. Then, when *making it and doing it* isn't enough, meet your goals by *counting it*, pushing accounting principles to their very edge. And when that isn't enough, cheat. As we now know, too many firms did exactly that.

The stated rationale for fixed-price stock options is that they "link the interests of management with the interests of shareholders." That turns out to be a falsehood. For managers don't *hold* the shares they acquire. They *sell* them, and promptly. Academic studies indicate that nearly *all* stock options are exercised as soon as they vest, and the stock is sold *immediately*. Indeed, the term *cashless exercise*—where the firm purchases the stock for the executive, sells it, and is repaid when the proceeds of the sale are delivered—became commonplace. (Happily, it is no longer legal.) We have rewarded our executives, not for long-term economic reality, but for short-term market perception.

Creating Wealth— for Management

Even if executives were required to hold their stock for an extended period, however, stock options are fundamentally flawed. They are not adjusted for the cost of capital, providing a free ride even for executives who produce only humdrum returns. They do not take into account dividends, so there is a perverse incentive to avoid paying them. Stock options reward the *absolute* performance of a stock rather than performance *relative* to peers or to a stock market index, so executive compensation tends to be like a lottery, creating unworthy centimillionaires in bull markets and eliminating rewards even for worthy performers in bear markets.

While these issues could be resolved by the use of restricted stock, or by raising the option price each year, or by linking the stock performance with a market index, such sensible programs were almost never used. Why? Because those alternative schemes require corporations to count the cost as an *expense*. (Heaven forbid!) The cost of fixed-price options alone is conspicuous by its absence on the company's expense statement. As the compensation consultants are wont to say, these stock options are "free."

The net result of the granting of huge options to corporate managers, all the while overstating earnings by ignoring them as an expense, is that total executive compensation went through the roof. In the early 1980s, the compensation of the average chief executive officer was 42 times that of the average worker; by the year 2000, the ratio had soared to 531(!) times. The rationale was that these executives had "created wealth" for their shareholders. But if we actually *measure* the success of corporate America, it's hard to see how that could be the case. During that two-decade period, while corporations had *projected* their earnings growth at an average annual rate of 11.5 percent, they actually delivered growth of 6 percent per year—only half of their goal, and even less than the 6.5 percent growth rate of our economy. How that lag can be the stuff to drive *average* CEO compensation to a cool $11 million in 2001 is one of the great anomalies of the age.

Examples That Prove the Point

The fact is that the executives had "created wealth" for themselves, but not for their share owners. And when the stock market values melted away, they had long since sold much of their stock. Let me give you a few examples:

- *AOL Time Warner*. In an extraordinary example of the delusions of grandeur that characterized the Information Age, the news of this marriage of the New Economy and the Old Economy as 2000 began sent the price of Time Warner soaring to a then-all-time high of $90 per share. But AOL's revenues began to tumble almost immediately, and the company recently reported losses totaling $98 billion(!). But in the first three years, the founder of AOL (and the chairman of the merged company) sold nearly *one-half billion dollars'* worth of his shares, mostly at boom-level prices. Today, the stock languishes at $10, down almost 90 percent from the high.
- *Sprint*. When they agreed to merge with WorldCom in October 1999, the directors accelerated the vesting of its executives' stock options. Although the merger scheme quickly fell apart, two senior executives quickly sold $290 million of their optioned shares at prices apparently in the $60 range. They also paid the firm's auditors $5.8 million(!) for a clever plan to circumvent the tax laws and pay not a penny of tax on these gains. (Yet! The IRS is now challenging the tax-evasion device.) Today, Sprint sells at about $13 per share, down 83 percent from its high.

• *General Electric.* While clearly a blue-chip company, the price of its shares has dropped from $60 to $23 per share since August 2000, a cool $370 billion reduction in its market value. Amid growing investor concern about its tendency to smooth its reported earnings by "creative accounting" practices, its once-legendary leader, Jack Welch, is not looking so good lately. Yet his total compensation from 1997 through 2000 came to nearly $550 million, plus another $200 million from the sale of option shares, some at prices of $55 or more. Now retired, he is still well paid: a pension of $357,000, plus another $377,000 for consulting services, a total of $734,000—*per month*! (He must enjoy an expensive lifestyle that leaves little to spare, for a recent report placed his monthly charitable giving at just $614.) Such is the world of executive compensation in corporate America today.

Clearly, *owners'* capitalism had been superseded by *managers'* capitalism, and managers' capitalism has created great distortions in our society. And chief executives, with all their fame, their jet planes, their perquisites, their pension plans, their club dues, and their Park Avenue apartments, seem to forget that they are employees of the corporation's owners, and the owners apparently have forgotten it, too. But their behavior has not gone unnoticed. They are now close to the bottom of the barrel in public trust. A recent survey showed that while 75 percent of the general public trust shopkeepers, 73 percent trust the military, and 60 percent trust doctors, only 25 percent trust corporate executives, slightly above the 23 percent that trust used-car dealers.

The Failure of the Gatekeepers

What happened? How did it all come to pass? Basically, we have had a failure of just about every gatekeeper we've traditionally relied on to make sure that corporations would be operated with honesty and integrity, and in the interests of their owners. Independent auditors became business partners of management. Government regulations were relaxed, and our elected officials not only didn't care, but actually aided and abetted the malfeasance. The elected representatives of the owners—the boards of directors—looked on the proceedings with benign neglect, apparently unmindful of the impending storm.

Pressure on Public Accountants to Accede to Management's Demands

Let's begin with our public accountants. It would seem obvious that they should have constituted the first line of defense against pushing accounting standards to the edge and beyond, and, hard as it may be to discover, at least some defense against fraud. But the accounting standards themselves had gradually become debased. "Cookie jar" reserves were created after corporate mergers, and off–balance sheet special-purpose enterprises flourished, creating debt invisible to the public eye and giving "financial engineering" a whole new meaning. Of course the pressure has always been on accountants to agree with the corporate clients who pay them for their services. But over the past decade, to that seemingly unavoidable conflict of interest has been added the conflict of being business partners with their clients, providing management consulting services whose revenues often dwarf their audit fees. In the year 2000, for example, U.S. corporations paid their auditors nearly $3 billion for auditing services, only one-half of the $6 billion paid for consulting.

This added pressure on accountants to accede to management's demands, coming as managers promised quarterly earnings growth that was impossible to deliver, led to a company's numbers becoming more important than a company's business—a direct contradiction to the advice given to his colleagues by James Anyon, America's first accountant, way back in 1912: "Think and act upon facts, truths, and principles, and regard figures only as things to express them . . . so proceeding, [you will be] a credit to one of the truest and finest professions in the land."[22] The

---

22. As quoted in David Boyle, *The Tyranny of Numbers* (London: HarperCollins, 2000), 8.

"creative accounting" of the recent era has taken us a long, long way from the wisdom of relying on figures to present facts.

On the regulatory and legislative front, our public servants were also pressed into relaxing existing regulations for accounting standards and disclosure. When proposals for reform came—for example, requiring that stock options *actually be counted* as a compensation expense, or prohibiting accountants from providing consulting services to the firms they audit—the outrage of our legislators, inspired (if that's the right word) both by political contributions and by the fierce lobbying efforts of both corporate America and the accounting profession, thwarted these long-overdue changes. Too many of our elected officials ought to be ashamed of themselves for their "play-for-pay" morality. Two centuries ago, Thomas Jefferson said, "I hope we shall crush in its birth the aristocracy of our monied corporations which dare already to challenge our government in a trial of strength, and bid defiance to the laws of our country." We didn't, of course, do so. But rather than defying our laws in this recent era of managers' capitalism, our monied corporations thwarted remedial legislation (it's a lot easier!), and compromised the highest interests of their investors.

The Mandate to the Board: Be Good Stewards of the Corporation's Property

That brings us to the board of directors. It is their job to be good stewards of the corporate property entrusted to them. In medieval England, the common use of the word *stewardship* meant the responsible use of a congregation's resources *in the faithful service of God*. In the corporate sense, the word has come to mean the use of the enterprise's resources in the faithful service of its owners. But somehow the system let us down. As boards of directors far too often turned over to the company's managers the virtually unfettered power to place their own interests first, both the word and the concept of stewardship became conspicuous by their absence from corporate America's values.

Reprise: Directors As "Rubber Stamps for Management"

Serving as rubber stamps for management, company directors have been responsible for approving option plans that are grossly excessive, audits in which the auditors are not independent appraisers of financial statements but partners of management, and mergers based on forcing the numbers rather than on improving the business. (As it turned out, according to *BusinessWeek*, 63 percent of all mergers have destroyed corporate value.) Directors also approved ethical codes in which words like "integrity," "trust," and "vision" were the order of the day, but corporate actions were another story. Some 60 percent of corporate employees, for example, report that they have observed violations of law or company policy at their firms, and 207 of 300 whistle-blowers report they have lost their jobs as a result.

Words Versus Deeds at Enron

Yet our society has lionized our boards of directors nearly as much as our vaunted CEOs. Early in 2001, for example, *Chief Executive* magazine told us that "dramatic improvements in corporate governance have swept through the American economic system, [thanks to] enlightened CEOs and directors who voluntarily put through so many [changes] designed to make the operations of boards more effective." In particular, the magazine praised a certain New Economy company, "with a board that works hard to keep up with things . . . and working committees with functional responsibilities where disinterested oversight is required," a company whose four highest values were stated as "Communication; Respect; Excellence; and Integrity—open, honest, and sincere. . . . We continue to raise the bar for everyone [because] the great fun here will be for all of us to discover just how good we can really be."[23] As it happens, we *do* now know just how good it could be: The company, so good that its board was named the third best among all of the thousands of boards in corporate America for 2000, is *bankrupt*. While

---

23. Robert W. Lear and Boris Yaritz, "Boards on Trial," *Chief Executive*, October 2000, 40.

its executives reaped billions in compensation, its employees are jobless, their retirement savings obliterated. Its reputation is shredded beyond repair. It was, of course, Enron.

The board of directors is the ultimate governing body of the corporation, and the directors are stewards charged with the responsibility of preserving and building the company over the long term. Yet the directors of corporate America couldn't have been unaware of the management's aggressive "earnings guidance"; nor of the focus on raising the price of the stock, never mind at what cost to the value of the corporation; nor of the fact that the lower the dividend, the more capital the company retains; nor that it was management that hired the consultants who recommended to the compensation committee higher compensation for that very same management, year after year, even when its actual accomplishments in building the business were hardly out of the ordinary. Surely it is fair to say that it is our corporate directors who should bear the ultimate responsibility for what went wrong with corporate America.

Oh No, the Board Shouldn't Bear the Ultimate Responsibility

Or should they? Why should the board bear the ultimate responsibility when it doesn't *have* the ultimate responsibility? Of course the directors' responsibility is large, indeed, but it is the stockholders themselves who bear the *ultimate* responsibility for corporate governance. And as investing has become institutionalized, stockholders have gained the *real*—as compared with the *theoretical*—power to exercise their will. Once owned largely by a diffuse and inchoate group of individual investors, each one with relatively modest holdings, today the ownership of stocks is concentrated—for better or worse—among a remarkably small group of institutions whose potential power is truly awesome. The 100 largest managers of pension funds and mutual funds alone now represent the ownership of one-half of all U.S. equities: *absolute control over corporate America*. Together, these 100 large institutional investors constitute the great 800-pound gorilla who can sit wherever he wants to sit at the board table.

But with all that power has come little interest in corporate governance. That amazing disconnection between the potential and the reality—awesome power, yet largely unexercised—reminds me of the original version of the motion picture *Mighty Joe Young*. In the film, the protagonist was a fierce gorilla who destroyed every object in his path. But whenever he heard the strains of "Beautiful Dreamer" he became serene and compliant. Not to push this analogy too far—especially for those who have not seen the film!—but I fear that, as institutional managers consider their responsibility for good corporate citizenship, they are hearing the sweet strains of "Beautiful Dreamer" playing in the background.

Worshiping at the Altar of Ephemeral Stock Prices

Yet mutual fund managers could hardly have been ignorant of what was going on in corporate America. Even before the stock market bubble burst, the industry's well-educated, highly trained, experienced professional analysts and portfolio managers must have been poring over company fiscal statements; evaluating corporate plans; and measuring the extent to which long-term corporate goals were being achieved, how cash flow compared with reported earnings, and the extent to which those ever-fallacious "pro forma" earnings diverged from the reality. Yet few, if any, voices were raised. Somehow, our professional investors either didn't understand, or understood but ignored, the house of cards that the stock market had become. We have worshiped at the altar of the precise but ephemeral price of the stock, forgetting that the eternal sovereign is the intrinsic value of the corporation—simply the discounted value of its future cash flows.

An Own-a-Stock Industry Becomes A Rent-a-Stock Industry

We have yet to accept our responsibility for our abject failure, for the fact is that we have become, not an *own-a-stock* industry, but a *rent-a-stock* industry. During the past year, for example, the average equity fund turned over its portfolio at a 110 percent rate—meaning that the average stock was held for just *11 months*.

When a company's stock may not even remain in a fund's portfolio by the time the company's next annual meeting rolls around, proxy voting and responsible corporate citizenship will rarely be found on the fund manager's agenda. What is more, money managers may avoid confrontation because even valid corporate activism could hurt the manager's ability to attract the assets of a corporation's pension account and 401(k) thrift plan, or limit its analysts' access to corporate information. Further, despite convincing information to the contrary, fund managers generally perceive only tenuous linkage between governance and stock price. But for whatever reason, the record clearly shows that the stock owners themselves—and especially the mutual fund industry—pay only sparse attention to corporate governance issues. "We have met the enemy, and he is us."

Actions and Reactions—The Stock Market Up 100%, then Down 50%

As Sir Isaac Newton said, "for every action there is an equal and opposite reaction," and the reaction to the stock market boom and the mismanagement of so many of our corporations, to state the obvious, is already upon us. The first reaction to the bull market, of course, was the bear market that holds us in its throes to this day. The stock market, having quickly doubled from the start of 1997 to the high in March 2000, then dropped by half through mid-October 2002. That combination of percentages—plus 100 percent, then minus 50 percent—of course produces a net gain of *zero*. (Think about it!) But with the modest recovery that then ensued, stocks are just 10 percent higher than their levels were when 1997 began.

The sharp decline, it seems to me, has brought us back to (or at least toward) normalcy in valuation. And even *after* the Great Bear Market, the return on stocks during 1982 through 2002 averaged 13 percent per year, surely an attractive outcome for long-term stock owners. Through the miracle of compounding, those who owned stocks in 1982 and still held them in 2002 had multiplied that capital *10 times* over. So for all of the stock market's wild and woolly extremes, *owners* who bought and held common stocks have been well compensated for the risks they assumed. For such investors, the coming of the bubble and then its going—the *boom* and then the *bust*—simply did not matter.

The Winners—Entrepreneurs, Corporate Executives, Wall Street Insiders

But that doesn't mean there weren't winners and losers during the mania—and lots of both. Simply put, the winners were those who *sold* their stocks in the throes of the halcyon era that is now history. The losers were those who bought them. Let's think first about the winners. A large proportion of these shares that were sold were those of corporate executives who had acquired vast holdings of their companies' stocks through options, and those of entrepreneurs whose companies had gone newly public as Wall Street investment banking firms underwrote huge volumes of initial stock offerings, many already defunct. *Fortune* magazine recently identified a group of executives in just 25 corporations in those categories, whose total share of sales came to $23 billion—nearly a billion dollars each.

Other winners included the financial intermediaries—investment bankers and brokers who sold the high-flying stocks to their clients, and mutual fund managers who sold more than *half a trillion*(!) dollars in speculative funds to the public. Why were they winners? Because the investment banking, brokerage, and management fees for their activities reached staggering levels. More than a few individual investment bankers saw their annual compensation reach well into the tens of millions, and at least a half-dozen owners of fund management companies accumulated personal wealth in the billion-dollar range, including one family said to be at the $30 billion level.

The Losers—The Great American Public

The losers, of course, were those who *bought* the stocks. "Greater fools"? Perhaps. But paradoxically, in order to avoid the dilution in their earnings that would otherwise have resulted from issuing those billions of optioned shares, the very corporations that issued those shares at dirt-cheap prices bought them back at the inflated prices of the day. But most of the buying came from the great American public—often in their personal accounts, and often through ever more popular 401(k) thrift plans—sometimes *directly*, by buying individual stocks; sometimes *indirectly*, through mutual funds. Greed, naïveté, the absence of common sense, and aggressive salesmanship all played a role in the rush to buy speculative stocks—technology, the Internet, telecommunications—that were part of the "New Economy." During the peak two years of the bubble, $425 billion of investor capital flowed into mutual funds favoring those types of speculative growth stocks, and $40 billion actually flowed out of those stodgy "Old Economy" value funds.

Clearly there was a massive transfer of wealth—a transfer, I believe, of as much as $2 trillion—during the late bubble, from public investors to corporate insiders and financial intermediaries. Such transfers, of course, are not without parallel all through human history. For whenever *speculation* takes precedence over *investment*, there is always a day of reckoning for the investors in the financial markets.

Fixing the Governance System

It's important to understand this history of what went wrong in corporate America and its impact on our financial markets, because only if we understand the root causes can we consider how to remedy them. So as I promised at the outset, I'm going to discuss the progress that is being made to right those wrongs. Newton's law holds here as well, for the reaction to the failures of our capitalistic system was swift in coming. Surprisingly, however, it was not the generalized problems of pushy earnings, faulty accounting, hyped expectations, imperial executives, loose governance, excessive speculation, and even the Great Bear Market that were the catalysts for reform. Rather, it was a handful of scandals—those few "bad apples," including Enron, Adelphia, WorldCom, Global Crossing—that galvanized the public's attention and generated the powerful reaction that, at long last, will help to bring the reform we need in our financial markets.

A Swift Reaction

This pervasive reaction to the unacceptable actions of those we trusted to be our corporate stewards came swiftly.

- Last July, Congress passed the Sarbanes-Oxley bill, requiring senior corporate managers to attest to the validity of their companies' financial statements, providing for disgorgement of profits by executives who sell stocks and later restate earnings, and replacing self-regulation of accountants with a new federal Public Company Accounting Oversight Board, as well as other salutary provisions.
- In August, the New York Stock Exchange approved a powerful set of corporate governance rules for its listed companies—most of the major corporations in America—including substantially greater director independence, and new standards for audit committees and compensation committees. It even contemplated a "lead director" who is independent of corporate management. These changes should at long last lead to a separation of the powers of governance from the powers of management, and help us to return to a system of owners' capitalism.
- Just last month, The Conference Board Blue-Ribbon Commission on Public Trust and Private Enterprise—on which I was privileged to serve—completed its recommendations of a powerful set of best practices for public corporations. Our report on executive compensation included a recommendation that *all* types of stock options be treated as corporate expense, at last making it clear that fixed-price options are not free. On corporate governance, we recommended an *independent* nominating/governance committee; the establishment and enforcement of codes of ethics; and the separation of

the chairman and CEO roles, making clear the distinction between ownership and management. On accounting standards, our Commission's recommendations include further strengthening of audit committees and auditor rotation, and a challenge to the remaining Big Four (also known as the Final Four) accounting firms to focus on quality audits and to eliminate all consulting and tax services that involve advocacy positions, including those grotesque tax shelters designed so executives can circumvent the law.

"If Men Were Angels, We Wouldn't Need Government"

Two centuries ago, James Madison said, "If men were angels, we wouldn't need *government*." Today, I say to our corporate leaders, "If chief executives were angels, we wouldn't need *corporate governance*." Through the reactions of Congress, the New York Stock Exchange, and The Conference Board Commission, to say nothing of the media, we're on our way to getting better governance right now.

Astonishingly, however, the reaction of institutional investors to the failings of our system has yet to occur. Even after the bear market that devastated the value of our clients' equity holdings, the only response we've heard from the mutual fund industry is the sound of silence. The reason for that silence seems to be that the overwhelming majority of mutual funds continue to engage, not in the process of long-term investing on the basis of intrinsic corporate *values*, but in the process of short-term speculation based on momentary stock *prices*. The typical fund manager has lots of interest in a company's price momentum—its quarterly earnings and whether or not they are meeting the guidance given to Wall Street. But when it comes to what a company is actually worth—its fundamental earning power, its balance sheet, its long-term strategy, its intrinsic value—there seems to be far less interest. When Oscar Wilde described the cynic as "a man who knows the price of everything but the value of nothing," he could have as easily been talking about fund managers.

Fixing the Investment System

It must be clear that we need not only good *managers* of corporate America, but good *owners*. That goal will not be easy to accomplish. For it will require shareholders—especially institutional shareholders—to abandon the focus on short-term speculation that has characterized the recent era and return at last to a focus on long-term investment. We need to return to behaving as *owners* rather than as *traders*, to return to principles of prudence and trusteeship rather than of speculation and salesmanship, and to return to acting as good stewards of the assets entrusted to our care. For example:

- Institutions and individual investors must begin to act as responsible corporate citizens, voting our proxies thoughtfully and communicating our views to corporate managements. We should be prepared to nominate directors and make business proposals in proxies, and regulators should facilitate these actions. The SEC's recent decision to require mutual funds to disclose how we vote our proxies is a long-overdue first step in this process.
- Share owners must demand that corporations focus the information provided to the investment community on long-term financial goals, cash flows, intrinsic values, and strategic direction. Quarterly earnings guidance, so omnipresent today, should be *eliminated*. So should efforts to meet financial targets through creative accounting techniques.
- Given the enormous latitude accorded by generally accepted accounting principles, owners must demand full disclosure of the impact of significant accounting policy decisions. Indeed, we ought to consider requiring that corporations report earnings both on a "most aggressive" basis (presumably what they are reporting today) and on a "most conservative" basis as well.
- Mutual funds must report to their owners not only the direct costs of mutual fund investing (such as management fees and sales loads), but the *indirect*

Taxing Short-Term Gains, Even for Tax-Exempt Pension Funds

costs, including the costs of past and expected portfolio turnover and its attendant tax impact. Funds must also desist from advertising short-term investment performance (and perhaps from any performance advertising at all).

- Policy makers must develop differential tax strategies aimed at stemming excessive speculation. Some years ago, for example, Warren Buffett suggested a 100 percent tax on short-term capital gains, paid not only by taxable investors, *but also by tax-exempt pension funds*. While that tax rate *might* seem a tad extreme, perhaps a 50 percent tax on very short-term gains on trading stocks would force investors to come to their senses.

WORDS FROM THOSE WHO KNOW BOGLE BEST

Sir David Tweedie, chairman, International Accounting Standards Board

I am writing to a soul mate! I thoroughly enjoyed reading your views—what a pity your October 2000 speech at New York University wasn't compulsory reading for all professional investors. I just loved your comment "Please don't write off too hastily the possibility that the *model* may be right and the *market* might be wrong." We were accused of not showing the assets of dot-com companies on balance sheets. I think we did show the [actual] assets—the assets that the market believed in simply did not exist!

I fully agree with your views on "the happy conspiracy." We are also as one on your views of share options expensing and pensions (which reveal overoptimistic future yield assumptions). I found your views on corporate governance equally refreshing. Perhaps you should rechristen yourself "the fighting *Téméraire*."

August 2002

- Perhaps most important of all, investor/owners must demand that corporations step up their dividend payouts. Despite the absence of evidence that earnings retention leads to sound capital allocations, the payout rate has been declining for years. Yet history tells us that higher dividend payouts are actually associated with higher future returns on stocks. Investing for income is a *long-term* strategy, and investing for capital gains is a *short-term* strategy; the turnover of dividend-paying stocks is at but one-half of the rate for non-dividend-paying stocks.

"Back to the Future"— Returning to a Culture of Stewardship

Calling for a return to the eternal principles of long-term investing is more than mere moralizing. Our very society depends on it, for our economic growth depends upon capital formation. Way back in 1936, Lord Keynes warned us, "When enterprise becomes a mere bubble on a whirlpool of speculation, the position is serious. *For when the capital development of a country becomes a by-product of the activities of a casino, the job is likely to be ill-done.*"[24] As a nation we can't afford to let that happen. The fact is that we need a whole new mind-set for institutional investors, one in which *speculation* becomes a mere bubble on a whirlpool of *investment*. In the mutual fund industry, we need to go "back to the future," to return to our traditional focus on stewardship and abandon the focus on salesmanship that has dominated our recent history.

While the changes I have suggested will help return us to our roots, however, the fact remains that there is more profit potential for financial services firms in marketing (generating huge assets to manage) than in management. For, as both simple mathematics and the investment record of the past clearly indicate, beating the market is a loser's game, simply because of the staggering toll taken by the costs

---

24. John Maynard Keynes, *The General Theory of Employment, Interest, and Money* (1936; New York: Harcourt, Brace, 1964), 159.

of financial intermediation. When fund investors realize that fact, they will vote with their feet, and send their hard-earned dollars to funds that get the message. By doing so, using Adam Smith's metaphor, "it is the individual who acts in his own interests to better his financial condition who will promote the natural progress of things toward improvement." Similarly, when an investor puts his money into mutual funds that invest rather than speculate, he earns the highest possible proportion of whatever returns the financial markets are generous enough to provide (of course, we know them to be low-cost market index funds), promoting the public interest without intending to or even knowing he is doing so.

That doesn't mean, however, that the trusted fiduciary, the honest businessman, or the good merchant should behave in an ethical way only because their clients have dragged them, kicking and screaming, into doing what's right. The fact is, as I noted at the outset, that in the long run *good ethics are good business, part of that virtuous circle that builds our society*. When in recent years our rule of conduct became "I can get away with it," or, more charitably, "I can do it because everyone else is doing it," integrity and ethics go out the window and the whole idea of capitalism is soured.

Man's Better Nature, the Grandeur and Dignity of Our Character

If my appeal to man's better nature seems hopelessly out of tune with the discouraging era I've described this evening, I can only remind you that Adam Smith, that patron saint of capitalism, would be on my side. Even before *The Wealth of Nations*, he wrote *The Theory of Moral Sentiments*, reminding us of the better nature that

> has lighted up the human heart, capable of counteracting the strongest impulses of self-love. . . . It is reason, principle, conscience, the inhabitant of the breast, the man within, the great judge and arbitrator of our conduct who calls to us with a voice capable of astonishing the most presumptuous of our passions that we are of the

multitude, in no respect better than any other in it . . . he who shows us the propriety of reining in the greatest interests of our own for the yet greater interests of others, the love of what is honorable and noble, of the grandeur, and dignity, and superiority of our characters.[25]

At last we are beginning a wave of reform in corporate governance and are undertaking the task of turning America's capital development process away from speculation and toward enterprise. It will be no mean task. For there's even more at stake than improving the *practices* of governance and investing. We must also establish a higher set of *principles*. This nation's founding fathers believed in high moral standards, in a just society, and in the virtuous conduct of our affairs. Those beliefs shaped the very character of our nation. If *character counts*—and I have absolutely no doubt that character *does* count—the ethical failings of today's business and financial model, the financial manipulation of corporate America, the willingness of those of us in the field of investment management to accept practices that we know are wrong, the conformity that keeps us silent, the selfishness that lets our greed overwhelm our reason, all erode the character we'll require in the years ahead, more than ever in the wake of this Great Bear Market and the investor disenchantment it reflects.

The motivations of those who seek the rewards earned by engaging in commerce and finance struck the imagination of no less a man than Adam Smith as "something grand and beautiful and noble, well worth the toil and anxiety." I can't imagine that the vast majority of our citizenry would use those words to describe

"I Have Absolutely No Doubt that Character Does Count"

---

25. Adam Smith, *The Theory of Moral Sentiments* (1759; Cambridge, England: Cambridge University Press, 2002), 158.

what capitalism is about today. The sooner the better when we can again apply those words to our business and financial leaders—*and mean them*.

The Good Citizen Promotes the Welfare of His Fellow Citizens

So there is much work to be done. But it's about much more than assuring that the bottom line of business is not only stated with probity, but focused on investing based on long-term corporate value rather than speculating on short-term stock prices. It is the enduring reality of intrinsic value—make no mistake, the worth of a corporation is neither more nor less than the discounted value of its future cash flows—not the ephemeral perception of the price of a stock that carries the day. And the enterprises that will endure are those that generate the most profits for their owners, something they do best when they take into account the interests of their customers, their employees, their communities, and indeed the interests of our society. *Please don't think of the ideals merely as foolish idealism.* They are the ideals that capitalism has depended upon from the very outset. Again, hear Adam Smith: "He is certainly not a good citizen who does not wish to promote, by every means of his power, the welfare of the whole society of his fellow citizens." So it's up to each one of us to speak up, to speak out, and to demand that our corporations and our fund managers represent our interests rather than their own—the owners first, not the managers. Please don't think that your voice doesn't matter. In the words of the motto I've tried to ingrain in the minds of our Vanguard crew members, "Even one person can make a difference."

While a call for virtue in the conduct of the affairs of corporate America—and investment America, too—may sound like a hollow "do-good" platitude, the fact is that in the long run the high road is the only possible road to national achievement and prosperity, to making the most of those priceless assets with which America has been endowed by her Creator. On this point, I am unable to find more compelling wisdom than some splendid words attributed, perhaps apocryphally, to Alexis de

Tocqueville. I hope these words will resound far beyond the parochial issues I've addressed here into the larger world around us, troubled as it is:

> I sought for the greatness and genius of America in her harbors and her rivers, in her fertile fields and boundless forests, and it was not there.
>
> I sought for the greatness and genius of America in her rich mines and her vast world commerce, and in her institutions of learning, and it was not there.
>
> I sought for the greatness and genius of America in her democratic Congress and her matchless Constitution, and it was not there.
>
> Not until I went into the churches of America and heard her pulpits flame with righteousness did I understand the secret of her genius and power.
>
> America is great because America is good, and if America ever ceases to be good, America will cease to be great.

And so it is with corporate America and investment America, too. If we return to goodness, we can again strive for greatness. Let's all of us together make sure that happens.

"If America Ever Ceases To Be Good, America Will Cease To Be Great"

PART V

The Vision of Service to Society

P ART V INCLUDES two chapters linked only by Bogle's passion for serving investors and society alike. The first essay—"Bogle on the Fiduciary Principle: No Man Can Serve Two Masters"—is a resounding call for a rejuvenated fiduciary society that is supported by new federal legislation, in order to "guarantee that our last-line owners . . . have their rights as investment principals protected." He comes to this overriding conclusion only after reflecting on his own 60 years of experience on the front lines of the mutual fund industry, as well as a historical review of centuries of teachings dating from the apostles Matthew and Luke ("No man can serve two masters"). He discusses the thinking of the nation's Founding Fathers on capitalism, and the more recent writings of American jurists such as Harlan Fiske Stone and Benjamin Cardozo. He concludes simply that "the concept of fiduciary duty is no longer merely an ideal to be debated. It is a vital necessity to be practiced."

Intertwined in Bogle's life's work and worldview are his beliefs about philanthropy—his "profound conviction that all of us who prosper in this great republic have a solemn obligation to recognize their good fortune by giving something back." In this essay, Bogle speaks straight from his heart on how his business and philanthropic philosophies are joined; his love and support, most notably, for Blair Academy and Princeton University; what "enough" wealth means to him; being a fiduciary pledged to serve others (he describes himself as "something of a financial failure" when he compares his wealth to the wealth accumulated by his peers); and why he views giving as both a joy and a duty of citizenship. Here, Bogle waxes philosophical, revealing his deeply held sentiments in their clearest form.

CHATPER 12: FIDUCIARY DUTY—NO MAN CAN SERVE TWO MASTERS[1]

I write at a time of financial and economic crisis in our nation and around the globe. I venture to assert that when the history of the financial era which has just drawn to a close comes to be written, most of its mistakes and its major faults will be ascribed to the failure to observe the fiduciary principle, the precept as old as holy writ, that "a man cannot serve two masters." No thinking man can believe that an economy built upon a business foundation can permanently endure without some loyalty to that principle. The separation of ownership from management, the development of the corporate structure so as to vest in small groups control over the resources of great numbers of small and uninformed investors, make imperative

---

1. Based on an essay published in the *Journal of Portfolio Management* (Fall 2009), which in turn was based on a lecture on business ethics delivered at Columbia University School of Business on April 1, 2009. Previously published as Chapter 14 of *Don't Count on It!* (2011).

*"Financial Institutions
Consider Only Last , if at All,
the Interests of Those Whose
Funds They Command"*

a fresh and active devotion to that principle if the modern world of business is to perform its proper function.

Yet those who serve nominally as trustees, but relieved, by clever legal devices, from the obligation to protect those whose interests they purport to represent, corporate officers and directors who award to themselves huge bonuses from corporate funds without the assent or even the knowledge of their stockholders . . . financial institutions which, in the infinite variety of their operations, consider only last, if at all, the interests of those whose funds they command, suggest how far we have ignored the necessary implications of that principle. The loss and suffering inflicted on individuals, the harm done to a social order founded upon business and dependent upon its integrity, are incalculable.[2]

Alas, except for the first sentence, the preceding words are not mine. Rather, they are the words of Harlan Fiske Stone, excerpted from his 1934—yes, 1934—address at the University of Michigan Law School, reprinted in the *Harvard Law Review* later that year.[3]

But his words are equally relevant—perhaps even more relevant—at this moment in history. They could hardly present a more appropriate analysis of the

---

2. H. F. Stone, address to the University of Michigan School of Law on June 15, 1934, reprinted in the *Harvard Law Review* (1934).

3. Harlan Fiske Stone (1872–1946) received his law degree at Columbia in 1898, and served as dean of Columbia Law School from 1910 to 1923. In 1925, President Calvin Coolidge appointed Stone as Associate Justice of the United States Supreme Court. In 1941, President Roosevelt appointed him as Chief Justice of the United States, and he served in that position until his death in 1946. A curious coincidence is that Justice Stone appeared on the cover of *Time* magazine on May 6, 1929, just two days before my own birth on May 8. In its profile story, *Time* accurately speculated that one day Stone would become the Chief Justice, in part because (in those backward sentences that distinguished the early style of the magazine), "Well he has always tackled the public interest."

causes of the present-day collapse of our financial markets and the economic crisis now facing our nation and our world.

One could easily react to Justice Stone's words by falling back on the ancient aphorism "The more things change, the more they remain the same," and move on to a new subject. But I hope financial professionals will react differently, and share my reaction: In the aftermath of that Great Depression and the stock market crash that accompanied it, we failed to take advantage of the opportunity to demand that those who lead our giant business and financial organizations—the stewards of so much of our nation's wealth—measure up to the stern and unyielding principles of fiduciary duty described by Justice Stone. So, 75 years later, for heaven's sake, let's not make the same mistake again. Justice Stone's stern words force us to fasten on ethical dilemmas faced by today's business leaders. Included among these leaders are the chiefs who manage our nation's publicly held corporations—today valued in the stock market at some $12 trillion—and the professional managers of "other people's money" who oversee equity investments valued at some $9 trillion of that total, owning 75 percent of all shares and therefore holding absolute voting control over those corporations. Like their counterparts in business, those powerful managers have not only an *ethical responsibility*, but a *fiduciary duty*, to those whose capital has been entrusted to their care.

Fiduciary Duty—Eight Centuries of Common Law

The concept of fiduciary duty has a long history, going back more or less eight centuries under English common law. Fiduciary duty is essentially a legal relationship of confidence or trust between two or more parties, most commonly a *fiduciary* or *trustee* and a *principal* or *beneficiary*, who justifiably reposes confidence, good faith, and reliance on his trustee. The fiduciary is expected to act at all times for the sole benefit and interests of the principal, with loyalty to those interests. A fiduciary must not put personal interests before that duty, and, importantly, must not be placed in a situation where his fiduciary duty to clients conflicts with a fiduciary duty to any other entity.

Way back in 1928, New York's Chief Justice Benjamin N. Cardozo put it well:

> Many forms of conduct permissible in a workaday world for those acting at arm's length are forbidden to those bound by fiduciary ties. A trustee is held to something stricter than the morals of the marketplace. . . . As to this there has developed a tradition that is unbending and inveterate. . . . Not honesty alone, but the punctilio of an honor the most sensitive, is then the standard of behavior. . . . Only thus has the level of conduct for fiduciaries been kept at a level higher than that trodden by the crowd.[4]

It has been said, I think, accurately, that fiduciary duty is the highest duty known to the law.

"A Shift from Moral Absolutism to Moral Relativism"

It is less ironic than it is tragic that the concept of fiduciary duty seems far *less* embedded in our society today than it was when Stone and Cardozo expressed their profound convictions. As ought to be obvious to all educated citizens, over the past few decades the balance between ethics and law, on the one hand, and the markets on the other has heavily shifted in favor of the markets. As I have often put it: We have moved from a society in which *there are some things that one simply does not do*, to one in which *if everyone else is doing it, I can do it, too*. I've described this change as a shift from moral absolutism to moral relativism. Business ethics, it seems to me, has been a major casualty of that shift in our traditional societal values. You will hardly be surprised to learn that I do not regard that change as progress.

---

4. *Meinhard v. Salmon*, 164 N.E. 545 (N.Y. 1928).

Trust and Honesty—It's Time to Restore Both

At least a few others share this view. In her book *Trust and Honesty*, published in 2006, Boston University Law School professor Tamar Frankel provides worthy insights on the diminishing role of fiduciary duty in our society. She is concerned—a concern that I suspect many investment professionals would share—that American culture has been moving toward dishonesty, deception, and abuse of trust, all of which have come to the fore in the present crisis. What we need, she argues, is "an effective way to increase trust [by] establishing trustworthy institutions and reliable systems," even as she despairs that the pressures brought out by the stock market and real estate bubbles have led to "deteriorating public morals . . . and burst into abuse of trust." (p. 99).[5]

In Professor Frankel's view, "we reduced the power of morality in law . . . emasculated the regulation of trusted persons [that is, fiduciaries] . . . abused the laws that govern fiduciaries' honesty . . . and opened the door to enormous losses to the public and the economic system" (p. 119). We also came to ignore the critical distinction between fiduciary law itself and a fiduciary relationship subject to contract law. What's more, she writes, "the movement from professions to businesses was accompanied by changes in the way the law was interpreted" (p. 146). We forgot the fundamental principle expressed by the apostles Matthew and Luke,[6] and repeated by Justice Stone: "No man can serve two masters."

My principal objection to moral relativism is that it obfuscates and mitigates the obligations that we owe to society, and shifts the focus to the benefits accruing to the individual. Self-interest, unchecked, is a powerful force, but a

---

5. Tamar Frankel, *Trust and Honesty: America's Business Culture at a Crossroad* (Oxford, England: Oxford University Press, 2006).
6. See Luke 16:13 and Matthew 6:34 of the King James Version of the New Testament.

force that, if it is to protect the interests of the community of all of our citizens, must ultimately be checked by society. The recent crisis—which I have described as "a crisis of *ethic* proportions"—makes it clear how serious that damage can become.

Causes of the Recent Crisis

The causes of the recent crisis are manifold. Metaphorically speaking, the collapse in our financial system has 1,000 fathers: the cavalier attitude toward risk of our bankers and investment bankers in holding a toxic mix of low-quality securities on enormously leveraged balance sheets; the laissez-faire attitude of our federal regulators, reflected in their faith that "free competitive markets" would protect our society against excesses; the Congress, which rolled back legislative reforms dating back to the Depression years; "securitization" in which the traditional link between borrower and lender—under which lenders demanded evidence of the borrowers' ability to meet their financial obligations—was severed; and reckless financial innovation in which literally tens of trillions of dollars of derivative financial instruments (such as credit default swaps) were created, usually carrying stupefying levels of risk and unfathomable levels of complexity.

The Dominant Power of Leaders of Corporate America and Investment America

The radical increase in the power and position of the leaders of corporate America and the leaders of investment America has been a major contributor to these failures. Today's dominant institutional ownership position of 75 percent of the shares of our (largely giant) public corporations compares with only about 8 percent a half-century ago. This remarkable increase in ownership has placed these managers—largely of mutual funds (holding 25 percent of all shares); private pension funds (12 percent); government retirement funds (9 percent); insurance companies (8 percent); and hedge funds and endowment funds—in a position to exercise great power and influence over corporate America.

But they have failed to exercise their power. In fact, the agents of investment in America have failed to honor the responsibilities that they owe to their principals—the last-line individuals who have much of their capital wealth committed to stock ownership, including mutual fund share owners and pension beneficiaries. The record is clear that, despite their controlling position, most institutions have failed to play an active role in board structure and governance, director elections, executive compensation, stock options, proxy proposals, dividend policy, and so on.

Given their forbearance as corporate citizens, these managers arguably played a major role in allowing the managers of our public corporations to exploit the advantages of their own agency, not only in executive compensation, perquisites, and mergers and acquisitions, but even in accepting the "financial engineering" that has come to permeate corporate financial statements, endorsed—at least tacitly—by their public accountants.

But the failures of our institutional investors go beyond governance issues to the very practice of their trade. These agents have also failed to provide the due diligence that our citizen/investors have every reason to expect of the investment professionals to whom they have entrusted their money. How could so many highly skilled, highly paid securities analysts and researchers have failed to question the toxic-filled leveraged balance sheets of Citicorp and other leading banks and investment banks and, lest we forget, AIG, as well as the ethics-skirting sales tactics of Countrywide Financial?[7] Even earlier, what were these professionals

"The Failures of Our Institutional Investors Go Beyond Governance Issues to the Very Practice of Their Trade"

---

7. I'm speaking here of the buy-side analysts employed directly by these managers. The conflicts of interest facing Wall Street's sell-side analysts were exposed by the investigations of New York Attorney General Eliot Spitzer in 2002–2003.

thinking when they ignored the shenanigans of special-purpose entities at Enron and cooking the books at WorldCom?

The Role of Institutional Managers

But the failure of our newly empowered agents to exercise their responsibilities to ownership is but a part of the problem we face. The field of institutional investment management—the field in which I've now plied my trade for more than 58 years—also played a major, if often overlooked, role. As a group, we veered off-course almost 180 degrees from stewardship to salesmanship, in which our focus turned away from prudent management and toward product marketing. We moved from a focus on long-term investment to a focus on short-term speculation. The driving dream of our adviser/agents was to gather ever-increasing assets under management, the better to build their advisory fees and profits, even as these policies came at the direct expense of the investor/principals whom, under traditional standards of trusteeship and fiduciary duty, they were duty-bound to serve.

Conflicts of interest are pervasive throughout the field of money management, albeit different in each sector. Private pension plans face one set of conflicts (i.e., minimizing plan contributions helps maximize a corporation's earnings), public pension plans another (i.e., political pressure to invest in pet projects of legislators). And labor union plans face yet another (i.e., pressure to employ money managers who are willing to "pay to play"). But it is in the mutual fund industry where the conflict between fiduciary duty to fund shareholder/clients often directly conflicts with the business interests of the fund manager.

Managers Exploiting Their Agency—A Clear Violation of the Language of the Investment Company Act of 1940

Perhaps we shouldn't be surprised that our money managers act first in their own behalf. Indeed, as Vice Chancellor Leo E. Strine, Jr., of the Delaware Court of Chancery has observed, "It would be passing strange if . . . professional money managers would, as a class, be less likely to exploit their agency than the managers of the corporations that make products and deliver services."[8] In the fund industry—the largest of all financial intermediaries—that failure to serve the interests of fund shareholders has wide ramifications. Ironically, the failure has occurred despite the clear language of the Investment Company Act of 1940, which demands that "mutual funds should be organized, managed, and operated in the best interests of their shareholders, rather than in the interests of [their] advisers."[9]

The Triumph of Speculation over Investment

As control over corporate America moved from owners to agents, our institutional money managers seemed to forget their duty to act solely in the interest of their own principals, those whose savings were entrusted to mutual funds and whose retirement security was entrusted to pension plans. These new investor/agents not only forgot the interests of their *principals*, but also seemed to forget their own investment *principles*. The predominant focus of institutional investment strategy turned from the wisdom of long-term investing, based on the enduring creation of intrinsic corporate values, to the folly of short-term speculation, focused on the ephemeral prices of corporate stocks. The own-a-stock strategy of yore became the rent-a-stock strategy of today.

In what I've called "the happy conspiracy" among corporate managers, directors, accountants, investment bankers, and institutional owners and renters of stocks, all kinds of bizarre financial engineering took place. Management became the master of its own numbers, and our public accountants too often went along.

---

8. Leo E. Strine, "Toward Common Sense and Common Ground? Reflections on the Shared Interests of Managers and Labor in a More Rational System of Corporate Governance," *Journal of Corporation Law* (Fall 2007): 7.

9. The Vanguard Group, Inc., 47 S.E.C. 450 (1981).

Loose accounting standards made it possible to create, often out of thin air, what passes for earnings, even under GAAP [generally accepted accounting principles] standards. One good example—which is already sowing the seeds of yet another financial crisis that is now emerging—is hyping the assumed future returns earned by pension plans, even as rational expectations for future returns deteriorated.

Benjamin Graham's Prescient Warning about a "New Element of Speculation"

Here, again, we can't say that we hadn't been warned well in advance. Speaking before the 1958 Convention of the National Federation of Financial Analysts Societies, Benjamin Graham, legendary investor and author of the classic *The Intelligent Investor*,[10] described "some contrasting relationships between the present and the past in our underlying attitudes toward investment and speculation in common stocks." He further commented:

> In the past, the speculative elements of a common stock resided almost exclusively in the company itself; they were due to uncertainties, or fluctuating elements, or downright weaknesses in the industry, or the corporation's individual setup.... But in recent years a new and major element of speculation has been introduced into the common-stock arena from outside the companies. It comes from the attitude and viewpoint of the stock-buying public and their advisers—chiefly us security analysts. This attitude may be described in a phrase: primary emphasis upon future expectations.... The concept of future prospects, and particularly of continued growth in the future, invites the application of formulas out of higher mathematics to establish the present value of the favored issues. But the combination of precise formulas with highly imprecise assumptions can be used to establish, or rather to justify, practically any value one wished, however high....

10. Benjamin Graham, *The Intelligent Investor*, rev. ed. (New York: HarperBusiness, 2003).

Given the three ingredients of a) optimistic assumptions as to the rate of earnings growth, b) a sufficiently long projection of this growth into the future, and c) the miraculous workings of compound interest—lo! the security analyst is supplied with a new kind of philosopher's stone which can produce or justify any desired valuation for a really "good stock."

Mathematics is ordinarily considered as producing precise and dependable results; but in the stock market the more elaborate and abstruse the mathematics the more uncertain and speculative are the conclusions we draw therefrom. . . . Whenever calculus is brought in, or higher algebra, you could take it as a warning signal that the operator was trying to substitute theory for experience, and usually also to give to speculation the deceptive guise of investment. . . .

Have not investors and security analysts eaten of the tree of knowledge of good and evil prospects? By so doing have they not permanently expelled themselves from that Eden where promising common stocks at reasonable prices could be plucked off the bushes?[11]

"Whenever Calculus Is Brought In . . . The Operator Was Trying To . . . Give Speculation the Deceptive Guise of Investment."

This obvious reference to Original Sin reflected Graham's deep concern about quantifying the unquantifiable (and doing so with false precision). The implications of that bite into the apple of quantitative investing were barely visible when Graham spoke in 1958. But by the late 1990s, this new form of investment behavior had become a dominant force that continues to be a major driver of the speculation that has overwhelmed our financial markets.

Consider with me now how the erosion in the conduct, values, and ethics of business that I have described has been fostered by the profound—and largely unnoticed—change that has taken place in the nature of our financial markets.

---

11. Ibid., 563–572.

That change reflects two radically different views of what investing is all about, two distinct markets, if you will. One is the real market of intrinsic business value. The other is the expectations market of momentary stock prices. The British economist John Maynard Keynes described this dichotomy as the distinction between *enterprise*—"forecasting the prospective yield of the asset over its whole life"—and *speculation*—"forecasting the psychology of the markets" (p. 155). Just as Keynes forecast, speculation came to overwhelm enterprise, the old ownership society became today's agency society, and the values of capitalism were seriously eroded.[12]

Justice Stone, Lord Keynes, Benjamin Graham ... How Many Warnings Do We Need Before We Get the Message?

It is little short of amazing how long ago these prescient warnings were issued. Justice Stone warned us in 1934. John Maynard Keynes warned us in 1936. Benjamin Graham warned us in 1958. Isn't it high time for us to heed the warnings of those three far-sighted intellectual giants? Isn't it high time we stand on their shoulders and shape national policy away from the moral relativism of peer conduct and greed and short-term speculation—gambling on expectations about stock prices? Isn't it high time to return to the moral absolutism of fiduciary duty, to return to our traditional ethic of long-term investment focused on building the intrinsic value of our corporations—prudence, due diligence, and active participation in corporate governance?

Yes, now *is* the time for reform. Today's agency society has ill-served the public interest. The failure of our money manager agents represents not only a failure of modern-day capitalism, but a failure of modern-day capitalists. As Lord Keynes warned us, "[W]hen enterprise becomes a mere bubble on a whirlpool of

---

12. John Maynard Keynes, *The General Theory of Employment, Interest, and Money* (1936; New York: Harcourt, Brace, 1964).

speculation, the job of capitalism will be ill-done" (p. 159). That is where we are today, and the consequences have not been pretty.

Graham's Eternal Truth: The Stock Market Is a Voting Machine in the Short Run, but a Weighing Machine in the Long Run

In all, our now-dominant money management sector has turned its focus away from the enduring nature of the intrinsic value of the goods and services created, produced, and distributed by our corporate businesses, and toward the ephemeral price of the corporation's stock—the triumph of perception over reality. We live in a world in which it is far easier to hype the price of a company's stock than it is to build the intrinsic value of the corporation itself. And we seem to have forgotten Benjamin Graham's implicit caution about the transience of short-term perception, compared to the durability of long-term reality: "In the short run, the stock market is a voting machine; in the long run it is a weighing machine."[13]

The Failure of Modern-Day Capitalism

My strong statements regarding the failure of modern-day capitalism are manifested in grossly excessive executive compensation; financial engineering; earnings "guidance," with massive declines in valuations if it fails to be delivered; enormous, casino-like trading among institutional investors; staggering political influence, borne of huge campaign contributions; and, in the financial arena, bestowal of wealth to traders and managers that is totally disproportionate to the value they add to investors' wealth. Indeed, the financial sector actually subtracts value from our society.

Finance is what is known to economists as a rent-seeking enterprise, one in which our intermediaries—money managers, brokers, investment bankers—act

---

13. Benjamin Graham and David Dodd, *Security Analysis* (1934, 1940; New York: McGraw-Hill, 2008).

as agents for parties on both sides of each transaction. Our intermediaries pit one party against another, so what would otherwise be a zero-sum game becomes a loser's game, simply because of the intermediation costs extracted by the various croupiers. (Other examples of rent seekers include casinos, the legal system, and government. Think about it!)

Ten Examples of What's Gone Wrong in the Mutual Fund Industry

I know something about how the financial system works, for I've been part of it for my entire 58-year career. The mutual fund industry—in which I've spent my entire career—is the paradigm of what's gone wrong with capitalism. Here are 10 examples of how far so many fund managers have departed from the basic fiduciary principle that "no man can serve two masters," despite the fact that the 1940 Act demands that the principal master must be the mutual fund shareholder:

1. The domination of fund boards by chairmen and chief executives who also serve as senior executives of the management companies that control the funds, an obvious conflict of interest and an abrogation of the fiduciary standard.
2. Focusing on short-term speculation over long-term investment, the ultimate triumph of expectations investing over enterprise investing, resulting in great financial benefits to fund managers and brokers, and commensurately great costs to fund investors.
3. Failure to exercise adequate due diligence in the research and analysis of the securities selected for fund portfolios, enabling corporate managers to engage in various forms of earnings management and speculative behavior, largely unchecked by the professional investment community.

4. Failure to exercise the rights and assume the responsibilities of corporate ownership, generally ignoring issues of corporate governance and allowing corporate managers to place their own financial interests ahead of the interests of their share owners.

5. Soaring fund expenses. As fund assets soared during the 1980s and 1990s, fund fees grew even faster, reflecting higher fee rates, as well as the failure of managers to adequately share the enormous economies of scale in managing money with fund shareholders. For example, the average expense ratio of the 10 largest funds of 1960 rose from 0.51 percent to 0.96 percent in 2008, an increase of 88 percent. (Wellington Fund was the only fund whose expense ratio declined; excluding Wellington, the increase was 104 percent.)

6. Charging fees to the mutual funds that managers control that are far higher than the fees charged in the competitive field of pension fund management. Three of the largest advisers, for example, charge an average fee rate of 0.08 percent of assets to their pension clients and 0.61 percent to their funds, resulting in annual fees of just $600,000 for the pension fund and *$56 million* for the comparable mutual fund, and presumably holding the same stocks in both portfolios.[14]

7. Diluting the value of fund shares held by long-term investors, by allowing hedge fund managers to engage in "time zone" trading. This vast, near-industry-wide scandal came to light in 2003. It involved some 23 fund managers, including many of the largest firms in the field—in effect, a

Soaring Fees for Mutual Fund Clients; Far Lower Fees for Pension Clients

---

14. These figures are based on 2002 data. In a March 2010 decision in the *Jones v. Harris Associates* case, the U.S. Supreme Court found that the effectiveness of the process by which mutual fund managers set the fee rates that they charge to the funds under their control needed improvement. I had provided an *amicus curiae* brief in favor of far sterner measures than the Court ultimately suggested.

conspiracy between mutual fund managers and hedge fund managers to defraud regular fund shareholders.

8. Pay-to-play distribution agreements with brokers, in which fund advisers use *fund* brokerage commissions ("soft" dollars) to finance share distribution, which primarily benefits the *adviser*.

9. Spending enormous amounts on advertising—almost a half-billion dollars in the past two years alone—to bring in new fund investors, using money obtained from existing fund shareholders. Much of this spending was to promote exotic and untested products that have proved to have far more ephemeral marketing appeal than enduring investment integrity.

10. Lending securities that are the property of the *fund* portfolios, but siphoning off a portion of the profits from lending to the *adviser*.

Justice Stone's Ancient Warning Still Applies

Given such failures as these, doesn't Justice Stone's warning that I cited at the outset seem even *more* prescient? Let me repeat the key phrases: "The separation of ownership from management, . . . corporate structure[s that] . . . vest in small groups control over the resources of great numbers of small and uninformed investors, . . . corporate officers and directors who award to themselves huge bonuses[,] . . . financial institutions which . . . consider only last, if at all, the interests of those whose funds they command." Just as we ignored the fiduciary principle all those years ago, we have clearly continued to ignore it in the recent era. The result in both cases, using Justice Stone's words, is: "The loss and suffering inflicted on individuals, the harm done to a social order founded upon business and dependent upon its integrity, are incalculable." Today, as you know, much of that harm can be calculated all too easily, amounting to several trillions of dollars. So, this time around, let's pay attention, and demand a return to fiduciary principles.

A Piece of History—A Warning to Wellington Partners in 1971

While the overwhelming majority of financial institutions operate primarily in the interests of their agents and at the expense of their principals, not quite all do. So I now draw on my personal experiences in the mutual fund industry to give you one example of my own encounter with this issue. As far back as 38 years ago, I expressed profound concern about the nature and structure of the fund industry. Only three years later, my convictions led to action, and 35 years ago this September, I founded a firm designed, to the best of my ability, to honor the principles of fiduciary duty.

I expressed these principles when doing so was distinctly counter to my own self-interest. Speaking to my partners at Wellington in September 1971—*1971!*—I cited the very same words of Justice Stone with which I opened my remarks this evening. I then added:

> I endorse that view, and at the same time reveal an ancient prejudice of mine: All things considered, absent a demonstration that the enterprise has substantial capital requirements that cannot be otherwise fulfilled, it is undesirable for professional enterprises to have public stockholders.
>
> This constraint is as applicable to money managers as it is to doctors, or lawyers, or accountants, or architects. In their cases, as in ours, it is hard to see what unique contribution public investors bring to the enterprise. They do not, as a rule, add capital; they do not add expertise; they do not contribute to the well-being of our clients.
>
> Indeed, it is possible to envision circumstances in which the pressure for earnings and earnings growth engendered by public ownership is antithetical to the responsible operation of a professional organization. Even though the field of money management has elements of both, there are, after all, differences between a business and a profession. . . . [So we must ask ourselves this question]: if it is a burden to our fund and counsel clients to be served by a public enterprise, should this burden exist in perpetuity?

"Public Ownership Is Antithetical to the Responsible Operation of a Professional Organization"

My candor may well have played a supporting role in my dismissal as chief executive of Wellington Management Company in January 1974. While it's a saga too complex to detail in this article, my being fired gave me the chance of a lifetime—the opportunity to create a new fiduciary-focused structure for our funds. I proposed just such a structure to the directors of the Wellington funds.[15] Wellington Management Company, of course, vigorously opposed my efforts.

Nonetheless, after months of study, the directors of the funds accepted my recommendation that we separate the activities of the funds themselves from their adviser and distributor, so that the funds could operate solely in the interests of our fund shareholders. Our new structure involved the creation of a new firm, The Vanguard Group of Investment Companies, owned by the funds, employing their own officers and staff, and operated on an at-cost basis, a truly *mutual* mutual fund firm.

Vanguard—Controlling Our Own Destiny

While Vanguard began with a limited mandate—to provide only administrative services to the funds—I realized that, if we were to control our own destiny, we would also have to provide both investment advisory and marketing services to our funds. So, almost immediately after Vanguard's operations commenced in May 1975, we began our move to gain substantial control over these two essential functions. By year's end, we had created the world's first index mutual fund, run by Vanguard.

---

15. The lecture at Columbia University, on which this article is based, is essentially the third part of a trilogy that chronicles the development of the fund industry and of Vanguard itself. The first two parts of the trilogy were presented in Chapter 12 and Chapter 13 of *Don't Count on It!*, "Re-Mutualizing the Mutual Fund Industry—The Alpha and the Omega" and "A New Order of Things: Bringing Mutuality to the 'Mutual' Fund."

Then, early in 1977, we abandoned the supply-driven broker/dealer distribution system that had been operated by Wellington since 1928 in favor of a buyer-driven no-load approach under our own direction. Later that year, we created the first-ever series of defined-maturity bond funds, segmented into short-, intermediate-, and long-term maturities, all focused on high investment quality. In 1981, Vanguard assumed responsibility for providing the investment advisory services to our new fixed-income funds as well as our established money market funds. (As you can imagine, none of these moves was without controversy!)

Sound Decisions, Made in a Cloud of Uncertainty

Since our formation in 1974, the assets of the Vanguard funds have grown from more than $1 billion to some *$1 trillion* currently, now the nation's largest manager of stock and bond mutual funds. Some 82 percent of that $1 trillion—$820 billion—is represented by passively managed index funds and "virtual" index funds tightly linked to various sectors of the fixed-income market. Some 25 external investment advisers serve our remaining (largely actively managed equity) funds, with Wellington Management advising by far the largest portion of those assets. Most of these funds have multiple advisers, the better to spread the risk of underperformance relative to their peers.

More than parenthetically, that long string of business decisions was made in a situation in which Vanguard's very existence was in doubt, because the Securities and Exchange Commission had initially refused to approve Vanguard's assumption of marketing and distribution responsibilities. But after a struggle lasting six (interminable!) years, the SEC reversed itself in February 1981. By unanimous vote, the Commission declared that

[t]he Vanguard plan is consistent with the provisions, policies, and purposes of the [Investment Company Act of 1940]. It actually furthers the Act's objectives . . . enhances the

funds' independence . . . benefits each fund within a reasonable range of fairness . . . [provides] substantial savings from advisory fee reductions [and] economies of scale . . . and promotes a healthy and viable mutual fund complex in which each fund can better prosper.[16]

"The Vanguard Plan . . . Promotes a Healthy and Viable Mutual Fund Complex in which Each Fund Can Better Prosper"

The SEC's words now seem prescient. With few exceptions, the Vanguard funds—and their shareholders—have prospered. Measured by Morningstar's peer-based rating system (comparing each fund with other funds having distinctly comparable policies and objectives), Vanguard ranked first in performance among the 50 largest fund complexes.

Vanguard has also provided shareholders with substantial savings from advisory fee reductions and economies of scale, in fact, the lowest costs in the field. Last year, over all, our funds' aggregate operating expense ratio came to 0.20 percent of average assets, compared to 1.30 percent for the average mutual fund. That 1.1 percentage-point saving, applied to $1 trillion of assets, now produces savings for our shareholders of some $11 billion annually. And, as the world of investing is at last beginning to understand, low costs are the single most reliable predictor of superior fund performance. As we read in Homer's *The Odyssey*, "fair dealing yields more profit in the end."

If you are willing to accept—based on these data—that Vanguard has achieved both *commercial* success (asset growth and market share) and *artistic* success (superior performance and low costs), you must wonder why, after 35 years of existence, no other firm has elected to emulate our shareholder-oriented structure. (A particularly ironic outcome, as I chose the name Vanguard in part because of its conventional

---

16. The Vanguard Group, Inc., 47 S.E.C. 450 (1981).

definition as "leader in a new trend.") The answer, I think, can be expressed succinctly: Under our at-cost structure, all of the profits go to the fund shareholders, not to the managers, resolving the transcendent conflict of interest of the mutual fund industry. In any event, the leader, as it were, has yet to find its first follower.

Vanguard represented my best effort to align the interests of fund investors and fund managers under established principles of fiduciary duty. I leave it to wiser—and surely more objective—heads than mine to evaluate whether or not I overstate or hyperbolize what we have accomplished. But I freely acknowledge that we owe our accomplishments to the three simple principles: the firm is (1) *structurally* correct (because we are owned by our fund investors); (2) *mathematically* correct (because it is a tautology that the lower the costs incurred in investing, the higher the returns); and (3) *ethically* correct (because we exist only by earning far greater trust and loyalty from our shareholders than any of our peers). Measured by repeated evaluations of loyalty by independent research firms, there has been no close rival for our #1 position. Please be appropriately skeptical of that self-serving claim, but look at the data. In a 2007 survey, one such group concluded, "Vanguard Group generates far more loyalty than any other company."[17]

"To Build the Financial World Anew"

Creating and restructuring Vanguard was no easy task. Without determination, expertise, luck, timing, and the key roles played by just a handful of individuals, it never could have happened. So when I suggest that we must now go beyond

17. Murray Coleman, "Few Firms Earn Loyalty of the Wealthy: Well-Heeled Investors Search for Consistency; Vanguard Rates Highest," *Wall Street Journal*, March 15, 2007, C13. Figures are based on data from Cogent Research. The Vanguard loyalty score (percentage of strong supporters minus strong detractors) was a positive 44. The fund industry scored a pathetic negative 12.

restructuring the nature and values of a single firm to restructuring the nature and values of the entire money management business—to build the financial world anew—I am well aware of how difficult it will be to accomplish that sweeping task.

And yet we dare not stand still.

For we meet at a time when, as never before in the history of the country, our most cherished ideals and traditions are being subjected to searching criticism. The towering edifice of business and industry, which had become the dominating feature of the American social structure, has been shaken to its foundations by forces, the full significance of which we still can see but dimly. What had seemed the impregnable fortress of a boasted civilization has developed unsuspected weaknesses, and in consequence we are now engaged in the altogether wholesome task of critical reexamination of what our hands have reared.

As you may have suspected, I've once again cited a section of Justice Stone's 1934 speech, and it's high time we take it seriously. For the fact is that there has been a radical change in our investment system from the ownership society of a half-century ago—which is gone, never to return—to our agency society of today—in which our agents have failed to serve their principals: mutual fund shareholders, pension beneficiaries, and long-term investors. Rather, the new system has served the agents themselves—our institutional managers.

"By Their Forbearance on Governance Issues, Our Money Managers Have Also Served the Managers of Corporate America"

Further, by their forbearance on governance issues, our money managers have also served the managers of corporate America. To make matters even worse, by turning to short-term speculation at the expense of long-term investment, the industry has also damaged the interests of the greater society, just as Lord Keynes warned.

Yet despite the extraordinary (and largely unrecognized) shift in the very nature of corporate ownership, we have failed to change the rules of the game.

Indeed, in the financial sector we have rolled back most of the historic rules regulating our securities issuers, our exchanges, and our investment advisers. While we should have been improving regulatory oversight and administering existing regulations with increasing toughness, both have been relaxed, ignoring the new environment, and therefore bear much of the responsibility for today's crisis.

The Inexorable Economic Forces of Change Demand Adaptation to Meet New Needs

Of course American society is in a constant state of flux. It always has been, and it always will be. I've often pointed out that our nation began as an agricultural economy, became largely a manufacturing economy, then largely a service economy, and most recently an economy in which the financial services sector had become the dominant element. Such secular changes are not new, but they are always different, so enlightened responses are never easy to come by. Justice Stone, once again, recognized that new forces demand new responses:

> It was in 1809 when Jefferson wrote: "We are a rural farming people; we have little business and few manufactures among us, and I pray God it will be a long time before we have much of either." Profound changes have come into American life since that sentence was penned. [These] inexorable economic forces [create] public problems [that] involve an understanding of the new and complex economic forces we have created, their relationship to the lives of individuals in widely separated communities engaged in widely differing activities, and the adaptation to those forces of old conceptions developed in a different environment to meet different needs.

To deal with the new and complex economic forces our failed agency society has created, of course we need a new paradigm: a fiduciary society in which the interest of investors comes first, and ethical behavior by our business and financial leaders represents the highest value.

The New Paradigm— Building a Fiduciary Society

While the challenges of today are inevitably different from those of the past, the principles are age-old. Consider this warning from Adam Smith way back in the eighteenth century: "Managers of other people's money [rarely] watch over it with the same anxious vigilance with which . . . they watch over their own. . . . [T]hey very easily give themselves a dispensation. Negligence and profusion must always prevail."[18] And so in the recent era, negligence and profusion have prevailed among our money manager/agents, even to the point of an almost complete disregard of their duty and responsibility to their principals. Too few managers seem to display the "anxious vigilance" over other people's money that once defined the conduct of investment professionals.

So what we must do is develop a new *fiduciary* society to guarantee that our last-line owners—those mutual fund shareholders and pension fund beneficiaries whose savings are at stake—have their rights as investment principals protected. These rights must include these six provisions:

Six Rights of Investors

1. The right to have money manager/agents act solely in their principals' behalf. The client, in short, must be king.
2. The right to rely on due diligence and high professional standards on the part of money managers and securities analysts who appraise securities for principals' portfolios.[19]

---

18. In those days, *profusion* was defined as a "lavish or wasteful expenditure or excess bestowal of money, substance, etc., squandering, waste" (*Oxford English Dictionary*, 2nd ed., vol. XII, 1989, p. 584).

19. Peter Fisher, widely respected BlackRock executive and former Treasury Department official, recently told the *Wall Street Journal* ("Principles for Change," March 29, 2009) that he believes we should force institutional investors to do a better job of analysis, and establish demanding minimum standards of competence.

3. The assurance that agents will act as responsible corporate citizens, restoring to their principals the neglected rights of ownership of stocks, and demanding that corporate directors and managers meet their fiduciary duty to their own shareholders.

4. The right to demand some sort of discipline and integrity in the mutual funds and financial products that they offer.

5. The establishment of advisory fee structures that meet a "reasonableness" standard based not only on *rates* but *dollar amounts*, and their relationship to the fees and structures available to other clients of the manager.

6. The elimination of all conflicts of interest that could preclude the achievement of these goals.

More than parenthetically, I should note that this final provision would seem to preclude the ownership of money management firms by financial conglomerates, now the dominant form of organization in the mutual fund industry. Among today's 40 largest fund complexes, only six remain privately held. The remaining 34 include 13 firms whose shares are held directly by the public, and an astonishing total of 21 fund managers are owned or controlled by U.S. and international financial conglomerates—including Goldman Sachs, Bank of America, Deutsche Bank, ING, John Hancock, and Sun Life of Canada. Painful as such a separation might be, conglomerate ownership of money managers is the single most blatant violation of the principle that "no man can serve two masters."

Of course it will take federal government action to foster the creation of this new fiduciary society that I envision. Above all else, it must be unmistakable that government intends, and is capable of enforcing, standards of trusteeship and fiduciary duty under which money managers operate with the *sole* purpose and in the *exclusive* benefit of the interests of their beneficiaries—largely the owners

Conglomerate Ownership of Money Managers Is the Single Most Blatant Violation of the Principle that "No Man Can Serve Two Masters"

of mutual fund shares and the beneficiaries of our pension plans. As corporate reformer Robert Monks accurately points out, "capitalism without owners will fail."

While government action is essential, however, the new system should be developed in concert with the private investment sector, an Alexander Hamilton–like sharing of the responsibilities in which the Congress establishes the fiduciary principle, and private enterprise establishes the practices that are required to observe it. This task of returning capitalism to its ultimate owners will take time, true enough. But the new reality—increasingly visible with each passing day—is that the concept of fiduciary duty is no longer merely an ideal to be debated. It is a vital necessity to be practiced.

So a lot is at stake in reforming the very nature of our financial system itself, which in turn is designed to force reform in our failed system of governance of our business corporations. The ideas I've passionately advocated in this article, however, are hardly widely shared among my colleagues and peers in the financial sector. But soon, perhaps, many others will ultimately see the light; for example, in March 2009, the idea of governance reform received encouraging support from Professor Andrew W. Lo of the Massachusetts Institute of Technology, one of today's most respected financial economists:

"There's Something Fundamentally Wrong with Current Corporate Governance Structures"

[T]he single most important implication of the financial crisis is about the current state of corporate governance . . . a major wake-up call that we need to change [the rules]. There's something fundamentally wrong with current corporate governance structures, [and] the kinds of risks that typical corporations face today.[20]

---

20. Andrew W. Lo, "Business Insight (A Special Report): Executive Briefing—Understanding Our Blind Spots: Financial Crisis Underscores Need to Transform Our View of Risk," *Wall Street Journal*, March 23, 2009.

In sum, the change in the rules that I advocate—applying to institutional money managers a federal standard of fiduciary duty to their clients—would be designed in turn to force money managers to use their own ownership position to demand that the managers and directors of the business corporations in whose shares they invest also honor their own fiduciary duty to the holders of their shares. Finally, it is these two groups that share the responsibility for the prudent steward-ship over both corporate assets and investment securities that have been entrusted to their care, not only reforming today's flawed and conflict ridden model, but developing a new model that, at best, will restore traditional ethical mores.

"The Punctilio of an Honor the Most Sensitive"

And so I await—with no great patience!—the return of the standard so beauti-fully described by Justice Cardozo all those years ago, excerpts from his words cited earlier in my remarks:

> Those bound by fiduciary ties . . . [are] held to something stricter than the morals of the marketplace . . . a tradition that is unbending and inveterate . . . Not honesty alone, but the punctilio of an honor the most sensitive . . . the level of conduct . . . higher than that trodden by the crowd.

In his profound 1934 speech that has been the inspiration for this essay, Justice Harlan Fiske Stone made one further prescient point on serving the common good:

> In seeking solutions for our social and economic maladjustments, we are too ready to place our reliance on what (the policeman's nightstick of) the state may command, rather than on what may be given to it as the free offering of good citizenship. . . . Yet we know that unless the urge to individual advantage has other curbs, and unless the more influential elements in society conduct themselves with a disposition to promote the common good, society cannot function . . . especially a society which has largely

measured its rewards in terms of material gains. . . . We must [square] our own ethical conceptions with the traditional ethics and ideals of the community at large. [There is] nothing more vital to our own day than that those who act as fiduciaries in the strategic positions of our business civilization, should be held to those standards of scrupulous fidelity which [our] society has the right to demand.

The 75th anniversary of Justice Stone's landmark speech reminds all of us engaged in the profession of investment management how far we have departed from those standards of scrupulous fidelity, and gives us yet one more opportunity to strengthen our resolve to meet that test, and build a better financial world.

CHAPTER 13: PHILANTHROPY—SERVING OUR COMMUNITY AND OUR NATION[21]

In my long career, I've been lucky to earn enough—actually, more than enough—to assure my wife's future well-being; to leave some resources behind for my six children (as Warren Buffett says, "enough so that they can do anything they want, but not enough that they can do nothing"); to leave a mite to each of my 12 grandchildren; and ultimately to add a nice extra amount to the modest-sized foundation that I created many years ago. The choice to share my financial blessings with those less fortunate reflects my profound conviction that all of us who prosper in this great republic have a solemn obligation to recognize their good fortune by giving something back.

I've been able to accumulate this wealth despite giving, for the past 30 years, one-half of my annual income to various philanthropic causes. I don't look at these contributions as "charity." I look at them as an attempt to repay the enormous

21. Excerpts from *Enough. True Measures of Money, Business, and Life* (2008), edited and expanded.

debts I've accumulated over a lifetime, including, among many others, the hospitals and research programs whose cardiologists and guardian angels shepherded me through my five-decade struggle with heart disease, the church in which many members of our family express their faith, and the Greater Philadelphia community through the United Way.

Supporting the Community

My belief that at least some of my giving should be directed to my community—that "charity begins at home"—was, I think, largely responsible for my receiving the Alexis de Tocqueville Society Award at the United Way's 75th Anniversary in 1996. Here are some excerpts from the citation:

The United Way Tocqueville Society

> Jack Bogle's extraordinary spirit breathes life into Tocqueville's observation of what is best about America. As a volunteer and philanthropist he has put his own stamp of excellence on the educational and not-for-profit organizations he has served, and through these organizations has helped thousands of people. As a business leader, Jack has enabled people of modest means to participate in the unprecedented growth of the securities market.
>
> Jack's leadership of Vanguard's United Way campaign and his extraordinary personal generosity have catapulted Vanguard well over the million dollar mark in funds contributed annually to health and human services in the Philadelphia region. Thank you for making the Philadelphia region a better place to live, work, and raise our families.

The National Constitution Center

I've also supported some major causes that have given me the opportunity to serve our society, most notably the magnificent National Constitution Center on Independence Mall in Philadelphia, whose mission is to return the values of our U.S. Constitution back into the mainstream of American life. I've served the

WORDS FROM THOSE WHO KNOW BOGLE BEST

Ambassador Joseph M. Torsella, President and CEO, National Constitution Center, 1997–2003 and 2006–2009; U.S. representative to the United Nations, 2011–2013

The world knows what you have meant to the Constitution Center, because I and others have shouted it from the mountaintops: If you hadn't lent your enormous credibility, talent, and integrity to our lonely cause, that beautiful tribute to the idea of America would still be just a gleam in someone's eye, and maybe not even that. . . .

I will never forget the way you were always so quick to defuse a tense situation with a quip, or to deflect credit to others. . . . I marvel that when I look back on our friendship and partnership of more than 10 years, although we have climbed so many steep mountains, I remember—most of all—a sense of joy in the effort and the journey. You've taught me that, Jack, and I'll be forever grateful.

April 2009

Richard Stengel, President and CEO, National Constitution Center, 2003–2006; managing editor, Time magazine, 2006–2013

Only a former president [Bill Clinton]—and a popular one at that—could ever fill your shoes as chairman of the National Constitution Center. I'm thrilled for you and for the Constitution Center. What a wonderful coup, and a fitting way to pass the baton. Your service to the NCC—and to the nation—has been enormous and incomparable. We are all in your debt. And most of all, I will always cherish the two and a half years we worked together. It was a special time—and a special relationship.

January 2007

"We Have Climbed So Many Steep Mountains"

"Your Service to the Nation Has Been Enormous and Incomparable"

Center for 25 years, including almost eight years as its chairman,[22] and was proud to preside at its grand opening in 2003.

On my retirement as chairman, the trustees kindly commemorated my tenure:

> During his service as Chairman, John C. Bogle … successfully completed the design of the world-class facility, opened to the public, initiated successful programs to increase the understanding of the Constitution of the United States, and expanded its outreach to a national scale.… [We recognize his] leadership, wisdom, integrity, practicality, and good fellowship, crucial to the Center's success.

Pretty heady praise! But all I can say is, "I did my best."

Supporting Education

"I Was Given Scholarships, and I Darn Well Had an Obligation to Return the Favor by Funding Scholarships for Others"

Most of all, I've also done my best to support the educational institutions that paved the way for my adult life and my career. At the top of my philanthropic agenda were Blair Academy, located in the hills of northern New Jersey, which fostered my academic discipline and opened my mind to a better understanding of mathematics, history, science, and the English language, opening for me the door of opportunity; and Princeton University, which helped hone my mind and my character, instilled in me the enormous respect and appreciation I've developed for the liberal arts, fostered my interest in Western civilization and the Enlightenment—its philosophers, writers, historians, musicians, and artists—to say nothing of my near-reverence for our Founding Fathers, and, yes, the eighteenth-century values that I hold high to this day.

"What goes around comes around." At both institutions, I was given scholarships, and I figured that I darn well had an obligation to return the favor by funding scholarships for other young human beings who needed them every bit

---

22. I was succeeded as chairman by former U.S. presidents William Jefferson Clinton and then George H.W. Bush, followed by former Florida governor Jeb Bush.

as much as my brothers and I did. So my greatest philanthropic delight has come with endowing Bogle Brothers Scholarships for the remarkable students at Blair and Princeton who have been the beneficiaries.

I've been at this task for a long time, ever since the moment came, years ago, when my income began to nicely exceed my family expenses. So far, some 150 Blair students and 130 Princeton students have been beneficiaries of those Bogle Brothers scholarships; and those numbers will grow, I expect, in perpetuity.

It's been the thrill of a lifetime to meet so many of these exceptional young men and women, and I've vicariously enjoyed their academic accomplishments. These fine citizens have already begun, or will soon begin, to realize their potential to serve not only our own nation but our global society as well. As I observe our younger generation in action, my confidence in our nation and my hopes for our future soar to the skies.

My Huge Debt to Blair Academy

"My Skills in Writing and Communication, Mathematics, and Leadership Began at Blair"

Truth be told, Blair and Princeton played vital but different roles in my life. In retrospect, attending Blair Academy was the seminal event of my career, even my life. At Blair I received a first-class education. Whatever skills I have developed in writing and communication, mathematics, and some sense of leadership began at Blair Academy. As for the first of these, thanks to my schoolmasters in English, Henry Adams and Marvin Garfield Mason, I learned—the hard way!—how to write, how to communicate with wisely chosen words and disciplined grammar, and the importance of building a solid vocabulary. I learned to love the English language, and then go out and use it! (Perhaps my 10 books and the 575 speeches and lectures would attest to that claim.)

Second, math. In my trade, I've always been known as a "numbers man." That reputation arises importantly from the serious math that began for me with my first foray into algebra at Blair in 1945. The remarkable schoolmaster Jesse Witherspoon Gage awarded me a 40 (yes, out of 100) on my first exam. But he demanded much of me and I responded as best I could. On my final exam, Mr. Gage awarded me a rare 100. In a sense, my entire career has been numbers-based—the mathematics of the financial markets, and "the relentless rules of humble arithmetic," a phrase favored by Justice Brandeis. Small wonder that I've often been called "Beta Bogle, the data devil" by my colleagues. And it all began at Blair.

And, third, at a young age, thanks to football coach Steve Kuk, I learned about leadership. No, I wasn't a great athlete, but in my senior year, Steve—who was also in charge of the dining room—named me as captain of the waiters. From Steve, I learned the ropes, not merely taking responsibility for my own actions, but taking the responsibility of setting high standards for others. I learned about getting things done and about trusting other human beings, and in turn being trusted. I learned, too, that leaders should also be servants—never more obvious than when I lined up next to those muscular guys on the kitchen staff to scoop ice cream for hundreds of students every Sunday. "Servant-leadership," writ large.

"I Learned About Trusting Other Human Beings and Being Trusted"

A Time for Leadership

With the great service that Blair Academy had given to me, I knew that I must serve the school in return. In the era following my graduation in 1947, the school, like many of its peers, had fallen on hard times. So in 1971, eager to help, I accepted the trustees' offer to join the board. Blair gradually began to return to its earlier position as a top academic institution. I knew that we still had far to go and, in 1986, I was honored to accept the trustees' invitation to serve as chairman of the board. During my career I had learned much about the importance of leadership, and, when the opportunity arose in 1989 to bring in a new headmaster, I was ready to capitalize on this opportunity of a lifetime to move Blair forward.

"Ready to Capitalize on the Opportunity of a Lifetime: To Move Blair Forward"

During our search, an extraordinary individual emerged from our list of candidates. He was Chandler Hardwick, a 35-year-old faculty member at Connecticut's Taft School, a fine teacher and communicator, a man with charisma and character and energy. Our search committee endorsed my strong recommendation, and Chan and his lovely wife Monie began their tenure at the school in June 1989. With their leadership and drive, their unflagging energy and enthusiasm, and their love for the school, Blair Academy embarked on a remarkable renaissance—in faculty strength and student quality, in new buildings and immaculate grounds, and in spirit and reputation. When the Hardwicks stepped down in 2013, they had served Blair Academy for 24 years, the second-longest tenure in the school's

"Thank You for Being Yourself, As If You Ever Could Have Been Anyone Else"

WORDS FROM THOSE WHO KNOW BOGLE BEST

T. Chandler Hardwick, headmaster, Blair Academy, 1989–2013

We at Blair Academy would argue that your impact here—both in the very important tangible and in the impossible-to-measure abstract—is the purest and finest of all your visions for making the world a better place. This campus, shaped by your leadership and vision, is forever changed. Yet we know it is in giving generations of Blair boys and girls the opportunity to come, study, and learn here that your greatest impact lies.

Thank you for being yourself, as if you ever could have been anyone else. Thank you for giving Monie and me the opportunity to build a legacy at Blair. We honor your values and your vision in our work at Blair, values and vision shared and confirmed in all we do and with a foundation both in the abstract ideals of any such enterprise and in the very real, fully human figure of you, Jack.

Gratefully,

Chan

May 2009

165-year history. Of course, I was deeply saddened. But I found consolation in the knowledge that we could not possibly ask more of this remarkable couple.

Supporting Princeton University

Yes, ever since the formative character development that Blair Academy cultivated in this young boy, I've been writing, and counting, and striving to be the best leader that I could be. (Alas, I'm not a "natural leader.") Of course, Princeton University also deserves great credit (if that's the right word) for my development, but, to state the obvious, I'd never have gained admission there were it not for Blair Academy.

At Princeton, as the (true!) legend of my blessed career goes, I majored in economics, but—given my inability to grasp the ideas in the first edition of Nobel-laureate-to-be in economic sciences Paul Samuelson's classic textbook—in 1948, I earned a well-deserved D in my first semester. If I didn't improve, I would lose my scholarship and, as a result, would have to depart the University. (Paradoxically, in 1993, Dr. Samuelson would write the foreword to my first book.) But, I pressed on, closed the semester with a C, and the crisis passed. Despite the turbulence of my college years—the demands of my jobs as waiter and then as manager of the athletic association ticket office along with the challenging academic tasks I faced—my grades got better and better.

"If I Didn't Improve, I Would Lose My Scholarship and Have to Depart the University"

I wrote my senior thesis on the infant mutual fund industry, a fortuitous choice that led me directly into the field in which I would spend my entire career. Largely because of my thesis, I graduated with high honors. The idealistic design for a fund industry that I set forth in that thesis, published in 2001 (a cool 50 years later!) has been described as a template for Vanguard, the mutual fund firm that I founded in 1974, which is now the largest fund manager in the world, responsible for $2 trillion of other people's money. Maybe . . . but maybe not.

Whatever the case, my work in economics took me to the books of Adam Smith and John Maynard Keynes, and their words and their philosophies have punctuated and guided my learning and my writing to this day. In the brilliant company of Smith, Keynes, and Samuelson—surely among the most influential figures in the history of economic thought—my own ideas found inspiration and reinforcement.

However much I have done to repay Princeton for my awesome debts to her, the University seems always to stay one step ahead of me, repeatedly honoring my life and career. In 1999, I was awarded its Woodrow Wilson Prize, presented to an alumnus who exemplifies "Princeton in the Nation's Service." In 2005, the trustees bestowed on me an honorary doctor of laws degree, describing me as "an idealistic economics major . . . an unrelenting crusader . . . an outspoken advocate for intelligent investing." And in 2008, I was named as one of the 25 most influential Princetonians in history. (It's always nice to be in the company of idealists like James Madison and Woodrow Wilson!)

In what I presume must be its final act of grace to this aging alumnus, here's how Princeton described me on the plaque gracing Bogle Hall, a small dormitory that is part of the Butler College complex, dedicated in 2010:

> Visionary Leader in the Vanguard of Finance
> Author and Philanthropist
> Selfless and Uplifting Friend and Counselor
> Benefactor and Faithful Son of Princeton.

"The University Seems Always One Step Ahead of Me"

WORDS FROM THOSE WHO KNOW BOGLE BEST

Shirley M. Tilghman, president, Princeton University

I would like to say how much your alma mater appreciates the course you have charted since leaving Princeton in 1951. It is not success per se but how you have achieved it that has made your life a source of pride and inspiration for us all.

At a time when the reckless pursuit of profit has tarnished the entire financial industry, the personal probity, responsible stewardship, and fundamental fairness that you championed at the helm of Vanguard are a welcome reminder that there is another—and better—way to approach investing. As you told a group of young alumni shortly before I moved to Nassau Hall, "enlightened idealism is sound economics," just as service to others should be the sine qua non of higher education. And service to others, especially the individual investor, has been a hallmark of your "battle for the soul of capitalism," to cite a book that has never been more timely. How nice to think it was your senior thesis that launched you on this path!

Thank you, Jack, for taking Princeton's informal motto to heart and bringing the values that this campus helped to shape to work with you each day.

March 2009

Honorary Doctorate Citation, May 31, 2005

John Clifton Bogle, Doctor of Laws

In 1951, as an idealistic economics major, he proposed in his senior thesis the then-revolutionary concept of an efficient and economical mutual fund run primarily for the benefit of the investor. Known as a pioneer of index fund investing, he is an unrelenting crusader against high fees and hidden costs and an outspoken advocate for intelligent investing. Honesty is an integral element of his management strategy, reflecting his precept that character counts, in investing as in other walks of life. We honor him today for over half a century of making sure that the individual investor's interest remains always in the vanguard.

"We Honor Him Today for Making Sure That the Individual Investor's Interest Remains Always in the Vanguard"

A Fiduciary's Modest Rewards

"About 20 Percent of the Nation's Wealthiest Individuals Have Made Their Fortunes in the Financial Field"

Despite the many gifts that I have been able to make so far during my long life—and those gifts that will follow—my only wish is that I had more to give to the worldly needs of those less fortunate human beings who surround us. Alas, those needs are infinite and my resources are finite. Despite what I suppose has been a successful career in finance, my rewards have been comparatively modest.

The rewards for many financial leaders have been little less than awesome. About 20 percent of the elite group named on the 2012 *Forbes* 400 listing of the nation's wealthiest individuals have made their fortunes in the financial field—through some combination of entrepreneurship, speculation, hard work, or sheer good luck. And most founders of large investment management firms (and often their successors) have accumulated truly enormous wealth. The wealth of the lowest-ranking financial person on the *Forbes* list is estimated at $1.3 billion, and the highest-ranking (Fidelity's Johnson family) has accumulated some $25 billion.

I have never played in that billion-dollar-plus major league; nor, for that matter, even in a hundred-million-dollar minor league. Why not? Simply because when I founded Vanguard in 1974, I created a firm in which the lion's share of the rewards would be bestowed on the shareholders of the truly *mutual* mutual funds who have entrusted their assets to our care. In fact, cumulative savings to our shareholders vis-à-vis the shareholders of our peers now exceed $150 billion—about $16 billion in 2012 alone. Largely as a result, Vanguard continues to be the highest-value provider in the industry. (Its costs are reimbursed by our mutual funds.)

In fact, in comparison to nearly all, if not all, of my peers, I'm something of a financial failure. (Perhaps they are amused by the fact that they are so much wealthier than I am!) Of course you could say that failure was intentional—not that I had any premonition that we would grow to such a huge size, nor, in truth, any idea of how much wealth I might be relinquishing by creating Vanguard's mutual structure. For when I created Vanguard I strongly believed—and still believe today—that it is the duty of fiduciaries to place first the interests of those who have entrusted their hard-earned assets to their care. So, it was an easy decision: Vanguard must be owned not by me but by its fund shareholders, and they must be the primary beneficiaries of the financial rewards of its success.

Sources of My Wealth

But I'm doing just fine, thank you, for three reasons. First, I was born and raised to save rather than spend. I don't go for extravagance, and it still hurts me a bit to spend on anything that is not a necessity. I can't remember a single year during my long career in which I've spent more than I earned. And I just can't imagine owing a yacht, or a jet plane, or a giant mansion on a grand estate. What, really, is the point? So I save and I give.

Second, ever since I began working in 1951, I've been blessed with a fabulous defined-contribution retirement plan, provided at the outset by Wellington Management, and then carried over to Vanguard, where I've continued to invest to this day. Wellington's first contribution to the plan was made in July 1951, 15 percent of my first month's salary of $250, or just $37.50. (Yes, even back then defined contribution pension plans were available.) I've continued investing at least 15 percent of my compensation—which grew substantially during the late 1980s through the mid-1990s—in my retirement and thrift savings plan.

"The Humble Wonders of the Tax-Deferred Retirement Plan"

My experience is a living testament to how the humble wonders of the tax-deferred retirement plan, soundly invested over the long term, can build an accumulation of wealth. My own retirement plan is by far the largest single item on our family balance sheet. (I prefer not to tell the world the exact amount.)

Third, I've invested wisely in both my retirement plan and my personal holdings, eschewing speculation and focusing exclusively on (you guessed it!) conservatively invested, low-cost mutual funds, first in Wellington Fund and then largely in Vanguard's index funds. Late in 1999, observing the generous bond yields then available, and concerned about the (obviously) speculative level of stock prices, I reduced equities to about 35 percent of my assets, increasing my bond position to about 65 percent. While stock and bond market fluctuations have swung that ratio around a bit (mostly favoring bonds), I haven't made a significant change in my asset allocation since then. Even in today's turbulent markets, I do my best to avoid the temptation to peek at the value of my fund holdings. (A good rule for all of us!)

So I've been truly blessed by the magical combination of my genetic Scottish thrift; my generous compensation when I ran Vanguard; my propensity to save whatever remains each year; my retirement savings plan; the mathematical miracle of tax-free compounding; the knowledge that in investing, costs matter enormously; and enough common sense to focus on a balanced asset allocation. It works!

Words from Those Who Know Bogle Best

Frank K. Martin, investment adviser; founder, Martin Capital Management; author of *A Decade of Delusions*

In the Company of Greatness

If there's one word that explains the popularity of Jack Bogle's books and his iconic status among investors worldwide, including purveyors of advice in the investment industry who scorn him publicly while admiring him privately, it's *integrity*. As a personal friend as well as a disciple, I have been a firsthand witness as this trait of character manifests itself in all that Bogle says and does. The word *integrity* is often applied where it doesn't fit and hasn't been earned, which makes it all the more fitting in this instance. How is it that integrity has become synonymous with the persona of Jack Bogle? As another remarkable and courageous man, German theologian Dietrich Bonhoeffer, observed, one can often find the significant in the trivial.

In 1974, Bogle made what at the time might have seemed like an inconsequential decision. As founder of the Vanguard Group, he decided that it should be organized as a "mutual" fund, owned by its investors, to whom the fund's profits would flow through lower costs. While he could not have known at the time the exact opportunity cost of his decision, he surely knew it would be huge.

In a world inclined to measure success in dollar terms, Jack Bogle would not even warrant honorable mention. And yet he has achieved his iconic status among tens of millions of investors while most men of wealth from the financial sector, save, perhaps, for a few like his friend Warren Buffett, have discovered something that money won't buy. Because of that crucial decision made years ago, Jack Bogle does not write to his legions of followers from a gilded cage. He writes as one of them, as their equal, as a man who has walked in their shoes. Their fears are his fears, their realities his realities.

It is his priceless integrity and incorruptible motives thus revealed that have long inspired me. As Charlie Munger likes to say, and I paraphrase, tell me a man's motives and I'll tell you the outcome. Jack Bogle's motives are unimpeachably transparent, making his honesty and candor all the more appealing. He says what he means, and means what he says. He is a man who has always been able to see the forest while most only see the trees. The subliminal message that percolates up through each book is the story of the life of Jack Bogle, the tireless champion of what is right and true, of what it means to live a life of integrity.

Frank Martin

August 2012

> *"Jack Bogle Does Not Write to His Legions of Followers from a Gilded Cage. He Writes As One of Them."*

My Philosophy of Life

Whoever cultivates the Golden Mean avoids both the poverty of a hovel and the envy of a palace.

Some two millennia ago, the Roman poet Horace set forth the standard of the Golden Mean. It is an equally valid standard today. My own resources surely place me within that Golden Mean, if clearly in the higher reaches among all U.S. citizens. We who are members of what *New York Times* columnist David Brooks has described as "the investor class" can feel proud of our good fortune and our thrift. But even as we thrive on the great benefits conferred to us as American citizens, we must remind ourselves that far too large a portion of our citizenry has not adequately shared in these benefits.

"'The Investor Class' Can Feel Proud of Our Good Fortune and Our Thrift"

The Declaration of Independence assures us "that all men are created equal, that they are endowed by their Creator with certain unalienable Rights, that among these are Life, Liberty, and the pursuit of Happiness." While we all may be *created* equal, however, the moment that birth takes place, inequality—of family, of wealth, of race, of education, and, yes, even of opportunity—begins for our citizens.

Our Constitution demands more. "We the People" are enjoined "to form a more perfect Union, establish Justice, insure domestic Tranquility,... promote the general Welfare, and secure the Blessings of Liberty to ourselves and our Posterity." These commitments—especially to *a more perfect* union, to *establish* justice, to *insure* domestic tranquility, to promote the *general* welfare—are more than mere words; they represent the challenge of our age.

In his second inaugural address, President Franklin D. Roosevelt beautifully expressed this challenge:

> The test of our progress is not whether we add more to the abundance of those who have much; it is whether we provide enough for those who have too little.

The joy of giving provides delightful pleasure. But giving is not only joy, it is duty—the solemn duty of those who have been favored by birth, by the genes that call for determination and hard work, by education, and by luck, to achieve financial success. We who have been blessed with prosperity in this land of opportunity and freedom have an obligation to share our resources with those less fortunate, and with the institutions that have shaped our lives and bestowed upon us our infinite blessings.

REWARDS FOR THE VISION—LETTERS OF APPRECIATION

I N PART VI, a chorus from all walks of career and life sings out its (generous) appreciation of Bogle's accomplishments. It starts with a philosophical primer by investment adviser, author, and Boglehead Allan Roth on what Jack Bogle means to millions of investors. His answer is as simple as it is poignant, as he presents comments from seven Bogleheads, including their founding leader, Taylor Larimore.

These letters are then followed by nine more from Vanguard shareholders, including a law professor, English teacher, Boston Coach driver, 89-year-old retiree, West Point cadet, and grounds maintenance worker. These are just a few of the thousands of Vanguard shareholders who have written to Bogle over the years. They express their appreciation for what Vanguard means to them and their families. Their stories illuminate the Vanguard founder's special place in the hearts and minds of many ordinary investors who deeply appreciate the Vanguard way.

In the third and final section—which begins with one poem and ends with another—we hear from 12 Vanguard crew members: We learn what working at Vanguard means to them. We also get a sense for their relationship with Bogle over the years, and how his philosophy of management focused on human beings is actually experienced within the ranks of Vanguard crew members. It is apparent from these letters that "human beingness" is felt and experienced, yet more examples of Bogle and Vanguard walking the walk that they talk.

CHAPTER 14: COMMENTS FROM BOGLEHEADS

The Bogleheads are, well, a happening. Spearheaded by Florida investor Taylor Larimore, this group of informed, help-one-another investors now has some 37,000 members. The members of the Bogleheads community add 12,000 to 25,000 posts on their website each month, with local chapters all over the world. They are smart, well-versed in investment principles, and simply interested in educating their fellow investors.

Allan Roth

Allan Roth is the founder of Wealth Logic and author of How a Second Grader Beats Wall Street: Golden Rules Any Investor Can Learn.

For many years, I've been asking people what money means to them. Reponses are typically words like *freedom*, *security*, *survival*, and *enjoyment*. Surprisingly, I rarely hear the word *happiness*, which begs the question: If money doesn't bring happiness, why do we place such importance on it? But before answering this, let's look at some research on happiness.

Many people perceive that the path to happiness lies in either reaching goals or acquiring possessions. All that separates us from being truly happy is getting that promotion, buying that big house, or cruising the neighborhood in that shiny new luxury car. In reality, the promotion brings more stress, the big house brings more maintenance, and the luxury car brings more anxiety about getting that first ding.

Former *Wall Street Journal* personal finance writer Jonathan Clements has written often on the subject of finding happiness and has arrived at his own conclusions based on the research. It turns out that happiness lies more in the journey than in reaching the destination. People are most happy when doing the activities they love. That can vary from spending time with family to doing charity work, traveling, and the like.

Money is really stored energy that allows us to do what we want with our lives. It does not bring happiness in itself; it only brings the freedom to pursue happiness. It brings the freedom to leave our jobs at an earlier age and concentrate full-time on what engages our interest and passion, regardless of whether it is financially gainful. Money brings choices. If we use this freedom wisely, we can make great strides toward finding our uniquely personal happiness. Money can also bring misery if we view the life choices it brings as creating stress.

What does all of this have to do with John C. Bogle? In 1975, Jack brought the first index mutual fund to the public. Since then, over $2 trillion has poured into stock and bond index funds. According to my estimates, the lower fees of these funds alone saved investors $25 billion in 2012. Beyond indexing, Jack Bogle has caused other active funds to lower costs and increase transparency, giving investors a bigger share of returns. In short, Bogle is responsible for consumers earning tens of billions of dollars each year that would have gone to Wall Street. That's a lot of freedom to pursue happiness.

Yet Jack Bogle's legacy goes far beyond giving investors a fair shake in keeping their share of the profits of capitalism rather than feeding the financial services industry. This legacy has given me and millions of others the freedom to pursue whatever gives our lives meaning. So why then at age 84, 17 years after a heart transplant, isn't Jack Bogle taking it easy and enjoying life? The answer is easy; his 61-year journey of helping the Main Street investor is a large part of what brings him happiness. How fortunate for us all that Jack Bogle's journey to find happiness has the added benefit of allowing us the stored energy to search for our own happiness.

"Money . . . Brings the Freedom to Pursue Happiness"

Jack Bogle's legacy is far more than the first investor-owned mutual fund family, popularizing no-load mutual funds, or even the first index fund available to Main Street investors. His legacy is that he gave millions of Main Street investors the freedom to pursue happiness.

Personally, Jack Bogle has given me the wisdom to press on regardless in doing my small part to spread the word on just how simple investing should be. My life journey is far more rewarding because of Mr. Bogle, as are those of countless others. What follows are just a few stories of life journeys changed by Jack Bogle.

William Bernstein

"A Man Who Takes the Time to Formulate Thoughtful and Constructive Written Answers to Silly Questions"

William Bernstein is an author and the founder of Efficient Frontier Advisors.

The hardest part of describing how Jack has benefited me, those in my immediate vicinity, and those who have read my books and website posts is doing so in just a few hundred words.

First, Jack answers his mail, no matter who it's from. A few years ago, I was cleaning out my files and came across several long single-spaced letters from him dating to the early 1990s, before I had published any books or started my website. Here, then, is a man who takes the time to formulate thoughtful and constructive written answers to silly questions from nobodies like me. Very impressive.

Second, he, more than anyone else, has shown the world, in a general sense, the folly of active management and, more specifically, the mendacity of the rest of the investment industry.

Third, he created the Vanguard Group, and instead of getting rich from it—and make no mistake about it, he would be a multibillionaire by now had he held on to his ownership stake—he gave it away to the company's customers, who benefit from the resultant reduction in fees. Imagine for a minute that you go out and buy a Ford, and every year that you own the vehicle the company sends you a check for a few hundred dollars—your share of its profits. Jack created a system that does just that for Vanguard's customers; invest $100,000 with Vanguard, and every year the company returns $1,000 or so to you in the form of expenses that are that much lower than the industry average.

Forcing Other Funds to Reduce Their Expenses

Even better, you don't even have to be a Vanguard shareholder to reap at least some of that benefit. Because of competition from Vanguard, other investment companies have been forced to reduce their expenses on their open-end mutual funds and exchange-traded funds (ETFs). It would be only a slight exaggeration to say that Jack, all by himself, has made me, my family, and our clients if not wealthy, at least comfortably well-to-do.

Fourth, Jack has taught the world the importance of long-term stay the-course discipline in investing and, more than anyone else, has shown investors, large and small, just how to estimate the returns of stocks and bonds. It's not that hard—you just have to add three numbers together. Had more people listened to him in the late 1990s and in 2008–2009, they'd have been a lot better off.

Last, and not least, his force of character has been a personal inspiration to all of us. To Warren Buffett's famous dictum, "How would this look on the front page of the *New York Times*?" add another: "What would Jack do?"

Rick Ferri

Rick Ferri is an author and the founder of Portfolio Solutions.

I remember the exact moment when John Bogle changed my life. I was sitting in the parking lot of the local House of Horrors one October night in 1996. My children were screaming inside as headless goblins chased them around with chainless chainsaws. All the while, I passed the time reading John Bogle's first book, *Bogle on Mutual Funds*.

I picked up the book at the local Barnes & Noble, a place I frequented quite regularly. Why not read a book on index funds? I had read nearly every book on how to beat the stock market, and nothing worked. Bogle's book was offering an alternative. He spoke about being the market, not beating the market. It might make sense.

My occupation as a stockbroker at Smith Barney had become terribly unsatisfying. All of the promises I sold to my clients turned out to be a mistake. The products make a lot of money for the company and very little for investors. There was a revolving door of products and no end to the lies.

I sat, listened to children screaming, and thought I was reading a book on index fund investing.

Wait . . . what am I reading here? This Bogle guy isn't talking just about index funds; he's talking about the lies, dishonesty, and unethical standards that define Wall Street and the mutual fund industry. He is describing my exact experience as a stockbroker! Wow! Bogle doesn't even know me and he's inside my head.

Stop—I needed to read the book again, from the beginning, every word.

My God! This Bogle guy is *so* right! It's the industry that's the problem, not me. I want to structure clients' portfolios in index funds but the industry won't let me. I want to limit portfolio turnover but the industry won't let me. I want to act as a fiduciary in the best interest of my clients but the industry won't let me.

A chemical reaction took place in my brain. I couldn't be a broker anymore. I had to do it another way—the Bogle way.

Unfortunately, I couldn't quit the brokerage industry in 1996 because I would have to pay back thousands of dollars in signing bonuses plus a lot of other benefits. So, I suffered through another three years of lies, deceit, and absolute nonsense until my contract ended.

Finally, in July 1999, I broke free of Wall Street and started an investment advisory firm based on John Bogle's principles. It was liberating—and challenging. I bet my career and all the money my wife and I had saved to start a firm that

"The Lies, Dishonesty, and Unethical Standards that Define Wall Street"

followed Bogle's philosophy, but I knew it would work because he was right, and if we also did what was right, the business couldn't lose.

It hasn't. Thank you, John Bogle!

Taylor Larimore

Taylor Larimore is a coauthor of The Bogleheads' Guide to Investing *and* The Bogleheads' Guide to Retirement Planning.

In 1994 I was fortunate to read *Bogle on Mutual Funds*. In the book, Jack's "Twelve Pillars of Wisdom," each backed up with his reasoning and academic research, were so logical that I drastically changed our complex portfolio of 15 managed funds to a seven-fund portfolio that incorporated *indexing* and *simplicity*. It was gratifying to see almost immediately that our Bogle-designed portfolio was outperforming the funds we had discarded.

In 1999, when I learned that Mr. Bogle was going to be the keynote speaker at "The Money Show" in Orlando, Florida, my wife Pat and I made the decision to go and hear the speech and, we hoped, meet him personally. We drove to Orlando and spent the first night in the convention hotel.

"Not Surrounded by Guards and Staff, Just Two Old Ladies Seeking Advice"

Next morning after breakfast, Pat and I were walking down the hallway toward the auditorium when I saw a tall gentleman in a light sweater talking to two elderly ladies. I instantly recognized Jack from pictures I had seen. He had been on the cover of the February 1991 issue of *Financial World* magazine (which I still have). We had expected John Bogle, chairman of a giant mutual fund company, to be surrounded by guards and staff—not two old ladies seeking advice.

Pat and I listened to the conversation. We were too starstruck to say anything. We followed Jack and the ladies into the auditorium, where he almost immediately went to the podium to speak before a crowd of several thousand. This is a portion of his exact words recorded by a member of the press:

I count that you'll have the opportunity to attend roughly 130 different seminars, masterminded by more than 100 speakers. It looks to me as if the great preponderance of them will offer you their secrets for success in the new millennium. Many speakers will offer you tempting solutions involving at best complexity and at worst financial legerdemain and witchcraft.

> I must confess that, no offense intended to the presenters, I wince when I see so many subjects that seem to offer easy roads for you to build your capital: "Wealth Creation and Preservation: Increasing Yields to 15–20 Percent," "The Possible Trillion-Dollar Opportunity of the Internet," "Finding Future Wealth in Diamond Mines," "High-Profit, Low-Risk Strategies" . . .

> I assume from the titles that these speakers will offer you the secrets of success. Let me offer mine: The one great secret of investment success is that there is no secret. . . . Investment success, it turns out, lies in simplicity as basic as the virtues of thrift, independence of thought, financial discipline, realistic expectations, and common sense.

"Investment Success
Lies in Simplicity"

I doubt if Mr. Bogle will be invited back to many more "Money Shows."

In 2000, I learned that Mr. Bogle was to be keynote speaker at a *Miami Herald*–sponsored financial convention in Miami. Mel [Lindauer] and I took a chance and invited Jack to a Florida seafood dinner prepared by Pat in our condominium. To our surprise, he accepted. We took a chance and invited *everyone* on the Morningstar Bogleheads forum to be our guests. Twenty-one Bogleheads showed up for what became a magical night. Our dinner that evening became the first Bogleheads reunion and initiated a friendship with Jack and his wife that has changed our lives, like so many others'.

> There is no one in the mutual fund industry with a greater combination of practical experience, perseverance, inventive genius, literary ability, kindness, modesty, desire to help others, and impeccable character.

Philip DeMuth

Philip DeMuth is an author and the founder of Conservative Wealth Management.

In 1994, I was a practicing psychologist investing a few dollars of my own on the side. I was buying Morningstar five-star funds that always seemed to turn into one-star funds during my tenure. Then some preternatural force guided my hand to *Bogle on Mutual Funds* at Barnes & Noble. I read it and did not understand a single word. So, I read it again. And again—five times in all, until I got it. I stopped asking my clients about sex and started asking them about their investment portfolios. I met Ben Stein and our friendship galvanized around the fact that we were both devotees of Jack's. That's how I became an investment adviser and author—all due to John C. Bogle.

Rick Van Ness

Rick Van Ness is the founder of FinancingLife.org.

An old saying that has been very true for me is: "When you are ready, a teacher will appear." Jack Bogle has been the third, and most influential, of three that I'll mention. The first was in 1978 when Andrew Tobias wrote his popular best seller with a chapter in it titled: "A Penny Saved Is Two Pennies Earned." This brilliant observation gave me a solid rationale for building a strong habit of automatic investments from every paycheck.

Ten years later, I met author Vicki Robin, who transformed the way I thought about financial independence. While my mind associated this phrase with wealth, Vicki described a life of freedom—where she could wake up every morning and volunteer for organizations she supported. Further, she viewed jobs as trading "life energy" for money. And this gave me a healthy framework for spending decisions.

I stumbled upon the Bogleheads forum. Wow. Who were these people who were being so helpful, so generous with their time and knowledge, and often anonymously? Inspired by their generosity, I decided to create bite-size

"The Bogleheads...
Were Being So Helpful,
So Generous With Their
Time and Knowledge"

educational videos to help others accumulate wealth and achieve financial independence. Creating these videos led me to the simple elegance of Jack Bogle's thinking. He writes so compellingly and so clearly. I knew I was on the right track.

By the time he wrote the book *Enough.*, I was convinced that Jack is as noble and unselfish as he appears—the very model of ethics and integrity. For me, he is also a role model of giving back—investing his energy into spreading his commonsense wisdom out through countless interviews, presentations, and books. I now understand why the Bogleheads' website has so many generous individuals more than willing to help others and share this wisdom.

Despite Jack Bogle's tireless efforts and this gem of a website, these commonsense investing principles are not common knowledge. I've decided to do whatever I can to help spread financial literacy. To date I have had nearly 100,000 views of these videos on YouTube, the Boglehead wiki, and my website at www.FinancingLife.org. I'm encouraged by the start and am working on more. Thank you to Jack, and to all other teachers who are so generous and wise.

"So Many Generous Individuals More Than Willing to . . . Share This Wisdom"

John Edwards

John Edwards is a Boglehead.

I've never met Jack Bogle, but his impact on my life will be far-reaching. I was fortunate to learn of his investment strategies at the start of my earning years. Jack's focus on simplicity in investing made his concepts approachable and understandable. Without Jack, my vision would have been shortsighted.

Like many youth, I felt as long as I kept my finger on the pulse of the market, I would easily outpace it. After all, for a class project in 1995, I was able to produce high simulated returns for a few months with little information. My short, uninformed experience was in still waters, though, and it established overconfidence.

"His Concepts Are Approachable and Understandable"

However, that experience was more than most people have before they prepare for retirement.

Thankfully, Jack's espousal of basic investment rules has expanded my knowledge and may, in the future, allow me a little wisdom. Because of Jack, I have diversified my holdings in total market index funds and kept costs low (this was made possible through Jack's commitment to the investor by introducing the world to the low-cost index fund); I have kept my investment strategy simple, and expect to stay the course during market manias and depressions. These concepts are so simple, yet they are difficult to follow.

Jack's influence has compelled my family to live below our means, allowing us the freedom of living responsibly without the worry of how we will pay for food or rent the next month. It is truly liberating to know we are doing all that we can to ensure a bright future and experience life's joy today without financial uncertainty. Mr. Bogle shares simple strategies; wise words are rarely complicated. When my son is ready to take responsibility for his financial path, he will learn of a man named Jack.

"Concepts that Are Simple, Yet Difficult to Follow"

Barb Dewey

Barb Dewey is a Boglehead.

John Bogle means more to me than wise investing. For even though this champion of the small investor has saved me many thousands of dollars since I first invested in his low-cost index funds in the late 1980s, it is his integrity that has come to mean the most, especially against the backdrop of the financial industry's role in the financial crisis. In the darkest moments of that crisis of rampant greed and lost humanity, I would look for John Bogle's integrity, for his advice not just to us small investors to stay the course if we've invested well (although that in itself would have been enough), but also for moral guidance.

*"I Would Look for John Bogle's
Integrity, for His Advice . . .
And Moral Guidance"*

What can we Main Streeters do about Wall Street greed? For that matter, what can Main Street do about its own greed? And what can Wall Street do to save itself? After some 60 years in the financial world, did John Bogle still believe in our financial system? Could the system be changed? What could be done to change it? To me, if he still basically believed in it, I knew I could and I would remain an investor.

Mr. Bogle's answers, of course, are in his many books and speeches and interviews. In them is all the wisdom in the world for the small investor, plenty to remind us to save regularly, appreciate the power of compounding, properly allocate assets based on risk tolerance, and continue to stay the course. Then there is his response to the big-picture questions about our financial industry, most notably in his most recent book, *The Clash of the Cultures: Investment vs. Speculation*. As I read it I thought, "Who better to answer these questions than a man of integrity?"

Chapter 15: Letters from Vanguard Clients

Dear Mr. Bogle:

The purpose of this letter is to praise you for the exceptional clarity and usefulness of your "Chairman's Letter" in the Annual Report 1993, and the inside-front-and-back-cover essay.

"You Aren't Pushing Vanguard,
Just Giving the Facts"

Clarity: Your language is straightforward, free of jargon, objective. You are honest with your readers, free of hype. You aren't pushing Vanguard, just giving the facts. The charts and figures are easy to understand.

Usefulness: Although I regularly read *Money* and *Kiplinger's*, and the *Wall Street Journal*, I find the general market analysis essay (front and back covers) the best compact, objective summary of advice to the average investor I have ever seen.

Moreover, your "Letter" is equally lucid, compact, and useful in laying out the facts of the five Vanguard index funds. I'm going to stay with Vanguard!

Sincerely,

Vanguard Shareholder

Brunswick, ME

March 1994

*"You Have Helped Me
Teach English Grammar"*

Dear Mr. Bogle:

This is a fan letter from an English teacher. I read your book *Bogle on Mutual Funds* right after its publication. I love your writing style! Your lucid exposition made financial concepts clear and confirmed many of my own impressions about the mutual fund industry and investor behavior. As time goes by, I am more and more convinced that your approach to the financial markets is correct. Thank you for sharing your wisdom with small investors like me. But that is not the only reason for this letter.

I want you to know how you have helped me teach English grammar. Like the financial markets, language is incredibly complex. Think about five basic sentence patterns, a lexicon of thousands of words, and infinite possibilities each time a sentence is generated. No wonder high school students find the study of advanced grammar overwhelming at times. Yet the workings of language can be understood on the basis of relatively simple underlying concepts. On page 302 of your book, you make the following statement: "When all else fails, fall back on simplicity." Mr. Bogle, that advice applies to the work my college-bound students find so intensely demanding.

"When All Else Fails, Fall Back on Simplicity"

Now when my students begin to struggle with new material, I ask them what they can always fall back on. Their answer: simplicity. And it works for them. When my young charges fall back on simple concepts from the earlier part of their studies, complex lessons become understandable. Maybe you and I have taught these youngsters a basic lesson in life.

Thank you again for taking the time to share your knowledge with the rest of us, for speaking out against the casino mentality in the current stock market, for crusading against high mutual fund expenses, and for helping me teach grammar to high school freshmen. I wish you all the best.

Sincerely,

Vanguard Shareholder

Orange, TX

February 1997

"... How Important It Is to Show Students that You Can Make Money, and Do So Honorably"

Dear Mr. Bogle,

As a satisfied Vanguard investor (since 1989), I really appreciate the hard work, leadership, and vision that you have provided since the founding of the company. Your book is also excellent, one that I recommend first when asked by friends, clients, and/or students about an authoritative resource on investment strategy.

As a law professor I use Vanguard as a prime example of how a company's fiduciary responsibilities not only *should* be met, but actually *are* met. The unique Vanguard corporate structure stands in dramatic contrast to the usual mutual fund setup. As Judge (later Justice) Cardozo once wrote, "Not honesty alone, but the punctilio of an honor the most sensitive, is then the standard of behavior." I cannot tell you how important it is to show students that you can make money, and do so honorably.

In any event, thanks again for your pioneering role in Vanguard and the mutual fund industry. Thanks, too, for making me a lot of money. Finally, please keep giving 'em hell, St. Jack!

Sincerely,

Attorney and Vanguard Shareholder

Chapel Hill, NC

April 1997

A Boston Coach Driver Gets a Call

Dear Mr. Bogle:

You may not remember me, but I was the Boston Coach driver who, in 1997, picked you and your lovely wife up at your son's home in Wellesley. To this day I do not know why I happened to start a conversation with you regarding mutual funds but it was my good fortune that I did. At the time I honestly did not know who you were. You suggested I invest in the Tax-Managed Capital Appreciation Fund, which I did. You even called me at home one evening.

My wife and I are now enrolled in Vanguard's Asset Management and Trust program. Thank you; we're very pleased to be on board with Vanguard, and look forward to the day when, with the help of our investments, we will be able to retire.

Sincerely,

Vanguard Shareholder

San Antonio, TX

July 26, 2002

"Your Writing Style Reaches Those of Us Who Are Less Knowledgeable"

Dear Mr. Bogle:

I have just finished your splendid book, *Character Counts*, and have had difficulty in putting it down. I had read *Bogle on Mutual Funds* and *Common Sense on Mutual Funds*, so I was prepared to appreciate *Character Counts*. Your writing style reaches those of us who are less knowledgeable concerning investments.

In 1948 a young man in a white suit, driving a white Lincoln from New York, drove to Clayton, Delaware, population 800, to see us about investing. My husband was a country doctor and I had taught school, and neither of us had any knowledge of investing. He sold us Wellington Fund, into which we paid $100.00 a month for 10 years. In 1958 we received a call telling us that the new Windsor Fund would be a suitable investment for us. We consented and our beloved Windsor has been with us since that time. We decided that all future investing would be done with Vanguard. What a blessing! Your *In the Vanguard* was an education in itself.

I will celebrate my 90th birthday August 31st and the present market situation has not worried me at all. I am with Vanguard! STAY THE COURSE!

With my very best wishes to you and your family, that you may spend years of happiness together. The secret of your success has been faith and hope. God bless you!

Sincerely,

Vanguard Shareholder

Dover-Foxcroft, ME

August 2002

*"The Only 'Magic' Is
Compounding"*

Dear Mr. Bogle,

I would like to thank you for the years you spent helping the average American learn to invest for the long term. There is no shortage of investment advice available at the local bookstore. However, your books are unique in that they profess the only "magic" to be that of compounding.

"Life Is Best when One Worries Least"

Vanguard has been wonderful, although we miss your presence and frank annual reports. You proved that character does indeed matter. One of the primary benefits of investing at Vanguard has been the almost complete lack of worry about our portfolio. Strange thing—life and its blessings are best when one worries least. And money is not worth worrying about, especially if one is a good steward.

Thank you again for your devotion to the average citizen. You will probably never know how much good you have done for so many people.

Sincerely yours,

Vanguard Shareholder

Wolfforth, TX

September 2002

A Cadet Says "Thank You"

"Honor, Integrity, Devotion to Family, Selflessness, Personal Courage, Sincerity, and Humility"

Mr. Bogle,

It's hard to believe it's been a month since your visit to West Point.

Your gift and letter were a wonderful surprise. I've started to read your book and can't wait to finish it over the summer. I'd like to thank you again for affording me the opportunity to spend the evening with you and your son. I've really come to believe that a humble disposition and sincere concern for others are absolutely essential for any effective leader.

That said, I was blown away by how purely you embodied these traits. Though you've certainly reached impressive heights as a professional, what I will remember more vividly about you is your dedication to and espousal of what's most important with regard to leadership—honor, integrity, devotion to family, selflessness, personal courage, sincerity, and humility. As you explained, even as the Army's mission is explicitly different from those of a typical financial firm, strong leadership in one parallels that of the other.

If you're ever having a rainy day, just remember that you were the only civilian speaker I've ever seen receive a standing ovation in my four years as a cadet.

Respectfully,

Cadet, U.S. Military Academy, Battalion Commander

West Point, NY

2006

Dear Mr. Bogle,

I'm not sure if you remember me, but I did the landscaping/ grounds maintenance work at the Vanguard office buildings when they were located in Chesterbrook and for the first

"I Have Learned a Lot About the Simplicity of Investing By Reading Your Books"

10 years after you built your corporate campus in Malvern. You were always very nice and often chatted with me when you ran into me on the campus. I always appreciated your taking the time to do that.

It is hard to believe that when Vanguard moved its headquarters into Chesterbrook in 1983, I wasn't sure what Vanguard did or what a mutual fund was. Now that I have been a Vanguard index investor for over 25 years, I realize that we have done well because we always took your advice and "stayed the course." I have learned a lot about the simplicity of investing by reading your books and the newspaper articles that you occasionally write—most recently in the *Wall Street Journal* a few weeks ago.

I just wanted to let you know that I and many of my friends really appreciate everything you have done for "the little guy." I hope everything is well with you and I'm looking forward to your next book.

Sincerely,

Vanguard Shareholder

Phoenixville, PA

September 2010

*"The Heavens Opened Up
and the Investment
Angels Sang"*

Dear Jack,

This thank-you note has been more than 10 years in the making. Though we only physically met yesterday, you have been on a journey with me, in my mind and in my heart, for a decade. It all began when I first opened up *Common Sense on Mutual Funds*. It was as if the heavens opened up and the investing angels sang.

Your words, your wisdom, your wit came flying through those pages (and all the pages since) and they changed my life and those of my family forever. In a short 10-year period, following the Bogle Truth, my husband and I have created a life for ourselves of financial knowledge and freedom. My family and I are first-generation Vietnamese immigrants. We came to the States literally with nothing but the clothes on our backs. We struggled for years and years, but managed to take this country up on her promise of a great life.

Thanks largely to you, this poor Vietnamese girl is completely debt free, including all mortgages and $200,000 in graduate school loans, and has a very sizable portfolio. The effect you've had on me will positively impact my family for generations. I thank you for all that you've done on behalf of all the people you'll never meet, but have helped.

Vanguard Shareholder

October 2012

CHAPTER 16: LETTERS FROM VANGUARD CREW MEMBERS

Ten Years After

How do I do justice to a champion bloke like Jack?
He's been more than an influence; he put me on a different tack.
It's been a full decade now since I chanced across his way,
A wonderful, exciting era, hard work and a fair share of play.

He took me in and led me, offered a "star to steer her by,"
Taught me business by example, and business principles by the bye.
If ever I had good fortune, it was the day I met this chap,
And it galls me now how slowly I saw what had fallen in my lap.

"A Gift He Uses to Enchant
... Sometimes to Preach"

If you look into his blue-gray eyes, as far as you can see,
There's Vanguard's farsighted vision, as pellucid as can be.
There's the face of a spirited fighter in that deep-furrowed brow.
You see the face of a man who's battled, and seen it through to victory now.

Though his scowl has withered many, his smile and laugh warm the soul.
And his memory, rarely faltering, spits out names, facts, stories of days of old.
Surely, the man has many talents, none better than "the speech,"
A gift he uses to enchant, to lead, oft to tutor, sometimes to preach.

Though it's been said by some that his cleric's collar is too tight,
For my part, I think the man's got it just about right.
The crew cut shows he's different, some say just a pain-in-the-ar**,
But after 10 years I know better; he's a true maverick, right-on iconoclast.

Ask anyone who has met him, Jack is a special friend.
And tears well up in the eyes and it's hard to comprehend
That a man can touch so many with his joy and inner grace.
The Jack Bogle/Vanguard legend will grow and never cease.

Well, I know I haven't done justice to this man I'm proud to know.
The impact's been so deep, the gratitude's tough to show.
And I don't expect him to comment, but I have an urge to say:
Where the hell without Bogle would Duffield be today?

Vanguard Crew Member, now 30-year veteran
April 18, 1995

"He Has Found for Himself... the Perfect Task and the Perfect Role Model"

Dear Mr. Bogle,

As my son started in his professional life [at Vanguard], he has searched for an object in life and a role to follow. With the heavy amount of medicine around him at home, he was torn back and forth and at times almost guilty that he hadn't followed in the area of medicine. If he had done that, I know he would have been outstanding. However, he has found for himself the perfect task and the perfect role model.

He has grown so quickly over the past years with you and the team at Vanguard. When the opportunity came for him to return to Vanguard after his first year at the Business School, there was no doubt in his mind where he would go. I would question him about greater financial opportunities elsewhere and so forth, and he said, "Dad, there is only one place that I really feel comfortable working, and it's because of the people there." Of course the person he had worked for entirely in the previous three years there had been you. Thank you for all you have done for my son and for the great example you have given.

More than all the rest, it was wonderful to see how well you have done after your heart transplant. The activities you have now bring back a sparkle to your life, and in talking to Dr. Roman DeSanctis, he knows how pleased you are. We hope that the result goes on for years and years.

Sincerely,

Boston Cardiologist, father of a Vanguard crew member

June 1998

Sitting a Young Office Cleaner Down to Discuss His Plans for the Future

Mr. Bogle,

Thanks for all the support and encouragement you have given to me over the years. You alone are responsible for my initial employment with Vanguard. I don't know if you remember sitting a young office cleaner down to discuss how

I was doing and what my plans were for the future, but it certainly made a lasting impression on me and one that will always be special. It is especially poignant in light of what was happening in your life and the life of the organization at that time. For the Chairman of the Board to take an interest in me at that time, well . . . this was certainly an organization I wanted to work for.

I've actually grown up with Vanguard and it will be difficult to acclimate myself to the realization that I'm no longer part of this organization. You should be justly proud of what you have built in Vanguard. From a small organization to the leader in the mutual fund industry is quite an accomplishment. The vast majority of the growth of this organization can be attributed to your values, insights, and efforts. "Bogle's folly" is now the envy of the mutual fund world.

Your leadership of this organization over the years has meant a tremendous amount to the employees. We're extremely proud to say that we work for the Vanguard shareholder and believe in Jack Bogle. Thanks again for all your encouragement and support. God bless!

Vanguard Crew Member

August 1998

"We're Proud To Say that We Work for the Vanguard Shareholder"

Mr. Bogle,

I've just come back from your book signing and wanted to send a brief note to say thank you. Not just for giving all of us crew members your new book and for taking time out of your busy schedule to personally sign each one—but most of all for this company. Vanguard is one of a kind, and I feel extremely fortunate and proud to be part of it.

Everything about Vanguard that you have fostered—its low-cost, high-value approach, its commitment to excellence, its dedication to its employees—makes me glad to come to work every day.

When you started Vanguard over 20 years ago, you probably had no idea of the impact you would have on the lives of so many people. But your vision of investing didn't just give the world the index fund and a low-cost way for the average investor to reap the rewards of the stock market. It also has given many of the 8,000 crew members here and their families—like mine—stability, security, and happiness in

"Your Vision . . . Has Given Many Crew Members . . . Stability, Security, and Happiness in Their Daily Lives"

their daily lives. And those returns pay dividends across a lifetime, and even across generations.

So thanks again for all you've done. I wish you the best of luck with your book. May it become a best seller.

Vanguard Crew Member

April 1999

"Thank You for the Inspirational Leadership You Have Provided"

Mr. Bogle,

I wanted to make sure that I wrote to you before I retire in August to thank you for the inspirational leadership you have provided to so many crew members, including myself, since founding The Vanguard Group. So many of us truly appreciate your strong sense of mission, your incredibly high ethical standards, and your belief that every individual crew member

"I Felt Embraced As a Valued
. . . Member of the Team"

can make a difference. For so many of my years working here, I felt embraced as a valued and contributing member of the team. It was a wonderful feeling!

I also want to thank you for all of your personal kindnesses to me over the years. No matter how busy, you never failed to say hello when you encountered me. Additionally, the encouragement you offered to my son was so very much appreciated.

Vanguard Veteran Crew Member

July 2001

Mr. Bogle,

I wanted to send you a personal note to say both good-bye and thanks for making me who I am today. I started with this company in November 1984 when we were approximately

600 crew members strong. I soon rose through the ranks of management and became an officer. One of the greatest days that I will remember forever was when you spoke at the Partnership Picnic after your heart transplant. I was so happy to see you and hear your words of inspiration and the courage that you displayed. I cried like a baby. Most were happy tears, but a lot were for the newer crew in the tent that just didn't know what they had missed out on with you and what a true hero you were to many. "Those were the days."

We loved Vanguard because of you. Thank you for all you have done over these many years to teach me, guide me, challenge me, stretch me, inspire me, and support me . . . all while having fun in the process. No one will ever live up to level of leadership that you provided the crew. I am absolutely convinced I would never have otherwise had the privilege of being led by such an individual as yourself. Best of times and healthy days ahead for you. Take care and Godspeed.

Former Veteran Vanguard Crew Member

October 2001

"Thank You for All You Have Done . . . To Teach Me, Guide Me, Challenge Me, Stretch Me, Inspire Me, and Support Me"

*"How Honored and
Privileged I Felt Working
at Vanguard with You"*

Mr. Bogle,

I wanted to take a moment to thank you for making my
Vanguard experience so special. It was like a dream coming to
work at the company created by such an amazing man (that's
you!). I have learned so much about mutual funds, the financial
industry, client service, and quality while working here. I wanted
you to know that when you would do a book signing, it would be
the highlight of my week! You have no idea how honored and
privileged I felt working at Vanguard with you. Thank you for
taking the time to have lunch with me (and four of my friends)—it
was absolutely the most memorable event of my Vanguard career!

Thanks for being an inspiration!

Warmest regards,

Vanguard Crew Member

(A tried-and-true Boglehead)

July 2003

P.S. I went to a special members only event at the National
Constitution Center yesterday. I was so impressed. I left with
a feeling that freedom and liberty really are to be cherished. I
also enjoyed your letter in the front of my pocket Constitution.
What a truly special place!

*"A Company That is Truly
Built on Character"*

Jack,

Finding your card and the autographed 1949 Benjamin Graham classic *The Intelligent Investor* in my mail was certainly the highlight of last week! I must confess that I didn't have this book on my bookshelf; now it has its own prominent spot reserved for when I finish it.

I do have wonderful memories of interviewing with you and others some 12 years ago. I know I have been most fortunate to have had the opportunity to work in a company that is *truly* built on character.

Vanguard's mission, its crew, its values, and its leadership are just as important to my satisfaction as the fun assignments I have had. As I now look upon those assignments, all have been personally rewarding.

I also appreciate your continuing to write (and write well, indeed!) and speak on the industry.

Without fail, I read the pieces you regularly circulate; sometimes several times. They are thought-provoking and refreshing, particularly in the sometimes harried context of my day-to-day responsibilities.

So, thanks for your vision in founding this special firm and launching it on an extraordinary course; thanks also for continuing your labors long beyond when others would have chosen to step back.

Vanguard Officer

June 2005

"It Is Wonderful that You Continue to . . . Connect with Crew Members"

Hi Jack,

It is wonderful that you continue to make the time to connect with crew members. As always, it was great to see you. I treasure my copies of your books, first because of the market wisdom they contain, but also because they carry your signature.

"Our Clients Love Your Book, *The Little Book of Common Sense Investing*"

I want to share with you the response I'm getting from clients on this latest masterpiece. I just sent a couple of dozen out to my clients, and they are writing and calling to express their appreciation. Not surprisingly, they love the book. In *every* case, your book, *The Little Book of Common Sense Investing*, has served to strengthen my relationship with them. One major client wrote: "I doubt there is anybody in the world who could write a book [about investing sensibly] that would do that better than John Bogle."

One client reaction in particular was especially meaningful. Around 1998, a long-time Vanguard shareholder who was working at that time as an investment adviser came to Malvern to meet with you. He persuaded his firm to move its entire client base into Vanguard funds, and later brought along several of his family members as well. Your inscription to him was, "Thanks for your confidence."

When I gave him the book, I asked him to open the front cover. I wish you could have seen the look on his face when he saw the inscription. Astonished joy is the closest I can come to describing his reaction. He was speechless, and clearly moved. He jumped up to show me his office, where, sitting in a prominent spot on his desk, is a picture of him taken with you at that 1998 meeting. The timing of the gift couldn't have been better.

Thanks again for taking the time to come over to sign your *Little Book*. You are my role model for how *not* to retire.

With heartfelt appreciation,

Vanguard Crew Member

May 2007

"... Could Not Have Described Your Personality and ... Principles any Better"

Mr. Bogle,

That major story in the *Philadelphia Inquirer*[1] last Sunday could not have described your personality and set of principles any better. I started working at Vanguard in April of 1988 and

1. Art Carey, "Market Moralist: To Jack Bogle, the Reckoning for Wall Street, 'with All Its Sins,' Reaffirms Vanguard's Pioneering Course in Funds," *Philadelphia Inquirer*, October 19, 2008.

"May the Wind Always Be at Your Back"

early in my second week of employment, I was walking from the cafeteria as you were walking in. You stopped me in the hallway, held out your hand, and said, "Hi, my name is Jack Bogle. You're new here, aren't you?" To say that I was taken aback and more than slightly tongue-tied would be an understatement, that someone in your position and with your credentials would even notice that someone was a new employee.

I never forgot how impressed and moved I was by that gesture of welcome. There are many in this world who feel that they deserve respect, but I can honestly say that you are among the very few who earn respect not only by your accomplishments, but by your very nature. I will always be proud to know that I had the opportunity to shake your hand when I started here and hope that I will get the honor to shake your hand one more time before I retire. Thank you for building a company that I have felt honored to work for and be a part of.

May the wind always be at your back.

Vanguard Crew Member

October 2008

This lovely short poem was given to Jack by a veteran Vanguard crew member. It was inscribed on a watercolor painting depicting—consistent with Vanguard's nautical heritage—a sturdy boat, sailing the seas.

Brave New Heart, with steady care, you sailed your flagship into waters uncharted
One person can make a difference—you challenged your stewards to believe
Great visionaries from Nelson to Morgan taught you to look as far as the eye could see
Legends abound, St. Jack, of your common sense and simplicity
Endless acres of diamonds have lit Vanguard's course to this celebration of your triumphant journey

SUPPORT FOR THE VISION— FOREWORDS TO BOGLE'S BOOKS

PART VII BEGINS with a wonderful essay by Jeremy Duffield, a longtime Vanguard crew member (recently retired) and longtime Bogle confidant. Duffield combines his own significant writing skills, insights, and close relationship as he narrates how Bogle's role as teacher and communicator is pivotal to his leadership and business success. He connects Bogle's many talents into a grand picture that depicts Bogle as both a leader and a legend.

Duffield's essay is followed by the poignant forewords and introductions to eight of Bogle's 10 books. Written by undisputed leaders in public life, finance, economics, and law, the introductions offer unique insights into the relevance of Bogle's themes for individual investors, the markets, and, critically, the very health of the nation. A few excerpts:

President William Jefferson Clinton: "Bogle is a brilliant and good man, . . . a reminder that what Alexis de Tocqueville said about our nation so long ago remains true: America is great because America is good, and if she ever ceases to be good, she will no longer be great."

Peter Bernstein: "Jack Bogle has written a book on investing unlike any investment book that I have ever encountered." Paul Volcker: Bogle's "strong sense of fiduciary responsibility, the objectivity of analysis, and the willingness to take a stand . . . set high standards for all." Arthur Levitt: "He is the free market's greatest friend: a faithful ally. And yet when he sees the corridors of finance and investment turned into a den of speculation and greed, he does not hold his tongue."

TEACHER, COMMUNICATOR PAR EXCELLENCE

Jeremy Duffield[1]

It's been a rare privilege to know and observe one of the world's great communicators over more than three decades. Jack Bogle is certainly a man who has changed an industry and countless lives with the power of his message and the voice and the pen that has carried it, a man who brought fresh and challenging ideas and steely conviction wrapped in a remarkable silken ability to convey them.

The trillions of dollars invested in index funds today are testimony to the notion that "no army can stop an idea whose time has come." However, such a counterintuitive notion that upended conventional wisdom and attacked the self-interest of a whole industry needs an awesome advocate to tell and retell the story, to make the case from every imaginable angle—a pontificating, pugilistic

---

1. Jeremy Duffield, Vanguard crew member 1980–2011, founder of Vanguard Investments Australia, 1996.

persuader to fight the fight that had to be won and to convince a skeptical and largely apathetic investor population that there was a better way.

Indexing Is "*Un*-American"

It's sort of amusing to imagine the counterfactual scenario, if Bogle hadn't been there to pick up the mantle of indexing in 1975 on behalf of retail investors. Would those dry advocates of indexing in the institutional funds management industry have ever spawned a retail wave of index usage? Unlikely. For the first 11 years, Bogle and Vanguard stood alone offering index mutual funds to investors, and only very slowly after that did competitors begrudgingly enter the market. That's a long time alone in the desert. A long time telling an unpopular story, with at first few ears to listen. After all, indexing was "*un*-American."[2]

If Bogle had patience and persistence, he also had a cause he believed in. Then, too, he had a rare set of communication skills, which any would-be world changer would do well to emulate, if they could. Let's consider those. What has made Bogle such a powerful communicator and teacher?

Thornton Wilder, three-time Pulitzer Prize winner, wrote: "The history of a writer is his search for his own subject, his myth-theme, hidden from him, but prepared for him in every hour of his life." This quote hit me as particularly apt because Jack's communications approach is so completely integrated with his life. It's not manufactured or separate, but reflects his life experience, his worldview and values, his times and his personality.

---

2. In the early days of indexing, the concept was not particularly popular among Vanguard's competitors. The Minneapolis-based Leuthold Group, which sold research to active managers, sent posters to clients depicting an angry Uncle Sam with the inscription "Help Stamp Out Index Funds/INDEX FUNDS ARE UN AMERICAN!"

Jack Bogle found his theme from an early age and built on it. His 1951 Princeton University thesis on the emerging mutual fund industry gave him a field of interest where he could apply the values he was brought up to believe in and that he would refine over the years.

"Fired with Enthusiasm"

The 1974 management blowup at Wellington Management Company left him "fired with enthusiasm." But "fired with enthusiasm" also described his dedicated approach to the challenge of making Vanguard the "best damn name in the mutual fund industry." The strategic move in 1977 to abandon commission-selling meant that the young Vanguard and its young leader would have to develop a distinctive voice outsized relative to its ability to pay for marketing clout. Communications ability became a core survival skill.

He was a man with a mission and a vision of how that mission could be achieved. But that meant wooing the press, and through the press, the public, with persuasive arguments about what Vanguard was doing that was different. It meant ensuring that clients believed Vanguard was acting in their best interests and had a distinctively better proposition. It meant making the case and telling the story—over and over again. It meant creating an inspired Vanguard crew, who got it and who would follow the mission and realize the vision.

"A Love for . . . the English Language"

Jack brought great strengths to this challenge: an undoubted flair for commonsense thinking; a willingness to dig into the data and do the work to prove the case (thus, his well-earned moniker as "Beta Bogle, the data devil"); and a love for and a wonderful facility with the English language.

Jack also brought a comprehensive, renaissance intelligence to the task. This allowed him to relate his work and his thinking to the ideas and quotations of contemporaries in fields far and wide. He does great credit to leading thinkers by capturing their ideas and impactful quotes, but also "stands on the shoulders of giants" to borrow their credibility and make his points. And, to add color, class, and resonance to his ideas, he borrows deeply from our cultural roots, ranging across the centuries from Aesop, Homer, Shakespeare, and the Founding Fathers to Jerzy Kosinski, Kurt Vonnegut, and Bob Seger.

White Hats and Black Hats

"Everyone Loves Champions, But Only if They Walk the Talk"

An ability to tell a great story was a key to Abraham Lincoln's success as a leader. And Jack Bogle knows how to build a speech around a story line. Bogle recognized instinctively that education begins with "romance," as philosopher Alfred North Whitehead argued. Most people don't naturally gravitate to learning investment theory; they need to be romanced into it.

One of the central stories in the pantheon was of course the creation story of Vanguard. Bogle used that terrific story over and over again to spark interest and create the company's and his own legend.

Another classic technique was the portrayal of so-called enemies, often described broadly enough to include the rest of the industry. Thus was the "white hat" formally drawn on his head, while the others were by default the "black hat" guys.

Everyone loves champions, but only if they walk the talk. And Bogle did and was seen to live up to what he said. Bogle in speech, on the page, and in person exudes integrity. And we are all aware of how short that precious commodity is these days.

Nothing takes the place of hard work and persistence. You can't be a great communicator on natural talent alone; it's 99 percent perspiration. Bogle learned the preacher's rule that one minute of sermon requires 20 minutes of preparation—all longhand on yellow legal pads. Communication meant showing up when given an audience, speaking with energy that belied his advancing years[3] (356 of his 575

---

3. His unflagging pace seemed to ignore the health challenges he faced beginning in 1960 when he suffered a serious heart attack, followed by some eight cardiac arrests and innumerable hospitalizations, culminating in a heart transplant in 1996.

speeches were given since 1999). And never a stump speech. Use common ideas and themes, but never take the easy route, never "Emily, pull out speech number 5." Always start again with the new audience in mind.

The Legacy of 10 Books

Enough.: His Business Achievements, Investment Thinking, the Role of Business in Society, Personal Life Philosophy

Alongside Vanguard, his 10 books are Jack's second monumental legacy to the world. Laying out with great clarity and grace his investment thinking, his business and social philosophy, they stand apart from other investment writers' work in their ability to inform, to educate, and, at the same time, to inspire. You might read *The Little Book of Common Sense Investing* to begin your Bogle journey, migrate to *Common Sense on Mutual Funds* for a deeper discussion on investing, and then switch to his books that take on broader issues of his approach to business and building Vanguard (*Character Counts*), or his struggles and issues with the mutual fund industry and the corporate world in general (*Don't Count on It!*, *The Battle for the Soul of Capitalism*, and *The Clash of the Cultures*).

It's *Enough.*, however, that brings together the broad threads of Bogle's thinking and shows a man who has achieved an unusual state of mind. *Enough.* shows how Jack Bogle has reconciled his business achievements, his investment thinking, his views about business in society, and his personal life philosophy. They merge in an amazingly consistent manner. Few can match that, I believe, and his example serves as inspiration to all.

Finally, we owe Jack Bogle a debt for asking more of us. As a communicator and educator, Bogle didn't stoop or use cheap tricks or comedy. He didn't pander or patronize. We might be entertained or enchanted by his stories and his deep and firm voice, but it was serious business and he asked us to pay attention, to think. And we benefited broadly, from our investment accounts to our personal lives. Thank you, Jack Bogle.

WORDS FROM THOSE WHO KNOW BOGLE BEST

John McPhee, author of 28 books, including *Annals of the Former World*, winner of the Pulitzer Prize for General Nonfiction; contributing editor to *The New Yorker* since 1963 (writing over 80 pieces); and the Ferris Professor of Journalism at Princeton University

In an August 1993 interview with In the Vanguard, *John Bogle talked about his love of writing*:

> Writing a book is a difficult process. The toughest part is touching paper with pen for the first time, which I did about a year ago. Let me tell you that it was hard work to the very last day, editing the manuscript, re-editing it, and then editing it some more.

John McPhee quickly responded with this note:

I endorse your *In the Vanguard* interview describing writing difficulties. And I have read every syllable of *Bogle on Mutual Funds*. The book is written with wonderful clarity. It is patient with the untutored but never condescending. The boxes work especially well. They are very interesting. There's a sense of discovery in coming upon them. Structurally, they serve to aerate the whole.

Spoken like a thesis-writing senior. Spoken like every ink-stained writing wretch who is not self-deluded. It is easier to shinny up a mile-high pole than to complete a piece of writing. Or so it seems. You got up there, though.

February 1994

James Grant, founder, *Grant's Interest Rate Observer*; author, *Money of the Mind*, *John Adams: Party of One*, and *Mr. Market Miscalculates*, among others

Dear Moses, or rather, Jack,

I enjoyed reading the text of the speech you gave at the Free Library of Philadelphia. . . . Has Fidelity, or, for that matter, Vanguard, called to check on your very well founded

---

Like Shinnying Up a Mile-High Pole . . . "You Got There"

"The Fellow Who Wrote Luke 16 Would Be Proud of You"

indictment of the mutual fund business? Never mind: I will now give you a piece of my mind about the "joy of writing." It is not a joy but an affliction, albeit one I have possibly brought on myself through sins unknown to me. May your mission live forever.

What an honor it was to have you at the Grant's Fall 2011 Conference. Never, in my 28 years of hosting these conferences, have I heard such love radiating from audience to speaker. Thank you.

December 2006 and November 2011

Warren E. Buffett, chairman, Berkshire Hathaway, Inc.

I think your book *Bogle on Mutual Funds* is absolutely terrific. Cogent, honest, and hard-hitting—a must read for every investor. I hope some journalists and the SEC get energized after reading it.

You are doing a real service for American investors by carrying on your crusade. The fellow who wrote Luke 16 would be proud of you.

Through your communications—both oral and written—you have saved American investors many billions of dollars. And, of course, if all of those who should have listened to you actually had done so, the total would be in the hundreds of billions.

Keep it up!

January 1999 and March 2009

CHAPTER 17: THE FOREWORDS

The Bogle books have included 10 forewords and introductions, each by a person of distinction and widespread respect. They appear here in the order of the publication date of each volume, from 1993 through 2012. The individual writers are Nobel laureate Paul Samuelson, economist Peter Bernstein, former Federal Reserve chairman Paul Volcker, former chancellor of Delaware Court of Chancery William Allen, the Honorable Peter G. Peterson, President William Jefferson Clinton, business icon and author Tom Peters, Yale University endowment manager David Swensen, former Federal Reserve vice chairman Alan Blinder, and former SEC chairman Arthur Levitt.

FOREWORD TO *BOGLE ON MUTUAL FUNDS* (1993)

Paul A. Samuelson[4]

The same surgeon general who required cigarette packages to say: "Warning, this product may be dangerous to your health" ought to require that 99 out of 100 books written on personal finance carry that same label. The exceptions are rare. Benjamin Graham's *The Intelligent Investor* is one. Now it is high praise when I endorse *Bogle on Mutual Funds* as another.

I do not speak for myself. What is one person's opinion worth? It is the statistical evidences of economic history that I speak for. Over half a century, professors of finance have studied various strategies for prudent investing. A jury of

---

4. Dr. Samuelson was professor emeritus, Massachusetts Institute of Technology, and a Nobel laureate in economic sciences. He died on December 13, 2009, at the age of 94, described by the *New York Times* as the "greatest economist of the twentieth century." He wrote this Foreword in Cambridge, Massachusetts, in June 1993.

economists is never unanimous—how could it be in such an inexact science?—but on these lessons of experience there is a remarkable degree of agreement.

"A Changing Group, Hard to Identify in Advance"

- Diversification does reduce, but not eliminate, risk. Buying many stocks, critics say, is "settling for mediocrity." When I was a trustee on the finance committee of the largest private pension equity fund in the world—which handled the old-age savings of the whole university community—we had 30 billion reasons to look into this critique alleging mediocrity. We discovered that the hundreds of money managers who believe in putting only a few eggs in one basket and then "watching fiercely those eggs," alas, produce long-term investment returns that are significantly below those of diversified portfolios. No exceptions? Yes, a few; but a changing group, hard to identify in advance, and prone to regress toward the mean even before you can spot them.

- For those not in the millionaire class, the need to diversify implies that the sensible and cost-efficient strategy is *not to handle personally* investments needed for those future days of retirement, of home purchases, and of sending offspring to college. "Leave the driving to Greyhound" is not counsel of cowardice and modesty. It's just plain good sense when you recon the facts about brokerage commissions and the need to keep tax records. All this applies even if you will not go all the way toward "index investing," my next topic.

- The most efficient way to diversify a stock portfolio is with a low-fee index fund. Statistically, a broadly based stock index fund will outperform most actively managed equity portfolios. A thousand money managers all look about equally good or bad. Each expects to do 3 percent or better than the mob. Each puts together a convincing story after the fact. Hardly 10 of 1,000 perform in a way that convinces a jury of experts that a long-term edge over indexing is likely. (For bond and money market portfolios, the canny investor will select among funds with high quality and lean costs.)

- Enough said about the testimony of economic science. Where John Bogle has added a new note is in connection with his emphasis upon low-cost, no-load investing. I have no association with The Vanguard Group of funds other than as a charter member investor, along with numerous children and innumerable grandchildren. So, as a disinterested witness in the court of opinion, perhaps my seconding his suggestions will carry some weight. John Bogle has changed a basic industry in the optimal direction. Of very few can this be said.

May I add a personal finding? Investing sensibly, besides being remunerative, can still be fun.

"A Disinterested Witness . . .
Seconding His Suggestions"

FOREWORD TO *COMMON SENSE ON MUTUAL FUNDS* (FIRST EDITION–1999)

Peter L. Bernstein[5]

Jack Bogle has written a book on investing unlike any investment book that I have ever encountered, because he discusses sensitive matters that other authors ignore.

---

5. Peter L. Bernstein was an economist and author of 10 books, including *Against the Gods: The Remarkable Story of Risk* (1996). He died on June 5, 2009, at the age of 90. No individual has made more influential and generous intellectual contributions to the field of economics and portfolio strategy. This Foreword was written in 1999.

I hesitate to speculate on why these topics receive such short shrift elsewhere, but I suspect that other experts have horizons that are more limited than Bogle's, or they have less concern for their readers' best interests.

People often forget that Bogle is much more than an investment professional who is deadly serious about how individual investors should manage their hard-earned wealth. He is first and foremost a fabulously successful businessman who has built one of the great mutual fund empires with skill and determination, always driving it in the direction of the vision that inspired him when he launched forth on this adventure many years ago. Readers of this book are therefore treated to a unique and unvarnished exposure of the nature of the mutual fund world and how it affects their pocketbooks.

Despite all the high-minded talk we hear from the corporate spinmasters, conflict of interest between seller and buyer is inherent in our economic system. Jack Bogle's goal was to build a business whose primary objective was to make money for his customers by minimizing the elements of that conflict of interest, but at the same time to be so successful that it would be able to continue to grow and sustain itself. That has been no easy task. The complexity of the job that Bogle set out for himself, however, has enabled him to look at the competition with a very special kind of eye. One of the loud and clear messages in this book is that he is less than pleased with what that eye sees.

We must look at the investment management industry (yes, it is an industry even more than it is a profession) as a *business* and within the framework of the economic system as a whole. The investment management business is extraordinarily profitable. As such, it responds to the iron law of capitalism that capital will flow to those areas where the expected return is the highest. Over the past

"He Is Less Than Pleased with What That Very Special Kind of Eye Sees"

10 years, the number of mutual funds has increased from 2,710 to 6,870, and the number of investment managers has exploded from 1,260 to 5,810. On the other hand, investment management defies the rest of the iron law of capitalism, which is that the very process by which high returns attract new capital inevitably brings down the rate of return as new competitors strive to take market share away from the old. Joseph Schumpeter, in a famous aphorism, referred to this process as "creative destruction." It is the essence of why our economic system has been so successful and why, despite its many glaring flaws, it continues to command such wide public acceptance.

Investment management firms never heard of such a thing. The growth in the number of managers far exceeds the rate of growth in the number of customers they serve. Willy-nilly, more and more people enter the field without in any way diminishing the profitability of those who have established themselves. Occasionally a start-up will fail to make it or an established firm goofs up in some horrible fashion and disappears from the scene, but the great mass of investment managers go right on earning a return on their own capital that most other industries can only envy.

Bogle's skill in dispensing uncommon wisdom about how to invest and how to understand the capital markets would be reason enough to read these pages. But the big message in this book is that what happens to the wealth of individual investors cannot be separated from the structure of the industry that manages those assets. Bogle's insight into what that structure means to the fortunes of the individuals whose welfare concerns him so deeply is what makes this book most rewarding. It is not only fun to read: It has a big payoff as well.

"The Wealth of Individual Investors Cannot Be Separated from the Structure of the Industry that Manages Those Assets"

FOREWORD TO *JOHN BOGLE ON INVESTING* (2001)

Paul A. Volcker[6]

Fiduciary Responsibility, Objectivity of Analysis, and Willingness to Take a Stand

If a modern-day Rip van Winkle were to wake up after a sleep of 50 years, he'd have a lot of trouble understanding today's financial markets or recognizing the names of the major participants. But if Rip happened to be, say, a Princeton professor who had monitored or read John Bogle's senior thesis, he wouldn't be at all surprised about one of the most significant developments in the world of the stock market and money management.

John Bogle didn't invent the business of mutual investment funds. They had started before he went to college, but were barely visible. His curiosity about the business was piqued by an article in a magazine as he was ruminating about a thesis topic. That bit of serendipity led not only to an honors thesis but to a life-long vocation.

Today, mutual funds are the dominant investment medium for American families. They directly own a large fraction of all traded stock and a sizable share of bonds and liquid assets as well.

The success of the industry is built on a solid base—the demonstrable value of diversifying risk and spreading costs by collective investment. Those were concepts intuitively recognized and emphasized by the Princeton senior.

John Bogle has not, of course, been alone in seeing the basic merit of mutual funds, now counted in the thousands. His great contribution—his single-minded mission—has been to insist that those funds should be managed, first and foremost, in a way truly to serve the interests of the investing public.

---

6. Paul Volcker was the twelfth chairman of the Board of Governors of the Federal Reserve, and served as chairman of President Barack H. Obama's Economic Recovery Advisory Board. This Foreword was written May 1, 2000.

That has meant strong emphasis on minimizing conflicts of interest and operating at the lowest possible cost. To those ends, the family of funds that John Bogle established a quarter of a century ago—The Vanguard Group—has remained independent of ties to other businesses. It has long led the industry in operating without sales charges and with minimal operating costs.

Early in its life, Vanguard established the industry's first index mutual fund. Over time, the stress on the value of index funds responded to the clear logic—a logic fully supported by the plain evidence—that most "active" money managers most of the time will not be able to beat the market. These days, after all, mutual funds largely are the market. On the average, they couldn't do better, even if they had no costs, operated with perfect efficiency, and incurred no taxes. With those hurdles to jump, very few funds can consistently outperform the averages.

That's not an easy conclusion for money managers to accept. John Bogle has not won many popularity contests among his professional colleagues. Moreover, he himself would readily confess that the unique form of governance and style of management that he instilled in Vanguard is not easy to replicate.

"Not an Easy Conclusion for Money Managers To Accept"

But from a distance, I, along with many others, have enormously admired the force and eloquence with which he has set forth his thinking. It is thinking that I find fully persuasive as an analytic matter and entirely consistent with the public interest. John Bogle's basic conviction that the mutual fund investor is entitled, in his words, to a "fair shake" should serve as the motto of every mutual fund.

This new volume happily makes that thinking easily available to a wider audience. John Bogle writes with unusual clarity and simplicity, clarity of the vision and simplicity of the written word. He has a rare ability to set out concisely and effectively the evidence to support his argument. A wry sense of humor can't quite disguise, and shouldn't disguise, his sense of frustration—even outrage—about some practices that permeate the industry that has been his life's work and personal passion.

All of us dependent on mutual funds or other collective investment institutions to manage our savings, and that is most of us, owe thanks to John Bogle for insisting that our interests be placed front and center.

Even more broadly, the strong sense of fiduciary responsibility, the objectivity of analysis, and the willingness to take a stand—qualities that permeate all his writings—set high standards for all those concerned with the growth and integrity of our open and competitive financial system.

INTRODUCTION TO *JOHN BOGLE ON INVESTING* (2001)

William T. Allen[7]

Let me introduce the great ideas in finance presented in this book by focusing on the author of them.

Virtue is a word that tends to embarrass us today. Perhaps we have lost a bit of the easy confidence that permitted earlier ages to believe in a fixed universe of good and evil. We are now very sensitive to the fact that in a diverse society we may not agree on the characteristics that constitute virtue, and today we may be on guard lest we be thought to impose our own contestable views of goodness on others who don't share them.

"Virtuous . . . Even If That Word Seems Quaint to Our Ears"

Yet in introducing the collected speeches of John Clifton Bogle I can start with no word other than virtuous to describe the author of these pieces, even if that word seems quaint to our ear. For John Bogle's life reflects such a deep commitment

---

7. William Allen is a professor of law and finance, and director of the Center for Law and Business at New York University, and former chancellor, Court of Chancery, State of Delaware.

to the concepts of duty, honor, candor, diligence, and service to others that the most complete summarization of the man is to say that he is a man of high virtue. In an age that sometimes seems to have tried to raise gratification of the self to the status of a virtue, his life reminds us that the value of a life is measured by how one affects the lives of others, not by either celebrity or balance sheet.

The power to affect the welfare of others positively is the aspect of business that gives it nobility. Bill Gates—arguably our most successful businessman—is, I suggest, not a great man because he is worth an astronomical sum. On that, I trust, we would all agree. If he is great, it is because, along with a team of others, he has done a great deal to bring the benefits of computers to millions of American homes. And in doing so has empowered others to achieve their various goals. His efforts have improved human welfare. The world is a noticeably better place because of his efforts.

A Great Businessman

Jack Bogle is a great businessman because he has changed the world in a way that confers huge benefits on countless citizens, allowing them to better achieve their goals. He envisioned a firm that would be different from all those that had gone before and indeed is different still in a fundamental way. He worked with his team—his crew—to build that business into a great enterprise. He is a great man because of the content of his vision and the impact it has had on others.

Vanguard is not simply a successful company. It is an idea of service that, while not selfless, is deeply committed to fairness and the delivery of value. It is a cliché for business to be committed to delivery of value to customers in order to deliver value to shareholders. But in the mutual fund business, at any rate, the best evidence suggested to Jack Bogle that an unconscionable share of value was being sidetracked from investors by excess costs. Of course neither Jack Bogle nor those who worked with him wear a sackcloth. In creating a successful enterprise,

Jack and his team created value that compensated them for their efforts. But his vision was from the beginning radically inconsistent with maximizing returns for the managers of the fund. The public was the principal beneficiary of his vision.

During decades in which average mutual funds charged fees of 150 basis points or considerably more, Vanguard's structure allowed it to offer comparable—actually superior—service for far less than a quarter as much. Today Vanguard manages about $500 billion in retirement and other savings. Thus, this year it will return some $4 billion more to its investors than they would have had if Jack Bogle had not had the vision to build this enterprise. But this estimated number *under-estimates* Vanguard's annual impact upon the savings and retirement portfolios of Americans. There is every reason to suppose that, had Vanguard never been founded, the average costs of management of mutual funds would remain as high as they were in 1970. Considering that the existence of the Vanguard philosophy has forced other funds to reduce their fees and costs materially, it would be difficult indeed to estimate how many billions of dollars of savings go into the retirement savings of working men and women across this country today as a result of Mr. Bogle's vision.

A Unique Enterprise that Reflects an Academic Theory

An interesting fact about this unique enterprise is that it reflects an academic theory. When Jack Bogle encountered the efficient market hypothesis, he understood it and its implications quickly and intuitively. His years of pupilage with Walter Morgan in Philadelphia had trained him to understand that in the long term it would be exceedingly difficult for any investment adviser to produce substantial excess returns over the returns of the market itself. Thus his famously successful business plan was simply to reduce costs and diversify risks. He applied theory to practice, inventing the index mutual fund as a commercial alternative to savings. The idea of course is simple, not fancy; in that it reflects the character of the man. For Vanguard's founder is, like his company, world-class in performance and straightforward and unaffected in manner.

"Strength of Character, Belief in Candor Rather Than Artifice, in Substance Rather than in Form, and in Performance Not Promises"

Perhaps these characteristics were inculcated in the young man at the Blair Academy or at Princeton University. Perhaps he learned them at the side of his older brother and his twin brother, who is now gone. Certainly the idea of fair sharing and of duty to another are concepts that brothers share. Almost certainly the boys learned at home the characteristics that shine in the man today: strength of character, belief in candor rather than artifice, in substance rather than in form, and in performance not promises.

Jack Bogle's life has not been without its moments of drama and tension and not without its keen and painful losses. The story of Vanguard's founding is an arresting business drama in which, at the beginning at least, the outcome did not seem foreordained. But Vanguard's rise to eminence in the world of finance attests to the soundness of its principles. The speeches that are collected in this volume capture in vivid outline the core concepts of Jack's vision and inevitably disclose as well the outstanding character of the man. That these two elements—vision and character—are inextricably linked is possibly the most fundamental and basic lesson that Jack Bogle's career teaches those of us interested in finance and investing.

FOREWORD TO *THE BATTLE FOR THE SOUL OF CAPITALISM* (2005)

The Honorable Peter G. Peterson[8]

Some, particularly those from the financial services industry, might say that Jack Bogle is cantankerous. Perhaps, but we now know that had we heeded his persistent

---

8. The Honorable Peter G. Peterson served as Secretary of Commerce, 1972–1973, cofounder of the Concord Coalition, and cofounder of the Blackstone Group. His foundation, the Peter G. Peterson Foundation, is dedicated to raising public awareness about the need for fiscal sustainability.

warnings about a troubled financial system we may well have avoided the stock market losses and corporate scandals we have witnessed in recent years. We now know that on many matters he was right and others were wrong.

"Cantankerous" simply may be a hapless attempt by some with interests to protect to dismiss a man who has done so much to elevate the standards of conduct in business over the years. Indeed, if cantankerous, he is far more than that. He is straight talking, straight thinking. He is tough on all of us: corporate executives, board members, and ultimately the owners of equities. But he also tries hard to be fair-minded.

"Concerned and Caring"

He is concerned and caring. Concerned because he knows that our current account deficits are at unheard-of levels—now running at a staggering annual rate of $700 billion a year. He knows that the United States is starved for savings and is outsourcing our need for capital to foreign sources at reckless and dysfunctional levels. He knows that foreign investor confidence, and, of course, domestic confidence, in the integrity of our capital markets is crucial to the health of our economy. To restore that integrity, he knows that fundamental reforms are needed in our corporations and our financial institutions as well.

It did not take this book to convince me of all this. I got to know Jack Bogle very well as a member of the Conference Board Commission on Public Trust and Private Enterprise that John Snow and I cochaired along with an extraordinary group of 10 other respected Americans. Jack was a firm advocate of directly confronting the really tough issues—such as the expensing of stock options; the need for an independent chairman (as he puts it in this book, companies need a "boss of the business and a boss of the board"); executive compensation based on long-term operating performance; truly independent compensation and audit committees that have the will and authority not only to hire and fire outside advisers but also to assure themselves that these advisers are not conflicted by providing

"Jack Was a Firm Advocate of Directly Confronting the Really Tough Issues"

services, such as consulting services by auditing firms where their perceived client is not the board but the management; and on and on.

Jack also has a stylish pen (one I wish I had!). He is a rarity, at least within our industry. He is highly literate. Who else could quote so easily and so relevantly from the likes of Demosthenes, Edward Gibbon, Alexander Hamilton, Thomas Jefferson, and Oscar Wilde?

His writing is also memorable. Jack has a knack for the colorful headline that helps the reader understand and remember the relevant observation or reform.

An "Own-a-Stock" Industry Becomes a "Rent-a-Stock" Industry

- To make the point that we have too few long-term investors, he reminds us of how we have gone from an "own-a-stock" to a "rent-a-stock" industry.
- To crystallize what went wrong, he describes our descent from "owners' capitalism" to "managers' capitalism."
- To punctuate the notion that many advisers have become too beholden to managements who hire them for fees for related services, he quotes Descartes: "A man is incapable of comprehending any argument that interferes with his revenue."
- To suggest the possibility that inappropriate behavior in the marketplace may have metastasized more than we may wish to acknowledge, he raises the provocative question "Bad apples or bad barrel?"
- To decry the state of affairs in the mutual fund industry, he says that these funds have gone from the "stewardship of shareholder investments to the salesmanship of asset gathering."

He rigorously defines the problems. He clearly outlines the needed reforms. This is a must-read book for anyone interested in how to restore badly needed integrity, and efficiency, to our capital markets.

FOREWORD TO *ENOUGH.* (2008)

William Jefferson Clinton[9]

My professor of ancient civilizations at Georgetown taught us that the United States became the greatest nation in history because our people had always believed in the two main pillars of Western civilization: that tomorrow can be better than today, and that we all have a personal moral obligation to make it so. He called it "future preference."

In recent years, some American finance leaders have strayed from these beliefs, making vast wealth in the moment without regard to its consequences for the future. In the United States and around the globe, we are still living with the repercussions of this business conduct, some of it illegal, all of it fruitless. We cannot continue on the same road we followed before the recent financial crises—not if we want to build a better tomorrow.

In *Enough.*, John C. Bogle offers a compelling account of what went wrong and some clear advice on how we can restore our financial system and create a more prosperous and equitable world. His book is an important call to action, to bring moral principles and integrity back into our financial affairs in a way that will support, not undermine, long-term economic growth.

With his own impeccable credentials in finance, Bogle reminds us that the United States was built upon a tradition of hard work, temperance, and duty, and shows why sacrificing these values in the pursuit of success sooner or later breeds destruction that harms many innocent people. In this meditation on ambition and

"Real Worth Comes in Making Long-Term Contributions to the Larger Communities"

---

9. William Jefferson Clinton was the 42nd President of the United States, from 1993 to 2001. He is at present the founding chairman of the Clinton Global Initiative.

society, Bogle argues that we cannot measure the meaning of our lives by quick profits. Instead, real worth comes in making long-term contributions to the larger communities of which even the most powerful financiers are simply facilitators, with a duty to help others build their dreams.

In our fast-moving digital age, with more than $2 trillion crossing borders every day before the current crisis, Bogle's analysis and argument seem, at first glance, strikingly old-fashioned. But our pervasive interdependence makes *Enough.* more relevant than ever. Our actions have profound consequences both within and beyond our borders. It is wrong to ignore them in pursuit of purely personal advantage. Future preference still matters. We have to get it back.

John Bogle is a brilliant and good man, and every concerned citizen can learn and benefit from the important lessons he shares in *Enough*. It is a reminder that what Alexis de Tocqueville said about our nation so long ago remains true: America is great because America is good, and if she ever ceases to be good, she will no longer be great. *Enough.* is about reclaiming both.

> *"Future Preference*
> *Still Matters. We Have*
> *to Get It Back."*

PROLOGUE TO *ENOUGH.* (2008)

Tom Peters[10]

In the late 1970s, I began a journey with Bob Waterman examining how good companies were managed that led to the publication of *In Search of Excellence*. Along the way we met an extraordinary cast of characters. There was Jim Burke, CEO of Johnson & Johnson, who when beset with the infamous Tylenol crisis in

---

10. Tom Peters is the coauthor of *In Search of Excellence*, and has written 16 books. This Prologue is dated April 2010.

1982 turned to J&J's quasi-religious "Credo." With the guidance of core values, the company handled the crisis with integrity and transparency that stands to this day as a memorial to the power of values-based organizations.

And then there was Delta Airlines, mired in crisis courtesy of the recession of the early 1980s—the company's balance sheet was helped enormously by the decision of Delta employees to buy their employer an airplane! There was McDonald's, living with rigor in the early 1980s on the bedrock established by founder Ray Kroc called QSC&V, or quality, service, cleanliness, and value. And then there was John Young of Hewlett-Packard, who managed by wandering around (MBWA), engaging with line employees on project specifics.

The key concept of our book was captured in six words: "Hard is soft. Soft is hard." As engineers, MBAs, and McKinsey consultants, we were firmly rooted in the virtues of measurement and metrics—but we also damn well knew how easy the numbers are to fudge! Purportedly hard numbers turn out again and again to be soft. Enron, circa 2000, masterminded by a Harvard Business School–McKinsey grad, and the derivatives, super-derivatives, and credit default swaps of the early 2000s, masterminded by PhDs, came about by numbers that were so soft they deflated.

"We Damn Well Knew How Easy the Numbers Are To Fudge!"

What matters? What is really "hard"? Integrity. Trust. Values that last (like J&J's Credo). Deep-rooted relationships. Good corporate citizenship. Listening—to the customer and to the frontline employee—and acting on what they tell us. Matchless quality, the bugbear of those early 1980s. And, yes, excellence. Those are the things they mostly didn't and don't teach in business schools, but that are the bedrock of effective enterprise.

It was memories of that startling journey that explained why, in the middle of the Great Recession of 2007, I picked up, for no particular reason, Jack Bogle's book, *Enough*. I quickly found, while standing in the bookstore in fact, that I couldn't put it down. It explains why I have now read it through four times; why I have bent some 57 pages to return to again and again; why I have given away over 50 copies to friends and associates; and why, I'm almost embarrassed to admit, I carry it with me as I travel from Angola to Abu Dhabi to China to Chicago—*Enough.* has taken on totemic significance. As I prepare a seminar in, say, Novosibirsk, Siberia, I thumb through the book and check myself as to whether I may have gone soaring off into some obscure theoretical corner and forgotten the lesson of the likes of Bill Hewlett's supposedly old-fashioned MBWA as practiced by John Young.

The Australian writer Peter Temple's thriller *The Broken Shore* won a bushel of prestigious global awards. Several prominent reviewers struck the same chord: in effect, "This is not a great thriller—this is a great *novel.*" That's precisely what I feel about *Enough.* It is not a great finance book. It is not a great business book. It is a great *book.* Period.

> ## *"Enough. Is Not A Great Finance Book. It Is Not a Great Business Book. It Is a Great Book. Period."*

Jack Bogle writes in plain English, and his reasoning is straightforward and based on a staggering sum of observations. Though he is a finance guy, not a single equation is unfurled as he takes us through finance, business, and life itself. It is not hyperbole to say, with some certainty at age 67, that this *is* clearly the best business book I've ever read, and as good a primer on life as I've read as well, save perhaps the works of Bogle's fellow Philadelphian, wise old Ben Franklin!

> ## *"The Sort of Excellence That Lit So Bright and True a Lamp"*

Jack Bogle and the organization he founded in 1974, The Vanguard Group, have been recognized far and wide and again and again for the sort of excellence that lit so bright and true a lamp for Bob Waterman and me in the 1980s. Jack Bogle is one the great financiers of our times and perhaps all times. He and Vanguard have contributed to the financial well-being and security of millions upon millions of people. His secret is a carefully formed belief that you will not, over the long haul, beat the market, and a belief that the best performance will therefore come from index funds that return their enhanced value, virtually in full, to investor/owners. His life and his life's work are built on a bedrock of integrity, transparency, simplicity, and value.

Interestingly, I've never met Jack and, alas, have not invested with Vanguard, which is to say that I have no vested interest whatsoever in making these remarks—and singling this book out as the matchless, perhaps life-changing gem that I think it unequivocally is. I have devoted my adult life to trying to help people manage organizations as effectively as possible, and have discovered, as Jack Bogle has, that being straightforward is best and that character and integrity and common sense and decency are the keys to running enterprises of all sorts—not to mention the life well lived in service to others.

"The Ten Commandments"   I will not reprise the best of the book in this Prologue. I tried to do so in a first draft, but was flummoxed by those 57 bent pages—each of abiding personal importance. Jack's straight talk is offered in spare and lucid prose that puts me to shame. However, I can give you a flavor of what is to follow by simply offering up the chapter titles (I was totally hooked on the book by the time I'd perused the Contents page):

1. "Too Much Cost, Not Enough Value"
2. "Too Much Speculation, Not Enough Investment"
3. "Too Much Complexity, Not Enough Simplicity"
4. "Too Much Counting, Not Enough Trust"
5. "Too Much Business Conduct, Not Enough Professional Conduct"
6. "Too Much Salesmanship, Not Enough Stewardship"
7. "Too Much Management, Not Enough Leadership"
8. "Too Much Focus on Things, Not Enough Focus on Commitment"

9. "Too Many Twenty-First-Century Values, Not Enough Eighteenth-Century Values"
10. "Too Much 'Success,' Not Enough Character"

Bogle's "Ten Commandments ... Encapsulate, Better Than Anything I've Come Across Before, the Life I Hope I Lead"

I'm inclined to hijack these chapter titles and make them my Ten Commandments. The concerns encapsulate, better than anything I've come across before, the life I hope I lead, the life I would surely like to lead—and the sorts of things I'd pray people might say about my endeavors when I check out.

I begin my lectures these days with two PowerPoint slides. The first recalls a celebration honoring the peerless hotelier Conrad Hilton. After a roast of sorts, Mr. Hilton was called to the podium and asked to share the secrets of his magnificent career. He faced the crowd, as the story is told, paused, and said, "Don't forget to tuck the shower curtain into the bathtub."

And with that he returned to his seat.

The second slide recalls a conference near Monterey, California, perhaps 20 years ago, during which I was chatting with the president of a very successful Midwestern community bank. As the financial crisis of 2007 engulfed us, I recalled his words clearly: "Tom, let me describe to you a successful lending officer. On Sunday after church, driving his family home, he takes a little detour to drive past a factory or distribution center he's lent money to. He doesn't go in or any such thing, just drives by, eyeballs the place, and continues home."

The shower curtain.

The simple drive by a business.

Enough.

Foreword to *Common Sense on Mutual Funds,* Fully Updated 10th Anniversary Edition (2010)

David F. Swensen[11]

Jack Bogle deserves the profound gratitude of the American public. First, he devotes enormous amounts of time and energy to showing investors how to navigate the treacherous marketplace for financial services. Second, he created Vanguard, a rare financial institution that places the interests of the investor front and center. Without Jack Bogle's efforts, Americans would face a financial landscape nearly barren of attractive alternatives.

Bogle offers disarmingly simple advice: employ low-cost index funds in a low-turnover, disciplined portfolio strategy. Unfortunately, few follow his sensible advice. The vast majority of investors play an active management game in which they lose two ways. First, they lose by choosing actively managed mutual funds that almost always fail to deliver on the promise of market-beating results. The shortfall comes from wildly excessive, ultimately counterproductive trading (with the attendant market impact and commissions) and from unreasonable management fees (that far exceed the managers' value added, if any). And, as Bogle points out, nearly all mutual fund managers behave as if taxes do not matter, thereby imposing an unnecessary and expensive tax burden (that often blindsides the investing public when they deal with the IRS on April 15).

Second, investors lose by trading mutual funds with eyes fixed unwaveringly on the rearview mirror. By dumping yesterday's faded idol and chasing today's

"Bogle Offers Disarmingly Simple Advice"

---

11. David F. Swensen is the chief investment officer at Yale University, and the author of two books on investment strategy.

hot prospect, mutual fund investors systematically sell low and buy high (which is a poor approach to making money). Moreover, the frenzied switching of funds often triggers a further tax burden. If investors followed Bogle's advice to use index funds, by dint of low costs they would beat the vast majority of fund managers. If investors followed Bogle's advice to take a steady approach to allocating assets, by avoiding perverse timing moves they would benefit from realizing nearly all that the markets have to offer.

Of course, as a financial professional I have my own views and offer two small amendments to Bogle's recipe for investment success. I would place a greater emphasis on the value of international diversification, particularly with respect to exposure to emerging markets. Second, I would limit holdings of bonds to full-faith-and-credit issues of the United States government. The experience of investors in the recent financial crisis (as well as the experience of investors in the market dislocations in 1998 and 1987) illustrates in high relief why exposure to credit risk (and optionality) undermines the very reason for holding bonds in the first place. That said, Jack Bogle gets the essential elements right. Follow his advice.

Sage Advice, Deserving Far More Attention Than It Receives

Bogle's sage advice deserves far more attention than it receives. Individual investors must educate themselves to have any hope of executing a successful investment program. Regardless of the approach that investors pursue, reading provides the essential underpinnings for an investor's education. Jack Bogle belongs to a small group of thoughtful author practitioners, including Burton Malkiel and Charles Ellis (dare I include myself?), who articulate a reasoned, thoughtful approach to investment. After reading *Common Sense on Mutual Funds*, move on to Malkiel's *A Random Walk Down Wall Street*, Ellis's *Winning the Loser's Game*, and my own *Unconventional Success*. This handful of books competes with the marketing hype of the mutual fund industry, the blathering blandishments of the brokerage community, and the enervating cacophony of television's talking heads. (Even after being eviscerated by Jon Stewart on *The Daily Show*, Jim Cramer continues unashamedly to offer seriously damaging advice to viewers of *Mad Money*. Across nearly every dimension of the investment world, Jim Cramer stands opposite Jack Bogle. Ignore Jim Cramer. Pay attention to Jack Bogle!)

Jack Bogle's accomplishments extend far beyond educating the investing public. His Vanguard offers investors an alternative in a mutual fund industry that overwhelmingly fails investors. As one of only two mutual fund complexes (TIAA-CREF, where I serve on the board, is the other) that operate without a profit motive, Vanguard gives investors a fair shake. Aside from Vanguard and TIAA-CREF, nearly all mutual fund management companies seek to generate profits and purport to serve investors. Unfortunately, when the profit motive comes into conflict with fiduciary responsibility, greed wins and profits triumph. The idea of serving investor interests disappears and the investor loses. As Jack Bogle so convincingly tells us, today's profit-motivated mutual fund companies pay close attention to marketing, make sure to collect high fees, and provide little in terms of actual investment management. Sensible investors avoid the active management morass, embrace the certainty of indexing, and select an investor-centric fund manager.

An Optimistic View of the World . . . with Caveats

In spite of his gloomy message about the fund industry's structural, operational, and performance failures, Jack Bogle retains an optimistic view of the world. I like to think of myself as a positive person, but I worry about the individual investor's chances for success. In recent years, the burden of providing for retirement has shifted dramatically from the employer to the employee. This policy shift creates a number of issues. First, individuals do not save enough. Second, not surprisingly, those who save tend to enjoy high incomes. Stunning statistics from the Federal Reserve Board's Survey of Consumer Finances indicate that 88 percent of the top-income quintile participate in defined contribution plans, in which they hold an average balance of more than $260,000; less than 11 percent of the bottom-income quintile participate in defined contribution plans, in which they hold an average balance of less than $2,000. Are retirement programs only for the rich? Third, rich or poor, investors face a substandard set of choices dominated by for-profit mutual funds. Fourth, investors take those substandard investment vehicles and use them to make consistently flawed timing decisions. The net result, as Jack Bogle points out, is that investors fail to capture a fair share of the rewards of investing in the world's security markets.

Jack Bogle gave the investing public two magnificent gifts—Vanguard, a rare investment management company that acts in the best interests of the investors, and *Common Sense on Mutual Funds*, a readily accessible guide on how to manage personal investment portfolios. Take advantage of Jack Bogle's gifts and pass them on to someone you love.

> *"Investors Fail To Capture a Fair Share of the Rewards of Investing"*

FOREWORD TO *DON'T COUNT ON IT!* (2011)

Alan S. Blinder[12]

Did someone say, *Don't count on it*? Or was it, don't count on *them*? As everybody knows, America's vaunted financial system let us down big-time during the

12. Alan Blinder is the Gordon S. Rentschler Memorial Professor of Economics at Princeton University, codirector of the Princeton Center for Economic Policy Studies, and former vice chairman, Federal Reserve Board. He wrote this Foreword in May 2010.

raucous first decade of the 2000s. The decade began with the spectacular stock market crash of 2000–2001, as corporate will-o'-the-wisps, previously hyped by unscrupulous "analysts" who should have known (and did know!) better, collapsed before our eyes. That searing financial shock was followed in close order by the accounting scandals at Enron, WorldCom, and others in 2001–2002, the mutual fund scandals in 2003, and then, of course, the mother of all financial collapses: the stunning series of financial crises that started in the summer of 2007 and eventually brought the entire financial system to the brink of ruin and the world economy to its knees. With all this going on, you might have thought that America's leaders, both political and financial, would have been frequently out on the hustings giving both detailed explanations and copious apologies. But you would have been wrong. The silence has been deafening.

Enter Jack Bogle, the conscience of Wall Street, if that's not an oxymoron. More accurately, Bogle never left. For decades his relentless voice, sharp pen, and indefatigable energy have been prodding the mutual fund industry in particular, and the financial industry more generally, to embrace higher business, fiduciary, and ethical standards. Indeed, the essay that lends its name to this volume originated as a speech at Princeton University (Bogle's alma mater and mine) in 2002, and a few of the others are older than that. Our financial leaders and public officials had plenty of time to set things straight. Would that they had listened to Bogle more. But, too often, his was a lonely voice in the wilderness.

That fine voice is in ample evidence here, in this worthy collection of 35 essays, many of them short and pithy. The essays range widely over the usual Bogle themes: the unconscionably high costs of financial intermediation, the disgraceful failure to abide by what should have been normal fiduciary standards, the inefficient absorption of too much high-priced talent into financial manipulation

"Jack Bogle, the Conscience of Wall Street, if That's Not an Oxymoron"

rather than into useful productive activities, the dismaying triumph of emotion over cool-headed reason in so many investment decisions, and the related—and sometimes ruinous—triumph of speculation over investment. If you've heard these themes expounded by Bogle before, listen again because the lessons still haven't sunk in. If you haven't, you're in for a real treat, for Bogle writes not only with passion and conviction, but also with verve, wit, and literary flair. Where else, in a book on finance, will you find references to (in chronological order) Horace, Benjamin Franklin, Edgar Allan Poe, and Steven Colbert?

Remember the Cost Matters Hypothesis: *Market* Gross Return, Minus Intermediation Costs, Equals *Investor* Net Return

As a veteran of the mutual fund industry, and a father of low-cost index funds, it is no surprise that Bogle directs much of his ire at the high costs of financial intermediation. He never tires of reminding investors of this fundamental identity:

> Gross returns on assets − Costs of operating the financial system
> = Net returns to investors

The identity implies, among other things, that an investment adviser, or broker, or mutual fund manager earns his keep only if the gross returns he adds by "beating the market" exceed the costs he subtracts. Armed with reams of evidence to the contrary, Bogle is skeptical that this happens often. In Chapter 4, for example, he estimates that, in 2007, the costs of intermediation in securities came to a staggering $528 billion. That was 3.8 percent of GDP and, by remarkable coincidence, almost exactly the amount of money that all businesses in America spent that year on new factories, offices, and stores. Were the benefits worth the Brobdingnagian costs? Bogle thinks not and he's probably right. It will not surprise you to see the

*"According to Saint Jack . . .
Fiduciary Duty Is the Highest
Duty Known to the Law"*

virtues of indexing—principally, the reduction of transaction costs—extolled by the man who brought us Vanguard. He should know—and he does.

The duties of a fiduciary have always commanded a central place in the Bogle pantheon of virtue and vice—and so it is here, in several essays that display both his strong moral sense and his limitless backbone. After all, as Bogle reminds us in the title of Chapter 19 (and elsewhere), "No man can serve two masters." (Too bad so many Wall Streeters served more than two.) According to Saint Jack, as he is sometimes called, "Fiduciary duty is the highest duty known to the law." It requires, among other things, that the fiduciary "act at all times for the sole benefit and interests of the principal" and never "put personal interests before that duty" or "be placed in a situation where his fiduciary duty to clients conflicts with a fiduciary duty to any other entity." Can you imagine how much milder the financial crisis would have been if Wall Street had adhered to those simple precepts? If not, read Bogle's essays on the subject. You'll see.

I could go on, but you've picked up this book to read Bogle, not Blinder. Let me just close with a wistful thought that sticks in my mind after reading these essays.

Once the financial cataclysm of 2007–2009 had passed its nadir, in about March 2009, policy makers, financial market experts, scholars, and others could turn their attention away from the emergency measures needed to prevent a total meltdown, and start thinking about the long-lasting structural reforms needed to build a sturdier and fairer financial system. It was a great national debate, which has already produced the landmark Dodd-Frank Wall Street Reform and Consumer Protection Act of 2010. And it's not over. As the debate has progressed, I must confess to a mischievous and, frankly, somewhat undemocratic thought: Wouldn't it be better just to turn the whole thing over to a small group of wise heads like Jack Bogle? When you finish this book, you'll see why.

FOREWORD TO *THE CLASH OF THE CULTURES* (2012)

Arthur Levitt[13]

*"The Inherent Conflicts
Between the Investor's
Interests and Those of Many
Financial Professionals"*

There is a motto that Jack Bogle uses from time to time (and he uses it in this book): "Even one person can make a difference." And while he uses it to elevate and praise the contributions of a single, relatively powerless person, that motto applies uniquely to Jack Bogle.

Here is a man whose contribution to American finance was not just a well-executed idea—the index fund—but a well-executed philosophy of investing and life. It is a philosophy that has the dual merit of simplicity and proven success.

Having known Bogle for several decades, I have come to appreciate his unique ability to speak to investors in a language that is accessible, lyrical, and yet also bracing. He points out with clarity the inherent conflicts present throughout our financial markets, most notably between the investor's interests and those of many financial professionals.

This is a critical complaint in his discussion of mutual funds. Many investors are under the mistaken impression that mutual funds are a secure and relatively matter-of-fact way to gain the benefit of diversification at low cost. In reality, as Bogle richly details here and elsewhere, mutual funds have a large incentive to benefit from the economics of their businesses, rather than look after their investors' long-term wealth. Thus we see some mutual funds not only charge outsized fees, but also practice portfolio management strategies that leave investors behind market index averages and overexposed to certain equities, sectors, and strategies.

---

13. Arthur Levitt was chairman of the U.S. Securities and Exchange Commission from 1993 to 2001, and is the author of *Take On the Street: What Wall Street and Corporate America Don't Want You to Know.*

Great Courage, Wisdom, and Forthrightness

That Bogle has stood against such practices for decades is no surprise to anyone who knows this man. He is a person of great courage, wisdom, and forthrightness. He has never lost the zeal or ability to go against conventional wisdom, and is strengthened by those moments when he stands alone. Jack Bogle is brilliant and persuasive, and his ability to get to the heart of often-complex issues of finance and markets is one of his greatest gifts.

He loves investing and loves what investing can do. He marvels at the miracles possible when corporations and their owners and managers jointly pursue long-term shareholder return to the exclusion of all else. He is the free market's greatest friend: a faithful ally. And yet when he sees the corridors of finance and investment turned into a den of speculation and greed, he does not hold his tongue. He knows the stakes are great.

The Clash of the Cultures is definitional, and could well serve as a philosophical and academic grounding for investors of every age. Throughout, his language is disarmingly straightforward. Because of his respect for the investor, he sidesteps glibness and oversimplification. He defines the difference between risk taking and recklessness. He correlates costs to returns. He explains why indexing works, and why active management usually doesn't. He traces the roots of today's markets to the rise of corporate agents and then investment managers—both of whom form an impenetrable and expensive "double-agency" layer separating the real investor/owners from active control over their assets.

"One of the Greatest Threats to the Strength of Financial Markets Is Groupthink"

While some Wall Street professionals may not agree with every word here—or even some of the words—I hope they read it. One of the greatest threats to the strength of financial markets is groupthink. When regulators, market professionals, investors, and policy makers all share the same assumptions, emerge from the same trading floors, nod to the same broad arguments, and expect the same outcomes, the result is as predictable as it is disastrous. Jack Bogle's iconoclasm is a useful tonic to groupthink. We need more like him.

There are many villains in this book: auditors, regulators, politicians, rating agencies, the Securities and Exchange Commission (which I led), the Federal Reserve, sell-side analysts, and the media. And their collective (as well as individual) sins have one primary victim: investors.

And he is right. Investors must remain the focus of any efforts to improve our financial markets. No matter the regulatory reform, the market practice, or the new financial product, if the investor's interests don't trump all others, we ought to question what purpose we are serving. One thinks of rules requiring ever more volumes of disclosures. The result is not better-informed investors, but the opposite. The disclosures, written in legalese and printed in agate type, might as well not exist to most investors. What we need is transparency: ways for investors to see information, understand it, and weigh the potential risks and opportunities of their investment options.

Transparency is at the core of effective market regulation, precisely because it empowers investors. Sadly, most efforts to improve transparency are fought by a well-funded mutual fund lobby and its related allies. One recent SEC proposal, to have money market funds mark to market their holdings every day, is one such example. This basic idea would not only give investors greater insight into their holdings; it would also impose a healthy appreciation for liquidity among mutual fund managers. Yet the mutual fund industry predictably has fought the idea.

"If the Investor's Interests Don't Trump All Others, We Ought To Question What Purpose We Are Serving"

Raising the Alarm

The industry would be wise to consider what Jack Bogle and others observe: If investors do not feel that mutual funds are protecting their interests, they will not participate in markets—and the markets themselves will suffer. If mutual funds wish to remain the gold standard for investor protections and stability, they ought to take seriously—and adopt—reforms and practices that add to those protections and that stability. We are but three years removed from one of the biggest financial crises of history, brought about by an excess of risk taking, leverage, and opaque financial products, combined with lax regulation. Surely mutual fund managers can see the value in avoiding a repeat of that catastrophic period. And if not, they can expect to reap what follows. Surely Jack Bogle and others inside the industry have done enough to raise the alarm.

"His Truth Telling Is the Key to His Personality"

Never is this clearer than in his insistence that fees and costs are draining all the promised value out of the pockets of investors. Investors must know that they inevitably earn the gross return of the stock market, but only before the deduction of the costs of financial intermediation are taken into account. If beating the market is a zero-sum game before costs, it is a loser's game after costs are deducted. Which is why costs must be made clear to investors, and, one hopes, minimized. Pointing this out routinely surely cannot earn Jack Bogle many friends on Wall Street, which depends on the mystery surrounding financial innovations—as they are called euphemistically. But Bogle doesn't care much about "stirring the pot." His friends have long learned to appreciate that his truth telling is the key to his personality.

Jack Bogle has spent a lifetime in study and active participation in financial markets. The amount of self-dealing and self-enrichment he has seen qualifies him to bear witness against not just a few individuals, but entire firms and certainly an entire industry. They should be glad that Jack Bogle is merely an expert witness, and not the judge and jury as well.

Vanguard by the Numbers, 1974–2013

Year	Total Assets* (Year-End) (millions)	Share of Industry Assets**	Total Fund Costs (millions)	Expense Ratio	Market Appreciation (millions)	Net Cash Flow (millions)	Net Cash Flow as a Percent of Assets 5-yr Moving Avg.	Number of Funds	Number of Crew Members	Crew/$Billion of Assets
1974	$ 1,457	5.9%	$ 10	0.66%	—	−$ 108	—	6	28	19
1975	1,781	5.7	12	0.66	$427	−103	—	8	47	26
1976	2,049	5.8	12	0.59	439	−171	—	10	97	47
1977	1,849	5.4	11	0.60	−62	−138	—	13	99	54
1978	1,919	5.4	12	0.62	71	−1	−5.9%	13	106	55
1979	2,380	5.6	14	0.58	308	153	−3.1	15	133	56
1980	3,026	5.4	17	0.58	531	115	−0.7	18	167	55
1981	4,110	5.8	22	0.53	203	881	7.0	20	272	66
1982	5,617	5.7	35	0.63	761	746	12.0	21	360	64
1983	7,258	5.9	44	0.61	890	751	14.7	24	431	59
1984	9,925	6.6	55	0.56	625	2,042	18.7	32	663	67
1985	16,408	5.2	86	0.53	2,269	4,214	26.2	36	886	54
1986	24,961	4.7	122	0.49	2,628	5,925	27.6	43	1,124	45
1987	27,007	4.1	106	0.39	−31	2,077	25.7	47	1,497	55
1988	34,172	4.4	134	0.39	3,638	3,526	25.6	52	1,588	46
1989	47,562	5.1	168	0.35	4,886	8,505	25.0	52	1,873	39
1990	55,711	5.4	186	0.33	−239	8,388	20.0	56	2,230	40
1991	77,027	6.2	244	0.32	8,878	12,438	17.2	56	2,631	34
1992	97,412	6.6	288	0.30	5,506	14,879	19.4	67	3,112	32
1993	125,755	6.5	378	0.30	10,512	17,832	20.5	68	3,520	28

(Continued)

Vanguard by the Numbers, 1974–2013 (Continued)

Year	Total Assets* (Year-End) (millions)	Share of Industry Assets**	Total Fund Costs (millions)	Expense Ratio	Market Appreciation (millions)	Net Cash Flow (millions)	Net Cash Flow as a Percent of Assets 5-yr Moving Avg.	Number of Funds	Number of Crew Members	Crew/$Billion of Assets
1994	$ 130,743	6.5%	$ 399	0.31%	−$ 1,503	$ 6,491	16.5%	74	3,545	27
1995	178,317	7.2	559	0.31	29,525	18,049	15.8	78	3,927	22
1996	236,006	7.8	691	0.29	25,116	32,573	15.0	82	4,798	20
1997	322,441	8.7	880	0.27	46,301	40,133	14.5	82	6,400	20
1998	431,693	9.8	1,195	0.28	52,438	56,814	14.4	87	8,113	19
1999	537,405	10.0	1,441	0.27	54,430	51,282	15.7	89	9,886	18
2000	561,236	10.6	1,511	0.27	−1,429	25,260	13.9	94	10,129	18
2001	577,942	11.4	1,544	0.27	−29,429	46,134	11.9	91	11,200	19
2002	555,789	12.0	1,438	0.26	−62,275	40,122	9.9	92	10,495	19
2003	689,980	12.0	1,798	0.26	103,191	31,001	7.5	92	10,007	15
2004	818,513	12.4	1,903	0.23	69,746	58,787	6.8	104	10,251	13
2005	928,862	12.6	2,007	0.22	52,233	58,116	7.3	104	11,205	12
2006	1,122,722	12.8	2,394	0.21	118,852	75,007	7.2	112	12,000	11
2007	1,304,606	13.1	2,451	0.19	73,206	108,679	7.8	118	11,944	9
2008	1,045,935	15.1	1,834	0.18	−343,570	84,900	8.0	118	12,534	12
2009	1,336,082	15.2	2,703	0.20	190,080	100,067	8.2	126	12,587	9
2010	1,563,797	15.7	2,798	0.18	149,865	77,850	7.9	141	12,483	8
2011	1,649,177	16.7	2,619	0.16	8,193	77,188	7.3	140	12,872	8
2012	1,973,502	17.4	2,880	0.15	182,120	142,204	7.1	140	13,500	7
2013****	$2,159,170	17.8%	$3,150	0.15%	$109,726	$ 75,942	6.6%	142	14,000	6

*U.S.-domiciled mutual fund assets.

**Percentage of assets of long-term mutual funds; money market funds are excluded.

REFERENCES

Baltzell, E. Digby. 1979. *Puritan Boston and Quaker Philadelphia*. New York: Free Press.

Bennis, Warren G. 2002. "Will the Legacy Live On?" *Harvard Business Review*, February 1.

Bogle, John C. 1993. *Bogle on Mutual Funds: New Perspectives for the Intelligent Investor*. New York: John Wiley & Sons.

Bogle, John C. 1999. *Common Sense on Mutual Funds: New Imperatives for the Intelligent Investor*. New York: John Wiley & Sons.

Bogle, John C. 2001. *John Bogle on Investing: The First 50 Years*. New York: McGraw-Hill. (Includes the complete text of John C. Bogle's Princeton University senior thesis, "The Economic Role of the Investment Company," 1951.)

Bogle, John C. 2002. *Character Counts: The Creation and Building of the Vanguard Group*. New York: McGraw-Hill.

Bogle, John C. 2002. Op-Ed, "Mutual Fund Secrecy." *New York Times*, December 14.

Bogle, John C. 2003. Lecture at the Community Forum Distinguished Speaker Series of the Bryn Mawr (Pennsylvania) Presbyterian Church, February 24.

Bogle, John C. 2004. "As the Index Fund Moves from Heresy to Dogma . . . What More Do We Need to Know?" Gary M. Brinson Distinguished Lecture at Washington State University.

Bogle, John C. 2005. *The Battle for the Soul of Capitalism*. New Haven, CT: Yale University Press.

Bogle, John C. 2007. *The Little Book of Common Sense Investing*. Hoboken, NJ: John Wiley & Sons.

Bogle, John C. 2008. *Enough. True Measures of Money, Business, and Life*. Hoboken, NJ: John Wiley & Sons.

Bogle, John C. 2009. *Common Sense on Mutual Funds: Fully Updated 10th Anniversary Edition*. Foreword by David F. Swensen. Hoboken, NJ: John Wiley & Sons.

Bogle, John C. 2011. *Don't Count on It!* Hoboken, NJ: John Wiley & Sons.

Bogle, John C. 2012. *The Clash of the Cultures: Investment vs. Speculation*. Hoboken, NJ: John Wiley & Sons.

"Bogle Issue." 2012. *Journal of Indexes*, Spring.

Boyle, David. 2000. *The Tyranny of Numbers*. London: HarperCollins.

Brennan, John, and Edward C. Johnson III. 2003. Op-Ed. *Wall Street Journal*, February 14.

Carey, Art. 2008. "Market Moralist: To Jack Bogle, the Reckoning for Wall Street, 'with All Its Sins,' Reaffirms Vanguard's Pioneering Course in Funds." *Philadelphia Inquirer*, October 19.

Coleman, Murray. 2007. "Few Firms Earn Loyalty of the Wealthy: Well-Heeled Investors Search for Consistency; Vanguard Rates Highest." *Wall Street Journal*, March 15, C13.

Ehrbar, A. F. 1976. "Index Funds—An Idea Whose Time Is Coming." *Fortune*, June.

"Ex-Fund Chief to Come Back?" 1974. *New York Times*, March 14.

Fisher, Peter. 2009. "Principles for Change." *Wall Street Journal*, March 29.

Frankel, Tamar. 2006. *Trust and Honesty: America's Business Culture at a Crossroad*. New York: Oxford University Press.

Frankel, Tamar. 2012. *The Ponzi Scheme Puzzle*. New York: Oxford University Press.

Gay, Jason. 2011. "What Tim Tebow Can't Do." *Wall Street Journal*, December 1. Accessed at http://online.wsj.com/article/SB10001424052970203833104577070351117638504.html.

Graham, Benjamin. 2003. *The Intelligent Investor*. Rev. ed. New York: HarperBusiness.

Graham, Benjamin, and David Dodd. 1934, 1940, 2008. *Security Analysis*. New York: McGraw-Hill.

Howell, Martin. 2003. *Predators and Profits: 100+ Ways for Investors to Protect Their Nest Eggs*. Upper Saddle River, NJ: Pearson Education.

Ibbotson, Roger G., and Rex A. Cinquefield. *Stocks, Bonds, Bills, and Inflation: Ibbotson SBBI Classic Yearbook*. Ibbotson Associates/Morningstar.

Isaac, William. 2010. *Senseless Panic: How Washington Failed America*. Foreword by Paul Volcker. Hoboken, NJ: John Wiley & Sons.

Keynes, John Maynard. 1936, 1964. *The General Theory of Employment, Interest, and Money*. New York: Harcourt, Brace.

Kinnel, Russel. 2005. "Mind the Gap." *Morningstar Advisor*, July 26.

Larimore, Taylor, Mel Lindauer, and Michael LeBoeuf. 2006. *The Bogleheads' Guide to Investing*. Hoboken, NJ: John Wiley & Sons.

Larimore, Taylor, Mel Lindauer, Richard A. Ferri, and Laura F. Dogu. 2009. *The Bogleheads' Guide to Retirement Planning*. Hoboken, NJ: John Wiley & Sons.

Lear, Robert W., and Boris Yaritz. 2000. "Boards on Trial." *Chief Executive*, October.

Lo, Andrew W. 2009. "Business Insight (A Special Report): Executive Briefing—Understanding Our Blind Spots: Financial Crisis Underscores Need to Transform Our View of Risk." *Wall Street Journal*, March 23.

Malkiel, Burton S. 1973. *A Random Walk Down Wall Street*. New York: W.W. Norton.

Mayo, Anthony J., and Nitin Nohria. 2005. *In Their Time: The Greatest Leaders of the Twentieth Century*. Boston: Harvard Business School Press.

Meinhard v. Salmon, 164 N.E. 545 (N.Y. 1928).

Monks, Robert, and Allen Sykes. 2002. *Capitalism without Owners Will Fail: A Policymakers' Guide to Reform*. London: Centre for the Study of Financial Innovation.

Pfaff, William. 2002. "A Pathological Mutation in Capitalism." *International Herald Tribune*, September 9, 8.

Reinker, Kenneth S., and Edward Tower. 2004. "Index Fundamentalism Revisited." *Journal of Portfolio Management*, Summer.

Sacks, Jonathan. 1998. *Morals and Markets*. 1998 Hayek Lecture. London: Institute of Economic Affairs.

Samuelson, P. A. 1974. "Challenge to Judgment." *Journal of Portfolio Management* 1 (1): 17–19.

Smith, Adam. 1759, 2002. *The Theory of Moral Sentiments*. Cambridge, UK: Cambridge University Press, 158.

Smith, Adam. 1776. *The Wealth of Nations*. London: Methuen & Co.

Stone, H. F. 1934. Address to the University of Michigan School of Law on June 15, reprinted in the *Harvard Law Review*.

Strine, Leo E. 2007. "Toward Common Sense and Common Ground? Reflections on the Shared Interests of Managers and Labor in a More Rational System of Corporate Governance." *Journal of Corporation Law*, Fall: 7.

Surowiecki, James. 2002. "A Virtuous Cycle." *Forbes*, December 23.

Swensen, David F. 2005. *Unconventional Success: A Fundamental Approach to Personal Investment*. New York: Free Press.

The Vanguard Group, Inc., 47 S.E.C. 450 (1981).

INDEX